Plays by
and about
Women

Plays
by
and about
Women

An Anthology

EDITED BY Victoria Sullivan AND James Hatch

Vintage Books

A DIVISION OF RANDOM HOUSE, NEW YORK

VINTAGE BOOKS EDITION, February 1974

Library of Congress Cataloging in Publication Data
Sullivan, Victoria, comp.
 Plays by and about women.
 CONTENTS: Sullivan, V. and Hatch J. Introduction.—Gerstenberg, A. Overtones.—Hellman, L. The children's hour. [etc.]
 1. Woman—Drama. 2. Drama—20th century.
I. Hatch, James Vernon, 1928– joint comp.
II. Title.
PN6120.W6S93 808.82'9'352 73–14734
ISBN 978-0-394-71896-5

Contents

Contents

Introduction

Here is an anthology devoted to twentieth-century plays by women. They are primarily about women and their problems: their struggles to attract prestigious men, their seeking of a coherent identity, and most recently, their anger at the bondage of outgrown stereotypes. All of the plays selected read well and play well. Several are experimental in form, while others are traditional, well-made plays. In the past, female playwrights have been largely ignored in standard drama anthologies, and therefore this group of eight plays should provide some new insights into how women view themselves in dramatic terms.

Drama directors, teachers and actresses will welcome these plays for very practical reasons: they provide roles for women. Since in the Western world action has generally been a male prerogative, most of the roles in play casts have been male, a phenomenon to which any aspiring actress can testify. The plays in this volume offer a total of eighty-five female parts, roles which run a dramatic range of age, class, type and genre from the working girls in *Rites* to the society matrons in *The Women* to the schoolteachers and pupils in *The Children's Hour* to the amorphously changing roles in *Calm Down Mother.*

As Kate Millett has pointed out in *Sexual Politics*, economics have played a role in keeping women "in their place." In the theatre, financial backers have been loath to risk the large amount of money necessary to mount a play by a woman in a society where patriarchal attitudes have reigned in relative security until recently. Occasional playwrights like Lillian Hellman and Clare Boothe have overcome this masculine hesitation, but they are the exceptions. Virginia Woolf claimed that "masterpieces are not single and solitary births; they are the outcome of many years of thinking in common," and women's creative problem has always been "that they had no tradition behind them, or one so short and partial that it was of little help. For we think back through our mothers if we are women. It is useless to go to the great men writers for help, however much one may go to them for pleasure."

Although the plays here are *about* women, the anthology is not strictly feminist in viewpoint, for the selections are plays first, not polemics. In fact, they are not even all positive in their assessment of women. Clare Boothe's *The Women* presents a picture of woman as a trivial social beast. Lillian Hellman's *The Children's Hour* treats lesbianism as a legitimately scandalous accusation. But each of the eight plays deals in some fashion, either positively or negatively, with the nature of women in Western society from a female point of view.

Art is a kind of mirror, with all its grotesqueries and distortions, and so these plays provide some real data on the characteristics of the uniquely female vision. Half of the selections date from before 1965 to provide historical perspective. Female consciousness, like black consciousness, while always present, is shaped by its time. Freud defined women in 1933 as basically passive, masochistic and narcissistic, a formula that had the effect of strongly prohibiting female creativity in any sphere other than childbearing, and Erikson's doctrine of "inner space" reinforced this attitude. Kate Millett labels the period 1930 to 1960 "the Counterrevolution," the period when earlier feminist gains were negated under the pressure of psychoanalytic theory and political reality, and when the twentieth-century version of the "feminine mystique" was born. The modern woman playwright, then, has had to fight against strong cultural taboos, refusing to acquiesce to the "anatomy is destiny" argument. She has had to be a very strong person indeed to invade the traditionally male world of the theatre.

The distance that women have traveled in their awareness of themselves can be measured by starting with *Overtones*, a one-act play written in 1913 in which two women are presented solely in their relationships to a man. The dramatist,

Alice Gerstenberg, reveals her characters through an expressionistic device; she gives each an inner and an outer persona, played by two different actresses. The audience hears not only what the characters say, but what they think and feel. To glimpse the social implications of the triangle in this play, consider the situation in reverse: two men competing to be the love-mate of a famous woman painter.

By contrast, *The Children's Hour*, first produced in 1934, considers two women in a noncompetitive relationship. Lillian Hellman, only twenty-six when she wrote it, already knew how to construct a taut, carefully crafted play.

The Children's Hour is dominated by women; in a cast of sixteen, only two are males. The story centers around Martha and Karen, who run a girls' boarding school. One of their pupils accuses them of lesbianism, an untrue charge that destroys them. "This is really not a play about lesbianism," Ms. Hellman said in an interview during the 1952 revival of the play, "but about a lie." It is a lie the school, the town and finally the women themselves come to believe. Women in positions of authority have always been particularly vulnerable to slander (the Gabrielle Russier case in France comes to mind); they are expected to be exemplary at the same time that they are suspected of hiding sinister perversions. If they were "normal," the reasoning goes, why would they desire careers?

In the play's denouement Martha says to Karen, "I've loved you like a friend, the way thousands of women feel about other women." Perhaps Lillian Hellman is suggesting that if a woman can learn to love herself, she will not be afraid to love another. Clare Boothe in *The Women* (1936) examines the problem specifically. Why is it that women do not love themselves?

Brooks Atkinson, then drama critic for the *New York Times*, wrote in his review that she "succeeded by spraying vitriol over the members of her sex" and declared that "Miss Boothe's writing was too poisonous for my taste." Not everyone agreed: *The Women* ran for 657 performances. Yet the myth persisted that *The Women* was a vitriolic attack upon the female sex. It is and is not.

The plot is slight: Mary loses her husband to a vamp, obtains a divorce, regrets it. The last scene shows her behaving "like a woman," clawing to get her man back. The overt evidence condemning women comes from the mouth of every character in the play:

> There's only one tragedy for a woman—losing her man. . . . This is a man's world. The sooner our girls are taught to accept the fact graciously. . . . But Mother dear, I don't want to be a little girl. I hate girls. They're so silly. . . . Women are natural enemies. . . . Pride, that's a luxury a woman in love can't afford.

Women speaking against women.

Clare Boothe herself said that *"The Women* is a satirical play about a numerically small group of ladies native to the Park Avenues of America." This is true in the sense that the women in the play have wealth and leisure, but the condition that encourages them to waste their lives and to destroy one another is general to women at all levels of the society.

No man is presented onstage in *The Women*, yet the characters are concerned with nothing else. The "girls" have no careers, no ambitions of their own. Says one professional woman:

> I wish I could get a man to foot my bills. I'm sick and tired, cooking my own breakfast, sloshing through the rain at 8 A.M., working like a dog. For what? Independence? A lot of independence you have on a woman's wages. I'd chuck it like that for a decent, or an indecent home.

The working "girls" speak:

> FIRST FITTER Look at that body. She's got him now.
> SECOND SALESGIRL You can't trust any man. That's all they want.
> CORSET MODEL *(plaintively, her hands on her lovely hips)* What else have we got to give?

Indeed, what else? This is the question Ms. Boothe asks women over and over throughout the play—a play whose scenes are set in the living room, at the hairdresser's, in the kitchen, the bathroom, the powder room, the fitting room, the world of segregated females who, if they are allowed into men's world, are so poorly paid and badly treated that they long to return to even the most unsatisfactory home.

An indictment of narcissism and frivolity, *The Women* thrusts an unflattering mirror at the female image. Still, to show women the worst of their sex is to challenge them to reveal the best—that struggle toward human definition and freedom which fascinates Doris Lessing in *Play with a Tiger*.

Play with a Tiger was first produced at the Comedy Theatre, London, on March 22, 1962. Ms. Lessing is probably best known as a novelist, and one of her major fictional concerns is a particular type of modern woman: the intellectual who refuses to make ideological and personal compromises in a world that demands them. The heroine of this play is a writer in her mid-thirties, Anna, who lives alone in a London flat. In the eyes of the world she is self-sufficient, charming, enterprising; but she knows that mere survival in a fragmenting world is an effort.

She wants a man, she is attractive to men, but she finds it impossible to break through the battle of the sexes and have a man on her own terms. So, although she has a number of friends and lovers, she is basically lonely. The action of the play is confined to one evening in her life, but the audience must assume that the action is repetitive, that although a crisis point is reached and passed (if not resolved) with one man, she will have to relive this crisis with other men.

Structurally, by abandoning the totally realistic set, Ms. Lessing broadens the psychological dimensions in the play. At certain points the walls of the apartment vanish, and the protagonists find themselves in an undefined atmosphere where they can re-create past selves, past experiences, past disguises. In the course of acting out this conscious regression, they reveal the early pressures that produced their adult personae.

Megan Terry's *Calm Down Mother,* first performed by the Open Theatre in March 1965 at the Sheridan Square Playhouse in New York City, is even more experimental in form. Subtitled "A Transformation for Three Women," it is played on an open stage with four chairs. In the transformation play, which has developed out of Open Theatre workshops, the actors—or, in this case, actresses—keep switching into new roles and situations without the aid of props, simply by means of acting technique. In this play the three women go through a series of short sketches focusing on female identity, or lack of identity, playing various archetypical female roles. The underlying theme linking these sketches is that anatomy may be destiny, that women's bodies define their roles, that "bellies" and "eggies" are the essential female elements. By giving this idea vivid life on the stage, Ms. Terry reveals its fearful limitations.

Natalia Ginzburg presents an equally frightening portrait of female limitation in *The Advertisement,* a play originally written in Italian, but given its world premiere in English translation by the National Theatre at the Theatre Royal, Brighton, England, on September 16, 1968.

The play revolves around Teresa, a woman who puts an advertisement in a newspaper in order to rent out a room in her large flat to a young female student. Once the student arrives, a slow unraveling of Teresa's passionate, absurd, unfortunate affair and marriage begins. Teresa, like Anna in *Play with a Tiger,* is lonely. She is also a compulsive talker. Her marriage lasted five years, and in the course of describing it to her young listener, she reveals herself as the self-indulgent victim of her own desperately chaotic personality. Her long-winded, egocentric monologues say something about the female state. Having been brought up with no particular goal except to catch a man, she cannot support herself economically or emotionally. Yet because of her demanding dependence and compulsive need to talk, no man can stand to live with her.

When the play was first performed, Irving Wardle, drama

critic for the *Times* of London, attacked it for being "the equivalent of a cheap woman's magazine story." He assumes that a complaining female protagonist is automatically less noble than Stanley Kowalski or Willy Loman. The implied standard of judgment behind Wardle's criticism is: men suffer greatly and are tragic; women suffer mawkishly and are bathetic.

There is little action in the play. In fact it has been successfully performed as a radio play by the BBC. Teresa is a woman who has been reduced to talk as her only form of action; her speeches are long and self-pitying; they ignore the response of the listener because they are old dreams and obsessions relived and so contain no freshness, no possibility of new growth.

Another National Theatre production, *Rites* by Maureen Duffy, first performed in its experimental theatre program on February 8, 1969, with a twelve-character all-female cast, is the perfect late-sixties foil to *The Women*. Fashionable New York matrons are replaced by London working-class women, and instead of the elegant-thirties powder room, the setting is a ladies' "loo" (public washroom).

Hostility toward men is expressed which is quite different from the veiled self-loathing of *The Women*. These lower-class women are neither educated nor consciously liberated, yet they possess a gut-level recognition of the inequities of the system. Ada, the head matron, is very much aware of her body as a commodity in the sexual market:

It's not much and you've got to tart it up a bit to sell it high. After all the goods are all the same when they get the wrapping off. You've got to make them pay for the wrapping off. It's the first law of finance.

Men are always "they" and "them" in this environment; they are not actually described as the enemy, but they are quite obviously felt to be such. There is a cynicism bred deep into all of these women which allows them to joke among themselves about the cultural myths of our times:

THIRD OFFICE GIRL   Dear Auntie Mabel, my friend is always begging me to do wrong. He says if I loved him I would be kind to him. What shall I do? I am frightened of losing him if I do not give in.

FIRST OFFICE GIRL   Dear worried Blue Eyes, on no account let him force you to anticipate the delights of the honeymoon. Two people should save themselves for each other. If this is all this boy wants from you he does not really love you and once he has had it he will quickly tire.

NORMA   Eddy always falls dead asleep after.

MEG   Men are made different.

FIRST OFFICE GIRL   That's for sure.

   (They scream with laughter)

Although a man might have written such dialogue, it does not seem likely; it is, in some strange way, too unsentimental for a man.

Consider two other pieces of dialogue:

FIRST OFFICE GIRL   Ent you goin in then Norma?

NORMA   I'm sick of old Villars and his, "Type this Miss Smith, file that Miss Smith, take it down Miss Smith, lick it, stamp on it, post it. In tray, out tray."

Or:

ADA   I'll tell you about your kind of love: a few moments of pleasure and then a lifetime kidding yourselves. Caught, bound, even if you don't know it. Or a lifetime looking, like Meg, and wailing what you've missed. Years of ministering to a stranger . . .

Such frustration finally unites all the women in the room for an act of ritualized violence against the enemy, the "rites" of the title. The act is horrifying but not surprising to an audience that has caught the cadence of anger boiling underground throughout the early portions of the play.

Such anger is doubly present in black women writers. From the production of Angelina Grimke's *Rachel* in 1916 to *Wine in the Wilderness* in 1969, over one hundred and twenty-five plays were written by black women in America.

The first to be performed professionally off-Broadway was *Gold Through the Trees* by Alice Childress in 1952. In 1959 Lorraine Hansberry became the first black woman to have a play staged on Broadway when *A Raisin in the Sun* opened. In 1964 Adrienne Kennedy won the "Obie," the off-Broadway award for the best play of the year, for *The Funnyhouse of a Negro.* In 1972 Micki Grant won two "Obie" awards for her musical, *Don't Bother Me I Can't Cope.*

Alice Childress' *Wine in the Wilderness* was first produced in a television series "On Being Black" in Boston, Massachusetts, on March 4, 1969. Abbey Lincoln played the role of Tommy; Israel Hicks played Bill, and it is these two who carry the conflict of the play.

Bill is an artist, he has an education and money; he is a man burdened with a pseudo-romantic vision of the mythical "black woman." Tommy has neither money nor recognition, but she has a vitality and a knowledge of what human beings are and should be. She is a grass-roots woman who has survived the rats, the roaches, the riots, and the landlords of Harlem. With Tommy, Ms. Childress has created a strong *new* black woman character to contrast with the traditional strong "Mammy" type. Bill's self-serving notion that he is "better" than Tommy not only is defeated but he comes to recognize that her ability to survive is the wine in the wilderness that has enabled the whole black race to survive in America.

To be a woman in the twentieth century is to be a creature caught in a time of change. And change is an opportunity for women to define themselves. Revolutions in consciousness produce art, not only art nurtured in anger and expressed in polemic, but art with passion, sensitivity and heightened awareness. The artist is a shaper, a person who gives form to chaos, one whose pain slowly emerges as perception. The theatre has been and will continue to be the stage upon which women create new women.

VICTORIA SULLIVAN & JAMES HATCH

Overtones

BY ALICE GERSTENBERG

CHARACTERS

HARRIET   a cultured woman

HETTY   her primitive self

MARGARET   a cultured woman

MAGGIE   her primitive self

TIME: *The present.*

SCENE: HARRIET'S *fashionable living room. The door at the back leads to the hall. In the center a tea table with a high-backed chair at each side.*

HARRIET'S *gown is a light, "jealous" green. Her counterpart,* HETTY, *wears a gown of the same design but in a darker shade.* MARGARET *wears a gown of lavender chiffon while her counterpart,* MAGGIE, *wears a gown of the same design in purple, a purple scarf veiling her face. Chiffon is used to give a sheer effect, suggesting a possibility of primitive and cultured selves merging into one woman. The primitive and cultured selves never come into actual physical contact but try to sustain the impression of mental conflict.* HARRIET *never sees* HETTY, *never talks to her but rather thinks aloud looking into space.* HETTY, *however, looks at* HARRIET, *talks intently and shadows her continually. The same is true of* MARGARET *and* MAGGIE. *The voices of the cultured women are affected and lingering, the voices of the primitive impulsive and more or less staccato.*

When the curtain rises HARRIET *is seated right of tea table, busying herself with the tea things.*

HETTY   Harriet. *(There is no answer)* Harriet, my other self. *(There is no answer)* My trained self.

HARRIET *(Listens intently)*   Yes?

       (From behind HARRIET'S *chair* HETTY *rises slowly)*

HETTY   I want to talk to you.

HARRIET   Well?

HETTY *(Looking at* HARRIET *admiringly)*   Oh, Harriet, you are beautiful today.

HARRIET   Am I presentable, Hetty?

HETTY   Suits me.

HARRIET   I've tried to make the best of the good points.

5

HETTY   My passions are deeper than yours. I can't keep on the mask as you do. I'm crude and real, you are my appearance in the world.

HARRIET   I am what you wish the world to believe you are.

HETTY   You are the part of me that has been trained.

HARRIET   I am your educated self.

HETTY   I am the rushing river; you are the ice over the current.

HARRIET   I am your subtle overtones.

HETTY   But together we are one woman, the wife of Charles Goodrich.

HARRIET   There I disagree with you, Hetty, I alone am his wife.

HETTY   (*Indignantly*) Harriet, how can you say such a thing!

HARRIET   Certainly. I am the one who flatters him. I have to be the one who talks to him. If I gave you a chance you would tell him at once that you dislike him.

HETTY   (*Moving away*) I don't love him, that's certain.

HARRIET   You leave all the fibbing to me. He doesn't suspect that my calm, suave manner hides your hatred. Considering the amount of scheming it causes me it can safely be said that he is my husband.

HETTY   Oh, if you love him—

HARRIET   I? I haven't any feelings. It isn't my business to love anybody.

HETTY   Then why need you object to calling him my husband?

HARRIET   I resent your appropriation of a man who is managed only through the cleverness of my artifice.

HETTY   You may be clever enough to deceive him, Harriet, but I am still the one who suffers. I can't forget he is my husband. I can't forget that I might have married John Caldwell.

HARRIET   How foolish of you to remember John, just because we met his wife by chance.

HETTY   That's what I want to talk to you about. She may be

here at any moment. I want to advise you about what to say to her this afternoon.

HARRIET By all means tell me now and don't interrupt while she is here. You have a most annoying habit of talking to me when people are present. Sometimes it is all I can do to keep my poise and appear *not* to be listening to you.

HETTY Impress her.

HARRIET Hetty, dear, is it not my custom to impress people?

HETTY I hate her.

HARRIET I can't let her see that.

HETTY I hate her because she married John.

HARRIET Only after you had refused him.

HETTY *(Turning to* HARRIET*)* Was it my fault that I refused him?

HARRIET That's right, blame me.

HETTY It was your fault. You told me he was too poor and never would be able to do anything in painting. Look at him now, known in Europe, just returned from eight years in Paris, famous.

HARRIET It was too poor a gamble at the time. It was much safer to accept Charles's money and position.

HETTY And then John married Margaret within the year.

HARRIET Out of spite.

HETTY Freckled, gauky-looking thing she was, too.

HARRIET *(A little sadly)* Europe improved her. She was stunning the other morning.

HETTY Make her jealous today.

HARRIET Shall I be haughty or cordial or caustic or—

HETTY Above all else you must let her know that we are rich.

HARRIET Oh, yes, I do that quite easily now.

HETTY You must put it on a bit.

HARRIET Never fear.

HETTY Tell her I love my husband.

HARRIET My husband—

HETTY Are you going to quarrel with me?

HARRIET *(Moves away)* No, I have no desire to quarrel with you. It is quite too uncomfortable. I couldn't get away from you if I tried.

HETTY *(Stamping her foot and following HARRIET)* You were a stupid fool to make me refuse John, I'll never forgive you—never—

HARRIET *(Stopping and holding up her hand)* Don't get me all excited. I'll be in no condition to meet her properly this afternoon.

HETTY *(Passionately)* I could choke you for robbing me of John.

HARRIET *(Retreating)* Don't muss me!

HETTY You don't know how you have made me suffer.

HARRIET *(Beginning to feel the strength of HETTY'S emotion surge through her and trying to conquer it)* It is not my business to have heartaches.

HETTY You're bloodless. Nothing but sham—sham—while I—

HARRIET *(Emotionally)* Be quiet! I can't let her see that I have been fighting with my inner self.

HETTY And now after all my suffering you say it has cost you more than it has cost me to be married to Charles. But it's the pain here in my heart—I've paid the price—I've paid —Charles is not your husband!

HARRIET *(Trying to conquer emotion)* He is.

HETTY *(Follows HARRIET)* He isn't.

HARRIET *(Weakly)* He is.

HETTY *(Towering over HARRIET)* He isn't! I'll kill you!

HARRIET *(Overpowered, sinks into a chair)* Don't—don't you're stronger than I—you're—

HETTY Say he's mine.

HARRIET He's ours.

HETTY *(The telephone rings)* There she is now.

    (HETTY hurries to 'phone but HARRIET regains her supremacy)

HARRIET *(Authoritatively)* Wait! I can't let the telephone girl down there hear my real self. It isn't proper. *(At phone)* Show Mrs. Caldwell up.

HETTY. I'm so excited, my heart's in my mouth.

HARRIET *(At the mirror)* A nice state you've put my nerves into.

HETTY Don't let her see you're nervous.

HARRIET Quick, put the veil on, or she'll see *you* shining through me.

> (HARRIET *takes a scarf of chiffon that has been lying over the back of a chair and drapes it on* HETTY, *covering her face. The chiffon is the same color of their gowns but paler in shade so that it pales* HETTY's *darker gown to match* HARRIET's *lighter one. As* HETTY *moves in the following scene the chiffon falls away revealing now and then the gown of deeper dye underneath.)*

HETTY Tell her Charles is rich and fascinating—boast of our friends, make her feel she needs us.

HARRIET I'll make her ask John to paint us.

HETTY That's just my thought—if John paints our portrait—

HARRIET We can wear an exquisite gown—

HETTY And make him fall in love again and—

HARRIET *(Schemingly)* Yes. (MARGARET *parts the portières back center and extends her hand.* MARGARET *is followed by her counterpart* MAGGIE) Oh, Margaret, I'm so glad to see you!

HETTY *(To* MAGGIE) That's a lie.

MARGARET *(In superficial voice throughout)* It's enchanting to see you, Harriet.

MAGGIE *(In emotional voice throughout)* I'd bite you, if I dared.

HARRIET *(To* MARGARET) Wasn't our meeting a stroke of luck?

MARGARET *(Coming down left of table)* I've thought of you so often, Harriet; and to come back and find you living in New York.

HARRIET *(Coming down right of table)* Mr. Goodrich has many interests here.

MAGGIE *(To* MARGARET) Flatter her.

MARGARET   I know, Mr. Goodrich is so successful.

HETTY *(To* HARRIET*)*   Tell her we're rich.

HARRIET *To* MARGARET*)*   Won't you sit down?

MARGARET *(Takes a chair)*   What a beautiful cabinet!

HARRIET   Do you like it? I'm afraid Charles paid an extravagant price.

MAGGIE *(To* HETTY*)*   I don't believe it.

MARGARET *(Sitting down. To* HARRIET*)*   I am sure he must have.

HARRIET *(Sitting down)*   How well you are looking, Margaret.

HETTY   Yes, you are not. There are circles under your eyes.

MAGGIE *(To* HETTY*)*   I haven't eaten since breakfast and I'm hungry.

MARGARET *(To* HARRIET*)*   How well you are looking, too.

MAGGIE *(To* HETTY*)*   You have hard lines about your lips, are you happy?

HETTY *(To* HARRIET*)*   Don't let her know that I'm unhappy.

HARRIET *(To* MARGARET*)*   Why shouldn't I look well? My life is full, happy, complete—

MAGGIE   I wonder.

HETTY *(In* HARRIET'S *ear)*   Tell her we have an automobile.

MARGARET *(To* HARRIET*)*   My life is complete, too.

MAGGIE   My heart is torn with sorrow; my husband cannot make a living. He will kill himself if he does not get an order for a painting.

MARGARET *(Laughs)*   You must come and see us in our studio. John has been doing some excellent portraits. He cannot begin to fill his orders.

HETTY *(To* HARRIET*)*   Tell her we have an automobile.

HARRIET *(To* MARGARET*)*   Do you take lemon in your tea?

MAGGIE   Take cream. It's more filling.

MARGARET *(Looking nonchalantly at tea things)*   No, cream, if you please. How cozy!

MAGGIE *(Glaring at tea things)*   Only cakes! I could eat them all!

HARRIET *(To* MARGARET*)*   How many lumps?

MAGGIE *(To* MARGARET*)*   Sugar is nourishing.

MARGARET *(To* HARRIET*)* Three, please. I used to drink very sweet coffee in Turkey and ever since I've—

HETTY I don't believe you were ever in Turkey.

MAGGIE I wasn't, but it is none of your business.

HARRIET *(Pouring tea)* Have you been in Turkey? Do tell me about it.

MAGGIE *(To* MARGARET*)* Change the subject.

MARGARET *(To* HARRIET*)* You must go there. You have so much taste in dress you would enjoy seeing their costumes.

MAGGIE Isn't she going to pass the cake?

MARGARET *(To* HARRIET*)* John painted several portraits there.

HETTY *(To* HARRIET*)* Why don't you stop her bragging and tell her we have an automobile?

HARRIET *(Offers cake across the table to* MARGARET*)* Cake?

MAGGIE *(Stands back of* MARGARET, *shadowing her as* HETTY *shadows* HARRIET. MAGGIE *reaches claws out for the cake and groans with joy)* At last!
(But her claws do not touch the cake.)

MARGARET *(With a graceful, nonchalant hand places cake upon her plate and bites at it slowly and delicately)* Thank you.

HETTY *(To* HARRIET*)* Automobile!

MAGGIE *(To* MARGARET*)* Follow up the costumes with the suggestion that she would make a good model for John. It isn't too early to begin getting what you came for.

MARGARET *(Ignoring* MAGGIE*)* What delicious cake.

HETTY *(Excitedly to* HARRIET*)* There's your chance for the auto.

HARRIET *(Nonchalantly to* MARGARET*)* Yes, it is good cake, isn't it? There are always a great many people buying it at Harper's. I sat in my automobile fifteen minutes this morning waiting for my chauffeur to get it.

MAGGIE *(To* MARGARET*)* Make her order a portrait.

MARGARET *(To* HARRIET*)* If you stopped at Harper's you must have noticed the new gowns at Henderson's. Aren't the shop windows alluring these days?

HARRIET Even my chauffeur notices them.

MAGGIE I know you have an automobile, I heard you the first time.

MARGARET I notice gowns now with an artist's eye as John does. The one you have on, my dear, is very paintable.

HETTY Don't let her see you're anxious to be painted.

HARRIET *(Nonchalantly)* Oh, it's just a little model.

MAGGIE *(To MARGARET)* Don't seem anxious to get the order.

MARGARET *(Nonchalantly)* Perhaps it isn't the gown itself but the way you wear it that pleases the eye. Some people can wear anything with grace.

HETTY Yes, I'm very graceful.

HARRIET *(To MARGARET)* You flatter me, my dear.

MARGARET On the contrary, Harriet, I have an intense admiration for you. I remember how beautiful you were—as a girl. In fact, I was quite jealous when John was paying you so much attention.

HETTY She is gloating because I lost him.

HARRIET Those were childhood days in a country town.

MAGGIE *(To MARGARET)* She's trying to make you feel that John was only a country boy.

MARGARET Most great men have come from the country. There is a fair chance that John will be added to the list.

HETTY I know it and I am bitterly jealous of you.

HARRIET Undoubtedly he owes much of his success to you, Margaret, your experience in economy and your ability to endure hardship. Those first few years in Paris must have been a struggle.

MAGGIE She is sneering at your poverty.

MARGARET Yes, we did find life difficult at first, not the luxurious start a girl has who marries wealth.

HETTY *(To HARRIET)* Deny that you married Charles for his money.

(HARRIET deems it wise to ignore HETTY's advice)

MARGARET But John and I are so congenial in our tastes, that we were impervious to hardship or unhappiness.

HETTY *(In anguish)* Do you love each other? Is it really true?

HARRIET *(Sweetly)* Did you have all the romance of starving for his art?

MAGGIE *(To* MARGARET*)* She's taunting you. Get even with her.

MARGARET Not for long. Prince Rier soon discovered John's genius, and introduced him royally to wealthy Parisians who gave him many orders.

HETTY *(To* MAGGIE*)* Are you telling the truth or are you lying?

HARRIET If he had so many opportunities there, you must have had great inducements to come back to the States.

MAGGIE *(To* HETTY*)* We did, but not the kind you think.

MARGARET John became the rage among Americans traveling in France, too, and they simply insisted upon his coming here.

HARRIET Whom is he going to paint here?

MAGGIE *(Frightened)* What names dare I make up?

MARGARET *(Calmly)* Just at present Miss Dorothy Ainsworth of Oregon is posing. You may not know the name, but she is the daughter of a wealthy miner who found gold in Alaska.

HARRIET I dare say there are many Western people we have never heard of.

MARGARET You must have found social life in New York very interesting, Harriet, after the simplicity of our home town.

HETTY *(To* MAGGIE*)* There's no need to remind us that our beginnings were the same.

HARRIET Of course Charles's family made everything delightful for me. They are so well connected.

MAGGIE *(To* MARGARET*)* Flatter her.

MARGARET I heard it mentioned yesterday that you had made yourself very popular. Some one said you were very clever!

HARRIET *(Pleased)* Who told you that?

MAGGIE Nobody!

MARGARET *(Pleasantly)* Oh, confidences should be suspected—respected, I mean. They said, too, that you are gaining some reputation as a critic of art.

HARRIET I make no pretences.

MARGARET Are you and Mr. Goodrich interested in the same things, too?

HETTY No!

HARRIET Yes, indeed, Charles and I are inseparable.

MAGGIE I wonder.

HARRIET Do have another cake.

MAGGIE (*In relief*) Oh, yes.

    (*Again her claws extend but do not touch the cake*)

MARGARET (*Takes cake delicately*) I really shouldn't—after my big luncheon. John took me to the Ritz and we are invited to the Bedfords' for dinner—they have such a magnificent house near the drive—I really shouldn't, but the cakes are so good.

MAGGIE Starving!

HARRIET (*To* MARGARET) More tea?

MAGGIE Yes!

MARGARET No, thank you. How wonderfully life has arranged itself for you. Wealth, position, a happy marriage, every opportunity to enjoy all pleasures; beauty, art—how happy you must be.

HETTY (*In anguish*) Don't call me happy. I've never been happy since I gave up John. All these years without him— a future without him—no—no—I shall win him back— away from you—away from you—

HARRIET (*Does not see* MAGGIE *pointing to cream and* MARGARET *stealing some*) I sometimes think it is unfair for anyone to be as happy as I am. Charles and I are just as much in love now as when we married. To me he is just the dearest man in the world.

MAGGIE (*Passionately*) My John is. I love him so much I could die for him. I'm going through hunger and want to make him great and he loves me. He worships me!

MARGARET (*Leisurely to* HARRIET) I should like to meet Mr. Goodrich. Bring him to our studio. John has some sketches to show. Not many, because all the portraits have been purchased by the subjects. He gets as much as four thousand dollars now.

HETTY *(To* HARRIET*)* Don't pay that much.

HARRIET *(To* MARGARET*)* As much as that?

MARGARET It is not really too much when one considers that John is in the foremost ranks of artists today. A picture painted by him now will double and treble in value.

MAGGIE It's a lie. He is growing weak with despair.

HARRIET Does he paint all day long?

MAGGIE No, he draws advertisements for our bread.

MARGARET *(To* HARRIET*)* When you and your husband come to see us, telephone first—

MAGGIE Yes, so he can get the advertisements out of the way.

MARGARET Otherwise you might arrive while he has a sitter, and John refuses to let me disturb him then.

HETTY Make her ask for an order.

HARRIET *(To* MARGARET*)* Le Grange offered to paint me for a thousand.

MARGARET Louis Le Grange's reputation isn't worth more than that.

HARRIET Well, I've heard his work well mentioned.

MAGGIE Yes, he is doing splendid work.

MARGARET Oh, dear me, no. He is only praised by the masses. He is accepted not at all by artists themselves.

HETTY *(Anxiously)* Must I really pay the full price?

HARRIET Le Grange thought I would make a good subject.

MAGGIE *(To* MARGARET*)* Let her fish for it.

MARGARET Of course you would. Why don't you let Le Grange paint you, if you *trust* him?

HETTY She doesn't seem anxious to have John do it.

HARRIET But if Le Grange isn't accepted by artists, it would be a waste of time to pose for him, wouldn't it?

MARGARET Yes, I think it would.

MAGGIE *(Passionately to* HETTY *across back of table)* Give us the order. John is so despondent he can't endure much longer. Help us! Help me! Save us!

HETTY *(To* HARRIET*)* Don't seem too eager.

HARRIET   And yet if he charges only a thousand one might consider it.

MARGARET   If you really wish to be painted, why don't you give a little more and have a portrait really worth while? John might be induced to do you for a little below his usual price considering that you used to be such good friends.

HETTY *(In glee)* Hurrah!

HARRIET *(Quietly to* MARGARET*)* That's very nice of you to suggest—of course I don't know—

MAGGIE *(In fear)* For God's sake, say yes.

MARGARET *(Quietly to* HARRIET*)* Of course, I don't know whether John would. He is very peculiar in these matters. He sets his value on his work and thinks it beneath him to discuss price.

HETTY *(To* MAGGIE*)* You needn't try to make us feel small.

MARGARET   Still, I might quite delicately mention to him that inasmuch as you have many influential friends you would be very glad to—to—

MAGGIE *(To* HETTY*)* Finish what I don't want to say.

HETTY *(To* HARRIET*)* Help her out.

HARRIET   Oh, yes, introductions will follow the exhibition of my portrait. No doubt I—

HETTY *(To* HARRIET*)* Be patronizing.

HARRIET   No doubt I shall be able to introduce your husband to his advantage.

MAGGIE *(Relieved)* Saved.

MARGARET   If I find John in a propitious mood I shall take pleasure, for your sake, in telling him about your beauty. Just as you are sitting now would be a lovely pose.

MAGGIE *(To* MARGARET*)* We can go now.

HETTY *(To* HARRIET*)* Don't let her think she is doing us a favor.

HARRIET   It will give me pleasure to add my name to your husband's list of patronesses.

MAGGIE *(Excitedly to* MARGARET*)* Run home and tell John the good news.

MARGARET *(Leisurely to* HARRIET*)* I little guessed when I came for a pleasant chat about old times that it would develop into business arrangements. I had no idea, Harriet, that you had any intention of being painted. By Le Grange, too. Well, I came just in time to rescue you.

MAGGIE *(To* MARGARET*)* Run home and tell John. Hurry, hurry!

HETTY *(To* HARRIET*)* You managed the order very neatly. She doesn't suspect that you wanted it.

HARRIET Now if I am not satisfied with my portrait I shall blame you, Margaret, dear. I am relying upon your opinion of John's talent.

MAGGIE *(To* MARGARET*)* She doesn't suspect what you came for. Run home and tell John!

HARRIET You always had a brilliant mind, Margaret.

MARGARET Ah, it is you who flatter, now.

MAGGIE *(To* MARGARET*)* You don't have to stay so long. Hurry home!

HARRIET Ah, one does not flatter when one tells the truth.

MARGARET *(Smiles)* I must be going or you will have me completely under your spell.

HETTY *(Looks at clock)* Yes, do go. I have to dress for dinner.

HARRIET *(To* MARGARET*)* Oh, don't hurry.

Maggie *(To* HETTY*)* I hate you!

MARGARET *(To* HARRIET*)* No, really I must, but I hope we shall see each other often at the studio. I find you so stimulating.

HETTY *(To* MAGGIE*)* I hate you!

HARRIET *(To* MARGARET*)* It is indeed gratifying to find a kindred spirit.

MAGGIE *(To* HETTY*)* I came for your gold.

MARGARET *(To* HARRIET*)* How delightful it is to know you again.

HETTY *(To* MAGGIE*)* I am going to make you and your husband suffer.

HARRIET My kind regards to John.

MAGGIE *(To* HETTY*)* He has forgotten all about you.

MARGARET *(Rises)* He will be so happy to receive them.

HETTY *(To* MAGGIE*)* I can hardly wait to talk to him again.

HARRIET I shall wait, then, until you send me word?

MARGARET *(Offering her hand)* I'll speak to John about it as soon as I can and tell you when to come.

> *(HARRIET takes MARGARET'S hand affectionately. HETTY and MAGGIE rush at each other, throw back their veils, and fling their speeches fiercely at each other.)*

HETTY I love him—I love him—

MAGGIE He's starving—I'm starving—

HETTY I'm going to take him away from you—

MAGGIE I want your money—and your influence.

HETTY and MAGGIE I'm going to rob you—rob you.

> *(There is a cymbal crash, the lights go out and come up again slowly, leaving only MARGARET and HARRIET visible.)*

MARGARET *(Quietly to HARRIET)* I've had such a delightful afternoon.

HARRIET *(Offering her hand)* It has been a joy to see you.

MARGARET *(Sweetly to HARRIET)* Good-bye.

HARRIET *(Sweetly to MARGARET as she kisses her)* Good-bye, my dear.

CURTAIN

The Children's Hour

BY LILLIAN HELLMAN

CHARACTERS

PEGGY ROGERS

MRS. LILY MORTAR

EVELYN MUNN

HELEN BURTON

LOIS FISHER

CATHERINE

ROSALIE WELLS

MARY TILFORD

KAREN WRIGHT

MARTHA DOBIE

DOCTOR JOSEPH CARDIN

AGATHA

MRS. AMELIA TILFORD

A GROCERY BOY

Act One

SCENE: *A room in the Wright-Dobie School for girls, a converted farm-house eighteen miles from the town of Lancet. It is a comfortable, unpretentious room used as an afternoon study-room and at all other times as the living room.*

A large door Left Center faces the audience. There is a single door Right. Against both back walls are bookcases. A large desk is at Right; a table, two sofas, and eight or ten chairs.

It is early in an afternoon in April.

AT RISE: MRS. LILY MORTAR *is sitting in a large chair Right Center, with her head back and her eyes closed. She is a plump, florid woman of forty-five with obviously touched-up hair. Her clothes are too fancy for a class-room.*

Seven girls, from twelve to fourteen years old, are informally grouped on chairs and sofas. Six of them are sewing with no great amount of industry on pieces of white material. One of the others, EVELYN MUNN, *is using her scissors to trim the hair of* ROSALIE, *who sits, nervously, in front of her. She has* ROSALIE'S *head bent back at an awkward angle and is enjoying herself.*

The eighth girl, PEGGY ROGERS, *is sitting in a higher chair than the others. She is reading aloud from a book. She is bored and she reads in a singsong, tired voice.*

PEGGY *(Reading)* "It is twice blest; it blesseth him that gives and him that takes: 'tis mightiest in the mightiest; it becomes the throned monarch better than his crown; his sceptre shows the force of temporal power, the attribute to awe and majesty, wherein . . ." *(*MRS. MORTAR *suddenly opens her eyes and stares at the hair-cutting. The children make efforts to warn* EVELYN. PEGGY *raises her voice until*

23

she is shouting) "doth sit the dread and fear of kings; but mercy is above . . ."

MRS. MORTAR Evelyn! What are you doing?

EVELYN *(Inanely. She lisps)* Uh—nothing, Mrs. Mortar.

MRS. MORTAR You are certainly doing something. You are ruining the scissors, for one thing.

PEGGY *(Loudly)* "But mercy is above. It . . ."

MRS. MORTAR Just a moment, Peggy. It is very unfortunate that you girls cannot sit quietly with your sewing and drink in the immortal words of the immortal bard. *(She sighs)* Evelyn, go back to your sewing.

EVELYN I can't get the hem thtraight. Honeth, I've been trying for three weekth, but I jutht can't do it.

MRS. MORTAR Helen, please help Evelyn with the hem.

HELEN *(Rises, holding up the garment EVELYN has been working on. It is soiled and shapeless, and so much has been cut off that it is now hardly large enough for a child of five. Giggling)* She can't ever wear *that*, Mrs. Mortar.

MRS. MORTAR *(Vaguely)* Well, try to do something with it. Make some handkerchiefs or something. Be clever about it. Women must learn these tricks. *(To PEGGY)* Continue. "Mightiest in the mightiest."

PEGGY " 'Tis mightiest in the mightiest; it becomes the throned monarch better than his crown; his sceptre—his sceptre shows the force of temporal power, the attribute to awe and majesty, wherein—"

LOIS *(From the back of the room chants softly and monotonously through the previous speech)* Ferebam, ferebas, ferebat, ferebamus, ferebatis, fere, fere—

CATHERINE *(Two seats away, the book propped in front of her)* Fere*bant*.

LOIS Ferebamus, ferebatis, fere*bant*.

MRS. MORTAR Who's doing that?

PEGGY *(The noise ceases. She hurries on)* "Wherein doth sit the dread and fear of kings; but mercy is above this sceptred sway, it is enthroned in the hearts of kings, it is an attribute to God himself—"

MRS. MORTAR *(Sadly, reproachfully)* Peggy, can't you

imagine yourself as Portia? Can't you read the lines with some feeling, some pity? *(Dreamily)* Pity. Ah! As Sir Henry said to me many's the time, pity makes the actress. Now, why can't *you* feel pity?

PEGGY   I guess I feel pity.

LOIS   Ferebamus, ferebatis, fere—fere—fere—

CATHERINE   Fere*bant*, stupid.

MRS. MORTAR   How many people in this room are talking? Peggy, read the line again. I'll give you the cue.

PEGGY   What's a cue?

MRS. MORTAR   A cue is a line or word given the actor or actress to remind them of their next speech.

HELEN   *(Softly)* To remind *him* or *her*.

ROSALIE   *(A fattish girl with glasses)* Weren't you ever in the movies, Mrs. Mortar?

MRS. MORTAR   I had many offers, my dear. But the cinema is a shallow art. It has no—no— *(Vaguely)* no fourth dimension. Now, Peggy, if you would only try to submerge yourself in this problem. You are pleading for the life of a man. *(She rises and there are faint sighs from the girls, who stare at her with blank, bored faces. She recites hammily, with gestures)* "But mercy is above this sceptred sway; it is enthroned in the hearts of kings, it is an attribute to God himself; and earthly power doth then show likest God's when mercy seasons justice."

LOIS   *(Almost singing it)* Utor, fruor, fungor, potior, and vescor take the dative.

CATHERINE   Take the *ablative*.

LOIS   Oh, dear. Utor, fruor, fung—

MRS. MORTAR   *(To LOIS, with sarcasm)* You have something to tell the class?

LOIS   *(Apologetically)* We've got a Latin exam this afternoon.

MRS. MORTAR   And you intend to occupy the sewing and elocution hour learning what should have been learnt yesterday?

CATHERINE   *(Wearily)* It takes her more than yesterday to learn it.

MRS. MORTAR Well, I cannot allow you to interrupt us like this.

CATHERINE But we're finished sewing.

LOIS *(Admiringly)* I bet you were good at Latin, Mrs. Mortar.

MRS. MORTAR *(Conciliated)* Long ago, my dear, long ago. Now, take your book over by the window and don't disturb our enjoyment of Shakespeare. *(CATHERINE and LOIS rise, go to window, stand mumbling and gesturing)* Let us go back again. "It is an attribute of—" *(At this point the door opens far enough to let MARY TILFORD, clutching a slightly faded bunch of wild flowers, squeeze cautiously in. She is fourteen, neither pretty nor ugly. She is an undistinguished-looking girl, except for the sullenly dissatisfied expression on her face)* "And earthly power doth then show likest God's when mercy seasons justice. We do pray for mercy, and that same prayer doth teach—"

PEGGY *(Happily)* You've skipped three lines.

MRS. MORTAR In my entire career I've never missed a line.

PEGGY But you did skip three lines. *(Goes to MRS. MORTAR with book)* See?

MRS. MORTAR *(Seeing MARY sidling along wall toward other end of the room, turns to her to avoid PEGGY and the book)* Mary!

HELEN *(In whisper to MARY)* You're going to catch it now.

MRS. MORTAR Mary!

MARY Yes, Mrs. Mortar?

MRS. MORTAR This is a pretty time to be coming to your sewing class, I must say. Even if you had no interest in your work you might at least remember that you owe me a little courtesy. Courtesy is breeding. Breeding is an excellent thing. *(Turns to class)* Always remember that.

ROSALIE Please, Mrs. Mortar, can I write that down?

MRS. MORTAR Certainly. Suppose you all write it down.

PEGGY But we wrote it down last week.

    (MARY giggles)

MRS. MORTAR Mary, I am still awaiting your explanation. Where have you been?

MARY I took a walk.

MRS. MORTAR So you took a walk. And may I ask, young lady, are we in the habit of taking walks when we should be at our classes?

MARY I am sorry, Mrs. Mortar, I went to get you these flowers. I thought you would like them and I didn't know it would take so long to pick them.

MRS. MORTAR *(Flattered)* Well, well.

MARY *(Almost in tears)* You were telling us last week how much you liked flowers, and I thought that I would bring you some and—

MRS. MORTAR That was very sweet of you, Mary; I always like thoughtfulness. But you must not allow anything to interfere with your classes. Now run along, dear, and get a vase and some water to put my flowers in. *(MARY turns, sticks out her tongue at HELEN, says: "A-a-a," and exits Left)* You may put that book away, Peggy. I am sure your family need never worry about your going on the stage.

PEGGY I don't want to go on the stage. I want to be a lighthouse-keeper's wife.

MRS. MORTAR Well, I certainly hope you won't read to him.
(The laughter of the class pleases her. PEGGY sits down among the other girls, who are making a great show of doing nothing. MRS. MORTAR returns to her chair, puts her head back, closes her eyes)

CATHERINE How much longer, O Catiline, are you going to abuse our patience? *(To LOIS)* Now translate it, and for goodness' sakes try to get it right this time.

MRS. MORTAR *(For no reason)* "One master passion in the breast, like Aaron's serpent, swallows all the rest."
(She and LOIS are murmuring during KAREN WRIGHT'S entrance. KAREN is an attractive woman of twenty-eight, casually pleasant in manner, without sacrifice of warmth or dignity. She smiles at the girls, goes to the desk. With her entrance there is an immediate change in the manner of the girls: they are fond of her and they respect her. She gives MORTAR, whose quotation has reached her, an annoyed look)

LOIS "Quo usque tandem a*bu*tere. . . ."

KAREN *(Automatically)* "Abu*tere.*" *(Opens drawer in desk)* What's happened to your hair, Rosalie?

ROSALIE It got cut, Miss Wright.

KAREN *(Smiling)* I can see that. A new style? Looks as though it has holes in it.

EVELYN *(Giggling)* I didn't mean to do it that bad, Mith Wright, but Rothalie'th got funny hair. I thaw a picture in the paper, and I wath trying to do it that way.

ROSALIE *(Feels her hair, looks pathetically at* KAREN*)* Oh, what shall I do, Miss Wright? *(Gesturing)* It's long here, and it's short here and—

KAREN Never mind. Come up to my room later and I'll see if I can fix it for you.

MRS. MORTAR And hereafter we'll have no more haircutting.

KAREN Helen, have you found your bracelet?

HELEN No, I haven't, and I've looked everywhere.

KAREN Have another look. It must be in your room somewhere.

    (MARY comes in Right, with her flowers in a vase. When she sees KAREN, she loses some of her assurance. KAREN looks at the flowers in surprise)

MARY Good afternoon, Miss Wright.

    (Sits down, looks at KAREN, who is staring hard at the flowers)

KAREN Hello, Mary.

MRS. MORTAR *(Fluttering around)* Peggy has been reading Portia for us.

    (PEGGY sighs)

KAREN *(Smiling)* Peggy doesn't like Portia?

MRS. MORTAR I don't think she quite appreciates it, but—

KAREN *(Patting PEGGY on the head)* Well, I didn't either. I don't think I do yet. Where'd you get those flowers, Mary?

MRS. MORTAR She picked them for me. *(Hurriedly)* It made her a little late to class, but she heard me say I loved flowers, and she went to get them for me. *(With a sigh)* The first wild flowers of the season.

KAREN   But not the very first, are they, Mary?

MARY   I don't know.

KAREN   Where did you get them?

MARY   Near Conway's cornfield, I think.

KAREN   It wasn't necessary to go so far. There was a bunch exactly like this in the garbage can this morning.

MRS. MORTAR   *(After a second)*   Oh, I can't believe it! What a nasty thing to do! *(To* MARY*)* And I suppose you have just as fine an excuse for being an hour late to breakfast this morning, and last week— *(To* KAREN*)* I haven't wanted to tell you these things before, but—

KAREN   *(Hurriedly, as a bell rings off stage)*   There's the bell.

LOIS   *(Walking toward door)*   Ad, ab, ante, in, de, inter, con, post prae— *(Looks up at* KAREN*)* I *can't* seem to remember the rest.

KAREN   Prae, pro, sub, super. Don't worry, Lois. You'll come out all right. *(*LOIS *smiles, exits.* MARY *attempts to make a quick exit)* Wait a minute, Mary. *(Reluctantly* MARY *turns back as the girls file out.* KAREN *moves the small chairs, clearing the room as she talks)* Mary, I've had the feeling —and I don't think I'm wrong—that the girls here were happy; that they liked Miss Dobie and me, that they liked the school. Do you think that's true?

MARY   Miss Wright, I have to get my Latin book.

KAREN   I thought it was true until you came here a year ago. I don't think you're very happy here, and I'd like to find out why. *(Looks at* MARY, *waits for an answer, gets none, shakes her head)* Why, for example, do you find it necessary to lie to us so often?

MARY   *(Without looking up)*   I'm not lying. I went out walking and I saw the flowers and they looked pretty and I didn't know it was so late.

KAREN   *(Impatiently)*   Stop it, Mary! I'm not interested in hearing that foolish story again. I *know* you got the flowers out of the garbage can. What I do want to know is why you feel you have to lie out of it.

MARY   *(Beginning to whimper)*   I *did* pick the flowers near

Conway's. You never believe me. You believe everybody but me. It's always like that. Everything I say you fuss at me about. Everything I do is wrong.

KAREN   You know that isn't true. (*Goes to* MARY, *puts her arm around her, waits until the sobbing has stopped*) Look, Mary, look at me. (*Raises* MARY'S *face with her hand*) Let's try to understand each other. If you feel that you *have* to take a walk, or that you just *can't* come to class, or that you'd like to go into the village by yourself, come and tell me—I'll try and understand. (*Smiles*) I don't say that I'll always agree that you should do exactly what you want to do, but I've had feelings like that, too—everybody has—and I won't be unreasonable about yours. But this way, this kind of lying you do, makes everything wrong.

MARY   (*Looking steadily at* KAREN)   I got the flowers near Conway's cornfield.

KAREN   (*Looks at* MARY, *sighs, moves back toward desk and stands there for a moment*)   Well, there doesn't seem to be any other way with you; you'll have to be punished. Take your recreation periods alone for the next two weeks. No horseback-riding and no hockey. Don't leave the school grounds for any reason whatsoever. Is that clear?

MARY   (*Carefully*)   Saturday, too?

KAREN   Yes.

MARY   But you said I could go to the boat-races.

KAREN   I'm sorry, but you can't go.

MARY   I'll tell my grandmother. I'll tell her how everybody treats me here and the way I get punished for every little thing I do. I'll tell her, I'll—

MRS. MORTAR   Why, I'd slap her hands!

KAREN   (*Turning back from door, ignoring* MRS. MORTAR'S *speech. To* MARY)   Go upstairs, Mary.

MARY   I don't feel well.

KAREN   (*Wearily*)   Go upstairs now.

MARY   I've got a pain. I've had it all morning. It hurts right here. (*Pointing vaguely in the direction of her heart*) Really it does.

KAREN Ask Dobie to give you some hot water and bicarbonate of soda.

MARY It's a bad pain. I've never had it before.

KAREN I don't think it can be very serious.

MARY My heart! It's my heart! It's stopping or something. I can't breathe.

> (*She takes a long breath and falls awkwardly to the floor*)

KAREN (*Sighs, shakes her head, kneels beside* MARY. *To* MRS. MORTAR) Ask Martha to phone Joe.

MRS. MORTAR (*Going out*) Do you think—? Heart trouble is very serious in a child.

> (KAREN *picks* MARY *up from the floor and carries her off Right. After a moment* MARTHA DOBIE *enters Center. She is about the same age as* KAREN. *She is a nervous, high-strung woman*)

KAREN (*Enters Right*) Did you get Joe?

MARTHA (*Nodding*) What happened to her? She was perfectly well a few hours ago.

KAREN She probably still is. I told her she couldn't go to the boat-races and she had a heart attack.

MARTHA Where is she?

KAREN In there. Mortar's with her.

MARTHA Anything really wrong with her?

KAREN I doubt it. (*Sits down at desk and begins to mark papers*) She's a problem, that kid. Her latest trick was kidding your aunt out of a sewing lesson with those faded flowers we threw out. Then she threatened to go to her grandmother with some tale about being mistreated.

MARTHA And, please God, Grandma will believe her and take her away.

KAREN Which would give the school a swell black eye. But we ought to do something.

MARTHA How about having a talk with Mrs. Tilford?

KAREN (*Smiling*) You want to do it? (MARTHA *shakes her head*) I hate to do it. She's been so nice to us. (*Shrugging her shoulders*) Anyway, it wouldn't do any good. She's too crazy about Mary to see her faults very clearly—and the kid knows it.

MARTHA How about asking Joe to say something to her? She'd listen to him.

KAREN That would be admitting that we can't do the job ourselves.

MARTHA Well, we can't, and we might as well admit it. We've tried everything we can think of. She's had more attention than any other three kids put together. And we still haven't the faintest idea what goes on inside her head.

KAREN She's a strange girl.

MARTHA That's putting it mildly.

KAREN *(Laughs)* It's funny. We always talk about the child as if she were a grown woman.

MARTHA It's not so funny. There's something the matter with the kid. That's been true ever since the first day she came. She causes trouble here; she's bad for the other girls. I don't know what it is—it's a feeling I've got that it's wrong somewhere—

KAREN All right, all right, we'll talk it over with Joe. Now what about our other pet nuisance?

MARTHA *(Laughs)* My aunt the actress? What's she been up to now?

KAREN Nothing unusual. Last night at dinner she was telling the girls about the time she lost her trunks in Butte, Montana, and how she gave her best performance of Rosalind during a hurricane. Today in the kitchen you could hear her on what Sir Henry said to her.

MARTHA Wait until she does Hedda Gabler standing on a chair. Sir Henry taught her to do it that way. He said it was a test of great acting.

KAREN You must have had a gay childhood.

MARTHA *(Bitterly)* Oh, I did, I did, indeed. God, how I used to hate all that—

KAREN Couldn't we get rid of her soon, Martha? I hate to make it hard on you, but she really ought not to be here.

MARTHA *(After a moment)* I know.

KAREN We can scrape up enough money to send her away. Let's do it.

MARTHA (*Goes to her, affectionately pats her head*) You've been very patient about it. I'm sorry and I'll talk to her today. It'll probably be a week or two before she can be ready to leave. Is that all right?

KAREN Of course. (*Looks at her watch*) Did you get Joe himself on the phone?

MARTHA He was already on his way. Isn't he always on his way over here?

KAREN (*Laughs*) Well, I'm going to marry him some day, you know.

MARTHA (*Looking at her*) You haven't talked of marriage for a long time.

KAREN I've talked of it with Joe.

MARTHA Then you *are* thinking about it—soon?

KAREN Perhaps when the term is over. By that time we ought to be out of debt, and the school should be paying for itself.

MARTHA (*Nervously playing with a book on the table*) Then we won't be taking our vacation together?

KAREN Of course we will. The three of us.

MARTHA I had been looking forward to some place by the lake—just you and me—the way we used to at college.

KAREN (*Cheerfully*) Well, now there will be three of us. That'll be fun, too.

MARTHA (*After a pause*) Why haven't you told me this before?

KAREN I'm not telling you anything we haven't talked about often.

MARTHA But you're talking about it as *soon* now.

KAREN I'm glad to be able to. I've been in love with Joe a long time. (MARTHA *crosses to window and stands looking out, her back to* KAREN. KAREN *finishes marking papers and rises*) It's a big day for the school. Rosalie's finally put an "l" in could.

MARTHA (*In a dull, bitter tone, not turning from window*) You really *are* going to leave, aren't you?

KAREN I'm not going to leave, and you know it. Why do you say things like that? We agreed a long time ago that my marriage wasn't going to make any difference to the school.

MARTHA But it will. You know it will. It can't help it.

KAREN That's nonsense. Joe doesn't want me to give up here.

MARTHA *(Turning from window)* I don't understand you. It's been so damned hard building this thing up, slaving and going without things to make ends meet—think of having a winter coat without holes in the lining again!— and now when we're getting on our feet, you're all ready to let it go to hell.

KAREN This is a silly argument, Martha. Let's quit it. You haven't listened to a word I've said. I'm not getting married tomorrow, and when I do, it's not going to interfere with my work here. You're making something out of nothing.

MARTHA It's going to be hard going on alone afterward.

KAREN For God's sake, do you expect me to give up my marriage?

MARTHA I don't mean that, but it's so—
    (Door Center opens and DOCTOR JOSEPH CARDIN *comes in. He is a large, pleasant-looking, carelessly dressed man of about thirty-five)*

CARDIN Hello, darling. Hi, Martha. What's the best news?

MARTHA Hello, Joe.

KAREN We tried to get you on the phone. Come in and look at your little cousin.

CARDIN Sure. What's the matter with her now? I stopped at Vernie's on the way over to look at that little black bull he bought. He's a baby! There's going to be plenty of good breeding done in these hills.

KAREN You'd better come and see her. She says she has a pain in her heart.
    (Goes out Right)

CARDIN *(Stopping to light a cigarette)* Our little Mary pops up in every day's dispatches.

MARTHA (*Impatiently*)   Go and see her. Heart attacks are nothing to play with.

CARDIN (*Looks at her*)   Never played with one in my life. (*Exits Right.*)

> (MARTHA *walks around room and finally goes to stare out window.* MRS. MORTAR *enters Right*)

MRS. MORTAR   *I* was asked to leave the room. (MARTHA *pays no attention*) It seems that I'm not wanted in the room during the examination.

MARTHA (*Over her shoulder*)   What difference does it make?

MRS. MORTAR   What difference does it make? Why, it was a deliberate snub.

MARTHA   There's very little pleasure in watching a man use a stethoscope.

MRS. MORTAR   Isn't it natural that the child should have me with her? Isn't it natural that an older woman should be present? (*No answer*) Very well, if you are so thick-skinned that you don't resent these things—

MARTHA   What are you talking about? Why, in the name of heaven, should *you* be with her?

MRS. MORTAR   It's—it's customary for an older woman to be present during an examination.

MARTHA (*Laughs*)   Tell that to Joe. Maybe he'll give you a job as duenna for his office.

MRS. MORTAR (*Reminiscently*)   It was I who saved Delia Lampert's life the time she had that heart attack in Buffalo. We almost lost her that time. Poor Delia! We went over to London together. She married Robert Laffonne. Not seven months later he left her and ran away with Eve Cloun, who was paying the Infant Phenomenon in Birmingham—

MARTHA   Console yourself. If you've seen one heart attack, you've seen them all.

MRS. MORTAR   So you don't resent your aunt being snubbed and humiliated?

MARTHA   Oh, Aunt Lily!

MRS. MORTAR   Karen is consistently rude to me, and you know it.

MARTHA I know that she is very polite to you, and—what's more important—very patient.

MRS. MORTAR Patient with me? *I*, who have worked my fingers to the bone!

MARTHA Don't tell yourself that too often, Aunt Lily; you'll come to believe it.

MRS. MORTAR I *know* it's true. Where could you have gotten a woman of my reputation to give these children voice lessons, elocution lessons? Patient with me! Here I've donated my services—

MARTHA I was under the impression you were being paid.

MRS. MORTAR That small thing! I used to earn twice that for one performance.

MARTHA The gilded days. It was very extravagant of them to pay you so much. *(Suddenly tired of the whole thing)* You're not very happy here, are you, Aunt Lily?

MRS. MORTAR Satisfied enough, I guess, for a poor relation.

MARTHA *(Makes a motion of distaste)* But you don't like the school or the farm or—

MRS. MORTAR I told you at the beginning you shouldn't have bought a place like this. Burying yourself on a farm! You'll regret it.

MARTHA We like it here. *(After a moment)* Aunt Lily, you've talked about London for a long time. Would you like to go over?

MRS. MORTAR *(With a sigh)* It's been twenty years, and I shall never live to see it again.

MARTHA Well, you can go any time you like. We can spare the money now, and it will do you a lot of good. You pick out the boat you want and I'll get the passage. *(She has been talking rapidly, anxious to end the whole thing)* Now that's all fixed. You'll have a grand time seeing all your old friends, and if you live sensibly I ought to be able to let you have enough to get along on.

(She begins to gather books, notebooks, and pencils)

MRS. MORTAR *(slowly)* So you want me to leave?

MARTHA That's not the way to put it. You've wanted to go ever since I can remember.

MRS. MORTAR You're trying to get rid of me.

MARTHA That's it. We don't want you around when we dig up the buried treasure.

MRS. MORTAR So? You're turning me out? At my age! Nice, grateful girl you are.

MARTHA Oh, my God, how can anybody deal with you? You're going where you want to go, and we'll be better off alone. That suits everybody. You complain about the farm, you complain about the school, you complain about Karen, and now you have what you want and you're still looking for something to complain about.

MRS. MORTAR *(With dignity)* Please do not raise your voice.

MARTHA You ought to be glad I don't do worse.

MRS. MORTAR I absolutely refuse to be shipped off three thousand miles away. I'm not going to England. I shall go back to the stage. I'll write to my agents tomorrow, and as soon as they have something good for me—

MARTHA The truth is I'd like you to leave soon. The three of us can't live together, and it doesn't make any difference whose fault it is.

MRS. MORTAR You wish me to go tonight?

MARTHA Don't act, Aunt Lily. Go as soon as you've found a place you like. I'll put the money in the bank for you tomorrow.

MRS. MORTAR You think I'd take your money? I'd rather scrub floors first.

MARTHA I imagine you'll change your mind.

MRS. MORTAR I should have known by this time that the wise thing is to stay out of your way when *he's* in the house.

MARTHA What are you talking about now?

MRS. MORTAR Never mind. I should have known better. You always take your spite out on me.

MARTHA Spite? *(Impatiently)* Oh, don't let's have any more of this today. I'm tired. I've been working since six o'clock this morning.

MRS. MORTAR Any day that he's in the house is a bad day.

MARTHA When *who* is in the house?

MRS. MORTAR Don't think you're fooling me, young lady. I wasn't born yesterday.

MARTHA Aunt Lily, the amount of disconnected unpleasantness that goes on in your head could keep a psychologist busy for years. Now go take your nap.

MRS. MORTAR I know what I know. Every time that man comes into this house, you have a fit. It seems like you just can't stand the idea of them being together. God knows what you'll do when they get married. You're jealous of him, that's what it is.

MARTHA *(Her voice is tense and the previous attitude of good-natured irritation is gone)* I'm very fond of Joe, and you know it.

MRS. MORTAR You're fonder of Karen, and I know that. And it's unnatural, just as unnatural as it can be. You don't like their being together. You were always like that even as a child. If you had a little girl friend, you always got mad when she liked anybody else. Well, you'd better get a beau of your own now—a woman of your age.

MARTHA The sooner you get out of here, the better. Your vulgarities are making me sick and I won't stand for them any longer. I want you to leave—

(At this point there is a sound outside the large doors Center. MARTHA *breaks off, angry and ashamed. After a moment she crosses to the door and opens it.* EVELYN *and* PEGGY *are to be seen on the staircase. For a second she stands still as they stop and look at her. Then, afraid that her anger with her aunt will color anything she might say to the children, she crosses the room again and stands with her back to them)*

MARTHA What were you doing outside the door?

EVELYN *(Hurriedly)* We were going upthtairth, Mith Dobie.

PEGGY We came down to see how Mary was.

MARTHA And you stopped long enough to see how we were. Did you deliberately listen?

PEGGY We didn't mean to. We heard voices and we couldn't help—

MRS. MORTAR *(Fake social tone)* Eavesdropping is something nice young ladies just don't do.

MARTHA *(Turning to face the children)* Go upstairs now. We'll talk about this later.

(Slowly shuts door as they begin to climb the stairs)

MRS. MORTAR You mean to say you're not going to do anything about that? *(No answer. She laughs nastily)* That's the trouble with these new-fangled notions of discipline and—

MARTHA *(Thoughtfully)* You know, it's really bad having you around children.

MRS. MORTAR What exactly does that mean?

MARTHA It means that I don't like them hearing the things you say. Oh, I'll "do something about it," but the truth is that this is their home, and things shouldn't be said in it that they can't hear. When you're at your best you're not for tender ears.

MRS. MORTAR So now it's my fault, is it? Just as I said, whenever he's in the house you think you can take it out on me. You've got to have some way to let out steam and—

(Door opens Right and CARDIN comes in)

MARTHA How is Mary?

(MRS. MORTAR, head in air, gives MARTHA a malicious half-smile and makes what she thinks is majestic exit Center)

MRS. MORTAR Good day, Joseph.

CARDIN What's the matter with the Duchess?

(Nods at door Center)

MARTHA Just keeping her hand in, in case Sir Henry's watching her from above. What about Mary?

CARDIN Nothing. Absolutely nothing.

MARTHA *(Sighs)* I thought so.

CARDIN I could have managed a better faint than that when I was six years old.

MARTHA Nothing the matter with her at all, then?

CARDIN *(Laughs)* No, ma'am, not a thing. Just a little something she thought up.

MARTHA But it's such a silly thing to do. She knew we'd

have you in. *(Sighs)* Maybe she's not so bright. Any idiots in your family, Joe? Any inbreeding?

CARDIN Don't blame her on me. It's another side of the family. *(Laughs)* You can look at Aunt Amelia and tell: old New England stock; never married out of Boston; still thinks honor is honor and dinner's at eight thirty. Yes, ma'am, we're a proud old breed.

MARTHA The Jukes were an old family, too. Look, Joe, have you any idea what is the matter with Mary? I mean, has she always been like this?

CARDIN She's always been a honey. Aunt Amelia's spoiling hasn't helped any, either.

MARTHA We're reaching the end of our rope with her. This kind of thing—

CARDIN *(Looking at her)* Aren't you taking this too seriously?

MARTHA *(After a second)* I guess I am. But you stay around kids long enough and you won't know what to take seriously, either. But I do think somebody ought to talk to Mrs. Tilford about her.

CARDIN You wouldn't be meaning me now, would you, Miss Dobie?

MARTHA Well, Karen and I were talking about it this afternoon and—

CARDIN Listen, friend, I'm marrying Karen, but I'm not writing Mary Tilford in the contract. (MARTHA *moves slightly.* CARDIN *takes her by the shoulders and turns her around to face him again. His face is grave, his voice gentle)* Forget Mary for a minute. You and I have got something to fight about. Every time anything's said about marrying—about Karen marrying me—you—*(She winces)* There it is. I'm fond of you. I always thought you liked me. What is it? I know how fond you are of Karen, but our marriage oughtn't to make a great deal of difference—

MARTHA *(Pushing his hands from her shoulders)* God damn you. I wish—*(She puts her face in her hands.* CARDIN *watches her in silence, mechanically lighting a cigarette. When she takes her hands from her face, she holds*

them out to him. Contritely) Joe, please, I'm sorry. I'm a
fool, a nasty, bitter—

CARDIN *(Takes her hands in one of his, patting them with his
other hand)* Aw, shut up.

> *(He puts an arm around her, and she leans her head
> against his lapel. They are standing like that when
> KAREN comes in Right)*

MARTHA *(To KAREN, as she wipes her eyes)* Your friend's
got a nice shoulder to weep on.

KAREN He's an admirable man in every way. Well, the angel child is now putting her clothes back on.

MARTHA The angel child's influence is abroad even while
she's unconscious. Her room-mates were busy listening at
the door while Aunt Lily and I were yelling at each other.

KAREN We'll have to move those girls away from one another.

> *(A bell rings from the rear of the house)*

MARTHA That's my class. I'll send Peggy and Evelyn down.
You talk to them.

KAREN All right. *(As MARTHA exits Center, KAREN goes toward door Right. As she passes CARDIN she kisses him)*
Mary!

> *(MARY opens door, comes in, stands buttoning the
> neck of her dress)*

CARDIN *(To MARY)* How's it feel to be back from the grave?

MARY My heart hurts.

CARDIN *(Laughing. To KAREN)* Science has failed. Try a
hairbrush.

MARY It's *my* heart, and it hurts.

KAREN Sit down.

MARY I want to see my grandmother. I want to—

> *(EVELYN and PEGGY timidly enter Center)*

KAREN Sit down, girls, I want to talk to you.

PEGGY We're awfully sorry, really. We just didn't think
and—

KAREN I'm sorry too, Peggy. *(Thoughtfully)* You and Evelyn never used to do things like this. We'll have to separate
you three.

EVELYN Ah, Mith Wright, we've been together almotht a year.

KAREN It was evidently too long. Now don't let's talk about it. Peggy, you will move into Lois's room, and Lois will move in with Evelyn. Mary will go in with Rosalie.

MARY Rosalie hates me.

KAREN That's a very stupid thing to say. I can't imagine Rosalie hating anyone.

MARY *(Starting to cry)* And it's all because I had a pain. If anybody else was sick they'd be put to bed and petted. You're always mean to me. I get blamed and punished for everything. *(To* CARDIN*)* I do, Cousin Joe. All the time for everything.

> *(*MARY *by now is crying violently and as* KAREN *half moves toward her,* CARDIN, *who has been frowning, picks* MARY *up and puts her down on the couch)*

CARDIN You've been unpleasant enough to Miss Wright. Lie here until you've stopped working yourself into a fit. *(Picks up his hat and bag, smiles at* KAREN*)* I've got to go now. She's not going to hurt herself crying. The next time she faints, I'd wait until she got tired lying on the floor.

> *(Passing* MARY, *he pats her head. She jerks away from him)*

KAREN Wait a minute. I'll walk to the car with you. *(To girls)* Go up now and move your things. Tell Lois to get her stuff ready.

> *(She and* CARDIN *exit Center. A second after the door is closed,* MARY *springs up and throws a cushion at the door)*

EVELYN Don't do that. She'll hear you.

MARY Who cares if she does? *(Kicks table)* And she can hear that, too.

> *(Small ornament falls off table and breaks on floor.* EVELYN *and* PEGGY *gasp, and* MARY'S *bravado disappears for a moment)*

EVELYN *(Frightened)* Now what are you going to do?

PEGGY *(Stooping down in a vain effort to pick up the pieces)* You'll get the devil now. Dr. Cardin gave it to Miss Wright.

I guess it was kind of a lover's gift. People get awfully angry about a lover's gift.

MARY   Oh, leave it alone. She'll never know we did it.

PEGGY   *We* didn't do it. You did it yourself.

MARY   And what will you do if I say *we* did do it? *(Laughs)* Never mind, I'll think of something else. The wind could've knocked it over.

EVELYN   Yeh. She'th going to believe that one.

MARY   Oh, stop worrying about it. I'll get out of it.

EVELYN   Did you really have a pain?

MARY   I fainted, didn't I?

PEGGY   I wish I could faint sometimes. I've never even worn glasses, like Rosalie.

MARY   A lot it'll get you to faint.

EVELYN   What did Mith Wright do to you when the clath left?

MARY   Told me I couldn't go to the boat-races.

EVELYN   Whew!

PEGGY   But we'll remember everything that happens and we'll give you all the souvenirs and things.

MARY   I won't let you go if I can't go. But I'll find some way to go. What were *you* doing?

PEGGY   I guess we shouldn't have done it, really. We came down to see what was happening to you, but the doors were closed and we could hear Miss Dobie and Mortar having an awful row. Then Miss Dobie opens the door and there we were.

MARY   And a lot of crawling and crying you both did too, I bet.

EVELYN   We were thort of thorry about lithening. I gueth it wathn't—

MARY   Ah, you're always sorry about everything. What were they saying?

PEGGY   What was who saying?

MARY   Dobie and Mortar, silly.

PEGGY   *(Evasively)*   Just talking, I guess.

EVELYN   Fighting, you mean.

MARY   About what?

EVELYN Well, they were talking about Mortar going away to England and—

PEGGY You know, it really wasn't very nice to've listened, and I think it's worse to tell.

MARY You do, do you? You just don't tell me and see what happens.

    (PEGGY sighs)

EVELYN Mortar got awful thore at that and thaid they juth wanted to get rid of her, and then they thtarted talking about Dr. Cardin.

MARY What about him?

PEGGY We'd better get started moving. Miss Wright will be back first thing we know.

MARY *(fiercely)* Shut up! Go on, Evelyn.

EVELYN They're going to be married.

MARY Everybody knows that.

PEGGY But everybody doesn't know that Miss Dobie doesn't want them to get married. How do you like that?

    (The door opens and ROSALIE WELLS sticks her head in)

ROSALIE I have a class soon. If you're going to move your things—

MARY Close that door, you idiot. *(ROSALIE closes door, stands near it)* What do you want?

ROSALIE I'm trying to tell you. If you're going to move your things—not that I want you in with me—you'd better start right now. Miss Wright's coming in a minute.

MARY Who cares if she is?

ROSALIE *(Starts for door)* I'm just telling you for your own good.

PEGGY *(Getting up)* We're coming.

MARY No. Let Rosalie move our things.

ROSALIE You crazy?

PEGGY *(Nervously)* It's all right. Evelyn and I'll get your things. Come on, Evelyn.

MARY Trying to get out of telling me, huh? Well, you won't get out of it that way. Sit down and stop being such a sissy.

Rosalie, you go on up and move my things and don't say a word about our being down here.

ROSALIE   And who was your French maid yesterday, Mary Tilford?

MARY *(Laughing)* You'll do for today. Now go on, Rosalie, and fix our things.

ROSALIE   You crazy?

MARY   And the next time we go into town, I'll let you wear my gold locket and buckle. You'll like that, won't you, Rosalie?

ROSALIE *(Draws back, moves her hands nervously)* I don't know what you're talking about.

MARY   Oh, I'm not talking about anything in particular. You just run along now and remind me the next time to get my buckle and locket for you.

ROSALIE *(Stares at her a moment)* All right, I'll do it this time, but just 'cause I got a good disposition. But don't think you're going to boss me around, Mary Tilford.

MARY *(Smiling)* No, indeed. (ROSALIE *starts for door)* And get the things done neatly, Rosalie. Don't muss my white linen bloomers—

 (The door slams as MARY laughs.)

EVELYN   Now what do you think of that? What made her tho agreeable?

MARY   Oh, a little secret we got. Go on, now, what else did they say?

PEGGY   Well, Mortar said that Dobie was jealous of them, and that she was like that when she was a little girl, and that she'd better get herself a beau of her own because it was unnatural, and that she never wanted anybody to like Miss Wright, and that was unnatural. Boy! Did Miss Dobie get sore at that!

EVELYN   Then we didn't hear any more. Peggy dropped a book.

MARY   What'd she mean Dobie was jealous?

PEGGY   What's unnatural?

EVELYN   Un for not. Not natural.

PEGGY   It's funny, because everybody gets married.

MARY   A lot of people don't—they're too ugly.

PEGGY *(Jumps up, claps her hand to her mouth)*   Oh, my God! Rosalie'll find that copy of *Mademoiselle de Maupin.* She'll blab like the dickens.

MARY   Ah, she won't say a word.

EVELYN   Who getth the book when you move?

MARY   You can have it. That's what I was doing this morning —finishing it. There's one part in it—

PEGGY   What part?
     (MARY laughs)

EVELYN   Well, what wath it?

MARY   Wait until you read it.

EVELYN   Don't forget to give it to me.

PEGGY   It's a shame about being moved. I've got to go in with Helen, and she blows her nose all night. Lois told me.

MARY   It was a dirty trick making us move. She just wants to see how much fun she can take away from me. She hates me.

PEGGY   No, she doesn't, Mary. She treats you just like the rest of us—almost better.

MARY   That's right, stick up for your crush. Take her side against mine.

PEGGY   I didn't mean it that way.

EVELYN *(Looks at her watch)*   We'd better get upthtairth.

MARY   I'm not going.

PEGGY   Rosalie isn't so bad.

EVELYN   What you going to do about the vathe?

MARY   I don't care about Rosalie and I don't care about the vase. I'm not going to be here.

EVELYN *and* PEGGY *(Together)*   Not going to be here! What do you mean?

MARY *(Calmly)*   I'm going home.

PEGGY   Oh, Mary—

EVELYN   You can't do that.

MARY   Can't I? You just watch. *(Begins to walk around the room)* I'm not staying here. I'm going home and tell Grandma I'm not staying any more. *(Smiles to herself)* I'll tell her I'm not happy. They're scared of Grandma—she

helped 'em when they first started, you know—and when
she tells 'em something, believe me, they'll sit up and listen. They can't get away with treating me like this, and
they don't have to think they can.

PEGGY *(Appalled)* You just going to walk out like that?

EVELYN What you going to tell your grandmother?

MARY Oh, who cares? I'll think of something to tell her. I
can always do it better on the spur of the moment.

PEGGY She'll send you right back.

MARY You let me worry about that. Grandma's very fond of
me, on account my father was her favorite son. I can manage *her* all right.

PEGGY I don't think you ought to go, really, Mary. It's just
going to make an awful lot of trouble.

EVELYN What'th going to happen about the vathe?

MARY Say I did it—it doesn't make a bit of difference any
more to me. Now listen, you two got to help. They won't
miss me before dinner if you make Rosalie shut the door
and keep it shut. Now, I'll go through the field to French's,
and then I can get the bus to Homestead.

EVELYN How you going to get to the thtreet-car?

MARY Taxi, idiot.

PEGGY How are you going to get out of here in the first
place?

MARY I'm going to walk out. You know where the front
door is, or are you too dumb even for that? Well, I'm going
right out that front door.

EVELYN Gee, I wouldn't have the nerve.

MARY Of course you wouldn't. You'd let 'em do anything to
you they want. Well, they can't do it to me. Who's got any
money?

EVELYN Not me. Not a thent.

MARY I've got to have at least a dollar for the taxi and a
dime for the bus.

EVELYN And where you going to find it?

PEGGY See? Why don't you just wait until your allowance
comes Monday, and then you can go any place you want.
Maybe by that time—

MARY I'm going today. *Now.*

EVELYN You can't *walk* to Lanthet.

MARY *(Goes to* PEGGY*)* You've got money. You've got two dollars and twenty-five cents.

PEGGY I—I—

MARY Go get it for me.

PEGGY No! No! I won't get it for you.

EVELYN You can't have *that* money, Mary—

MARY Get it for me.

PEGGY *(Cringes, her voice is scared)* I won't. I won't. Mamma doesn't send me much allowance—not half as much as the rest of you get—I saved this so long—you took it from me last time—

EVELYN Ah, she wanth that bithycle tho bad.

PEGGY I haven't gone to the movies, I haven't had any candy, I haven't had anything the rest of you get all the time. It took me so long to save that and I—

MARY Go upstairs and get me the money.

PEGGY *(Hysterically, backing away from her)* I won't. I won't. I won't.

    *(*MARY *makes a sudden move for her, grabs her left arm, and jerks it back, hard and expertly.* PEGGY *screams softly.* EVELYN *tries to take* MARY'S *arm away. Without releasing her hold on* PEGGY, MARY *slaps* EVELYN'S *face.* EVELYN *begins to cry)*

MARY Just say when you've had enough.

PEGGY *(Softly, stiflingly)* All—all right—I'll get it.

    *(*MARY *smiles, nods her head as the Curtain falls)*

Act Two

SCENE 1

SCENE: *Living room at* MRS. TILFORD'S. *It is a formal room, without being cold or elegant. The furniture is old, but excellent. The exit to the hall is Left; glass doors Right lead to a dining room that cannot be seen.*

AT RISE: *Stage is empty. Voices are heard in the hall.*

AGATHA *(Off-stage)* What are *you* doing here? Well, come on in—don't stand there gaping at me. Have they given you a holiday or did you just decide you'd get a better dinner here? (AGATHA *enters Left, followed by* MARY. AGATHA *is a sharp-faced maid, not young, with a querulous voice)* Can't you even say hello?

MARY Hello, Agatha. You didn't give me a chance. Where's Grandma?

AGATHA Why aren't you in school? Look at your face and clothes. Where have you been?

MARY I got a little dirty coming home. I walked part of the way through the woods.

AGATHA Why didn't you put on your middy blouse and your old brown coat?

MARY Oh, stop asking me questions. Where's Grandma?

AGATHA Where ought any clean person be at this time of day? She's taking a bath.

MARY Is anybody coming for dinner?

AGATHA She didn't say anything about you coming.

MARY How could she, stupid? She didn't know.

AGATHA Then what are you doing here?

MARY Leave me alone. I don't feel well.

AGATHA Why don't you feel well? Who ever heard of a person going for a walk in the woods when they didn't feel well?

MARY Oh, leave me alone. I came home because I was sick.

AGATHA You look all right.

MARY But I don't feel all right. *(Whining)* I can't even come home without everybody nagging at me.

AGATHA Don't think you're fooling me, young lady. You might pull the wool over some people's eyes, but—I bet you've been up to something again. *(Stares suspiciously at* MARY, *who says nothing)* Well, you wait right here till I get your grandmother. And if you feel so sick, you certainly won't want any dinner. A good dose of rhubarb and soda will fix you up.

> *(Exits Left.* MARY *makes a face in the direction* AGATHA *has gone and stops sniffling. She looks nervously around the room, then goes to a low mirror and tries several experiments with her face in an attempt to make it look sick and haggard.* MRS. TILFORD, *followed by* AGATHA, *enters Left.* MRS. TILFORD *is a large, dignified woman in her sixties, with a pleasant, strong face)*

AGATHA *(To* MRS. TILFORD, *as she follows her into the room)* Why didn't you put some cold water on your chest? Do you want to catch your death of cold at your age? Did you have to hurry so?

MRS. TILFORD Mary, what are you doing home?

> *(*MARY *rushes to her and buries her head in* MRS. TILFORD'S *dress, crying.* MRS. TILFORD *lets her cry for a moment while she pats her head, then puts an arm around the child and leads her to a sofa)*

MRS. TILFORD Never mind, dear; now stop crying and tell me what is the matter.

MARY *(Gradually stops crying, fondling* MRS. TILFORD'S *hand)* It's so good to see you, Grandma. You didn't come to visit me all last week.

MRS. TILFORD I couldn't, dear. But I was coming tomorrow.

MARY I missed you so. *(Smiling up at* MRS. TILFORD*)* I was awful homesick.

MRS. TILFORD I'm glad that's all it was. I was frightened when Agatha said you were not well.

AGATHA Did I say that? I said she needed a good dose of

rhubarb and soda. Most likely she only came home for Wednesday night fudge cake.

MRS. TILFORD We all get homesick. But how did you get here? Did Miss Karen drive you over?

MARY I—I walked most of the way, and then a lady gave me a ride and—
    (Looks timidly at MRS. TILFORD*)*

AGATHA Did she have to walk through the woods in her very best coat?

MRS. TILFORD Mary! Do you mean you left without permission?

MARY *(Nervously)* I ran away, Grandma. They didn't know—

MRS. TILFORD That was a very bad thing to do, and they'll be worried. Agatha, phone Mrs. Wright and tell her Mary is here. John will drive her back before dinner.

MARY *(As* AGATHA *starts toward telephone)* No, Grandma, don't do that. Please don't do that. Please let me stay.

MRS. TILFORD But, darling, you can't leave school any time you please.

MARY Oh, please, Grandma, don't send me back right away. You don't know how they'll punish me.

MRS. TILFORD I don't think they'll be that angry. Come, you're acting like a foolish little girl.

MARY *(Hysterically, as she sees* AGATHA *about to pick up the telephone)* Grandma! Please! I can't go back! I can't! They'll kill me! They will, Grandma! They'll kill me!
    *(*MRS. TILFORD *and* AGATHA *stare at* MARY *in amazement. She puts her head in* MRS. TILFORD'S *lap and sobs)*

MRS. TILFORD *(Motioning with a hand for* AGATHA *to leave the room)* Never mind phoning now, Agatha.

AGATHA If you're going to let her—
    *(*MRS. TILFORD *repeats the gesture.* AGATHA *exits Right, with offended dignity)*

MRS. TILFORD Stop crying, Mary.

MARY *(Raising her head from* MRS. TILFORD'S *lap)* It's so nice here, Grandma

MRS. TILFORD I'm glad you like being home with me, but at your age you can hardly—*(More seriously)* What made you say such a terrible thing about Miss Wright and Miss Dobie? You know they wouldn't hurt you.

MARY Oh, but they would. They—I—*(Breaks off, looks around as if hunting for a clue to her next word; then dramatically)* I fainted today!

MRS. TILFORD *(Alarmed)* Fainted?

MARY Yes, I did. My heart—I had a pain in my heart. I couldn't help having a pain in my heart, and when I fainted right in class, they called Cousin Joe and he said I didn't. He said it was maybe only that I ate my breakfast too fast and Miss Wright blamed me for it.

MRS. TILFORD *(Relieved)* I'm sure if Joseph said it wasn't serious, it wasn't.

MARY But I did have a pain in my heart—honest.

MRS. TILFORD Have you still got it?

MARY I guess I haven't got it much any more, but I feel a little weak, and I was so scared of Miss Wright being so mean to me just because I was sick.

MRS. TILFORD Scared of Karen? Nonsense. It's perfectly possible that you had a pain, but if you had really been sick your Cousin Joseph would certainly have known it. It's not nice to frighten people by pretending to be sick when you aren't.

MARY I didn't *want* to be sick, but I'm always getting punished for everything.

MRS. TILFORD *(Gently)* You mustn't imagine things like that, child, or you'll grow up to be a very unhappy woman. I'm not going to scold you any more for coming home this time, though I suppose I should. Run along upstairs and wash your face and change your dress, and after dinner John will drive you back. Run along.

MARY *(Happily)* I can stay for dinner?

MRS. TILFORD Yes.

MARY Maybe I could stay till the first of the week. Saturday's your birthday and I could be here with you.

MRS. TILFORD   We don't celebrate my birthday, dear. You'll have to go back to school after dinner.

MARY   But—(*She hesitates, then goes up to* MRS. TILFORD *and puts her arms around the older woman's neck. Softly*) How much do you love me?

MRS. TILFORD (*Smiling*)   As much as all the words in all the books in all the world.

MARY   Remember when I was little and you used to tell me that right before I went to sleep? And it was a rule nobody could say another single word after you finished? You used to say: "Wor-rr-ld," and then I had to shut my eyes tight.

MRS. TILFORD   And sometimes you were naughty and didn't shut them.

MARY   I miss you an awful lot, Grandma.

MRS. TILFORD   And I miss you, but I'm afraid my Latin is too rusty—you'll learn it better in school.

MARY   But couldn't I stay out the rest of this term? After the summer maybe I won't mind it so much. I'll study hard, honest, and—

MRS. TILFORD   You're an earnest little coaxer, but it's out of the question. Back you go tonight. (*Gives* MARY *a playful slap*) Let's not have any more talk about it now, and let's have no more running away from school ever.

MARY (*Slowly*)   Then I really have to go back there tonight?

MRS. TILFORD   Of course.

MARY   You don't love me. You don't care whether they kill me or not.

MRS. TILFORD   Mary.

MARY   You don't! You don't! You don't care what happens to me.

MRS. TILFORD (*Sternly*)   But I *do* care that you're talking this way.

MARY (*Meekly*)   I'm sorry I said that, Grandma. I didn't mean to hurt your feelings. (*Puts her arms around* MRS. TILFORD'S *neck*) Forgive me?

MRS. TILFORD   What made you talk like that?

MARY *(In a whisper)* I'm scared, Grandma, I'm scared. They'll do dreadful things to me.

MRS. TILFORD Dreadful? Nonsense. They'll punish you for running away. You deserve to be punished.

MARY It's not that. It's not anything I do. It never is. They —they just punish me anyhow, just like they got something against me. I'm afraid of them, Grandma.

MRS. TILFORD That's ridiculous. What have they ever done to you that is so terrible?

MARY A lot of things—all the time. Miss Wright says I can't go to the boat-races and—*(Realizing the inadequacy of this reply, she breaks off, hesitates, hunting for a more telling reply, and finally stammers)* It's—it's after what happened today.

MRS. TILFORD You mean something else besides your naughtiness in pretending to faint and then running away?

MARY I *did* faint. I didn't pretend. They just said that to make me feel bad. Anyway, it wasn't anything that I did.

MRS. TILFORD What was it, then?

MARY I can't tell you.

MRS. TILFORD Why?

MARY *(Sulkily)* Because you're just going to take their part.

MRS. TILFORD *(A little annoyed)* Very well. Now run upstairs and get ready for dinner.

MARY It was—it was all about Miss Dobie and Mrs. Mortar. They were talking awful things and Peggy and Evelyn heard them and Miss Dobie found out, and then they made us move our rooms.

MRS. TILFORD What has that to do with you? I don't understand a word you're saying.

MARY They made us move our rooms. They said we couldn't be together any more. They're afraid to have us near them, that's what it is, and they're taking it out on me. They're scared of you.

MRS. TILFORD For a little girl you're imagining a lot of big things. Why should they be scared of me? Am I such an unpleasant old lady?

MARY They're afraid you'll find out.

MRS. TILFORD Find out what?

MARY *(Vaguely)* Things.

MRS. TILFORD Run along, Mary. I hope you'll get more coherent as you get older.

MARY *(Slowly starting for the door)* All right. But there're a lot of things. They have secrets or something, and they're afraid I'll find out and tell you.

MRS. TILFORD There's not necessarily anything wrong with people having secrets.

MARY *(Coming back in the room again)* But they've got funny ones. Peggy and Evelyn heard Mrs. Mortar telling Miss Dobie that she was jealous of Miss Wright marrying Cousin Joe.

MRS. TILFORD You shouldn't repeat things like that.

MARY But that's what she said, Grandma. She said it was unnatural for a girl to feel that way.

MRS. TILFORD What?

MARY I'm just telling you what she said. She said there was something funny about it, and that Miss Dobie had always been like that, even when she was a little girl, and that it was unnatural—

MRS. TILFORD Stop using that silly word, Mary.

MARY *(Vaguely realizing that she is on the right track, hurries on)* But that was the word *she* kept using, Grandma, and then they got mad and told Mrs. Mortar she'd have to get out.

MRS. TILFORD That was probably not the reason at all.

MARY *(Nodding vigorously)* I bet it was, because honestly, Miss Dobie does get cranky and mean every time Cousin Joe comes, and today I heard her say to him: "God damn you," and then she said she was just a jealous fool and—

MRS. TILFORD You have picked up some fine words, haven't you, Mary?

MARY That's just what she said, Grandma, and one time Miss Dobie was crying in Miss Wright's room, and Miss Wright was trying to stop her, and she said that all right, maybe she wouldn't get married right away if—

MRS. TILFORD How do you know all this?

MARY   We couldn't help hearing because they—I mean Miss Dobie—was talking awful loud, and their room is right next to ours.

MRS. TILFORD   Whose room?

MARY   Miss Wright's room, I mean, and you can just ask Peggy and Evelyn whether we didn't hear. Almost always Miss Dobie comes in after we go to bed and stays a long time. I guess that's why they want to get rid of us—of me —because we hear things. That's why they're making us move our room, and they punish me all the time for—

MRS. TILFORD   For eavesdropping, I should think. *(She has said this mechanically. With nothing definite in her mind, she is making an effort to conceal the fact that* MARY'S *description of the life at school has shocked her)* Well, now I think we've had enough gossip, don't you? Dinner's almost ready, and I can't eat with a girl who has such a dirty face.

MARY   *(Softly)*   I've heard other things, too.

MRS. TILFORD   *(Abstractedly)*   What? What did you say?

MARY   I've heard other things. Plenty of other things, Grandma.

MRS. TILFORD   What things?

MARY   Bad things.

MRS. TILFORD   Well, what were they?

MARY   I can't tell you.

MRS. TILFORD   Mary, you're annoying me very much. If you have something to say, then say it and stop acting silly.

MARY   I mean I can't say it out loud.

MRS. TILFORD   There couldn't possibly be anything so terrible that you couldn't say it out loud. Now either tell the truth or be still.

MARY   Well, a lot of things I don't understand. But it's awful, and sometimes they fight and then they make up, and Miss Dobie cries and Miss Wright gets mad, and then they make up again, and there are funny noises and we get scared.

MRS. TILFORD   Noises? I suppose you girls have a happy time imagining a murder.

MARY   And we've seen things, too. Funny things. *(Sees the impatience of her grandmother)* I'd tell you, but I got to whisper it.

MRS. TILFORD Why must you whisper it?

MARY I don't know. I just got to.
> *(Climbs on the sofa next to* MRS. TILFORD *and begins whispering. At first the whisper is slow and hesitant, but it gradually works itself up to fast, excited talking. In the middle of it* MRS. TILFORD *stops her)*

MRS. TILFORD *(Trembling)* Do you know what you're saying? *(Without answering,* MARY *goes back to the whispering until the older woman takes her by the shoulders and turns her around to stare in her face)* Mary! Are you telling me the truth?

MARY Honest, honest. You just ask Peggy and Evelyn and ——*(After a moment* MRS. TILFORD *gets up and begins to pace about the room. She is no longer listening to* MARY, *who keeps up a running fire of conversation)* They know too. And maybe there're other kids who know, but we've always been frightened and so we didn't ask, and one night I was going to go and find out, but I got scared and we went to bed early so we wouldn't hear, but sometimes I couldn't help it, but we never talked about it much, because we thought they'd find out and——Oh, Grandma, don't make me go back to that awful place.

MRS. TILFORD *(Abstractedly)* What?
> *(Starts to move about again)*

MARY Don't make me go back to that place. I just couldn't stand it any more. Really, Grandma, I'm so unhappy there, and if only I could stay out the rest of the term, why, then——

MRS. TILFORD *(Makes irritated gesture)* Be still a minute. *(After a moment)* No, you won't have to go back.

MARY *(Surprised)* Honest?

MRS. TILFORD Honest.

MARY *(Hugging* MRS. TILFORD*)* You're the nicest, loveliest grandma in all the world. You——you're not mad at me?

MRS. TILFORD I'm not mad at you. Now go upstairs and get ready for dinner. *(*MARY *kisses her and runs happily out*

Left. MRS. TILFORD *stands staring after her for a long moment; then, very slowly, she puts on her eyeglasses and crosses to the phone. She dials a number)* Is Miss Wright —is Miss Wright in? *(Waits a second, hurriedly puts down the receiver)* Never mind, never mind. *(Dials another number)* Dr. Cardin, please. Mrs. Tilford. *(She remains absolutely motionless while she waits. When she does speak, her voice is low and tense)* Joseph? Joseph? Can you come to see me right away? Yes, I'm perfectly well. No, but it's important, Joseph, very important. I must see you right away. I—I can't tell you over the phone. Can't you come sooner? It's not about Mary's fainting—I said it's not about Mary, Joseph; in one way it's about Mary—*(Suddenly quiet)* But will the hospital take so long? Very well, Joseph, make it as soon as you can. *(Hangs up the receiver, sits for a moment undecided. Then, taking a breath, she dials another number)* Mrs. Munn, please. This is Mrs. Tilford. Miriam? This is Amelia Tilford. I have something to tell you—something very shocking, I'm afraid—something about the school and Evelyn and Mary—

CURTAIN

SCENE 2

SCENE: *The same as Scene 1. The curtain has been lowered to mark the passing of a few hours.*

AT RISE: *Mary is lying on the floor playing with a puzzle.* AGATHA *appears lugging blankets and pillows across the room. Almost at the door, she stops and gives* MARY *an annoyed look.*

AGATHA And see to it that she doesn't get my good quilt all dirty, and let her wear your green pajamas.

MARY Who?

AGATHA Who? Don't you ever keep your ears open? Rosalie Wells is coming over to spend the night with you.

MARY You mean she's going to sleep *here?*

AGATHA You heard me.

MARY What for?

AGATHA Do I know all the crazy things that are happening around here? Your grandmother phones Mrs. Wells all the way to New York, three dollars and eighty-five cents and families starving, and Mrs. Wells wanted to know if Rosalie could stay here until tomorrow.

MARY *(Relieved)* Oh. Couldn't Evelyn Munn come instead?

AGATHA Sure. We'll have the whole town over to entertain you.

MARY I won't let Rosalie Wells wear my new pajamas.

AGATHA *(Exits as the front door-bell rings)* Don't tell me what you won't do. You'll act like a lady for once in your life. *(Off-stage)* Come on in, Rosalie. Just go on in there and make yourself at home. Have you had your dinner?

ROSALIE *(Off-stage)* Good evening. Yes'm.

AGATHA *(Off-stage)* Hang up your pretty coat. Have you had your bath?

ROSALIE *(Off-stage)* Yes, ma'am. This morning.

AGATHA *(Off-stage)* Well, you better have another one.

(She is climbing the stairs as ROSALIE *comes into the room.* MARY, *lying in front of the couch, is hidden from her. Gingerly* ROSALIE *sits down on a chair)*

MARY *(Softly)* Whooooooo. (ROSALIE *jumps)* Whooooooo. (ROSALIE, *frightened, starts hurriedly for the door.* MARY *sits up, laughs)* You're a goose.

ROSALIE *(Belligerently)* Oh, so it's you. Well, who likes to hear funny noises at night? You could have been a werewolf.

MARY A werewolf wouldn't want you.

ROSALIE You know everything, don't you? (MARY *laughs.* ROSALIE *comes over, stands staring at puzzle)* Isn't it funny about school!?

MARY What's funny about it?

ROSALIE Don't act like you can come home every night.

MARY Maybe I can from now on. *(Rolls over on her back luxuriously)* Maybe I'm never going back.

ROSALIE Am I going back? I don't want to stay home.

MARY What'll you give to know?

ROSALIE Nothing. I'll ask Mamma.

MARY Will you give me a free T. L. if I tell you?

ROSALIE *(Thinks for a moment)* All right. Lois Fisher told Helen that you were very smart.

MARY That's an old one. I won't take it.

ROSALIE You got to take it.

MARY Nope.

ROSALIE *(Laughs)* You don't know, anyway.

MARY I know what I heard, and I know Grandma phoned your mother in New York to come and get you right away. You're just going to spend the night here. I wish Evelyn could come instead of you.

ROSALIE But what's happened? Peggy and Helen and Evelyn and Lois went home tonight, too. Do you think somebody's got scarlet fever or something?

MARY No.

ROSALIE Do *you* know what it is? How'd you find out? *(No answer)* You're always pretending you know everything. You're just faking. *(Flounces away)* Never mind, don't bother telling me. I think curiosity is very unladylike, any-how. I have no concern with your silly secrets.

MARY Suppose I told you that I just may have said that you were in on it?

ROSALIE In on what?

MARY The secret. Suppose I told you that I *may have* said that you told me about it?

ROSALIE Why, Mary Tilford! You can't do a thing like that. I didn't tell you about anything. (MARY *laughs*) Did you tell your grandmother such a thing?

MARY Maybe.

ROSALIE Did you?

MARY Maybe.

ROSALIE Well, I'm going right up to your grandmother and tell her I didn't tell you anything—whatever it is. You're just trying to get me into trouble and I'm not going to let you.

　　(Starts for door)

MARY Wait a minute, I'll come with you.

ROSALIE What for?

MARY I want to tell her about Helen Burton's bracelet.

ROSALIE *(Sits down suddenly)* What about it?

MARY Just that you stole it.

ROSALIE Shut up. I didn't do any such thing.

MARY Yes, you did.

ROSALIE *(Tearfully)* You made it up. You're always making things up.

MARY You can't call me a fibber, Rosalie Wells. That's a kind of a dare and I won't take a dare. I guess I'll go tell Grandma, anyway. Then she can call the police and they'll come for you and you'll spend the rest of your life in one of these solitary prisons and you'll get older and older, and when you're very old and can't see anymore, they'll let you out maybe with a big sign on your back saying you're a thief, and your mother and father will be dead and you won't have any place to go and you'll beg on the streets—

ROSALIE I didn't steal anything. I borrowed the bracelet

and I was going to put it back as soon as I'd worn it to the movies. I never meant to keep it.

MARY Nobody'll believe that, least of all the police. You're just a common ordinary thief. Stop that bawling. You'll have the whole house down here in a minute.

ROSALIE You won't tell? Say you won't tell.

MARY Am I a fibber?

ROSALIE No.

MARY Then say: "I apologize on my hands and knees."

ROSALIE I apologize on my hands and knees. Let's play with the puzzle.

MARY Wait a minute. Say: "From now on, I, Rosalie Wells, am the vassal of Mary Tilford and will do and say whatever she tells me under the solemn oath of a knight."

ROSALIE I won't say that. That's the worst oath there is. *(MARY starts for the door)* Mary! Please don't—

MARY Will you swear it?

ROSALIE *(Sniffling)* But then you could tell me to do anything.

MARY And you'd have to do it. Say it quick or I'll—

ROSALIE *(Hurriedly)* From now on, I, Rosalie Wells, am the vassal of Mary Tilford and will do and say whatever she tells me under the solemn oath of a knight.

> *(She gasps, and sits up straight as* MRS. TILFORD *enters)*

MARY Don't forget that.

MRS. TILFORD Good evening, Rosalie, you're looking very well.

ROSALIE Good evening, Mrs. Tilford.

MARY She's getting fatter every day.

MRS. TILFORD *(Abstractedly)* Then it's very becoming. *(Door-bell rings)* That must be Joseph. Mary, take Rosalie into the library. There's some fruit and milk on the table. Be sure you're both fast asleep by half past ten.

> *(Leans down, kisses them both.* ROSALIE *starts to exit Right, sees* MARY, *stops and hesitates)*

MARY Go on, Rosalie. *(Waits until* ROSALIE *reluctantly exits)* Grandma.

MRS. TILFORD Yes?

MARY Grandma, Cousin Joe'll say I've got to go back. He'll say I really wasn't—
    (CARDIN *enters and she runs from the room*)

CARDIN Hello, Amelia. (*Looks curiously at the fleeing* MARY) Mary home, eh?

MRS. TILFORD (*Watching* MARY *as she leaves*) Hello, Joseph. Sit down. (*He sits down, looks at her curiously, waits for her to speak*) Whisky?

CARDIN Please. How are you feeling? Headaches again?

MRS. TILFORD (*Puts drink on table*) No.

CARDIN Those are good powders. Bicarbonate of soda and water. Never hurt anybody yet.

MRS. TILFORD Yes. How have you been, Joseph?

CARDIN My good health is monotonous.

MRS. TILFORD (*Vaguely, sparring for time*) I haven't seen you the last few weeks. Agatha misses you for Sunday dinners.

CARDIN I've been busy. We're getting the results from the mating-season right about now.

MRS. TILFORD Did I take you away from a patient?

CARDIN No. I was at the hospital.

MRS. TILFORD How's it getting on?

CARDIN Just the same. No money, badly equipped, a lousy laboratory, everybody growling at everybody else— Amelia, you didn't bring me here to talk about the hospital. We're talking like people waiting for the muffins to be passed around. What's the matter with you?

MRS. TILFORD I—I have something to tell you.

CARDIN Well, out with it.

MRS. TILFORD It's a very hard thing to say, Joseph.

CARDIN Hard for you to say to *me*? (*No answer*) Don't be worried about Mary. I guessed that she ran home to tell you about her faint. It was caused by nothing but bad temper and was very clumsily managed, at that. Amelia, she's a terribly spoilt—

MRS. TILFORD I heard about the faint. That's not what is worrying me.

CARDIN *(Gently)* Are you in some trouble?

MRS. TILFORD We all are in trouble. Bad trouble.

CARDIN We? Me, you mean? Nothing's the matter with me.

MRS. TILFORD When did you last see Karen?

CARDIN Today. This afternoon.

MRS. TILFORD Oh. Not since seven o'clock?

CARDIN What's happened since seven o'clock?

MRS. TILFORD Joseph, you've been engaged to Karen for a long time. Are your plans any more definite than they were a year ago?

CARDIN You can get ready to buy the wedding present. We'll have the wedding here, if you don't mind. The smell of clean little girls and boiled linen would worry me.

MRS. TILFORD Why has Karen decided so suddenly to make it definite?

CARDIN She has not suddenly decided anything. The school is pretty well on its feet, and now that Mrs. Mortar is leaving—

MRS. TILFORD I've heard about their putting Mrs. Mortar out.

CARDIN Putting her out? Well, maybe. But a nice sum for a trip and a promise that a good niece will support you for the rest of your life is an enviable way of being put out.

MRS. TILFORD *(Slowly)* Don't you find it odd, Joseph, that they want so much to get rid of that silly, harmless woman?

CARDIN I don't know what you're talking about, but it isn't odd at all. Lily Mortar is not a harmless woman, although God knows she's silly enough. She's a nasty, tiresome, spoilt old bitch. If you're forming a Mortar Welfare Society, you're wasting your time. *(Gets up, puts down his glass)* It's not like you to waste your time. Now, what's it that's really on your mind?

MRS. TILFORD You must not marry Karen.

CARDIN *(Shocked, he grins)* You're a very impertinent lady. Why must I—*(imitates her)* not marry Karen?

MRS. TILFORD Because there's something wrong with Karen—something horrible.

(The door-bell is heard to ring loud and long)

CARDIN   I don't think I can allow you to say things like that, Amelia.

MRS. TILFORD   I have good reason for saying it. *(Breaks off as she hears voices off-stage)* Who is that?

KAREN *(Off-stage)*   Mrs. Tilford, Agatha. Is she in?

AGATHA *(Off-stage)*   Yes'm. Come on in.

MRS. TILFORD   I won't have her here.

CARDIN *(Angrily)*   What are you talking about?

MRS. TILFORD   I won't have her here.

CARDIN *(Picks up his hat)*   Then you don't want me here either. *(Turns to face* KAREN, *who, with* MARTHA, *has rushed in)* Darling, what?—

KAREN *(Stops when she sees him, puts her hand over her eyes)*   Is it a joke, Joe?

MARTHA *(With great force to* MRS. TILFORD*)*   We've come to find out what you are doing.

CARDIN *(Kissing* KAREN*)*   What is it?

KAREN   It's crazy! It's crazy! What did she do it for?

CARDIN   What are you talking about? What do you mean?

MRS. TILFORD   You shouldn't have come here.

CARDIN   What is all this. What's happened?

KAREN   I tried to reach you. Hasn't she told you?

CARDIN   Nobody's told me anything. I haven't heard anything but wild talk. What is it, Karen? *(She starts to speak, then dumbly shakes her head)* What's happened, Martha?

MARTHA *(Violently)*   An insane asylum has been let loose. How do we know what's happened?

CARDIN   What was it?

KAREN   We didn't know what it was. Nobody would talk to us, nobody would tell us anything.

MARTHA   I'll tell you, I'll tell you. You see if you can make any sense out of it. At dinner-time Mrs. Munn's chauffeur said that Evelyn must be sent home right away. At half past seven Mrs. Burton arrived to tell us that she wanted Helen's things packed and that she'd wait outside because she didn't want to enter a place like ours. Five minutes later the Wells's butler came for Rosalie.

CARDIN   What was it?

MARTHA   It was a madhouse. People rushing in and out, the children being pushed into cars—

KAREN   *(Quiet now, takes his hand)*   Mrs. Rogers finally told us.

CARDIN   What? What?

KAREN   That—that Martha and I are—in love with each other. In love with each other. Mrs. Tilford told them.

CARDIN   *(For a moment stands staring at her incredulously. Then he walks across the room, stares out of the window, and finally turns to MRS. TILFORD)*   Did you tell them that?

MRS. TILFORD   Yes.

CARDIN   Are you sick?

MRS. TILFORD   You know I'm not sick.

CARDIN   *(Snapping the words out)*   Then what did you do it for?

MRS. TILFORD   *(Slowly)*   Because it's true.

KAREN   *(Incredulously)*   You think it's true, then?

MARTHA   You fool! You damned, vicious—

KAREN   Do you realize what you're saying?

MRS. TILFORD   I realize it very well. And—

MARTHA   You realize nothing, nothing, nothing.

MRS. TILFORD   And that's why I don't think you should come here. *(Quietly, with a look at MARTHA)* I shall not call you names, and I will not allow you to call me names. It comes to this: I can't trust myself to talk about it with you now or ever.

KAREN   What's she talking about, Joe? What's she mean? What is she trying to do to us? What is everybody doing to us?

MARTHA   *(Softly, as though to herself)*   Pushed around. We're being pushed around by crazy people. *(Shakes herself slightly)* That's an awful thing. And we're standing here—*(CARDIN puts his arm around KAREN, walks with her to the window. They stand there together)* We're standing here taking it. *(Suddenly with violence)* Didn't you know we'd come here? Were we supposed to lie down and grin while you kicked us around with these lies?

MRS. TILFORD   This can't do any of us any good, Miss Dobie.

MARTHA *(Scornfully imitating her)*   "This can't do any of us any good." Listen, listen. Try to understand this: you're not playing with paper dolls. We're human beings, see? It's our lives you're fooling with. *Our* lives. That's serious business for us. Can you understand that?

MRS. TILFORD *(For the first time she speaks angrily)*   I can understand that, and I understand a lot more. *You've* been playing with a lot of children's lives, and that's why I stopped you. *(More calmly)* I know how serious this is for you, how serious it is for all of us.

CARDIN *(Bitterly)*   I don't think you do know.

MRS. TILFORD   I wanted to avoid this meeting because it can't do any good. You came here to find out if I had made the charge. You've found out. Let's end it there. *I don't want you in this house.* I'm sorry this had to be done to you, Joseph.

CARDIN   I don't like your sympathy.

MRS. TILFORD   Very well. There's nothing I mean to do, nothing I want to do. There's nothing anybody can do.

CARDIN *(Carefully)*   You have already done a terrible thing.

MRS. TILFORD   I have done what I had to do. What they are may possibly be their own business. It becomes a great deal more than that when children are involved.

KAREN *(Wildly)*   It's not true. Not a word of it is true; can't you understand that?

MRS. TILFORD   There won't be any punishment for either of you. But there mustn't be any punishment for me, either —and that's what this meeting is. This—this thing is your own. Go away with it. I don't understand it and I don't want any part of it.

MARTHA *(Slowly)*   So you thought we would go away?

MRS. TILFORD   I think that's best for you.

MARTHA   There must be something we can do to you, and, whatever it is, we'll find it.

MRS. TILFORD   That will be very unwise.

KAREN   You are right to be afraid.

MRS. TILFORD   I am not afraid, Karen.

CARDIN But you *are* old—and you *are* irresponsible.

MRS. TILFORD *(Hurt)* You know that's not true.

KAREN *(Goes to her)* I don't want to have anything to do with your mess, do you hear me? It makes me feel dirty and sick to be forced to say this, but here it is: there isn't a single word of truth in anything you've said. We're standing here defending ourselves—and against what? Against a lie. A great, awful lie.

MRS. TILFORD I'm sorry that I can't believe that.

KAREN Damn you!

CARDIN But you can believe this: they've worked eight long years to save enough money to buy that farm, to start that school. They did without everything that young people ought to have. You wouldn't know about that. That school meant things to them: self-respect, and bread and butter, and honest work. Do you know what it is to try so hard for anything? Well, now it's gone. *(Suddenly hits the side of the table with his hand)* What the hell did you do it for?

MRS. TILFORD *(Softly)* It had to be done.

CARDIN Righteousness is a great thing.

MRS. TILFORD *(Gently)* I know how how you must feel.

CARDIN You don't know anything about how I feel. And you don't know how they feel, either.

MRS. TILFORD I've loved you as much as I loved my own boys. I wouldn't have spared them; I couldn't spare you.

CARDIN *(Fiercely)* I believe you.

MARTHA What is there to do to you? What can we do to you? There must be something—something that makes you feel the way we do tonight. You don't want any part of this, you said. But you'll get a part. More than you bargained for. *(Suddenly)* Listen: are you willing to stand by everything you've said tonight?

MRS. TILFORD Yes.

MARTHA All right. That's fine. But don't get the idea we'll let you whisper this lie: you made it and you'll come out with it. Shriek it to your town of Lancet. We'll *make* you shriek it—and we'll make you do it in a court room. *(Qui-*

etly) Tomorrow, Mrs. Tilford, you will have a libel suit on your hands.

MRS. TILFORD That will be very unwise.

KAREN Very unwise—for you.

MRS. TILFORD It is you I am thinking of. I am frightened for you. It was wrong for you to brazen it out here tonight; it would be criminally foolish of you to brazen it out in public. That can bring you nothing but pain. I am an old woman, Miss Dobie, and I have seen too many people, out of pride, act on that pride. In the end they punish themselves.

MARTHA And you feel that you are too old to be punished? That we should spare you?

MRS. TILFORD You know that is not what I meant.

CARDIN *(Turns from the window)* So you took a child's word for it?

MARTHA *(Looks at him, shakes her head)* I knew it, too.

KAREN That is really where you got it? I can't believe—it couldn't be. Why, she's a child.

MARTHA She's not a child any longer.

KAREN Oh, my God, it all fits so well now. That girl has hated us for a long time. We never knew why, we never could find out. There didn't seem to be any reason—

MARTHA There wasn't any reason. She hates everybody and everything.

KAREN Your Mary's a strange girl, a bad girl. There's something very awful the matter with her.

MRS. TILFORD I was waiting for you to say that, Miss Wright.

KAREN I'm telling you the truth. We should have told it to you long ago. *(Stops, sighs)* It's no use.

MARTHA Where is she? Bring her out here and let us hear what she has to say.

MRS. TILFORD You cannot see her.

CARDIN Where is she?

MRS. TILFORD I won't have that, Joseph.

CARDIN I'm going to talk to her.

MRS. TILFORD *I won't have her go through with that again.* *(To* KAREN *and* MARTHA*)* You came here demanding explanations. It was I who should have asked them from you. You attack me, you attack Mary. I've told you I didn't mean you any harm. I still don't. You claim that it isn't true; it may be natural that you should say that, but I *know* that it is true. No matter what you say, you know very well I wouldn't have acted until I was absolutely sure. All I wanted was to get those children away. That has been done. There won't be any talk about it or about you—I'll see to that. You have been in my house long enough. Get out.

KAREN *(Gets up)* The wicked very young, and the wicked very old. Let's go home.

CARDIN Sit down. *(To* MRS. TILFORD*)* When two people come here with their lives spread on the table for you to cut to pieces, then the honest thing to do is to give them a chance to come out whole. Are you honest?

MRS. TILFORD I've always thought so.

CARDIN Then where is Mary? *(After a moment she moves her head to door Right. Quickly* CARDIN *goes to the door and opens it)* Mary! Come here.

(After a moment MARY *appears, stands nervously near door. Her manner is shy and afraid)*

MRS. TILFORD *(Gently)* Sit down, dear, and don't be afraid.

MARTHA *(Her lips barely moving)* Make her tell the truth.

CARDIN *(Walking about in front of* MARY*)* Look: everybody lies all the time. Sometimes they have to, sometimes they don't. I've lied myself for a lot of different reasons, but there was never a time when, if I'd been given a second chance, I wouldn't have taken back the lie and told the truth. You're lucky if you ever get that chance. I'm telling you this because I'm about to ask you a question. Before you answer the question, I want to tell you that if you've l—, if you made a mistake, you must take this chance and say so. You won't be punished for it. Do you get all that?

MARY *(Timidly)* Yes, Cousin Joe.

CARDIN *(Grimly)* All right, let's get started. Were you telling your grandmother the truth this afternoon? The exact truth about Miss Wright and Miss Dobie?

MARY *(Without hesitation)* Oh, yes.

> *(KAREN sighs deeply, MARTHA, her fists closed tight, turns her back to the child. CARDIN smiles as he looks at MARY)*

CARDIN All right, Mary, that was your chance; you passed it up. *(Pulls up a chair, sits down in front of her)* Now let's find out things.

MRS. TILFORD She's told you. Aren't you through?

CARDIN Not by a long shot. You've started something, and I'm going to finish it for you. Will you answer some more questions, Mary?

MARY Yes, Cousin Joe.

MARTHA Stop that sick, sweet tone.

> *(MRS. TILFORD half rises; CARDIN motions her back)*

CARDIN Why don't you like Miss Dobie and Miss Wright?

MARY Oh, I do like them. They just don't like me. They never have liked me.

CARDIN How do you know?

MARY They're always picking on me. They're always punishing me for everything that happens. No matter what happens, it's always me.

CARDIN Why do you think they do that?

MARY Because—because they're—because they—*(Stops, turns)* Grandma, I—

CARDIN All right, we'll skip that one. Did you get punished today?

MARY Yes, and it was just because Peggy and Evelyn heard them and so they took it out on me.

KAREN That's a lie.

CARDIN Sssh. Heard what, Mary?

MARY Mrs. Mortar told Miss Dobie that there was something funny about her. She said that she had a funny feeling about Miss Wright, and Mrs. Mortar said that was unnatural. That was why we got punished, just because—

KAREN That was not the reason they got punished.

MRS. TILFORD *(To MARTHA)* Miss Dobie?

MARTHA My aunt is a stupid woman. What she said was

unpleasant; it was said to annoy me. It meant nothing more than that.

MARY   And, Cousin Joe, she said every time you came to the school Miss Dobie got jealous, and that she didn't want you to get married.

MARTHA   *(To* CARDIN*)*   She said that, too. For God's sake can't you see what's happening? This—this child is taking little things, little family things, and making them have meanings that—*(Stops, suddenly regards* MARY *with a combination of disgust and interest)* Where did you learn so much in so little time?

CARDIN   What do you think Mrs. Mortar meant by all that, Mary?

MRS. TILFORD   Stop it, Joseph!

MARY   I don't know, but it was always kind of funny and she always said things like that and all the girls would talk about it when Miss Dobie went and visited Miss Wright late at night—

KAREN   *(Angrily)*   And we go to the movies at night and sometimes we read at night and sometimes we drink tea at night. Those are guilty things, too, Mrs. Tilford.

MARY   And there are always funny sounds and we'd stay awake and listen because we couldn't help hearing and I'd get frightened because the sounds were like—

MARTHA   Be still!

KAREN   *(With violence)*   No, no. You don't want her still now. What else did you hear?

MARY   Grandma, I—

MRS. TILFORD   *(Bitterly to* CARDIN*)*   You are trying to make her name it, aren't you?

CARDIN   *(Ignoring her, speaks to* MARY*)*   Go on.

MARY   I don't know; there were just sounds.

CARDIN   But what did you think they were? Why did they frighten you?

MARY   *(Weakly)*   I don't know.

CARDIN   *(Smiles at* MRS. TILFORD*)*   She doesn't know.

MARY   *(Hastily)*   I saw things, too. One night there was so much noise I thought somebody was sick or something and

I looked through the keyhole and they were kissing and saying things and then I got scared because it was different sort of and I—

MARTHA *(Her face distorted, turns to* MRS. TILFORD*)* That child—that child is sick.

KAREN Ask her again how she could see us.

CARDIN How could you see Miss Dobie and Miss Wright?

MARY I—I—

MRS. TILFORD Tell him what you whispered to me.

MARY It was at night and I was leaning down by the keyhole.

KAREN *There's no keyhole on my door.*

MRS. TILFORD What?

KAREN There—is—no—keyhole—on—my—door.

MARY *(Quickly)* It wasn't her room, Grandma, it was the other room, I guess. It was *Miss Dobie's* room. I saw them through the keyhole in Miss Dobie's room.

CARDIN How did you know anybody was in Miss Dobie's room?

MARY I told you, I told you. Because we heard them. Everybody heard them—

MARTHA I share a room with my aunt. It is on the first floor at the other end of the house. It is impossible to hear anything from there. *(To* CARDIN*)* Tell her to come and see for herself.

MRS. TILFORD *(Her voice shaken)* What is this, Mary? Why did you say you saw through a keyhole? *Can* you hear from your room?—

MARY *(Starts to cry)* Everybody is yelling at me. I don't know what I'm saying with everybody mixing me all up. I did see it! I did see it!

MRS. TILFORD *What* did you see? *Where* did you see it? I want the truth, now. The truth, whatever it is.

CARDIN *(Gets up, moves his chair back)* We can go home. We are finished here. *(Looks around)* It's not a pleasant place to be.

MRS. TILFORD *(Angrily)* Stop that crying, Mary. Stand up.

(MARY *gets up, head down, still crying hysterically.*
MRS. TILFORD *goes and stands directly in front of her*)

MRS. TILFORD   *I want the truth.*

MARY   All—all right.

MRS. TILFORD   What is the truth?

MARY   It was Rosalie who saw them. I just said it was me so
I wouldn't have to tattle on Rosalie.

CARDIN *(Wearily)*   Oh, my God!

MARY   It *was* Rosalie, Grandma, she told us all about it. She
said she had read about it in a book and she knew. *(Desperately)* You ask Rosalie. You just ask Rosalie. She'll tell you.
We used to talk about it all the time. That's the truth, that's
the honest truth. She said it was when the door was open
once and she told us all about it. It was just trying to save
Rosalie, and everybody jumps on me.

MRS. TILFORD *(To CARDIN)*   Please wait a minute. *(Goes to
library door)* Rosalie!

CARDIN   You're giving yourself an awful beating, Amelia,
and you deserve whatever you get.

MRS. TILFORD *(Stands waiting for ROSALIE, passes her hand
over her face)*   I don't know. I don't know, any more.
Maybe it's what I do deserve. *(As ROSALIE, frightened,
appears at the door, making bows to everybody, she takes
the child gently by the hand, brings her down Center,
talking nervously)* I'm sorry to keep you up so late, Rosalie. You must be tired. *(Speaks rapidly)* Mary says there's
been a lot of talk in the school lately about Miss Wright and
Miss Dobie. Is that true?

ROSALIE   I—I don't know what you mean.

MRS. TILFORD   That things have been said among you
girls.

ROSALIE *(Wide-eyed, frightened)*   What things? I never—I
—I—

KAREN *(Gently)*   Don't be frightened.

MRS. TILFORD   What was the talk about, Rosalie?

ROSALIE *(Utterly bewildered)*   I don't know what she
means, Miss Wright.

KAREN   Rosalie, Mary has told her grandmother that certain

things at school have been—er—puzzling you girls. You, particularly.

ROSALIE History puzzles me. I guess I'm not very good at history, and Helen helps me sometimes, if that—

KAREN No, that's not what she meant. She says that you told her that you saw certain—certain acts between Miss Dobie and myself. She says that once, when the door was open, you saw us kissing each other in a way that—*(Unable to bear the child's look, she turns her back)* women don't kiss one another.

ROSALIE Oh, Miss Wright, I didn't, didn't, I didn't. I *never* said such a thing.

MRS. TILFORD *(Grimly)* That's true, my dear?

ROSALIE I never saw any such thing. Mary always makes things up about me and everybody else. *(Starts to weep in excitement)* I never said any such thing ever. Why, I never even could have thought of—

MARY *(Staring at her, speaks very slowly)* Yes, you did, Rosalie. You're just trying to get out of it. I remember just when you said it. I remember it, because it was the day Helen Burton's bracelet was—

ROSALIE *(Stands fascinated and fearful, looking at MARY)* I never did. I—I—you're just—

MARY It was the day Helen's bracelet was stolen, and nobody knew who did it, and Helen said that if her mother found out, she'd have the thief put in jail.

KAREN *(Puzzled, as are the others, by the sudden change in ROSALIE's manner)* There's nothing to cry about. You must help us by telling the truth. Why, what's the matter, Rosalie?

MARY Grandma, there's something I've got to tell you that—

ROSALIE *(With a shrill cry)* Yes. Yes. I did see it. I told Mary. What Mary said was right. I said it, I said it—

> *(Throws herself on the couch, weeping hysterically;* MARTHA *stands leaning against the door;* KAREN, CARDIN, *and* MRS. TILFORD *are staring at* ROSALIE; MARY *slowly sits down as the Curtain falls)*

Act Three

SCENE: *The same as Act One. Living room of the school.*
AT RISE: *The room has changed. It is not dirty, but it is dull and dark and uncared for. The windows are tightly shut, the curtains tightly drawn.* KAREN *is sitting in a large chair, Right Center, feet flat on floor.* MARTHA *is lying on the couch, her face buried against the pillows, her back to* KAREN. *It is a minute or two after the rise of the curtain before either speaks.*

MARTHA   It's cold in here.

KAREN   Yes.

MARTHA   What time is it?

KAREN   I don't know. What's the difference?

MARTHA   None. I was hoping it was time for my bath.

KAREN   Take it early today.

MARTHA   *(Laughs)*   Oh, I couldn't do that. I look forward all day to that bath. It's my last touch with the full life. It makes me feel important to know that there's one thing ahead of me, one thing I've *got* to do. You ought to get yourself something like that. I tell you, at five o'clock every day you comb your hair. How's that? It's better for you, take my word. You wake up in the morning and you say to yourself, the day's not entirely empty, life is rich and full: at five o'clock I'll comb my hair.

   (They fall back into silence. A moment later the phone rings. Neither of them pays the slightest attention to it. But the ringing becomes too insistent. KAREN *rises, takes the receiver off, goes back to her chair and sits down)*

KAREN   It's raining.

MARTHA   Hungry?

KAREN   No. You?

76

MARTHA No, but I'd like to be hungry again. Remember how much we used to eat at college?

KAREN That was ten years ago.

MARTHA Well, maybe we'll be hungry in another ten years. It's cheaper this way.

KAREN What's the old thing about time being more nourishing than bread?

MARTHA Yeah? Maybe.

KAREN Joe's late today. What time is it?

MARTHA *(Turns again to lie on her side)* We've been sitting here for eight days asking each other the time. Haven't you heard? There isn't any time any more.

KAREN It's been days since we've been out of this house.

MARTHA Well, we'll have to get off these chairs sooner or later. In a couple of months they'll need dusting.

KAREN What'll we do when we get off?

MARTHA God knows.

KAREN *(Almost in a whisper)* It's awful.

MARTHA Let's not talk about it. *(After a moment)* What about eggs for dinner?

KAREN All right.

MARTHA I'll make some potatoes with onions, the way you used to like them.

KAREN It's a week ago Thursday. It never seemed real until the last day. It seems real enough now, all right.

MARTHA Now and forever after.

KAREN *(Suddenly)* Let's go out.

MARTHA *(Turns over, stares at her)* Where to?

KAREN We'll take a walk.

MARTHA Where'll we walk?

KAREN Why shouldn't we take a walk? We won't see anybody, and suppose we do, what of it? We'll jus—

MARTHA *(Slowly gets up)* Come on. We'll go through the park.

KAREN They might see us. *(They stand looking at each other)* Let's not go. *(MARTHA goes back, lies down again)* We'll go tomorrow.

MARTHA *(Laughs)* Stop kidding yourself.

KAREN But Joe says we've got to go out. He says that all the people who don't think it's true will begin to wonder if we keep hiding this way.

MARTHA If it makes you feel better to think there *are* such people, go ahead.

KAREN He says we ought to go into town and go shopping and act as though—

MARTHA Shopping? That's a sound idea. There aren't three stores in Lancet that would sell us anything. Hasn't he heard about the ladies' clubs and their meetings and their circulars and their visits and their—

KAREN *(Softly)* Don't tell him.

MARTHA *(Gently)* I won't. *(There are footsteps in the hall, and the sound of something being dragged)* There's our friend.

> *(A GROCERY BOY appears lugging a box. He brings it into the room, stands staring at them, giggles a little. Walks toward KAREN, stops, examines her. She sits tense, looking away from him. Without taking his eyes from KAREN, he speaks)*

GROCERY BOY I knocked on the kitchen door but nobody answered.

MARTHA You said that yesterday. All right. Thanks. Goodbye.

KAREN *(Unable any longer to stand the stare)* Make him stop it.

GROCERY BOY Here are the things.

> *(Giggles, moves toward MARTHA, stands looking at her. Suddenly MARTHA thrusts her hand in the air)*

MARTHA I've got eight fingers, see? I'm a freak.

GROCERY BOY *(Giggling)* There's a car comin' here. *(Gets no answer, starts backing out of door, still looking. Familiarly)* Good-bye.

> *(Exits)*

MARTHA *(Bitterly)* You still think we should go into town?

KAREN I don't know. I don't know about anything any more. *(After a moment)* Martha, Martha, Martha—

MARTHA *(Gently)* What is it, Karen?

KAREN   What are we going to do? It's all so cold and unreal and—. It's like that dark hour of the night when, half awake, you struggle through the black mess you've been dreaming. Then, suddenly, you wake up and you see your own bed or your own nightgown and you know you're back again in a solid world. But now it's all the nightmare; there is no solid world. Oh, Martha, *why* did it happen? *What* happened. What are we doing here like this?

MARTHA   Waiting.

KAREN   For what?

MARTHA   I don't know.

KAREN   We've got to get out of this place. I can't stand it any more.

MARTHA   You'll be getting married soon. Everything will be all right then.

KAREN   *(Vaguely)* Yes.

MARTHA   *(Looks up at the tone)* What is it?

KAREN   Nothing.

MARTHA   There mustn't be anything wrong between you and Joe. Never.

KAREN   *(Without conviction)* Nothing's wrong. *(As footsteps are heard in the hall, her face lights up)* There's Joe now.

  (MRS. MORTAR, small suitcase in hand, stands in the doorway, her face pushed coyly forward)

MRS. MORTAR   And here I am. Hello, hello.

MARTHA   *(She has turned over on her back and is staring at her aunt. She speaks to KAREN)* The Duchess, isn't it? Returned at long last. *(Too jovially)* Come on in. We're delighted to see you. Are you tired from your journey? Is there something I can get you?

MRS. MORTAR   *(Surprised)* I'm very glad to see you both, and *(looks around)* I'm very glad to see the old place again. How is everything?

MARTHA   Everything's fine. We're splendid, thank you. You're just in time for tea.

MRS. MORTAR   You know, I should like some tea, if it isn't too much trouble.

MARTHA No trouble at all. Some small sandwiches and a little brandy?

MRS. MORTAR *(Puzzled finally)* Why, Martha.

MARTHA Where the hell have you been?

MRS. MORTAR Around, around. I had a most interesting time. Things—

MARTHA Why didn't you answer my telegrams?

MRS. MORTAR Things have changed in the theater—drastically changed. I might say.

MARTHA *Why didn't you answer my telegrams?*

MRS. MORTAR Oh, Martha, there's your temper again.

MARTHA Answer me and don't bother about my temper.

MRS. MORTAR *(Nervously)* I was moving around a great deal *(Conversationally)* You know, I think it will throw a very revealing light on the state of the new theater when I tell you that the Lyceum in Rochester now has a toilet back-stage.

MARTHA To hell with the toilet in Rochester. Where were you?

MRS. MORTAR Moving around, I tell you.

KAREN What difference does it all make now?

MRS. MORTAR Karen is quite right. Let bygones be bygones. As I was saying, there's an effete something in the theater now, and that accounts for—

MARTHA *(To KAREN)* Isn't she wonderful? *(To MRS. MORTAR)* Why did you refuse to come back here and testify for us?

MRS. MORTAR Why, Martha, I didn't refuse to come back at all. That's the wrong way to look at it. I was on a tour; that's a moral obligation, you know. Now don't let's talk about unpleasant things any more. I'll go up and unpack a few things; tomorrow's plenty of time to get my trunk.

KAREN *(Laughs)* Things have changed here, you know.

MARTHA She doesn't know. She expected to walk right up to a comfortable fire and sit down and she very carefully waited until the whole thing was over *(Leans forward, speaking to MRS. MORTAR)* Listen, Karen Wright and Martha Dobie brought a libel suit against a woman called Tilford because her grandchild had accused them of having what the judge called "sinful sexual knowledge of one another." (MRS. MORTAR *holds up her hand in protest, and* MARTHA *laughs*) Don't like that, do you? Well, a great part of the defense's case was based on remarks made by Lily Mortar, actress, in the toilets of Rochester, against her niece, Martha. And a greater part of the defense's case rested on the telling fact that Mrs. Mortar would not appear in court to deny or explain those remarks. Mrs. Mortar had a moral obligation to the theater. As you probably read in the papers, we lost the case.

MRS. MORTAR   I didn't think of it that way, Martha. It couldn't have done any good for all of us to get mixed up in that unpleasant notoriety— (*Sees* MARTHA'S *face. Hastily*) But now that you've explained it, why, I do see it your way, and I'm sorry I didn't come back. But now that I am here, I'm going to stand shoulder to shoulder with you. I know what you've gone through, but the body and heart *do* recover, you know. I'll be here working right along with you and we'll—

MARTHA   There's an eight o'clock train. Get on it.

MRS. MORTAR   Martha.

MARTHA   You've come back to pick the bones dry. Well, there aren't even bones anymore. There's nothing here for you.

MRS. MORTAR   (*Sniffling a little*) How can you talk to me like that?

MARTHA   Because I hate you. I've always hated you.

MRS. MORTAR   (*Gently*) God will punish you for that.

MARTHA   He's been doing all right.

MRS. MORTAR   When you wish to apologize, I will be temporarily in my room. (*Starts to exit, almost bumps into* CARDIN, *steps back with dignity*) How do you do?

CARDIN   (*Laughs*) Look who's here. A little late, aren't you?

MRS. MORTAR   So it's you. Now, I call *that* loyal. A lot of men wouldn't still be here. They would have felt—

MARTHA   Get out of here.

KAREN *(Opening door)* I'll call you when it's time for your train.

    (MRS. MORTAR looks at her, exits)

CARDIN Now, what do you think brought her back?

KAREN God knows.

MARTHA I know. She was broke.

CARDIN *(Pats MARTHA on the shoulder)* Don't let her worry you this time, Martha. We'll give her some money and get rid of her. *(Pulls KAREN to him)* Been out today, darling?

KAREN We started to go out.

CARDIN *(Shakes his head)* Feel all right?

    (KAREN leans over to kiss him. Almost imperceptibly he pulls back)

KAREN Why did you do that?

MARTHA Karen.

CARDIN Do what?

KAREN Draw back that way.

CARDIN *(Laughs, kisses her)* If we sit around here much longer, we'll all be bats. I sold my place today to Foster.

KAREN You did what?

CARDIN We're getting married this week. Then we're going away—all three of us.

KAREN You can't leave here. I won't have you do this for me. What about the hospital and—

CARDIN Shut up, darling, it's all fixed. We're going to Vienna and we're going quick. Fischer wrote that I can have my old place back.

KAREN No! No! I'm not going to let you.

CARDIN It's already done. Fischer can't pay me much, but it'll be enough for the three of us. Plenty if we live cheap.

MARTHA I couldn't go with you, Joe.

CARDIN Nonsense, Martha, we're all going. We're going to have fun again.

KAREN *(Slowly)* You don't want to go back to Vienna.

CARDIN No.

KAREN Then why?

CARDIN Look: I don't want to go to Vienna; I'd rather have

stayed here. But then you don't want to go to Vienna; you'd rather have stayed here. Well, to hell with that. We *can't* stay here, and Vienna offers enough to eat and sleep and drink beer on. Now don't object any more, please, darling. All right?

KAREN   All right.

MARTHA   I can't go. It's better for all of us if I don't.

CARDIN   *(Puts his arm around her)*   Not now. You stay with us now. Later on, if you want it that way. All right?

MARTHA   *(smiles)*   All right.

CARDIN   Swell. I'll buy you good coffee cakes and take you both to Ischl for a honeymoon.

MARTHA   *(Picking up grocery box, she starts for door)*   A big coffee cake with a lot of raisins. It would be nice to like something again
      (Exits)

CARDIN   *(With a slightly forced heartiness)*   I'll be going back with a pretty girl who belongs to me. I'll show you off all over the place—to Dr. Engelhardt, and the nurse at the desk, and to the fat gal in the cake shop, and to Fischer. *(Laughs)* The last time I saw him was at the railroad station. He took me back of the baggage car. *(With an imitation of an accent)* "Joseph" he said, "you'll be a good doctor; I would trust you to cut up my Minna. But you're not a great doctor, and you never will be. Go back where you were born and take care of your sick. Leave the fancy work to the others." I came home.

KAREN   You'll be coming home again some day.

CARDIN   No. Let's not talk about it. *(After a moment)* You'll need some clothes?

KAREN   A few. Oh, your Dr. Fischer was so right. This is where you belong.

CARDIN   I need an overcoat and a suit. You'll need a lot of things—heavy things. It's cold there now, much colder than you'd expect—

KAREN   I've done this to you. I've taken you away from everything you want.

CARDIN But it's lovely in the mountains, and that's where we'll go for a month.

KAREN They—*they've* done it. They've taken away every chance we had. Everything we wanted, everything we were going to be.

CARDIN And we've got to stop talking like that. *(Takes her by the shoulder)* We've got a chance. But it's just one chance, and if we miss it we're done for. It means that we've got to start putting the whole business behind us now. *Now,* Karen. What you've done, you've done—and that's that.

KAREN What *I've* done?

CARDIN *(Impatiently)* What's been done to you.

KAREN What did you mean? *(When there is no answer)* What did you mean when you said: "What you've done"?

CARDIN *(Shouting)* Nothing. Nothing. *(Then very quietly)* Karen, there are a lot of people in this world who've had bad trouble in their lives. We're three of those people. We could sit around the rest of our lives and exist on that trouble, until in the end we had nothing else and we'd want nothing else. That's something I'm not coming to and I'm not going to let you come to.

KAREN I know. I'm sorry. *(After a moment)* Joe, can we have a baby right away?

CARDIN *(Vaguely)* Yes, I guess so. Although we won't have much money now.

KAREN You used to want one right away. You always said that was the way you wanted it. There's some reason for your changing.

CARDIN My God, we *can't* go on like this. Everything I say to you is made to mean something else. We don't talk like people any more. Oh, let's get out of here as fast as we can.

KAREN *(As though she is finishing the sentence for him)* And every word will have a new meaning. You think we'll be able to run away from that? Woman, child, love, lawyer —no words that we can use in safety any more. *(Laughs bitterly)* Sick, high-tragic people. That's what we'll be.

CARDIN *(Gently)* No, we won't, darling. Love is casual—

that's the way it should be. We must find that out all over again. We must learn again to live and love like other people.

KAREN It won't work.

CARDIN What?

KAREN The two of us together.

CARDIN *(Sharply)* Stop talking like that.

KAREN It's true. *(Suddenly)* I want you to say it now.

CARDIN I don't know what you're talking about.

KAREN Yes, you do. We've both known for a long time. I knew surely the day we lost the case. I was watching your face in court. It was ashamed—and sad at being ashamed. Say it now, Joe. Ask it now.

CARDIN I have nothing to ask. Nothing— *(Quickly)* All right. Is it—was it ever—

KAREN *(Puts her hand over his mouth)* No. Martha and I have never touched each other. *(Pulls his head down on her shoulder)* That's all right, darling. I'm glad you asked. I'm not mad a bit, really.

CARDIN I'm sorry, Karen, I'm sorry. I didn't mean to hurt you, I—

KAREN I know. You wanted to wait until it was all over, you really never wanted to ask at all. You didn't know for sure; you thought there might be just a little truth in it all. *(With great feeling)* You've been good to me and loyal. You're a fine man. *(Afraid of tears, she pats him, walks away)* Now go and sit down, Joe. I have things to say. They're all mixed up and I must get them clear.

CARDIN Don't let's talk any more. Let's forget and go ahead.

KAREN *(Puzzled)* Go ahead?

CARDIN Yes, Karen.

KAREN You believe me, then?

CARDIN Of course I believe you. I only had to hear you say it.

KAREN No, no, no. That isn't the way things work. Maybe you believe me. I'd never know whether you did or not. You'd never know whether you did, either. We couldn't do it that way. Can't you see what would happen? We'd be hounded by it all our lives. I'd be frightened, always, and in the end my own fright would make me—would make me hate you. *(Sees slight movement he makes)* Yes, it would; I know it would. I'd hate you for what I thought I'd done to you. And I'd hate myself, too. It would grow and grow until we'd be ruined by it. *(Sees him about to speak)* Ah, Joe, you've seen all that yourself. You knew it first.

CARDIN *(Softly)* I didn't mean it that way; I don't now.

KAREN *(Smiles)* You're still trying to spare me, still trying to tell yourself that we might be all right again. But we won't be all right. Not ever, ever, ever. I don't know all the reasons why. Look, I'm standing here. I haven't changed. *(Holds out her hands)* My hands look just the same, my face is the same, even my dress is old. We're in a room we've been in so many times before; you're sitting where you always sit; it's nearly time for dinner. I'm like everybody else. I can have all the things that everybody has. I can have you and a baby, and I can go to market, and we can go to the movies, and people will talk to me and— *(Suddenly notices the pain in his face)* Oh, I'm sorry. I mustn't talk like that. That couldn't be true any more.

CARDIN It could be, Karen. We'll make it be like that.

KAREN No. That's only what we'd like to have had. It's what we can't have now. Go home, darling.

CARDIN *(With force)* Don't talk like that. No matter what it is, we can't leave each other. I can't leave you—

KAREN Joe, Joe. Let's do it now and quick; it will be too hard later on.

CARDIN No, no, no. We love each other. *(His voice breaks)* I'd give anything not to have asked questions, Karen.

KAREN It had to be asked sooner or later—and answered. You're a good man—the best I'll ever know—and you've been better to me than—But it's no good now, for either of us; you can see that.

CARDIN It can be. You say I helped you. Help me now; help me to be strong and good enough to—*(Goes toward her with his arms out)* Karen!

KAREN (*Drawing back*) No Joe! (*Then, as he stops*) Will you do something for me?

CARDIN No. I won't—

KAREN Will you—will you go away for two days—a day— and think this all over by yourself—away from me and love and pity? Will you? And then decide.

CARDIN (*After a long pause*) Yes, if you want, but it won't make any difference. We will—

KAREN Don't say anything. Please go now. (*She sits down, smiles, closes her eyes. For a moment he stands looking at her, then slowly puts on his hat*) And all my heart goes with you.

CARDIN (*At door, leaving*) I'll be coming back.
        (*Exits, slowly, reluctantly, closing door*)

KAREN (*A moment after he has gone*) No, you won't. Never, darling.
        (*Stays as she is until* MARTHA *enters Right*)

MARTHA (*Goes to lamp, lights it*) It gets dark so early now. (*Sits down, stretches, laughs*) Cooking always makes me feel better. Well, I guess we'll have to give the Duchess some dinner. When the hawks descend, you've got to feed 'em. Where's Joe? (*No answer*) Where's Joe?

KAREN Gone.

MARTHA A patient? Will he be back in time for dinner?

KAREN No.

MARTHA (*Watching her*) We'll save dinner for him, then. Karen! What's the matter?

KAREN (*In a dull tone*) He won't be back any more.

MARTHA (*Speaking slowly and carefully*) You mean he won't be back any more tonight?

KAREN He won't be back at all.

MARTHA (*Quickly, walks to* KAREN) What happened? (KAREN *shakes her head*) What happened, Karen?

KAREN He thought that we had been lovers.

MARTHA (*Tensely*) I don't believe you.
        (*Wearily* KAREN *turns her head away*)

KAREN All right.

MARTHA (*Automatically*) I don't believe it. He's never said a word all these months, all during the trial— *(Suddenly grabs* KAREN *by the shoulder, shakes her)* Didn't you tell him? For God's sake, didn't you tell him it wasn't true?

KAREN Yes.

MARTHA He didn't believe you?

KAREN I guess he believed me.

MARTHA *(Angrily)* Then what have you done?

KAREN What had to be done.

MARTHA It's all wrong. It's silly. He'll be back in a little while and you'll clear it all up— *(Realizes why that can't be, covers her mouth with her hand)* Oh, God, I wanted that for you so much.

KAREN Don't. I feel sick to my stomach.

MARTHA *(Goes to couch opposite* KAREN, *puts her head in her arms)* What's happened to us? What's really happened to us?

KAREN I don't know. I want to be sleepy. I want to go to sleep.

MARTHA Go back to Joe. He's strong; he'll understand. It's too much for you this way.

KAREN *(Irritably)* Stop talking about it. Let's pack and get out of here. Let's take the train in the morning.

MARTHA The train to where?

KAREN I don't know. Some place; any place.

MARTHA A job? Money?

KAREN In a big place we could get something to do.

MARTHA They'd know about us. We've been famous.

KAREN A small town, then.

MARTHA They'd know more about us.

KAREN *(As a child would say it)* Isn't there anywhere to go?

MARTHA No. There'll never be any place for us to go. We're bad people. We'll sit. We'll be sitting the rest of our lives wondering what's happened to us. You think this scene is strange? Well, get used to it; we'll be here for a long time. *(Suddenly pinches* KAREN *on the arm)* Let's pinch each other sometimes. We can tell whether we're still living.

KAREN *(Shivers, listlessly gets up, starts making a fire in the fireplace)* But this isn't a new sin they tell us we've done. Other people aren't destroyed by it.

MARTHA They are the people who believe in it, who want it, who've chosen it. We aren't like that. We don't love each other. *(Suddenly stops, crosses to fireplace, stands looking abstractedly at* KAREN. *Speaks casually)* I don't love you. We've been very close to each other, of course, I've loved you like a friend, the way thousands of women feel about other women.

KAREN *(Only half listening)* Yes.

MARTHA Certainly that doesn't mean anything. There's nothing wrong about that. It's perfectly natural that I should be fond of you, that I should—

KAREN *(Listlessly)* Why are you saying all this to me?

MARTHA Because I love you.

KAREN *(Vaguely)* Yes, of course.

MARTHA I love you that way—maybe the way they said I loved you. I don't know. *(Waits, gets no answer, kneels down next to* KAREN*)* Listen to me!

KAREN What?

MARTHA *I have loved you the way they said.*

KAREN You're crazy.

MARTHA There's always been something wrong. Always— as long as I can remember. But I never knew it until all this happened.

KAREN *(For the first time looks up, horrified)* Stop it!

MARTHA You're afraid of hearing it; I'm more afraid than you.

KAREN *(Puts her hands over her ears)* I won't listen to you.

MARTHA Take your hands down. *(Leans over, pulls* KA-REN's *hands away)* You've got to know it. I can't keep it any longer. I've got to tell you how guilty I am.

KAREN *(Deliberately)* You are guilty of nothing.

MARTHA I've been telling myself that since the night we heard the child say it; I've been praying I could convince myself of it. I can't. I can't any longer. It's there. I don't know how, I don't know why. But I did love you. I do love you. I resented your marriage; maybe because I wanted you, maybe because I wanted you all along; maybe I couldn't call it by a name; maybe it's been there ever since I first knew you—

KAREN *(Tensely)* It's a lie. You're telling yourself a lie. We never thought of each other that way.

MARTHA *(Bitterly)* No, of course *you* didn't. But who says I didn't? I never felt that way about anybody but you. I've never loved a man—*(Stops. Softly)* I never knew why before. Maybe it's that.

KAREN *(Carefully)* You are tired and sick.

MARTHA *(As though she were talking to herself)* It's funny; it's all mixed up. There's something in you, and you don't know it and you don't do anything about it. Suddenly a child gets bored and lies—and there you are, seeing it for the first time. *(Closes her eyes)* I don't know. It all seems to come back to *me*. In some way I've ruined your life. I've ruined my own. I didn't even *know*. *(Smiles)* There's a big difference between us now, Karen. I feel all dirty and— *(Puts out her hand, touches* KAREN'S *head)* I can't stay with you any more, darling.

KAREN *(In a shaken, uncertain tone)* All this isn't true. You've never said it; we'll forget it by tomorrow—

MARTHA Tomorrow? That's a funny word. Karen, we would have had to invent a new language, as children do, without words like tomorrow.

KAREN *(Crying)* Go and lie down, Martha. You'll feel better.

(MARTHA *looks around the room, slowly, carefully. She is very quiet. Exits Right, stands at door for a second looking at* KAREN, *then slowly shuts the door behind her.* KAREN *sits alone without moving. There is no sound in the house until, a few minutes after* MARTHA'S *exit, a shot is heard. The sound of the shot should not be too loud or too strong. For a few seconds after the noise has died out,* KAREN *does not move. Then, suddenly, she springs from the chair, crosses the room, pulls open door Right. Almost at the same moment footsteps are heard on the staircase)*

MRS. MORTAR What was that? Where is it? *(Enters door Center, frightened, aimlessly moving about)* Karen! Martha! Where are you? I heard a shot. What was—*(Stops as she sees* KAREN *reappear Right. Walks toward her, still talking. Stops when she sees* KAREN'S *face)* What—what is it? *(*KAREN *moves her hands, shakes her head slightly, passes* MRS. MORTAR, *and goes toward window.* MRS. MORTAR *stares at her for a moment, rushes past her through door Right. Left alone,* KAREN *leans against the window,* MRS. MORTAR *re-enters crying. After a minute)* What shall we do? What shall we do?

KAREN *(In a toneless voice)* Nothing.

MRS. MORTAR We've got to get a doctor—right away. *(Goes to phone, nervously, fumblingly starts to dial)*

KAREN *(Without turning)* There isn't any use.

MRS. MORTAR We've got to do something. Oh, it's awful. Poor Martha. I don't know what we can do—*(Puts phone down, collapses in chair, sobs quietly)* You think she's dea—

KAREN Yes.

MRS. MORTAR Poor, poor, Martha. I can't realize it's true. Oh, how could she—she was so—I don't know what—*(Looks up, still crying, surprised)* I'm—I'm frightened.

KAREN Don't cry.

MRS. MORTAR I can't help it. How can I help it? *(Gradually the sobs cease, and she sits rocking herself)* I'll never forgive myself for the last words I said to her. But I was good to her, Karen, and you know God will excuse me for that once. I always tried to do everything I could. *(Suddenly)* Suicide's a sin. *(No answer. Timidly)* Shouldn't we call somebody to—

KAREN In a little while.

MRS. MORTAR She shouldn't have done it, she shouldn't have done it. It was because of all this awful business. She would have got a job and started all over again—she was just worried and sick and—

KAREN That isn't the reason she did it.

MRS. MORTAR What—why—?

KAREN *(Wearily)* What difference does it make now?

MRS. MORTAR *(Reproachfully)* You're not crying.

KAREN No.

MRS. MORTAR What will happen to me? I haven't anything. Poor Martha—

KAREN She was very good to you; she was good to us all.

MRS. MORTAR Oh, I know she was, Karen, and I was good to her, too. I did everything I could. I—I haven't any place to go. *(After a few seconds of silence)* I'm afraid. It seems so queer—in the next room.
> *(Shivers)*

KAREN Don't be afraid.

MRS. MORTAR It's different for you. You're young.

KAREN Not any more.
> *(The sound of the door-bell ringing.* MRS. MORTAR *jumps.* KAREN *doesn't move. It rings again)*

MRS. MORTAR *(Nervously)* Who is it? *(The bell rings again)* Shall I answer it? *(*KAREN *shrugs)* I think we'd better. *(Exits down the hall through Center doors. Returns in a minute followed by* MRS. TILFORD'S *maid,* AGATHA, *who stands in the door)* It's a woman. *(No answer)* It's a woman to see you, Karen. *(Getting no answer, she turns to* AGATHA*)* You can't come in now; we've had a—we've had trouble here.

AGATHA Miss Karen, I've *got* to speak to you.

KAREN *(Turns slowly, mechanically)* Agatha.

AGATHA *(Goes to* KAREN*)* Please, Miss Karen. We've tried so hard to get you. I been phoning here all the time. Trying to get you. Phoning and phoning. Please, please let her come in. Just for a minute, Miss Karen. Please—

MRS. MORTAR Who wants to come in here?

AGATHA Mrs. Tilford. *(Looks at* KAREN*)* Don't you feel well? *(*KAREN *shakes her head)* You ain't mad at *me?*

MRS. MORTAR That woman can't come in here. She caused all—

KAREN I'm not mad at you, Agatha.

AGATHA Can I—can I get you something?

KAREN No

AGATHA You poor child. You look like you got a pain some-where. (*Hesitates, takes* KAREN'S *hands*) I only came cause she's so bad off. She's got to see you, Miss Karen, she's just got to. She's been sittin' outside in the car, hoping you'd come out. She can't get Dr. Joe. He—he won't talk to her any more. I wouldn't a come—I always been on your side —but she's sick. If only you could see her, you'd let her come for just a minute.

KAREN I couldn't do that, Agatha.

AGATHA I don't blame you. But I had to tell you. She's old. It's going to kill her.

KAREN (*Bitterly*) Kill her? Where is Mrs. Tilford?

AGATHA Outside.

KAREN All right.

AGATHA (*Presses* KAREN'S *arm*) You always been a good girl.

　　　(*Hurriedly exits*)

MRS. MORTAR You going to allow that woman to come in here? With Martha lying there? How can you be so feeling-less? (*She starts to cry*) I won't stay and see it. I won't have anything to do with it. I'll never let that woman—

　　　(*Rushes sobbing from the room. A second after,* MRS. TILFORD *appears in the doorway Center. Her face, her walk, her voice have changed. She is feeble*)

MRS. TILFORD Karen, let me come in.

　　　(*Without turning,* KAREN *bows her head.* MRS. TIL-FORD *enters, stands staring at the floor*)

KAREN Why have you come here?

MRS. TILFORD I had to come. (*Stretches out her hand to* KAREN, *who does not turn. She drops her hand*) I know now; I know it wasn't true.

KAREN What?

MRS. TILFORD (*Carefully*) I know it wasn't true, Karen.

KAREN (*Stares at her, shudders*) You know it wasn't true? I don't care what you know. It doesn't matter any more. If that's what you had to say, you've said it. Go away.

MRS. TILFORD (*Puts her hand to her throat*) I've *got* to tell you.

KAREN I don't want to hear you.

MRS. TILFORD Last Tuesday Mrs. Wells found a bracelet in Rosalie's room. The bracelet had been hidden for several months. We found out that Rosalie had taken the bracelet from another girl, and that Mary—*(Closes her eyes)* that Mary knew that and used it to force Rosalie into saying that she had seen you and Miss Dobie together. I—I've talked to Mary. I've found out. *(KAREN suddenly begins to laugh, high and sharp)* Don't do that, Karen. I have only a little more to say. I've talked to Judge Potter. He will make all arrangements. There will be a public apology and an explanation. The damage suit will be paid to you in full and—and any more that you will be kind enough to take from me. I—I must see that you won't suffer any more.

KAREN We're not going to suffer any more. Martha is dead. *(MRS. TILFORD gasps, shakes her head as though to shake off the truth, feebly falls into a chair, and covers her face. KAREN watches her for a minute)* So you've come here to relieve your conscience? Well, I won't be your confessor. It's choking you, is it? *(Violently)* And you want to stop the choking, don't you? You've done a wrong and you have to right that wrong or you can't rest your head again. You want to be "just," don't you, and you wanted us to help you be just? You've come to the wrong place for help. You want to be a "good" woman again, don't you? *(Bitterly)* Oh, I know. You told us that night you had to do what you did. Now you "have" to do this. A public apology and money paid, and you can sleep again and eat again. That done and there'll be peace for you. You're old, and the old are callous. Ten, fifteen years left for you. But what of me? It's a whole life for me. A whole God-damned life. *(Suddenly quiet, points to door Right)* And what of her?

MRS. TILFORD *(She is crying)* You are still living.

KAREN Yes. I guess so.

MRS. TILFORD *(With a tremendous effort to control herself)* I didn't come here to relieve myself. I swear to God I didn't. I came to try—to try anything. I knew there wasn't any relief for me, Karen, and that there never would be again. *(Tensely)* But what I am or why I came doesn't matter. The only thing that matters is you and—You, now.

KAREN There's nothing for me.

MRS. TILFORD Oh, let's try to make something for you. You're young and I—I can help you.

KAREN *(Smiles)* You can help me?

MRS. TILFORD *(With great feeling)* Take whatever I can give you. Take it for yourself and use it for yourself. It won't bring me peace, if that's what's worrying you. *(Smiles)* Those ten or fifteen years you talk about! They will be bad years.

KAREN I'm tired, Mrs. Tilford. *(Almost tenderly)* You will have a hard time ahead, won't you?

MRS. TILFORD Yes.

KAREN Mary?

MRS. TILFORD I don't know.

KAREN You can send her away.

MRS. TILFORD No. I could never do that. Whatever she does, it must be to me and no one else. She's—she's—

KAREN Yes. Your very own, to live with the rest of your life. *(For a moment she watches* MRS. TILFORD'S *face)* It's over for me now, but it will never end for you. She's harmed us both, but she's harmed you more, I guess. *(Sits down beside* MRS. TILFORD*)* I'm sorry.

MRS. TILFORD *(Clings to her)* Then you'll try for yourself.

KAREN All right.

MRS. TILFORD You and Joe.

KAREN No. We're not together anymore.

MRS. TILFORD *(Looks up at her)* Did I do that, too?

KAREN I don't think anyone did anything, any more.

MRS. TILFORD *(Makes a half-movement to rise)* I'll go to him right away.

KAREN No, it's better now the way it is.

MRS. TILFORD But he must know what I know, Karen. You must go back to him.

KAREN *(Smiles)* No, not any more.

MRS. TILFORD You must, you must—*(sees her face, hesitates)* Perhaps later, Karen?

KAREN Perhaps.

MRS. TILFORD *(After a moment in which they both sit silent)* Come away from here now, Karen. *(KAREN shakes her head)* You can't stay with—
(Moves her hand toward door Right)

KAREN When she is buried, then I will go.

MRS. TILFORD You'll be all right?

KAREN I'll be all right, I suppose. Good-bye, now.
(They both rise. MRS. TILFORD speaks, pleadingly)

MRS. TILFORD You'll let me help you? You'll let me try?

KAREN Yes, if it will make you feel better.

MRS. TILFORD *(With great feeling)* Oh, yes, oh, yes, Karen.
(Unconsciously, KAREN begins to walk toward the window)

KAREN *(Suddenly)* Is it nice out?

MRS. TILFORD It's been cold. *(KAREN opens the window slightly, sits on the ledge. MRS. TILFORD with surprise)* It seems a little warmer, now.

KAREN It feels very good.
(They smile at each other)

MRS. TILFORD You'll write me some time?

KAREN If I ever have anything to say. Good-bye, now.

MRS. TILFORD You will have. I know it. Good-bye, my dear.
(KAREN smiles, shakes her head as MRS. TILFORD exits. She does not turn, but a minute later she raises her hand)

KAREN Good-bye.

CURTAIN

The Women

BY CLARE BOOTHE

CHARACTERS

JANE	SECOND SALESWOMAN
NANCY *(Miss Blake)*	A FITTER
PEGGY *(Mrs. John Day)*	CORSET MODEL
SYLVIA *(Mrs. Howard Fowler)*	PRINCESS TAMARA
EDITH *(Mrs. Phelps Potter)*	CRYSTAL ALLEN
MARY *(Mrs. Stephen Haines)*	EXERCISE INSTRUCTRESS
MRS. WAGSTAFF	MAGGIE
FIRST HAIRDRESSER	MISS TRIMMERBACK
SECOND HAIRDRESSER	MISS WATTS
PEDICURIST	A NURSE
OLGA	LUCY
EUPHIE	COUNTESS DE LAGE
A MUD-MASK	MIRIAM AARONS
COOK *(Ingrid)*	HELENE
MISS FORDYCE	FIRST CUTIE
LITTLE MARY	SECOND CUTIE
MRS. MOREHEAD	FIRST SOCIETY WOMAN
FIRST SALESGIRL	SECOND SOCIETY WOMAN
SECOND SALESGIRL	SADIE
HEAD SALESWOMAN *(Miss Shapiro)*	CIGARETTE GIRL
	A DOWAGER
FIRST MODEL *(Miss Myrtle)*	A DEBUTANTE

A GIRL IN DISTRESS

Act One

SCENE 1

MARY HAINES' *living room. Today, Park Avenue living rooms are decorated with a significant indifference to the fact that ours is still a bi-sexual society. Period peacock alleys, crystal-hung prima-donna roosts, they reflect the good taste of their mistresses in everything but a consideration of the master's pardonable right to fit in his own home decor.* MARY HAINES' *living room is not like that. It would be thought a comfortable room by a man. This, without sacrificing its own subtle, feminine charm. Above the fireplace there is a charming portrait of* MARY'S *children—a girl of 11, a boy of 5 or 6.* R., *a door to the living quarters.* L., *another to the hall.* C., *a sofa, armchair, tea-table group; and in the good light from the window, a bridge-table group.*

As curtain rises, JANE, *a pretty and quite correct little Irish-American maid, is arranging the tea-table. Four women are playing bridge in a smoking-car cloud of smoke. They are:*

NANCY, *who is sharp, but not acid, sleek but not smart, a worldly and yet virginal 35. And her partner—*

PEGGY, *who is pretty, sweet, 25.* PEGGY'S *character has not, will never quite "jell." And—*

SYLVIA, *who is glassy, elegant, feline, 34. And her partner—*

EDITH, *who is a sloppy, expensively dressed (currently, by Lane Bryant) matron of 33 or 34. Indifferent to everything but self,* EDITH *is incapable of either deliberate maliciousness or spontaneous generosity.*

SYLVIA So I said to Howard, "What do you expect me to do? Stay home and darn your socks? What do we all have money for? Why do we keep servants?"

NANCY You don't keep them long, God knows—*(Placing pack of cards)* Yours, Peggy.

PEGGY   Isn't it Mrs. Potter's? I opened with four spades.
   (SYLVIA *firmly places pack before* PEGGY. PEGGY,
   wrong again, deals)

SYLVIA   Second hand, you did. And went down a thousand.
   (*Patronizingly*) Peggy, my pet, you can't afford it.

PEGGY   I can too, Sylvia. I'm not a pauper.

SYLVIA   If your bridge doesn't improve, you soon will be.

NANCY   Oh, shut up, Sylvia. She's only playing till Mary
   comes down.

SYLVIA   (*Querulously*)   Jane, what's Mrs. Haines doing upstairs?

JANE   (*Reproachfully*)   It's that lingerie woman you sent
   her, Mrs. Fowler.

SYLVIA   I didn't expect Mrs. Haines to buy anything. I was
   just trying to get rid of the creature. (JANE *exits*) Peggy,
   bid.

PEGGY   Oh, mine? By.

SYLVIA   (*Looking at* PEGGY)   She *won't* concentrate.

NANCY   She's in love, bless her. After the child's been married as long as you girls, she may be able to concentrate on
   vital matters like bridge.

SYLVIA   (*Bored*)   Another lecture on the modern Woman?

NANCY   At the drop of a hat. By.

SYLVIA   I consider myself a perfectly good wife. I've sacrificed a lot for Howard Fowler—two spades. I devote as
   much time to my children as any of my friends.

NANCY   Except Mary.

SYLVIA   Oh, Mary, of course. Mary is an exception to all of
   us.

NANCY   Quite right. (*They are waiting for Peggy again*)
   Peggy?

PEGGY   (*Uncertainly*)   Two no trumps?
   (EDITH *rises suddenly. Plainly she feels squeamish*)

SYLVIA   (*Wearily*)   Edith, not *again?*

EDITH   I shouldn't have eaten that alligator pear. Morning
   sickness! I heave the whole darn day. This is positively the
   last time I go through this lousy business for any man! Four
   spades. If men had to bear babies, there'd never be—

NANCY —more than one child in a family. And he'd be a boy. By.

(EDITH *sinks on edge of her chair, lays down cards*)

PEGGY I wish I were having a baby. We can't afford one now.

SYLVIA And you'll never be able to, until you know Goren. (*Arranging* EDITH'S *cards*) Honestly, Edith! Why didn't you show a slam?

EDITH (*Rising hurriedly*) Oh, I *have* got to unswallow. Wait till you've had four, Peggy. You'd wish you'd never gotten past the bees and flowers. (*Exits precipitously*)

NANCY (*Disgusted*) Poor, frightened, bewildered madonna!

SYLVIA I'm devoted to Edith Potter. But she does get me down. You'd think she had a hard time. Dr. Briggs says she's like shelling peas. She ought to go through what *I* went through. Nobody *knows!*

NANCY No clubs, partner?

SYLVIA I had a Caesarean. You should see my stomach—It's a slam!

NANCY Are you sure?

SYLVIA Got the king, Peggy? (PEGGY *obligingly plays king*) Thanks, dear, it's a slam. And the rubber. (*Rises, lights fresh cigarette, goes to armchair and perches*) But I've kept my figure. I must say, I don't blame Phelps Potter for playing around.

PEGGY Oh, does her husband . . . ?

SYLVIA Oh, Phelps has made passes at all us girls. I do think it's bad taste for a man to try to make his wife's friends, *especially* when he's bald and fat. I told him once, "Phelps Potter," I said, "the next time you grab at me, I'm going straight to Edith."

NANCY And did you?

SYLVIA Certainly not. I wouldn't say anything to hurt Edith for the world. Besides, it isn't necessary. I'll say one thing for Edith. She's not as dumb as *some* of my friends. She's on to her husband.

PEGGY (*Bravely*) Do you think *he* is on to her?

SYLVIA   What do you mean?

PEGGY   If he could only hear her talk about him!

SYLVIA   Listen, Peggy, do we know how men talk about us when we're not around?

NANCY   I've heard rumors.

SYLVIA   Exactly. Peggy, you haven't been married long enough to form a realistic opinion of your husband.

PEGGY   Well, if I had one, I'd keep it to myself. Do you think I'd tell anybody in the world about the quarrels John and I have over money? I'd be too proud!

(*Enter* EDITH. *Goes to tea-table, gathers handful of sandwiches*)

SYLVIA   All over, dear?

EDITH   Oh, that was a false alarm. What happened?

SYLVIA   Only a slam, dear. You do underbid.

EDITH   I'll bet you had me on the pan.

SYLVIA   I never say behind my friends' backs what I won't say to their faces. I said you ought to diet.

EDITH   There's no use dieting in my condition. I've got to wait until I can begin from scratch. Besides, I've got the most wonderful cook. She was with Mary. She said Mary let her go because she was too extravagant. I think this cook Mary has is too, too homey. (*Examines sandwich*) Water cress. I'd just as soon eat my way across a front lawn.

SYLVIA   I think Mary's gone off terribly this winter. Have you noticed those deep lines here? (*Draws finger around her mouth*)

NANCY   Smiling lines. Tragic, aren't they?

SYLVIA   Perhaps they are. Maybe a woman's headed for trouble when she begins to get too—smug.

NANCY   Smug? Don't you mean happy?

PEGGY   Mr. Haines adores her so!

SYLVIA   (*Flashing* EDITH *a significant glance*) Yes, doesn't he.

NANCY   (*Coldly*) You just can't bear it, Sylvia, can you?

SYLVIA   Bear what?

NANCY   Mary's happiness. It gets you down.

SYLVIA   Nancy Blake, if there's one thing I can say for myself, I've never been jealous of another woman. Why should I be jealous of Mary?

NANCY Because she's contented. Contented to be what she is.

SYLVIA Which is what?

NANCY A woman.

EDITH And what, in the name of my revolting condition, am I?

NANCY A female.

SYLVIA Really. And what are you, pet?

NANCY What nature abhors, I'm—a virgin—a frozen asset.

EDITH I wish I were a virgin again. The only fun I ever had was holding out on Phelps. Nancy, you ought to thank God every night you don't have to make sacrifices for some man.

PEGGY I wish I could make a little money, writing the way you do, Miss Blake.

NANCY If you wrote the way I do, that's just what you'd make.

SYLVIA You're not exactly a popular author, are you, dear?

NANCY Not with you. Well, good news, Sylvia. My book is finished and once again I'm about to leave your midst.

PEGGY Oh, I wish we could afford to travel. Where do you go this time, Miss Blake?

NANCY Africa, shooting.

SYLVIA Well, darling, I don't blame you. I'd rather face a tiger any day than the sort of things the critics said about your last book.

> (*Enter* MARY. *A lovely woman in her middle 30's. She is what most of us want our happily married daughters to be like. She is carrying several white boxes*)

MARY Sorry, girls. (*Teasing*) Sylvia, must you always send me woebegone creatures like that lingerie woman? It's been a very expensive half hour for me.

PEGGY (*Looking at* SYLVIA) For me too, Mrs. Haines.

MARY (*Laughing*) Nonsense, Peggy, you were playing for me. Here. (*Hands* PEGGY *a box*) Don't open it now. It's a bed-jacket. Or a tea cozy. Or something padded. I wouldn't know. I was crying so hard:

SYLVIA You didn't believe that woman's sob story?

MARY Of course I did. *(She really didn't)* Anyway, she's a lot worse off than you and I. *(Putting down another box)* Edith, wee garments—

EDITH Darling, how sweet! *(It comes over her again)* Oh, my God! I'm sick as a cat. *(Sits)*

SYLVIA It's a girl. Girls always make you sicker.

NANCY Even before they're born?

EDITH I don't care what it is. I've lost everything including my curiosity. Why did God make it take nine months?

NANCY *(Helpfully)* It takes an elephant seven years.

EDITH I wish I were an elephant. I'll look like one anyway before I'm finished. And it would be heaven not to worry for seven years.

MARY *(Laughing)* Oh, Edith, it is rather trying. But when it's all over, isn't it the grandest thing in the world to have them?

JANE *(Entering with tea-kettle)* Ma'am, Mr. Haines would like to speak to you on the phone.

MARY Oh, I can feel what it is in my bones, Jane. *(To others)* Stephen's going to be kept at the office again tonight. *(Exits)*

SYLVIA Give him my love, pet.

MARY *(Off stage)* I will.

SYLVIA *(She never lets anything pass)* Nancy, you couldn't be more wrong about me and Mary.

NANCY Still rankling?

SYLVIA Jealous? As a matter of fact, I'm sorry for her.

NANCY Oh-ho? Why?

SYLVIA *(Mysteriously)* Well, for all *we* know she may be living in a fool's paradise with Stephen.

NANCY Let's check that one for a moment, Sylvia. Jane, are the children in?

JANE Yes, Miss. Just back from the Park. *(EDITH rises— SYLVIA, in pantomime, signals her not to leave the room. This is not lost on NANCY. For a moment she hesitates at door)*

PEGGY Oh, I'd love to see Mrs. Haines' little girl, Miss
Blake—

NANCY *(Following* PEGGY*)* Come along, child. Anyway, it's
our turn to go on the pan. But we don't have to worry.
You've got a poor man. I've got no man at all.
(They exit)

EDITH *(Goes to tea-table—pours 2 cups.* JANE *empties ash
trays)* This is positively the last time I play bridge with
Nancy. She never misses a chance to get in a dig. What has
a creature like her got but her friends? *(*JANE *exits, closing
door,* L. SYLVIA *stealthily closes door,* R.*)* The way she kept
at you about Mary made me so nervous, I thought I'd
scream. And in my condition—

SYLVIA Edith, I've got to tell you! I'll burst if I wait!

EDITH I *knew* you had something!
*(She brings her well-laden plate and tea-cup and set-
tles herself happily beside* SYLVIA *on sofa)*

SYLVIA You'll die! Stephen Haines is cheating on Mary!

EDITH I don't believe you; is it true?

SYLVIA Wait till you hear. *(Now she is into it)* You know I
go to Michael's for my hair. You ought to go, pet. I despise
whoever does yours. Well, there's the most wonderful new
manicurist there. *(Shows her scarlet nails)* Isn't that divine? Jungle Red—

EDITH Simply divine. Go on.

SYLVIA It all came out in the most extraordinary way, this
morning. I tried to get you on the phone—

EDITH I was in the tub. Go on.

SYLVIA This manicurist, she's marvelous, was doing my
nails. I was looking through *Vogue*, the one with Mary in
the Junior League Ball costume—

EDITH —in that white wig that flattered her so much?

SYLVIA *(Nodding)* Well, this manicurist: "Oh, Mrs.
Fowler," she says, "is that that Mrs. Haines who's so awfully
rich?"

EDITH Funny how people like that think people like us are
awfully rich.

SYLVIA I forget what she said next. You know how those
creatures are, babble, babble, babble, babble, and never

let up for a minute! When suddenly she says: "I know the girl who's being *kept* by Mr. Haines!"

EDITH No!

SYLVIA I swear!

EDITH *(Thrilled)* Is she someone *we* know?

SYLVIA No! That's what's so awful about it. She's a friend of this manicurist. Oh, it wouldn't be so bad if Stephen had picked someone in his own class. But a blond floosie!

EDITH But how did Stephen ever meet a girl like that?

SYLVIA How do men ever meet girls like that? That's what they live for, the rats!

EDITH But—

SYLVIA I can't go into all the details now. They're utterly fantastic—

EDITH You suppose Mary knows?

SYLVIA No. Mary's the kind who couldn't help showing it if she knew.

EDITH *(Nodding, her mouth full of her third cake)* She has no self-control. Well, she's bound to find out. If a woman's got any instincts, she feels when her husband's off the reservation. I know *I* would.

SYLVIA Of course you would, darling. Not Mary—*(Rises, walks about, wrestling with* MARY'S *sad problem)* If only there were some way to warn her!

EDITH *(Horrified, following her)* Sylvia! You're not going to tell her?

SYLVIA Certainly not. I'd *die* before I'd be the one to hurt her like that!

EDITH Couldn't someone shut that manicurist up?

SYLVIA A good story like that? A lot girls like that care whose life they ruin.

EDITH *Isn't* it a dirty trick?

SYLVIA Isn't it *foul?* It's not as though only Mary's friends knew. We could keep our mouths shut.

EDITH I know plenty that I never *breathe* about my friends' husbands!

SYLVIA So do I! *(They exchange a sudden glance of sharp suspicion)* Anyway, the whole thing's disgustingly unfair to Mary. I feel absolutely sick about it, just knowing about it—

EDITH   I adore Mary—

SYLVIA   I *worship* her. She's my dearest friend in all the world—

> (*Voices off stage. They sit down at card-table and begin to play solitaire hastily. Enter* NANCY *and* PEGGY)

NANCY   Well, Sylvia, feeling better?

SYLVIA   (*Innocently*) Meaning what?

NANCY   Must've been a choice piece of gossip. You both look so *relaxed.*

SYLVIA   Nancy, were you listening at that door?

PEGGY   Oh, Mrs. Fowler, we were in the nursery.

> (MARY *enters*)

SYLVIA   (*Quickly*) Well, darling, how is Stephen, the old dear? And did you give him my love?

MARY   I did. Stephen's not so well, Sylvia.

SYLVIA   Oh? What's the trouble?

MARY   Nervous indigestion. That's why I have such a plain cook now.

EDITH   Phelps has had indigestion for years. You should hear that man rumble in the night. Like a truck on cobblestones.

SYLVIA   There's nothing—worrying Stephen?

MARY   Oh, no, he's just been working too hard. He's not coming home tonight.

SYLVIA   Are you sure it's *work,* darling, and not a beautiful blonde?

MARY   Stephen? (*Laughing, and perhaps a little smugly, too*) Oh, Sylvia.

EDITH   (*Afraid* SYLVIA *will go too far*) Sylvia, let's play another rubber.

SYLVIA   Stephen's a very attractive man.

MARY   Isn't he? I can't imagine why he hasn't deserted me for some glamorous creature long ago.

NANCY   (*Alarmed*) Mary, you do sound smug.

MARY   Oh, let me be, Nancy. How can you be too sure of what you believe in most?

SYLVIA I wouldn't be sure of the Apostle Paul. I always tell Howard, "If you ever manage to make a fool of me, I'll deserve what I get."

NANCY You certainly will. *(Faces* SYLVIA *squarely)* Now, Sylvia, let's have it.

SYLVIA Have what?

NANCY Just what did you mean when you said Mary was living in a fool's paradise?

MARY What?

SYLVIA *(Angrily)* Nancy, don't be absurd. *(A pause. Then, wriggling out of it)* Oh, Mary, I was just trying to make a typical Nancy Blake wisecrack about marriage. I said, "A woman's paradise is always a fool's paradise!"

MARY That's not bad, is it, Nancy? Well, Sylvia, whatever I'm living in, I like it. Nancy, cut.

SYLVIA *(Examines her nails minutely, suddenly shows them to* MARY*)* Mary, how do you like my new polish?

NANCY *(Not looking)* Too, too—too!

SYLVIA You can't imagine how it stays on. I get it at Michael's—There's a terrific new manicurist there—

EDITH *(Protestingly)* Oh, Sylvia—

SYLVIA Olga's her name. She's out of this world.

EDITH Will you cut, Sylvia?

SYLVIA It's called Jungle Red.

NANCY Just the thing for tearing your friends apart.

SYLVIA I'll be damned, Nancy, if I'll let you ride me any more!

MARY Now, Sylvia, Nancy's just being clever too.

SYLVIA She takes a crack at everything about me. Even my nails!

MARY *(Laughing)* Well, I like it. I really do! It's new and chic. *(Pats her hand)* Michael's, Olga, Jungle Red? I'll remember that. *(Cuts cards)* You and I, Sylvia. I feel lucky today.

SYLVIA *(With a sweet, pitying smile)* Do you, darling? Well, you know what they say, "Lucky in cards—"

CURTAIN

SCENE 2

An afternoon, a few days later. A hairdressing booth in Michael's. An elegantly functioned cubbyhole. R., a recessed mirror in wall. L., from high partition pole, a curtain to floor. Rear wall is a plain partition. C., swivel hairdressing chair. Above it from an aluminum tree, the hanging thicket of a permanent-wave machine. In wall, gadgets for curling irons, electric outlets which connect with wires to drying machine, hand drier, manicurists' table-light, stools for pedicurists, and manicurist, OLGA. *As curtain rises, the booth is, to put it mildly, full.*

The COUNTESS DE LAGE, *an amiable, silly, fat and forty heiress-type, is in chair, having her hair dyed.* OLGA, *at her* R., *is doing her nails. Her fat bare feet rest in the lap of the* PEDICURIST. 1ST HAIRDRESSER *applies the dye.* 2ND HAIRDRESSER, *watch in hand, times the operation. The* COUNTESS, *apparently inured to public execution, smokes, reads magazine on her lap, occasionally nibbles a sandwich which* OLGA *passes her from a tray near her instruments.*

COUNTESS   That stuff is burning my scalp! Mon Dieu *(Pronounced Mon Doo)*

2ND HAIRDRESSER   Be brave! One minute more!

COUNTESS *(In pain)*   O-o-oo!

1ST HAIRDRESSER   It's going to be so worth it, Countess.

COUNTESS   It's dribbling down my neck!

2ND HAIRDRESSER   Be brave!

COUNTESS   O-o-o-o! My nerves—Oo—my God! *(To* PEDICURIST*)* My sandwich— *(*OLGA *hands her sandwich)*

2ND HAIRDRESSER   Ten seconds. We must suffer to be beautiful.

> *(Curtain parts, a figure in flowing white half-enters. It is, judging by the voice, a woman, but its face is completely obliterated by a mud-mask)*

MUD MASK Whoops——I thought I was in here. Why, hiya, Countess de Lage. *(Coyly)* Guess who I am?
> *(A second face appears over this intruder's shoulder. It's the colored maid, EUPHIE. She clutches the shoulder of the mud-mask)*

EUPHIE Mustn't talk, Miss Aarons. You'll crack your mud-mask.

MIRIAM I was half-cracked to let you put this glop on me
> *(Exits followed by EUPHIE)*

COUNTESS Who was that?

1ST HAIRDRESSER Miriam Aarons.

COUNTESS Who?

1ST HAIRDRESSER Miriam Aarons. She's playing in "The Vanities."

COUNTESS Does she know me?

OLGA Oh, everybody knows you, Countess de Lage. *(Full of awe)* You're in the society columns almost every day.

COUNTESS Miriam Aarons? It's a funny thing about me. I have no memory for names or faces. Well, I suppose she came to one of my parties. I never know who the Count's going to ask. For an aristocrat, mon dieu, is he democratic!

OLGA I've seen pictures of the Count. He's awful handsome . . .

COUNTESS *(Thoughtfully)* What does a mud mask do for you?

1ST HAIRDRESSER Tightens the chin and throat muscles.

2ND HAIRDRESSER Brings on a natural glow——

PEDICURIST Miriam Aarons has lovely skin.

1ST HAIRDRESSER Not lovelier than yours, Countess!

1ST, 2ND HAIRDRESSERS, PEDICURIST, OLGA *(In fawning chorus)* Oh, yours is lovely. Why, not nearly as lovely. You have lovely skin.

COUNTESS I do think it's rather good for a woman my age!

1ST HAIRDRESSER You mustn't talk as if you were an old woman, Countess dear!

COUNTESS *(Lying)* After all, I'm 45.

1ST HAIRDRESSER Mustn't tell anyone.

2ND HAIRDRESSER You don't look a day over 40.

CHORUS OF HAIRDRESSERS, PEDICURIST, OLGA   You look so young! Why not a day . . . ! You certainly don't look your age. Not a day over 40!

1ST HAIRDRESSER   Haven't you slimmed down since last year?

COUNTESS *(With satisfaction)*   My last divorce took off ten pounds. *(A pause)* I think I'll have a mud mask.

1ST HAIRDRESSER *(To 2ND HAIRDRESSER)*   Tell the desk Countess de Lage is working in a mud.

(Exit 2ND HAIRDRESSER)

COUNTESS *(Admiring her nail polish on one hand)*   Tres gai, n'est-ce pas?

OLGA   Oh, no, we don't have "tray gay." That's Jungle Red. Everybody's wild about it. Mrs. Howard Fowler wears it. You know Mrs. Fowler—the best dressed woman in New York?

1ST HAIRDRESSER *(To COUNTESS)*   There, dear. The agony's over! We'll move to the shampoo. *(Calling off)* Euphie! Clear this booth.

PEDICURIST *(Rising, gathering up her pedicure basket, and the Countess' stockings)*   We won't put your stockings on yet, Countess. We don't want to smear your beautiful big toe.

(PEDICURIST and HAIRDRESSER help COUNTESS to her feet. COUNTESS, leaning on their arms, has to walk on her heels, her toes still wadded with cotton)

COUNTESS *(Singing)*   Allons enfants de la patrie! On to the mud mask!

(EUPHIE opens curtain. 1ST HAIRDRESSER, PEDICUR-IST, COUNTESS exit. During the ensuing dialogue EU-PHIE cleans the floor of the booth with a long-handled sweeper, brush and pan, and OLGA puts manicure things away in her basket)

OLGA   That old gasoline truck! Fifty-two, if she's a day. One more permanent and she won't have a hair left on her head!

EUPHIE *(Viewing dustpan)*   She sure does shed.

OLGA   I'll bet this husband sheds *her* in a year. A woman is a fool to marry a man ten years younger. Know what I heard a client under the dryer tell a friend? The Count's a pansy!

> (OLGA *exits, pantomiming "pansy." Enter* 2ND HAIR-DRESSER)

2ND HAIRDRESSER Countess de Lage forgot her bag.
> (*She retrieves the bag from the floor. It is open. She is about to close it. Looks in. Laughs. Pulls out a leather whiskey flask, shows it without comment to* EUPHIE, *then drops it back in bag, and exits.* EUPHIE *starts to follow, then holds back curtain. Enter* MARY, *followed by* NANCY)

MARY (*To* EUPHIE) Thank you.

EUPHIE Yes Ma'am. (*Exits*)

MARY (*To* NANCY) So, as I say, I woke up this morning, and for no good reason I felt the time has come to change my hair-do—
> (*Enter* 2ND HAIRDRESSER)

2ND HAIRDRESSER Mr. Michael will be ten minutes, madam. Anyone in particular for your manicure?

MARY I'd like the girl who does Mrs. Fowler's nails.

2ND HAIRDRESSER Olga. I'll see. (*Exits*)

NANCY God, I'd love to do Mrs. Fowler's nails, right down to the wrist, with a nice big buzz saw.

MARY Sylvia's all right. She's a good friend underneath.

NANCY Underneath what?

MARY Nancy, you don't humor your friends enough.

NANCY So that's the big idea coming here? You're humoring Sylvia?

MARY Oh, you did hurt her. I had it all over again at lunch. (*She catches a glimpse of herself in mirror*) Nancy, am I getting old?

NANCY Who put that in your head? Sylvia?

MARY Tell me the truth.

NANCY Beauty is in the eye of the beholder, and twaddle to that effect.

MARY But it's such a scary feeling when you see those little wrinkles creeping in.

NANCY Time's little mice.

MARY And that first gleam of white in your hair. It's the way you'd feel about autumn, if you knew there'd never be another spring—

NANCY *(Abruptly)* There's only one tragedy for a woman.

MARY Growing old?

NANCY Losing her man.

MARY That's why we're all so afraid of growing old.

NANCY Are you afraid?

MARY Well, I was very pretty when I was young. I never thought about it twice then. Now I know it's why Stephen loved me.

NANCY Smart girl.

MARY Now I think about it all the time.

NANCY Love is not love which alters when it alteration finds. Shakespeare.

MARY Well, he told me, on my birthday, I'd always look the same to him.

NANCY Nice present. No jewels?

MARY It rained that day. He brought me a bottle of perfume called "Summer Rain."

NANCY How many ounces?

MARY Nancy, you've never been in love.

NANCY Says who?

MARY *(Surprised)* Have you?

NANCY Yes.

MARY You never told me.

NANCY You never asked— *(Wistfully)* Neither did *he*. *(OLGA enters with fresh bowl of water)* Here, innocent. *(Gives book to MARY)* The book my readers everywhere have been waiting for with such marked apathy.

MARY "All the Dead Ladies"?

NANCY Originally called, "From the Silence of the Womb." My publisher thought that would make too much noise.

MARY What's it about? *(OLGA begins to file MARY's nails)*

NANCY Women I dislike: "Ladies—"

MARY Oh, Nancy!

OLGA *(Putting MARY's hand in water)* Soak it, please.

NANCY   No good? Too bad. It's a parting shot. I'm off.

MARY   Off?

NANCY   Africa.

MARY   But not today?

NANCY   I knew if I told you you'd scurry around and do things. A party. Steamer baskets of sour fruit. Not nearly as sour as the witty cables your girl friends would send me —So don't move. No tears. For my sake—just soak it. Good-bye, Mary—

MARY   Good-bye, Nancy. I'll miss you.

NANCY   I doubt it. Practically nobody ever misses a clever woman. *(Exits)*

OLGA   Funny, isn't she?

MARY   She's a darling.

OLGA   She's a writer? How do those writers think up those plots? I guess the plot part's not so hard to think up as the end. I guess anybody's life'd make a interesting plot if it had a interesting end—Mrs. Fowler sent you in? *(MARY, absorbed in NANCY'S book, nods)* She's sent me three clients this week. Know the Countess de Lage? Well, she inherited this fortune when her first husband died and—

MARY   *(Shortly)*   I don't know her—

OLGA   Soak it, please. Know Mrs. Potter?

MARY   Yes.

OLGA   She's pregnant again.

MARY   *(She wants to read.)*   I know.

OLGA   Soak it, please. *(Puts MARY'S hand in water. Begins on other hand)* Know Mrs. Stephen Haines?

MARY   I certainly do—

OLGA   I guess Mrs. Fowler's told you about her! Mrs. Fowler feels awfully sorry for her.

MARY   *(Laughing)*   Oh, she does! Well, I don't. I—

OLGA   You would if you knew this Crystal Allen.

MARY   Crystal Allen?

OLGA   Yes, you know. The girl who's living with Mr. Haines? *(MARY starts violently)* Don't you like the file? Mrs. Potter says it sets her unborn child's teeth on edge.

MARY   *(Indignant)*   Whoever told you such a thing?

OLGA Oh, I thought you knew. Didn't Mrs. Fowler—?

MARY No—

OLGA Then you will be interested. You see, Crystal Allen is a friend of mine. She's really a terrible man-trap. Soak it, please. (MARY, *dazed, puts her hand in the dish*) She's behind the perfume counter at Saks'. So was I before I got fi—left. That's how she met him.

MARY Met Stephen Haines?

OLGA Yeah. It was a couple of months ago. Us girls weren't busy. It was an awful rainy day, I remember. So this gentleman walks up to the counter. He was the serious type, nice-looking, but kind of thin on top. Well, Crystal nabs him. "I want some perfume," he says. "May I awsk what type of woman for?" Crystal says, very ritzy. That didn't mean a thing. She was going to sell him our feature, Summer Rain, anyway. "Is she young?" Crystal says. "No," he says, sort of embarrassed. "Is she the glamorous type?" Crystal says. "No, thank God," he says. "Thank God?" Crystal says and bats her eyes. She's got those eyes which run up and down a man like a searchlight. Well, she puts perfume on her palm and in the crook of her arm for him to smell. So he got to smelling around and I guess he liked it. Because we heard him tell her his name, which one of the girls recognized from Igor Cassini's column— Gee, you're nervous— Well, it was after that I left. I wouldn't of thought no more about it. But a couple of weeks ago I stopped by where Crystal lives to say hello. And the landlady says she'd moved to the kind of house where she could entertain her gentleman friend— "What gentleman friend?" I says. "Why, that Mr. Haines that she's had up in her room all hours of the night," the landlady says— (MARY *draws her hand away*) Did I hurt?

MARY No. But I don't really need a manicure.

OLGA Just polish? One coat, or two? (*Picks up a red bottle*)

MARY None. (*Rises, goes to chair, where she left her purse*)

OLGA But I thought that's what you came for? All Mrs. Fowler's friends—

MARY I think I've gotten what all Mrs. Fowler's friends came for. *(Puts dollar bill on table)*

OLGA *(Picks up bill)* Oh, thanks— Well, good-bye. I'll tell her you were in, Mrs.—?

MARY Mrs. Stephen Haines.

OLGA Mrs.—? Oh, gee, gee! Gee, Mrs. Haines—I'm sorry! Oh, isn't there something I can do?

MARY Stop telling that story!

OLGA Oh, sure, sure, I will!

MARY And please don't tell anyone— *(Her voice breaks)* that you told it to *me*—

OLGA Oh, I won't, gee I promise! Gee, that would be kind of humiliating for you! *(Defensively)* But in a way, Mrs. Haines, I'm kinda *glad* you know. Crystal's a terrible girl —I mean, she's terribly clever. And she's terribly pretty, Mrs. Haines—I mean, if I were you I wouldn't waste no time getting Mr. Haines away from her—

(MARY turns abruptly away)

MARY Thank you. Goodday.

(OLGA eyes bill in her hand distastefully, suddenly puts it down on table and exits. MARY, alone, stares blankly in mirror, then, suddenly focusing on her image, leans forward, searching her face between her trembling hands. A drier goes on in next booth. A shrill voice rises above its drone)

VOICE—Not too hot! My sinus! So she said: "I wouldn't want anybody in the world to know," and *I* said: "My dear, you know you can trust *me!*"

CURTAIN

SCENE 3

An hour later. MARY'S *boudoir. Charming, of course. A door to bedroom,* R. *A door to hall,* L. *A chaise-longue, next to it, a table with books, flowers, a phone. A dressing table.*

As curtain rises, MARY *is discovered on chaise-longue, twisting a damp handkerchief in her hands. Jane enters from hall, carrying a tea tray.*

JANE You looked like you needed a cup of tea when you came in, ma'am.

MARY I do. I have a sudden headache. And, Jane—my mother will be here in a few minutes. A cup for her.

JANE Yes, ma'am.

(*Enter* MISS FORDYCE. *She is a raw-boned, capable English spinster of 32*)

MISS FORDYCE May I see you, Mrs. Haines?

MARY Of course, Miss Fordyce.

MISS FORDYCE It's about little Mary—Really, Mrs. Haines, you'll have to talk to your child. She's just smacked her little brother, hard. Pure temper.

MARY What did little Stevie do to her, Miss Fordyce?

MISS FORDYCE Well, you see, it happened while I was down getting my tea. When I came up, she'd had such a tantrum, she'd made herself ill. She positively refuses to discuss the incident with me. But I'm quite sure the dear boy hadn't done a thing.

MARY You're very apt to take the boy's side, Miss Fordyce.

MISS FORDYCE Not at all. But in England, Mrs. Haines, our girls are not so wretchedly spoiled. After all, this is a man's world. The sooner our girls are taught to accept the fact *graciously—*

MARY (*Gently*) Send her in to me, Miss Fordyce. (*Exit* MISS FORDYCE) Oh, Jane, I don't understand it. Miss Fordyce

119

really prefers Mary, but she insists we all make a little god of Stevie. *(Exits to bedroom, leaving door open)*

JANE Them English ones always stand up for the boys. But they say since the War, ma'am, there's six women over there to every man. Competition is something fierce! Over here, men aren't so scarce. You can treat them the way they deserve—

> *(Enter LITTLE MARY. She is a broad-browed, thoughtful little girl, physically well developed for her age)*

LITTLE MARY Where's Mother?

JANE You're going to catch it. Smacking your little brother. *(Mimicking MISS FORDYCE)* Such a dear, sweet little lad— shame. *(LITTLE MARY does not answer)* I'll bet you wish you were Mother's girl, instead of Daddy's girl today, don't you? *(LITTLE MARY doesn't answer)* What's the matter, the cat got your tongue?

> *(Enter MARY, wearing negligee)*

MARY Hello, darling— Aren't you going to kiss me? *(LITTLE MARY doesn't move)* What red eyes!

LITTLE MARY I was mad. I threw up. When you throw up, doesn't it make you cry?

MARY *(Smiling)* Stevie tease you? *(LITTLE MARY, embarrassed, looks at JANE. JANE snickers, takes hint and goes out)* Well, darling?

LITTLE MARY Mother, I don't know how to begin.

MARY *(Sitting on chaise-longue, and putting out her hand)* Come here. *(LITTLE MARY doesn't budge)* Would you rather wait until tonight and tell Dad?

LITTLE MARY *(Horrified)* Oh, Mother, I couldn't tell him! *(Fiercely)* And I'd be killed to death before I'd tell skinny old Miss Fordyce—

MARY That's not the way for my dear little girl to talk.

LITTLE MARY *(Setting her jaw)* I don't want to be a dear little girl. *(She suddenly rushes to MARY'S outstretched arms in tears)* Oh, Mother dear, Mother dear!

MARY Baby, what?

LITTLE MARY What brother said!

MARY What did he say, the wretched boy?

LITTLE MARY *(Disentangling herself)* He said I had bumps!

MARY Bumps? You don't mean mumps?

LITTLE MARY No, bumps. He said I was covered with disgusting bumps!

MARY *(Alarmed)* Mary, where?

LITTLE MARY *(Touching her hips and breasts with delicate, ashamed finger tips) Here* and *here!*

MARY Oh— *(Controlling her relieved laughter, and drawing* LITTLE MARY *to her side)* Of course you have bumps, darling. Very pretty little bumps. And you have them because—you're a little girl.

LITTLE MARY *(Wailing)* But, Mother dear. I don't want to be a little girl. I hate girls! They're so silly, and they tattle, tattle—

MARY Not really, Mary.

LITTLE MARY Yes, Mother, I know. Oh, Mother, what *fun* is there to be a lady? What can a lady do?

MARY *(Cheerfully)* These days, darling, ladies do all the things men do. They fly aeroplanes across the ocean, they go into politics and business—

LITTLE MARY *You* don't, Mother.

MARY Perhaps I'm happier doing just what I do.

LITTLE MARY What do you do, Mother?

MARY Take care of you and Stevie and Dad.

LITTLE MARY You don't, Mother. Miss Fordyce and the servants do.

MARY *(Teasing)* I see. I'm not needed around here.

LITTLE MARY *(Hugging her)* Oh, Mother, I don't mean that. It wouldn't be any fun at all without you. But, Mother, even when the ladies *do* do things, they stop it when they get the lovey-dovies.

MARY The what?

LITTLE MARY Like in the movies, Mother. Ladies always end up so *silly. (Disgusted)* Lovey-dovey, lovey-dovey all the time!

MARY Darling, you're too young to understand—

LITTLE MARY But, Mother—

MARY "But Mother, but Mother!" There's one thing a woman can do, no man can do.

LITTLE MARY *(Eagerly)* What?

MARY Have a child. *(Tenderly)* Like you.

LITTLE MARY Oh, that! Everybody knows that. But is that any fun, Mother dear?

MARY Fun? No. But it is—joy. *(Hugging her)* Of a very special kind.

LITTLE MARY *(Squirming away)* Well, it's never sounded specially exciting to me— I love you, Mother. But I bet you anything you like, Daddy has more *fun* than you! *(She slips away from* MARY. *Then sees* MARY'S *dispirited face, turns and kisses her warmly)* Oh, I'm sorry, Mother. But you just don't *understand!* *(A pause)* Am I to be punished, Mother?

MARY *(She is thinking about something else)* What do you think?

LITTLE MARY I smacked him awful hard— Shall I punish myself?

MARY It will have to be pretty bad.

LITTLE MARY *(Solemnly)* Then I won't go down to breakfast with Daddy tomorrow, or the next day—O. K., Mother?

MARY O. K.

> (LITTLE MARY *walks, crestfallen, to door as* JANE *enters with extra cup and saucer.* LITTLE MARY *sticks out her tongue)*

LITTLE MARY There's my tongue! So what? *(Exits skipping)*

JANE *(Laughing)* She never lets anybody get the best of her, does she, Mrs. Haines?

MARY My poor baby. She doesn't want to be a woman, Jane.

JANE Who does?

MARY Somehow, I've never minded it, Jane.

> *(Enter* MRS. MOREHEAD. *She is a bourgeois aristocrat of 55.* MARY *rises, kisses her)*

MRS. MOREHEAD Hello, child, 'Afternoon, Jane.

JANE 'Afternoon, Mrs. Morehead. *(Exits to bedroom)*

MARY Mother, dear! *(She walks slowly to dressing table)*

MRS. MOREHEAD *(Cheerfully)* Well, what's wrong? *(Sits)*

MARY *(Turning)* How did you know something's wrong?

MRS. MOREHEAD Your voice on the phone. Is it Stephen?

MARY How did you know?

MRS. MOREHEAD You sent for *Mother.* So it must be he. *(A pause)*

MARY I don't know how to begin, Mother.

MRS. MOREHEAD *(Delighted to find that her instincts were correct)* It's a woman! Who is she?

MARY Her name is Crystal Allen. She—she's a salesgirl at Saks'.

> (MRS. MOREHEAD'S *cheerful and practical manner discourages tears, so she begins to cream and tonic her face instead)*

MRS. MOREHEAD She's young and pretty, I suppose.

MARY Well, yes. *(Defensively)* But common.

MRS. MOREHEAD *(Soothingly)* Of course— Stephen told you?

MARY No. I—I found out—this afternoon.

MRS. MOREHEAD How far has it gone?

MARY He's known her about three months.

MRS. MOREHEAD Does Stephen know you know?

MARY *(Shaking her head)* I—I wanted to speak to you first. *(The tears come anyway)* Oh, Mother dear, what am I going to say to him?

MRS. MOREHEAD *Nothing.*

MARY *Nothing.*

MRS. MOREHEAD My dear, I felt the same way twenty years ago.

MARY Not, Father?

MRS. MOREHEAD Mary, in many ways your father was an exceptional man. *(Philosophically)* That, unfortunately, was not one of them.

MARY Did you say nothing?

MRS. MOREHEAD Nothing. I had a wise mother, too. Listen, dear, this is not a new story. It comes to most wives.

MARY But Stephen—

MRS. MOREHEAD Stephen is a man. He's been married twelve years—

MARY   You mean, he's tired of me!

MRS. MOREHEAD   Stop crying. You'll make your nose red.

MARY   I'm not crying. *(Patting tonic on her face)* This stuff stings.

MRS. MOREHEAD   *(Going to her)*   Stephen's tired of himself. Tired of feeling the same things in himself year after year. Time comes when every man's got to feel something new —when he's got to feel young again, just because he's growing old. Women are just the same. But when *we* get that way we change our hairdress. Or get a new cook. Or redecorate the house from stem to stern. But a man can't do over his office, or fire his secretary. Not even change the style of his hair. And the urge usually hits him hardest just when he's beginning to lose his hair. No, dear, a man has only one escape from his old self: to see a different self— in the mirror of some woman's eyes.

MARY   But, Mother—

MRS. MOREHEAD   This girl probably means no more to him than that new dress means to you.

MARY   But, Mother—

MRS. MOREHEAD   "But Mother, but Mother!" He's not giving anything to her that belongs to you, or you would have felt that yourself long ago.

MARY   *(Bewildered)*   Oh, I always thought I would. I love him so much.

MRS. MOREHEAD   And he loves you, baby. *(Drawing MARY beside her on chaise-longue)* Now listen to me: Go away somewhere for a month or two. There's nothing like a good dose of another woman to make a man appreciate his wife. Mother knows!

MARY   But there's never been a lie between us before.

MRS. MOREHEAD   You mean, there's never been a *silence* between you before. Well, it's about time. Keeping still, when you *ache* to talk, is about the only sacrifice spoiled women like us ever have to make.

MARY   But I'd forgive him—

MRS. MOREHEAD   Forgive him? *(Impatiently)* For what⸱

For being a man? Accuse him, and you'll never get a chance to forgive him. He'd have to justify himself—

MARY How can he!

MRS. MOREHEAD *(Sighing)* He can't and he *can*. Don't make him try. Either way you'd lose him. And remember, dear, it's being together at the *end* that really matters. *(Rising)* One more piece of motherly advice: Don't confide in your girl friends!

MARY I think they all know

MRS. MOREHEAD They think you don't? *(MARY nods)* Leave it that way. If you let them advise you, they'll see to it, in the name of friendship, that you lose your husband and your home. I'm an old woman, dear, and I know my sex. *(Moving to door)* I'm going right down this minute and get our tickets.

MARY Our—tickets?

MRS. MOREHEAD You're taking me to Bermuda, dear. My throat's been awfully bad. I haven't wanted to worry you, but my doctor says—

MARY Oh, Mother darling! Thank you!

MRS. MOREHEAD Don't thank me, dear. It's rather—*nice* to have you need Mother again.

(Exits. Phone rings. MARY answers it)

MARY Yes?—Oh, Stephen— Yes, dear?—*(Distressed)* Oh, Stephen! Oh, no—I'm not angry. It's—it's just that I wanted to see the play. Yes, I can get Mother to go with me.... Stephen, will you be very late? *(It's a bit of struggle, but she manages a cheerful voice)* Oh, it's—all right. Have a good time. Of course, I know it's just business—No, dear —I won't wait up—Stephen. I love— *(A click. The other end has hung up. JANE enters. MARY turns her back. Her face would belie the calmness of her voice.)* Jane— The children and I will be having dinner alone—

CURTAIN

SCENE 4

Two months later. A dressmaker's shop. We see 2 fitting booths, the same in appointment: triplex pier glasses, dress-racks, smoking stands, 2 small chairs. They are divided by a mirrored partition. At rear of each booth, a curtain and a door, off a corridor, which leads to "the floor."

As curtain rises booth on L. is empty. Other booth is cluttered with dresses. 2 salesgirls are loading them over their arms.

1ST GIRL *(With vivid resentment against a customer who has just departed)* Well, now we can put them all back again. Makes you drag out everything in the damn store, and doesn't even buy a brassiere!

2ND GIRL And that's the kind who always needs one.

1ST GIRL This isn't her type. That isn't her type. I'd like to tell her what her type is. .

2ND GIRL I'd like to know.

1ST GIRLS It's the type that nobody gives a damn about! Gee, I'd like to work in a men's shop once. What can a man try on?

2ND GIRL Ever see a man try on hats? What they go through, you'd think a head was something peculiar.

(Both girls exit. 1ST SALESWOMAN enters booth on R., hereafter called "MARY'S booth")

1ST SALESWOMAN Miss Myrtle, step in here a moment.

(MODEL, a handsome wench, in a slinky negligee, enters)

MODEL Yes, Miss Shapiro.

1ST SALESWOMAN If I've told you once, I've told you a thousand times, when you're modeling that dress, your stomach must lead. If you walk like this *(Pantomimes)* you take away all the seduction. *This* is seduction!

126

(Shows MODEL *her rather unconvincing conception of a seductive walk)*

MODEL I'll try, Miss Shapiro. *(Tearfully)* But if you had my appendix!

1ST SALESWOMAN Well, Miss Myrtle, you can take your choice: You will either lose your job or lose your appendix!

(Exit MODEL. *In* R. *booth, hereafter called* "CRYSTAL'S *booth," enter* 2ND SALESWOMAN*)*

2ND SALESWOMAN *(To* 1ST *and* 2ND GIRLS *who have returned for another load of dresses)* Quickly, please, I have a client waiting.

*(2ND GIRL *exits with last of clothes as enter* CRYSTAL, *followed by* SALESWOMAN. 3RD SALESWOMAN *is seen crossing corridor from* R. *to* L.*)*

1ST SALESWOMAN *(*MARY'S *Booth. Giving little white slip to* SALESWOMAN *who passes)* Bring down Mrs. Haines' fittings.

(Exits, leaving booth empty)

2ND SALESWOMAN *(*CRYSTAL'S *Booth)* Will you open a charge?

CRYSTAL *(Taking off gloves and hat)* Please.

2ND SALESWOMAN May I have the name?

CRYSTAL *(Quite self-assured)* Allen. Miss Crystal Allen. The Hotel Waverly.

2ND SALESWOMAN May I have your other charges? Saks, Bergdorf, Cartier—?

CRYSTAL *(Putting it on)* Oh, I'll be opening those in the next few days—

2ND SALESWOMAN Then may I have your bank?

CRYSTAL I've no checking account either, at the moment.

(Enter MARY *in her booth with fitter and* 1ST SALES-WOMAN, *who carried her try-on gown. During following scene* MARY *undresses, gets into gay evening gown, fits)*

1ST SALESWOMAN *(To* MARY, *as they enter)* Shall we show the things that came in while you were away?

MARY Please. But I'd like to see some younger things than I usually wear.

2ND SALESWOMAN (*In* CRYSTAL'S *Booth*) I'm sorry, Miss Allen, but we must have one business reference—

CRYSTAL I—er—am a friend of Miss Miriam Aarons. You know, the musical comedy star?

2ND SALESWOMAN (*Coolly*) Oh, yes, Miss Aarons. One of our new accounts. (*A pause, then decides to level, in a dramatic way*) Miss Aarons had an *excellent* business reference.

CRYSTAL (*Making the same decision*) Such as Howard Fowler, the broker?

2ND SALESWOMAN (*Brightly*) Why, yes, I believe he is her broker!

CRYSTAL (*Lightly, she was prepared for this*) Well, if a broker's reference will do, it's Mr. Stephen Haines, 40 Wall Street.

2ND SALESWOMAN (*Writing*) That will do. (*A pause*) Mrs. Haines is a very old client of ours.

CRYSTAL (*Unprepared for that*) Oh?

2ND SALESWOMAN Will you try on now, or finish seeing the collection?

CRYSTAL Have the models show in here. By the way, I've never met Mrs. Haines.

2ND SALESWOMAN She's lovely

CRYSTAL So—I'd rather you didn't mention to her that I gave her husband as a reference. (*Beguiling*) Do you mind?

2ND SALESWOMAN (*With a faint smile*) Oh, of course not, Miss Allen. (*Indulgently*) We understand.

CRYSTAL (*Angrily*) Do you! What do you understand?

2ND SALESWOMAN (*Flustered*) I mean—

CRYSTAL (*Very injured*) Never mind.

2ND SALESWOMAN Please, I hope you don't think I meant—

CRYSTAL (*Laughing and very charming again*) Of course not. Oh, it's dreadful, living in a strange city alone. You have to be so careful not to do anything people can misconstrue. You see, I don't know Mrs. Haines yet. So I'd hate to get off on the wrong foot before I've met her *socially*.

2ND SALESWOMAN *(Sounds convinced)* Naturally. Women are funny about little things like that. We never discuss one client with another.

    (MARY'S booth—enter SYLVIA)

SYLVIA Yoo-hoo! May I come in?

MARY *(Not at all pleased to see her)* Hello, Sylvia.

2ND SALESWOMAN *(In CRYSTAL'S Booth)* What are you most interested in, Miss Allen, evening gowns?

CRYSTAL Until I—I organize my social life—I won't have much use for evening gowns.

2ND SALESWOMAN I'll show you some smart daytime things. *(Deliberately toneless)* And we have very exciting negligees—

    (They exit. MARY'S Booth: SYLVIA circles around MARY, appraising her fitting with a critical eye)

MARY Oh, sit down, Sylvia.

SYLVIA *(To the Fitter)* I don't like that underslung line. *(Demonstrating on MARY)* It cuts her across the fanny. Makes her look positively duck-bottomed.

MARY *(Pulling away)* It's so tight, Mrs. Fowler can't sit down.

1ST SALESWOMAN Mrs. Fowler, shall I see if your fittings are ready?

SYLVIA They'll call me.

MARY *(Pointing to dress 1ST SALESWOMAN has over her arm)* Have you seen that?

1ST SALESWOMAN *(Holding up dress)* It's a lovely shape on. It doesn't look like a thing in the hand. *(Hands dress to someone outside and calls)* Tell Princess Tamara to show this model.

SYLVIA *(Settling in chair and smoking cigarette)* So you had a marvelous time in Bermuda.

MARY I had a good rest.

SYLVIA *(With unconscious humor)* Howard wants *me* to take a world cruise. By the way, dear, how is Stephen?

MARY Splendid. *(Smiling, and very glad to be able to tell SYLVIA this)* He's not nearly so busy. He hasn't spent an evening—in the office, since I've come home. *(Enter 1ST*

MODEL *in an elaborate negligee.* MARY *shakes her head, very practical)* Pretty, but I never need a thing like that—

SYLVIA Of course *you* don't. A hot little number, for intimate afternoons. *(Exit* 1ST MODEL*)* Howard says nobody's seen Stephen in the Club, in the afternoon, for months—

MARY *(Thought flashes across her mind that* STEPHEN *could, of course, have revised his extra-marital schedule, from an evening to an afternoon one, but she quickly dismisses it. Stephen has never let anything interfere with his hours downtown)* Don't worry so much about Stephen, Sylvia. He's my concern.

> *(Enter* 2ND MODEL *in a corset. She is prettily fashioned from head to toe. She does a great deal for the wisp of lace she wears. It does nothing that nature didn't do better for her)*

2ND MODEL This is our new one-piece lace foundation garment. *(Pirouettes)* Zips up the back, and no bones. *(She exits)*

SYLVIA Just that uplift, Mary, you need. I always said you'd regret nursing. Look at me. I don't think there's another girl our age who can boast of bazooms like mine. I've taken care of them. Ice water every morning, camphor at night.

MARY Doesn't it smell rather like an old fur coat?

> *(PRINCESS TAMARA passes in corridor)*

SYLVIA Who cares?

MARY Well, doesn't Howard?

SYLVIA *(Laughing harshly)* Howard! With his prostate condition?

1ST SALESWOMAN *(Calling out door)* Princess Tamara, show in here.

> *(Enter* PRINCESS TAMARA *in a very extreme evening gown. She is Russian, regal, soignée)*

MARY Oh, Tamara, how lovely!

TAMARA You must have it. Stephen would be amazed.

MARY He certainly would. It's too extreme for me.

SYLVIA *(Rises)* And you really haven't the figure. *(Yanks at gown)* Tamara, you wear it wrong. I saw it in *Vogue. (Jerks)* Up here, and down there.

TAMARA *(Slapping* SYLVIA'S *hand down)* Stop mauling me!

1ST SALESWOMAN Princess!

TAMARA What do you know how to wear clothes?

SYLVIA *I* am not a model, Tamara, but no one disputes how *I* wear clothes!

TAMARA No one has mistaken you for the Duchess of Windsor yet?

1ST SALESWOMAN Princess Tamara, please apologize.

MARY *(To* SALESWOMAN*)* It's just professional jealousy. They both wear clothes so beautifully. They're really friends!

SYLVIA *(Maliciously)* You mean Tamara and *Howard* are friends.

TAMARA *(Disgusted at the thought)* Do you accuse me of flirting with *your* husband?

SYLVIA *(Pleasantly)* Go as far as you can, Tamara! If I know Howard, you're wasting valuable time.

TAMARA *(Very angry)* Perhaps I am. But perhaps somebody else is not! *(SALESWOMAN gives her an angry shove)* You are riding for a fall-off, Sylvia dear!

(Exit TAMARA *angrily, followed by* SALESWOMAN*)*

SYLVIA Did you get that inyouendo? I'd like to see Howard Fowler put anything over on me. Oh, I've always hated that girl, exploiting her title the way she does!

(CRYSTAL and 2ND SALESWOMAN *enter* CRYSTAL'S *Booth)*

2ND SALESWOMAN *(Calling down corridor)* Princess Tamara, show in here, to Miss Allen.

(MARY'S SALESWOMAN enters MARY'S booth, picking up the call)

1ST SALESWOMAN Girls, show in Number 3 to Miss Allen.

SYLVIA *(Alert)* Did you say Miss Allen?

1ST SALESWOMAN Yes.

SYLVIA Not—Crystal Allen?

1ST SALESWOMAN Why, yes—I just saw her on the floor. She's so attractive I asked her name.

SYLVIA *(Watching MARY closely)* Oh, so Crystal Allen gets her things here now?

(MARY sits down suddenly)

1ST SALESWOMAN She's a new client—Why, Mrs. Haines, are you ill?
> (MARY *has caught* SYLVIA'S *eye in the mirror.* SYLVIA *knows now that* MARY *knows*)

MARY No, no. I'm just tired.
> (*Tamara enters* CRYSTAL'S *Booth*)

FITTER We've kept you standing too long—

1ST SALESWOMAN I'll get you a glass of sherry. (*Exit* MARY'S *fitter and* SALESWOMAN. SYLVIA *closes door*)

CRYSTAL (CRYSTAL'S *Booth. Admiring* TAMARA'S *extreme evening gown*) I'm going to have that, if I have to wear it for breakfast.

2ND SALESWOMAN Send it in here, Princess.
> (TAMARA *exits*)

SYLVIA (MARY'S *Booth*) Mary, you do know! (*Deeply sympathetic*) Why didn't you confide in me?

MARY Sylvia, go away.

SYLVIA (*Fiercely*) Stephen is a louse. Spending your money on a girl like that.

MARY Sylvia, please mind your own affairs.

SYLVIA She's already made a fool of you before all your friends. And don't you think the salesgirls know who gets the bills?

MARY (*Distraught*) I don't care, I tell you. I don't care!

SYLVIA Oh, yes, you do. (*Pointing to* MARY'S *stricken face in mirror*) Don't be an ostrich, Mary. (*A pause*) Go in there and face her down.

MARY I'm going home. (*She rises and begins to dress*)

1ST SALESWOMAN (*Half enters*) Mrs. Haines' sherry—

SYLVIA (*Taking it from her, and closing door in her face*) All right. You've caught her cold. It's *your* chance to humiliate her. Just say a few *quiet* words. Tell her you'll make Stephen's life *hell* until he gives her up.

MARY Stephen will give her up when he's tired of her.

SYLVIA When he's tired of her? Look where she was six months ago. Look where she is now. She probably has an apartment to go with those kinds of clothes.

MARY Stephen's not in love with that girl.

SYLVIA Maybe not. But you don't know women like that when they get hold of a man.

MARY Sylvia, please let me decide what is best for me, and my home.

> (CRYSTAL, *in her booth, has been undressing, admiring herself as she does so in mirror. Now she slips into a "really exciting" negligee. During the scene going on in* MARY'S *Booth she tries to get out of the negligee easily. She can't*)

SYLVIA Well, she may be a perfectly marvelous influence for Stephen, but she's not going to do your children any good.

MARY *(Turning to her)* What do you mean?

SYLVIA *(Mysteriously)* Never mind.

MARY *(Going to her)* Tell me!

SYLVIA Far be it from *me* to tell you things you don't care to hear. I've known this all along. *(Nobly)* Have I *uttered?*

MARY *(Violently)* What have my children to do with this?

SYLVIA *(After all,* MARY'S *asking for it)* It was while you were away. Edith saw them. Stephen, and that tramp, and your children—together, lunching in the Park.

MARY It's not true!

SYLVIA Why would Edith lie? She said they were having a hilarious time. Little Stevie was eating his lunch sitting on that woman's lap. She was kissing him between every bite. When I heard that, I was positively *heart-sick,* dear! *(Sees she has scored. Celebrates by tossing down* MARY'S *sherry)*

CRYSTAL (CRYSTAL'S *Booth)* Oh, go get that evening gown. This thing is too complicated to get out of.

2ND SALESWOMAN Right away, Miss Allen. *(Exits)*

SYLVIA (MARY'S *Booth)* But, as you say, dear, it's your affair, not mine. *(Goes to door, looking very hurt that* MARY *has refused her good advice)* No doubt that girl will make a perfectly good stepmamma for your children!

> (Exits. MARY, *now dressed, is alone. She stares at partition which separates her from that still unmeasured enemy to her well-ordered domesticity, "The other woman." Her common sense dictates she should go*

home, but now she violently experiences the ache to talk. She struggles against it, then goes, bitterly determined, to door. Exits. A second later, a knock on CRYSTAL'S door. CRYSTAL is alone)

CRYSTAL Come in! *(Enter MARY. She closes door)* I beg your pardon?

MARY *I* am—Mrs. Stephen Haines.

CRYSTAL *(Her poise is admirable)* Sorry—I don't think I know you!

MARY Please don't pretend.

CRYSTAL So Stephen finally told you?

MARY No. I found out.

(2ND SALESWOMAN half enters)

CRYSTAL Stay out of here!

(Exit SALESWOMAN)

MARY I've known about you from the beginning.

CRYSTAL Well, that is news.

MARY I've kept still up to now—

CRYSTAL Very smart of you.

(2ND SALESWOMAN pantomimes down corridor to another girl to join her. Enters MARY'S booth. One by one, during rest of this scene, FITTER, SALESWOMAN, and MODELS tiptoe into MARY'S booth and plaster their ears against partition)

MARY But you've gone a little too far—You've been seeing my children. I won't have you touching my children!

CRYSTAL For God's sake, don't get hysterical. What do I care about your children? I'm sick of hearing about them.

MARY You won't have to hear about them any more. When Stephen realizes how humiliating all this has been to me, he'll give you up instantly.

CRYSTAL Says who? The dog in the manger?

MARY That's all I have to say. *(Turns to go)*

CRYSTAL That's plenty. Maybe you'll find you've said too much. Stephen's not tired of me yet, Mrs. Haines.

MARY *(Contemptuous)* Stephen is just amusing himself with you.

CRYSTAL And he's amusing himself plenty.

MARY You're very hard.

CRYSTAL I can be soft—on the *right* occasions. What do you expect me to do? Burst into tears and beg you to forgive me?

MARY I found exactly what I expected!

CRYSTAL That goes double!

MARY *(Turning to door)* You'll have to make other plans, Miss Allen.

CRYSTAL *(Going to her)* Listen, I'm taking my marching orders from Stephen.

MARY Stephen doesn't love you.

CRYSTAL He's doing the best he can in the circumstances.

MARY He couldn't love a girl like you.

CRYSTAL What do you think we've been doing for the past six months? Crossword puzzles? What have you got to kick about? You've got everything that matters. The name, the position, the money—

MARY *(Losing control of herself again)* Nothing matters to me but Stephen—!

CRYSTAL Oh, can the sob-stuff, Mrs. Haines. You don't think this is the first time Stephen's ever cheated? Listen, I'd break up your smug little roost if I could. I have just as much right as you have to sit in a tub of butter. But I don't stand a chance!

MARY I'm glad you know it.

CRYSTAL Well, don't think it's just because he's *fond* of you—

MARY Fond?

CRYSTAL You're not what's stopping him—You're just an old *habit* with him. It's just those brats he's afraid of losing. If he weren't such a sentimental fool about those kids, he'd have walked out on *you* months ago.

MARY *(Fiercely)* That's not true!

CRYSTAL Oh, yes, it is. I'm telling you a few plain truths you won't get from Stephen.

MARY Stephen's always told me the truth—!

CRYSTAL *(Maliciously)* Well, look at the record. *(A pause)*

Listen, Stephen's satisfied with this arrangement. So don't force any issue, unless you want plenty of trouble.

MARY You've made it impossible for me to do anything else—!

CRYSTAL *(Rather pleased)* Have I?

MARY You haven't played fair—!

CRYSTAL Where would any of us get if we played fair?

MARY Where do you hope to get?

CRYSTAL Right where *you* are, Mrs. Haines!

MARY You're very confident.

CRYSTAL The longer you stay in here, the more confident I get. Saint or no saint, Mrs. Haines, you are a hell of a stupid *woman!*

MARY (MARY *stares at her wide-eyed at the horrid thought that this may be the truth. She refuses to meet the challenge. She equivocates)* I probably am. I—*(Suddenly ashamed that she has allowed herself to be put so pathetically on the defensive)* Oh, why am I standing here talking to you? This is something for Stephen and me to settle! *(Exits)*

CRYSTAL *(Slamming door after her)* Oh, what the hell!

2ND SALESWOMAN (MARY'S *booth)* So that's what she calls meeting Mrs. Haines *socially.*

1ST SALESWOMAN Gee, I feel sorry for Mrs. Haines. She's so nice.

NEGLIGEE MODEL She should have kept her mouth shut. Now she's in the soup.

1ST SALESWOMAN It's a terrible mistake to force a decision on a man who's hot for another woman.

1ST MODEL Allen's smart. She knows that.

1ST SALESWOMAN She'll get him sure.

1ST FITTER Look at that body. She's got him now.

2ND SALESWOMAN You can't trust any man. *That's* all they want.

CORSET MODEL *(Plaintively, her hands on her lovely hips)* What else have we got to give?

CURTAIN

SCENE 5

Two weeks later. Small exercise room in Elizabeth Arden's beauty-salon. R., *a mirrored wall. Rear, a door.* L., *cabinet victrola beneath open window. On floor, a wadded pink satin mat. As curtain rises,* SYLVIA, *in a pair of shorts, is prone on mat, describing lackadaisical arcs with her legs, to the sensuous rhythm of a tango record.* INSTRUCTRESS, *a bright, pretty girl in a pink silk bathing suit, stands above her, drilling her in a carefully cultured voice. Until the cue "stretch,"* INSTRUCTRESS' *lines are spoken through* SYLVIA'S *prattle, which she is determined, for the honor of the salon, to ignore, and, if possible, to discourage. From word "up," this is a hopeless task.*

INSTRUCTRESS Up—over—up—down. Up—stretch—up—together. Up—stretch—up—

SYLVIA Of course, my sympathies are for Mrs. Haines. They always are for a woman against a man—

INSTRUCTRESS *(Louder)* Up—over—up—down. Up—stretch—up—together. Up—

SYLVIA But she did behave like an awful idiot—

INSTRUCTRESS Stretch—up—together. Please don't try to talk, Mrs. Fowler.

SYLVIA But you know how some women are when they lose their heads—

INSTRUCTRESS *(Grimly)* Stretch—up—together—up—

SYLVIA They do things they regret all their lives—

INSTRUCTRESS *(Grabs* SYLVIA'S *languid limb and gives it a corrective yank)* Ster-retch!

SYLVIA Ouch, my scars!

INSTRUCTRESS *(Callously)* This is very good for adhesions. Up—

SYLVIA *(Resolutely inert)* It's got me down.

INSTRUCTRESS Rest. (SYLVIA *groans her relief)* And relax

137

your diaphragm muscles, Mrs. Fowler, *(Bitterly)* if you can. *(Goes to victrola, changes record for a fox-trot)*

SYLVIA Of course, I do wish Mrs. Haines would make up her mind if she's going to get a divorce. It's terrible on all her friends, not knowing. Naturally, you can't ask them anywhere—

INSTRUCTRESS Of course not. Now, on your side. *(SYLVIA rolls to her side, reclining on her elbow)* Ready? Up—down—up—down—(*Snaps her fingers.* SYLVIA *flaps a limp leg up, down)* Don't bend the knee—

SYLVIA *(Thoughtfully)* Of course, for the children's sake, I think Mrs. Haines ought to stay. *(Piously)* I know I would. *(Her knees look bent, not to say broken)*

INSTRUCTRESS *(Imploring)* Don't crook it, please.

SYLVIA And she ought not to have faced Mr. Haines with the issue. When a man's got himself in that deep he has to have time to taper it off—

INSTRUCTRESS *(Straightening out SYLVIA's offending member with considerable force)* Thigh in, not out.

SYLVIA *(Pained, but undaunted)* But Mrs. Haines never listens to any of her friends. She is a very peculiar woman.

INSTRUCTRESS She must be. Now, please—up—down—up —down—

SYLVIA *(Redoubling her efforts, and her errors)* Oh, I tell everybody whatever she wants to do is the right thing. I've got to be loyal to Mrs. Haines, you know. . . . Oh, I'm simply exhausted. *(Flops over, flat on her stomach, panting)*

INSTRUCTRESS Then suppose you try something simple— like crawling up the wall?

   (SYLVIA lifts a martyred face. INSTRUCTRESS *changes record for a waltz)*

SYLVIA *(Scrambling to her feet)* What I go through to keep my figure! Lord, it infuriates me at dinner parties when some fat lazy man asks, "What do you do with yourself all day, Mrs. Fowler?" *(Sits alongside the rear wall)*

INSTRUCTRESS You rotate on your buttocks. *(SYLVIA ro-*

tates, then lies back, her knees drawn up to her chin, the soles of her feet against wall) Arms flat. Now you crawl slowly up the wall.

SYLVIA *(Crawling)* I wish you wouldn't say that. It makes me feel like vermin—

INSTRUCTRESS *(Kneeling beside her)* Don't talk.

SYLVIA There's a couple of people I'd like to exterminate, too—

INSTRUCTRESS Let's reverse the action. (SYLVIA *crawls down, as* PEGGY *enters in exercise suit.* INSTRUCTRESS *brightens)* How do you do, Mrs. Day? *(To* SYLVIA*)* Down slowly—

PEGGY *(Gaily)* How do you do? Hello, Sylvia.

SYLVIA You're late again, Peggy.

PEGGY *(Crestfallen)* I'm sorry.

SYLVIA *(Sitting up)* After all, dear, I am paying for this course.

PEGGY You know I'm grateful, Sylvia—

SYLVIA Well, don't cry about it. It's only fifty dollars.

PEGGY That's a lot to me—

SYLVIA *(Sweetly)* To you, or just to your husband, dear?

INSTRUCTRESS Please, ladies. Let us begin with posture. (SYLVIA *rises)* A lady always enters a room erect.

SYLVIA Lots of my friends exit horizontally.

(PEGGY *and* SYLVIA *go to mirrored wall, stand with backs to it)*

INSTRUCTRESS Now—knees apart. Sit on the wall. *(They sit on imaginary seats)* Relax. *(They bend forward from waist, finger tips brushing floor)* Now, roll slowly up the wall . . . pressing each little vertebra against the wall as hard as you can . . . shoulders back, and where they belong. Heads back. Mrs. Fowler, lift yourself behind the ears. Pretend you're just a silly little puppet dangling on a string. Chin up. *(She places her hand at level of* PEGGY'S *straining chin)* No, Mrs. Day, your chin is resting comfortably on a little table. Elbows bent—up on your toes—arms out—shove with the small of your back—you're off!

(SYLVIA *and* PEGGY, *side by side, mince across room*)

PEGGY *(Whispering)* Oh, Sylvia, why do you always insinuate that John is practically a—miser?

INSTRUCTRESS *(She refers to* PEGGY'S *swaying hips)* Tuck under!

SYLVIA You have your own little income, Peggy. And what do you do with it? You give it to John—

INSTRUCTRESS Now, back, please! *(They mince backwards across room)*

PEGGY *(Staunchly)* John makes so little—

INSTRUCTRESS *(She refers to* SYLVIA'S *relaxed tummy)* Steady center control!

SYLVIA Peggy, you're robbing John of his manly sense of responsibility. You're turning him into a gigolo. A little money of her own she lets no man touch is the only protection a woman has. *(They are against mirror again)*

INSTRUCTRESS Now, are you both the way you were when you left the wall?

SYLVIA *(Brightly)* Well, I am.

INSTRUCTRESS No, Mrs. Fowler, you're not. *(She imitates* SYLVIA'S *posture, showing how* SYLVIA'S *posterior protrudes, against the dictates of fashion, if not of nature)* Not this, Mrs. Fowler—("Bumps.") That! *(She leads* SYLVIA *forward)* Try it, please. *(Facing one another, they do an elegant pair of "bumps")* Now, relax on the mat. *(This piece of business defies description, but to do the best one can: Girls stand side by side, arms straight above their heads. At* INSTRUCTRESS' *count of "one," each drops a hand, limp, from wrist. At "two," the other hand drops, then their heads fall upon their breasts, their arms flap to their sides, their waists cave in, their knees buckle under, and they swoon, or crumble like boneless things, to the mat.* INSTRUCTRESS *has changed record)* Now, ready? Bend—stretch, you know. Begin— *(They do another leg exercise on mat)* Bend—stretch—bend—down—plenty of pull on the hamstrings, please! Bend—stretch—bend—down—

(Enter EDITH. *She is draped in a white sheet. Her head is bound in a white towel. Her face is undergoing a "tie-up," that is, she wears broad white straps under her chin and across her forehead. She appears very distressed)*

EDITH Oh, Sylvia! Hello, Peggy—

SYLVIA *(Sitting up)* Why, Edith, what are you doing up here?

EDITH Having a facial, downstairs. Oh, Sylvia, I'm so glad you're here. I've done the most *awful* thing. I—

INSTRUCTRESS We're right in the middle of our exercise, Mrs. Potter—

SYLVIA *(To* INSTRUCTRESS*)* Will you tell them outside—I want my paraffine bath now? There's a dear.

INSTRUCTRESS But, Mrs. Fowler—

SYLVIA *(Cajoling)* I'm simply exhausted.

INSTRUCTRESS You've hardly moved a muscle.

SYLVIA *(With elaborate patience)* Look, whose carcass is this? Yours or mine?

INSTRUCTRESS It's yours, Mrs. Fowler, but I'm paid to exercise it.

SYLVIA You talk like a horse-trainer.

INSTRUCTRESS Well, Mrs. Fowler, you're getting warm. *(Exits)*

EDITH I've done the most *ghastly* thing. Move over. *(PEGGY and* SYLVIA *move over,* EDITH *plumps between them on mat)* But it wasn't until I got here, in the middle of my facial, that I realized it—I could bite my tongue off when I think of it—

SYLVIA Well, what is it, Edith?

EDITH I was lunching with Frances Jones, and—

SYLVIA Edith Potter, I know exactly what you're going to say!

EDITH I forget she—

SYLVIA You forgot she's Dolly de Peyster.

EDITH But I never read her awful column—

SYLVIA *(Fiercely)* You told her something about me? What did you tell her?

EDITH   Oh, darling, you know I never give you away. *(Remorsefully)* I—I—told her all about Stephen and Mary—

SYLVIA   *(Relieved)* Oh! That!

EDITH   It wasn't until the middle of my facial—

PEGGY   Oh, Edith! It will be in all those dreadful tabloids!

EDITH   I know—I've been racking my brains to recall what I said—I think I told her that when Mary walked into the fitting room, she yanked the ermine coat off the Allen girl—

SYLVIA   You didn't!

EDITH   Well, I don't know whether I said ermine or *sable*—but I know I told her that Mary *smacked* the Allen girl!

PEGGY   Edith!

EDITH   Well, that's what Sylvia told me!

SYLVIA   I didn't!

EDITH   You did, too!

SYLVIA   *(Hurt)* Anyway, I didn't expect you to tell it to a cheap reporter—

EDITH   Well, it doesn't really make much difference. The divorce is practically settled—

SYLVIA   *(Eagerly)* Who says so?

EDITH   You did!

SYLVIA   *(Patiently)* I said, Mary couldn't broadcast her domestic difficulties, and not expect them to wind up in a scandal.

PEGGY   Mary didn't broadcast them!

SYLVIA   Who did?

PEGGY   *You* did. You—you're all making it impossible for her to do anything now but get a divorce!

SYLVIA   You flatter us. We didn't realize how much influence we had on our friends' lives!

PEGGY   Everybody calling her up, telling her how badly she's been treated—

SYLVIA   As a matter of fact, I told her she'd make a great mistake. What has any woman got to gain by a divorce? No matter how much he gives her, she won't have what they have together. And you know as well as I do, he'd marry that girl. What he's spent on her he'd have to, to protect his investment. *(Sorrowfully)* But I have as much influence on Mary as I have on *you*, Peggy.

(INSTRUCTRESS *re-enters*)

INSTRUCTRESS The paraffine bath is ready, Mrs. Fowler.

SYLVIA *(Rises)* Well, don't worry, Edith, I'll give de Peyster a ring. I can fix it.

EDITH How?

SYLVIA *(Graciously)* Oh, I'll tell her you were lying.

EDIGH You'll do no such thing!

SYLVIA *(Shrugging)* Then let the story ride. It will be forgotten tomorrow. You know the awful things they printed about—what's her name?—before she jumped out the window? Why, I can't even remember her name, so who cares, Edith? *(Exits)*

INSTRUCTRESS Mrs. Potter, you come right back where you belong.

EDITH Why, you'd think this was a boarding school!

INSTRUCTRESS But, Mrs. Potter, it's such a foolish waste of money—

EDITH Listen, relaxing is part of my facial.

INSTRUCTRESS *(Coolly)* Then you should relax completely, Mrs. Potter, from the chin up. *(Exits)*

EDITH Honestly, the class feeling you run into these days! *(Struggles to her feet)* I'm so tired of paying creatures like that to insult me—

PEGGY *(Going to her)* Edith! Let's call Mary up and warn her!

EDITH About what?

PEGGY The newspapers!

EDITH My dear, how could we do that, without involving Sylvia—

PEGGY But it's *her* fault—Oh, she's such a dreadful woman!

EDITH Oh, she can't help it, Peggy. It's just her tough luck she wasn't born deaf and dumb. But what can we do about it? She's always gotten away with murder. Why, she's been having an affair for a year with that young customers' man in Howard's office.

PEGGY *(Shocked)* Edith!

EDITH Right under Howard's nose! But Howard doesn't care! So what business is it of yours or mine? *(Earnestly)* Peggy, take a tip from me—keep out of other women's troubles. I've never had a fight with a girl friend in all my life. Why? I hear no evil, I see no evil, I speak no evil!

CURTAIN

SCENE 6

A few days later.

MARY'S *pantry, midnight.* L., *a swinging door to kitchen. Rear, a sink under curtained window. A small, built-in re-frigerator.* C., *a table, 2 chairs.*

As curtain rises, JANE, *the maid, and* MAGGIE, *the new cook, are having a midnight snack.* MAGGIE, *a buxom, mid-dle-aged woman, wears wrapper and felt bedroom slippers.*

JANE *(Folding tabloid newspaper she has been reading to* MAGGIE*)* So he says, "All you can do with a story like that is live it down, Mary."

MAGGIE I told you they'd begin all over. Once a thing like that is out between a married couple, they've got to fight it out. Depends which they get sick of first, each other, or the argument.

JANE It's enough to make you lose your faith in marriage.

MAGGIE Whose faith in marriage?

JANE You don't believe in marriage?

MAGGIE Sure I do. For women. *(Sighs)* But it's the sons of Adam they got to marry. Go on.

JANE Well, finally he said to the madam, "I gave her up, didn't I? And I was a swine, about the way I did it." How do you suppose he did it, Maggie?

MAGGIE Maybe he just said, "Scram, the wife is onto us."

JANE Well, the madam didn't believe him. She says, "Stephen, you really ain't seen her?"

MAGGIE He lied in his teeth—

JANE Oh, the way he said it, I kind of believed him. But the madam says, "Oh, but can I ever trust you again?"

MAGGIE You can't trust none of 'em no further than I can kick this lemon pie.

JANE Oh, it was terrible sad. He said, "Mary dear Mary, Mary, dear Mary, Mary—"

145

MAGGIE Dear Mary. But it ain't exactly convincing.

JANE Then, I guess he tried to kiss her. Because she says, "Please don't. I'll never be able to kiss you again without thinking of her in your arms."

MAGGIE *(Appreciatively)* Just like in the movies—imagine him taking up with a girl like that.

JANE He was telling the madam: She's a virgin.

MAGGIE She is? Then what's all the rumpus about?

JANE Oh, she ain't a virgin now. She was.

MAGGIE So was Mae West—once.

JANE He told the madam he'd been faithful for twelve years.

MAGGIE Well, that's something these days; that beats Lindbergh's flight. Did the madam believe him?

JANE She said, "How do I know you've been faithful?"

MAGGIE Listen, if they lay off six months, they feel themselves busting out all over with haloes.

JANE Anyway, he says this girl was really a nice girl. So sweet and interested in him and all. And how it happened one night, unexpected, in her room—

MAGGIE Did he think it was going to happen in Roxy's?

JANE He said she wouldn't take nothing from him for months—

MAGGIE Only her education. Oh, that one knew her onions. She certainly played him for a sucker.

JANE That's what the madam said. She said, "Stephen, can't you see that girl's only interested in you for your money?"

MAGGIE Tch, tch, tch. I'll bet that made him sore. A man don't like to be told no woman but his wife is fool enough to love him. It drives 'em nutty.

JANE Did it! "Mary, I told you what kind of girl she is," he says. You know—I just told you—

MAGGIE I had her number. You didn't convey no information.

JANE Well, then they both got sore.

MAGGIE *(Rises, goes out for coffee)* I knew it.

JANE So he began to tell her all over what a good husband he'd been. And how hard he'd worked for her and the kids.

And she kept interrupting with what a good wife she'd been and how proud she was of him. Then they began to exaggerate themselves—

MAGGIE *(Enters with coffeepot)* Listen, anybody that's ever been married knows that line backwards and forwards. What happened?

JANE Well, somewhere in there the madam says, "Stephen, you do want a divorce. Only you ain't got the courage to ask it." And he says, "Oh, my God, no, I don't, Mary. Haven't I told you?" And she says, "But you don't love me!" And he says, "But oh, my God, Mary, I'm awful *fond* of you." And she says, very icy, "Fond, fond? Is that all?" and he says, "No, Mary, there's the children." Maggie, that's the thing I don't understand. Why does she get so mad every time he says they've got to consider the children? If children ain't the point of being married, what is?

MAGGIE A woman don't want to be told she's being kept on just to run a kindergarten. *(Goes to icebox for bottle of cream)*

JANE Well, the madam says, "Stephen, I want to keep the children out of this. I haven't used the children. I ain't asked you to sacrifice yourself for the children." Maggie, that's where he got so terrible mad. He says, "But why, in God's name, Mary? You knew about us all along. Why did you wait until now to make a fool of me?"

MAGGIE As if he needed her help.

JANE So then, suddenly she says, in a awful low voice, "Stephen, oh, Stephen, we can't go on like this. It ain't worthy of what we been to each other!" And he says, "Oh, no, it's not, Mary!"

MAGGIE Quite a actress, ain't you?

JANE My boy friend says I got eyes like Joan Crawford.

MAGGIE Did he ever say anything about your legs? Have a cup of coffee. *(Pours coffee)*

JANE That's when the madam says what you could have knocked me down with a feather! The madam says, "Stephen, I want a divorce. Yes, Stephen, *I* want a divorce!"

MAGGIE Tch. Tch. Abdicating!

JANE   Well, Maggie, you could have knocked him down with a feather!

MAGGIE *(Waving coffeepot)* I'd like to knock him down with this.

JANE   "My God! Mary," he says, "you don't mean it!" So she says, in a funny voice, "Yes, I do. You've killed my love for you, Stephen."

MAGGIE   He's just simple-minded enough to believe that.

JANE   So he says, "I don't blame you. My God, how can I blame you?"

MAGGIE   My God, he can't!

JANE   So then she said it was all over, because it was only the children he minded losing. She said that made their marriage a mockery.

MAGGIE   A mockery?

JANE   Something funny.

MAGGIE   I ain't going to die laughing.

JANE   He said she was talking nonsense. He said she was just upset on account of this story in the papers. He said what else could she expect if she was going to spill her troubles to a lot of gabby women? He said she should go to bed until she could think things over. He was going out for a breath of fresh air.

MAGGIE   The old hat trick.

JANE   So the madam says, "You're going to see that girl." And he says, "Oh, for God's sake, Mary, one minute you never want to see me again, the next I can't even go out for a airing!"

MAGGIE   You oughtn't to let none of 'em out except on a leash.

JANE   And she says, "Are you going to see her, or ain't you?" And he says, "Well, what difference does it make, if you're going to divorce me?" And she says, "It don't make no difference to you, I guess. Please go, Stephen. And don't come back *ever.*" *(Begins to cry)*

MAGGIE *(Impatiently)* Yes?

JANE   I didn't hear his last words. Because naturally, when he said he was going, I scooted down the hall. But I heard her call, "Stephen?" and he stops on the landing and says, "Yes, Mary?" and she says, "Nothing. Just don't slam the front door—the servants will hear you!" So I came down here. Oh, Maggie, what's going to happen?

MAGGIE She's going to get a divorce.

JANE Oh, dear. I'm so sad for her.

MAGGIE I ain't.

JANE What?

MAGGIE She's indulging a pride she ain't entitled to. Marriage is a business of taking care of a man and rearing his children. It ain't meant to be no perpetual honeymoon. How long would any husband last if he was supposed to go on acting forever like a red-hot Clark Gable? What's the difference if he don't love her?

JANE How can you say that, Maggie!

MAGGIE That don't let her off her obligation to keep him from making a fool of himself, does it?

JANE Do you think he'll marry that girl?

MAGGIE When a man's got the habit of supporting some woman, he just don't feel natural unless he's doing it.

JANE But he told the madam marrying her was the furthest thing from his mind.

MAGGIE It don't matter what he's got in his mind. It's what those two women got in theirs will settle the matter.

JANE But the madam says it's up to *him*. She said, "You love her, or you love me, Stephen."

MAGGIE So what did he say to that?

JANE Nothing for a long time. Just walked up and down—up and down—up and—

MAGGIE He was thinking. Tch—tch. The first man who can think up a good explanation how he can be in love with his wife *and* another woman is going to win that prize they're always giving out in Sweden!

CURTAIN

SCENE 7

A month later. MARY'S *living room. The room is now denuded of pictures, books, vases, etc. Rug is rolled up. Curtains and chairs covered with slips.*

As curtain rises, MARY, *dressed for traveling, is pacing up and down.* MRS. MOREHEAD, *dressed for the street, watches her from sofa.*

MRS. MOREHEAD   What time does your train go?

MARY *(Looking at her wrist watch)*   An hour. His secretary ought to be here. I never knew there could be so many papers to sign.

MRS. MOREHEAD   You showed everything to your lawyers—

MARY   They always say the same thing! I'm getting a "raw deal"—

MRS. MOREHEAD *(Alarmed)*   But, Mary—

MARY   Oh, I know it's not true. Stephen's been very generous.

MRS. MOREHEAD   Oh, I wouldn't say that. If Stephen is a rich man now, he owes it largely to you.

MARY   Stephen would have gotten where he is with or without me.

MRS. MOREHEAD   He didn't have a penny when you married him.

MARY   Mother, are you trying to make me bitter, too?

MRS. MOREHEAD *(Helplessly)*   I'm sure I don't know what to say. If I sympathize with Stephen, you accuse me of taking his side. And when I sympathize with you, I'm making you bitter. The thing for me to do is keep still. *(Pause. Then, emphatically)* You're both making a terrible mistake!

MARY   Mother, please!

MRS. MOREHEAD   But the children, Mary. The children—

MARY   What good will it do them to be brought up in a

150

home full of quarrelling and suspicion? They'll be better off just with me.

MRS. MOREHEAD No, they won't. A child needs both its parents in one home.

MARY A home without love?

MRS. MOREHEAD He's terribly fond of you—

MARY Mother, don't use that word! Oh, Mother, please. Every argument goes round in circles. And it's too late now—

MRS. MOREHEAD It's never too late when you love. Mary, why don't you call this thing off? I'm sure that's what Stephen's waiting for.

MARY *(Bitterly)* Is it? He hasn't made any sign of it to me. Isn't he the one to come to me?

MRS. MOREHEAD You're the one, Mary, who insisted on the divorce.

MARY But don't you see, if he hadn't wanted it, he'd have fought me—

MRS. MOREHEAD Stephen's not the fighting kind.

MARY Neither am I.

MRS. MOREHEAD Damn these modern laws!

MARY Mother!

MRS. MOREHEAD Damn them, I say! Fifty years ago, when women couldn't get divorces, they made the best of situations like this. And sometimes, out of situations like this, they made very good things indeed! *(Enter JANE, R.)*

JANE Mr. Haines' secretary, ma'am.

MRS. MOREHEAD Tell her to come in. *(Exit JANE)* Now, go bathe your eyes. Don't let that adding-machine see you like this. And don't be long. Remember, you have one more unpleasant task.

MARY Mary?

MRS. MOREHEAD The child must be told.

MARY *(Miserably, a little guiltily)* I have been putting it off. Because—

MRS. MOREHEAD Because you hope at the last minute a miracle will keep you from making a mess of your life. Have you thought: Stephen might marry that girl?

MARY *(Very confident)* He won't do that.

MRS. MOREHEAD What makes you so sure?

MARY Because, deep down, Stephen does love me—But he won't find it out until I've—really gone away—*(At door)* You'll take good care of the children, Mother? And make them write to me to Reno once a week? And please, Mother, don't spoil them so. *(Exits L.)*

MRS. MOREHEAD Gracious! You'd think I'd never raised children of my own! *(Enter* MISS WATTS *and* MISS TRIMMERBACK, R. *They are very tailored, plain girls.* MISS WATTS, *the older and plainer, carries brief-case)* How do you do, Miss Watts?

MISS WATTS How do you do, Mrs. Morehead? This is Miss Trimmerback from our office.

MISS TRIMMERBACK How do you do?

MISS WATTS She's a notary. We have some papers for Mrs. Haines to sign.

MRS. MOREHEAD Anything I can do?

MISS WATTS The children will be with you? *(*MRS. MOREHEAD *nods)* Any incidental bills, Mrs. Morehead, send to the office. But you understand, bills arriving after the divorce will be assumed by Mrs. Haines under the terms of the settlement.

MRS. MOREHEAD Mrs. Haines will be with you in a minute. Please don't bother her with unnecessary details. She's—she's pressed for time. *(Exits R.)*

MISS TRIMMERBACK Gee, don't you feel sorry for Mrs. Haines?

MISS WATTS *(Bitterly)* I don't feel sorry for any woman who thinks the world owes her breakfast in bed.

MISS TRIMMERBACK You don't like her.

MISS WATTS Oh, she never interfered at the office.

MISS TRIMMERBACK Maybe that's why he's been a success.

MISS WATTS He'd have gotten further without her. Everything big that came up, he was too cautious, because of her and the kids. *(Opens brief-case, takes out papers and pen, arranges papers, for signing, on table)* Well, thank heavens it's almost over. He and I can go back to work. *(Sits)*

MISS TRIMMERBACK   What about Allen?

MISS WATTS *(Guardedly)* What about her?

MISS TRIMMERBACK   Is he going to marry her?

MISS WATTS   I don't butt into his private affairs. Oh, I hold no brief for Allen. But I must say knowing *her* gave him a new interest in his work. Before her, he was certainly going stale. That had me worried.

MISS TRIMMERBACK *(Sinking on sofa)* Well, she's lucky, I'll say.

MISS WATTS   Oh?

MISS TRIMMERBACK   I wish I could get a man to foot my bills. I'm sick and tired cooking my own breakfast, sloshing through the rain at 8 A.M., working like a dog. For what? Independence? A lot of independence you have on a woman's wages. I'd chuck it like that for a decent, or indecent, home.

MISS WATTS   I'm sure you would.

MISS TRIMMERBACK   Wouldn't you?

MISS WATTS   I have a home.

MISS TRIMMERBACK   You mean Plattsburg, where you were born?

MISS WATTS   The office. That's my home.

MISS TRIMMERBACK   Some home! I see. The office-wife?

MISS WATTS *(Defiantly)* He could get along better without Mrs. Haines or Allen than he could without me.

MISS TRIMMERBACK   Oh, you're very efficient, dear. But what makes you think you're indispensable?

MISS WATTS   I relieve him of a thousand foolish details. I remind him of things he forgets, including, very often these days, his good opinion of himself. I never cry and I don't nag. I guess I *am* the office-wife. And a lot better off than Mrs. Haines. He'll never divorce me!

MISS TRIMMERBACK *(Astonished)* Why, you're in love with him! *(Both rise, face each other angrily)*

MISS WATTS   What if I am? I'd rather work for him than marry the kind of dumb cluck I could get—*(Almost tearful)* just because he's a *man*—

   (Enter MARY, *L.)*

MARY Yes, Miss Watts.

MISS WATTS *(Collecting herself quickly)* Here are the inventories of the furniture, Mrs. Haines. I had the golf cups, the books, etchings, and the ash stands sent to Mr. Haines' club. *(Pauses)* Mr. Haines asked if he could also have the portrait of the two children.

MARY *(Looking at blank space over mantel)* Oh, but—

MISS WATTS He said it wouldn't matter, if you really didn't *care* for him to have it.

MARY It's in storage.

MISS WATTS *(Laying paper on table)* This will get it out. Sign there. The cook's letter of reference. Sign here. *(MARY sits, signs)* The insurance papers. You sign here. *(MISS TRIMMERBACK signs each paper after MARY)* The transfer papers on the car. What do you want done with it?

MARY Well, I—

MISS WATTS I'll find a garage. Sign here. What do you want done if someone meets your price on this apartment?

MARY Well, I thought—

MISS WATTS This gives us power of attorney until you get back. Sign here.

MARY But—I—

MISS WATTS Oh, it's quite in order, Mrs. Haines. Now, Mr. Haines took the liberty of drawing you a new will. *(Places blue, legal-looking document before* MARY*)*

MARY *(Indignantly)* But—really—

MISS WATTS If anything were to happen to you in Reno, half your property would revert to him. A detail your lawyers overlooked. Mr. Haines drew up a codicil cutting himself out—

MARY But I don't understand legal language, Miss Watts. I —I must have my lawyer—

MISS WATTS As you please. *(Stiffly)* Mr. Haines suggested this for *your* sake, not his. I'm sure you realize he has nothing but your interests at heart. *(A pause)* Sign here. *(MARY signs,* MISS WATTS *signs)* We need three witnesses. *(Enter* JANE, R., *with box of flowers)* Your maid will do.

MARY Jane, please witness this. It's my will.

JANE *(In tears)* Oh, Mrs. Haines! *(Signs)*

MISS WATTS *(Gathering all the papers)* You can always make changes, in the event of your remarriage. *(MARY rises)* And don't hesitate to let me know at the office if there is anything *I* can ever do for you.

MARY *(Coldly)* There will be nothing, Miss Watts.

MISS WATTS *(Cheerfully)* Oh, there are always tag ends to a divorce, Mrs. Haines. And you know how Mr. Haines hates to be bothered with inconsequential details. Good day, Mrs. Haines, and pleasant journey to you!

> *(Exit* MISS WATTS, R., *followed by* MISS TRIMMERBACK*)*

JANE *(Sniveling as she places box on table)* Mr. Haines said I was to give you these to wear on the train.

> *(Exits abruptly.* MARY *slowly opens box, takes out corsage of orchids and card. Reads aloud: "What can I say? Stephen." Then throws them violently in the corner. Enter* MRS. MOREHEAD, LITTLE MARY, *dressed for street)*

MRS. MOREHEAD All set, dear?

MARY *(Grimly)* All set—Mary, Mother wants to talk to you before she goes away.

MRS. MOREHEAD Brother and I will wait for you downstairs. *(Exits* MRS. MOREHEAD*)*

MARY Mary, sit down, dear. *(LITTLE MARY skips to sofa, sits down. A pause.* MARY *discovers it's going to be even more painful and difficult then she imagined)* Mary—

LITTLE MARY Yes, Mother?

MARY Mary—

LITTLE MARY *(Perplexed by MARY'S tone, which she feels bodes no good to her)* Have I done something wrong, Mother?

MARY Oh, no darling, no. *(She sits beside LITTLE MARY, and takes her hands)* Mary, you know Daddy's been gone for some time.

LITTLE MARY *(Sadly)* A whole month.

MARY Shall I tell you why?

LITTLE MARY *(Eagerly)* Why?

MARY *(Plunging in)* You know, darling, when a man and woman fall in love what they do, don't you?

LITTLE MARY They kiss a lot—

MARY They get married—

LITTLE MARY Oh, yes. And then they have those children.

MARY Well, sometimes married people don't stay in love.

LITTLE MARY What, Mother?

MARY The husband and the wife—fall out of love.

LITTLE MARY Why do they do that?

MARY Well, they do, that's all. And when they do, they get unmarried. You see?

LITTLE MARY No.

MARY Well, they do. They—they get what is called a divorce.

LITTLE MARY *(Very matter of fact)* Oh, do they?

MARY You don't know what a divorce is, but—

LITTLE MARY Yes, I do. I go to the movies, don't I? And lots of my friends have mummies and daddies who are divorced.

MARY *(Relieved, kisses her)* You know I love you very much, don't you, Mary?

LITTLE MARY *(A pause)* Of course, Mother.

MARY Your father and I are going to get a divorce. That's why I'm going away. That's why—Oh, darling, I can't explain to you quite. But I promise you, when you are older you will understand. And you'll forgive me. You really will! Look at me, baby, please!

LITTLE MARY *(Her lips begin to tremble)* I'm looking at you, Mother—Doesn't Daddy love you any more?

MARY No, he doesn't.

LITTLE MARY Don't you love him?

MARY I—I—no, Mary.

LITTLE MARY Oh, Mother, why?

MARY I—I don't know—But it isn't either Daddy's or Mother's fault.

LITTLE MARY But, Mother, when you love somebody I thought you loved them until the day you die!

MARY With children, yes. But grown-ups are different. They can fall out of love.

LITTLE MARY I won't fall out of love with you and Daddy when I grow up. Will you fall out of love with me?

MARY Oh, no, darling, that's different, too.

LITTLE MARY *(Miserable)* I don't see *how*.

MARY You'll have to take my word for it, baby, it is. This divorce has nothing to do with our love for you.

LITTLE MARY But if you and Daddy—

MARY *(Rising and drawing* LITTLE MARY *up to her)* Darling, I'll explain it better to you in the taxi. We'll go alone in the taxi, shall we?

LITTLE MARY But, Mother, if you and Daddy are getting a divorce, which one won't I see? Daddy or you?

MARY You and Brother will live with me. That's what happens when—when people get divorced. Children must go with their mothers. But you'll see Daddy—sometimes. Now, darling, come along.

LITTLE MARY Please, Mother, wait for me downstairs.

MARY Why?

LITTLE MARY I have to go to the bathroom.

MARY Then hurry along, dear—
(Sees orchids on floor, and as she moves to door, stoops, picks them up, goes out. LITTLE MARY *stands looking after her, stricken. Suddenly she goes to back of chair, hugs it as if for comfort. Then she begins to cry and beat back of chair with her fists)*

LITTLE MARY Oh, please, please, Mother dear—Oh! Daddy, Daddy darling! Oh, why don't you do something—*do something*—Mother dear!

CURTAIN

Act Two

SCENE 1

A month later.

A room in a lying-in hospital. L., *a door to corridor.* R., *a window banked to sill with expensive flowers.* C., *a hospital bed, in which* EDITH, *propped up in a sea of lace pillows, lies with a small bundle at her breast. A white-uniformed nurse sits by window. The droop of her shoulders is eloquent:* EDITH *is a trying patient. As curtain rises,* EDITH *reaches across bundle to bedside table for a cigarette. She can't make it.*

EDITH *(Whining)* Nurse!

NURSE *(Rising wearily)* Yes, Mrs. Potter.

EDITH Throw me a cigarette.

NURSE Can't you wait, at least until you're through nursing?

EDITH How many children have you nursed? I've nursed four. *(*NURSE *lights her cigarette,* EDITH *shifts bundle slightly)* Ouch! Damn it! It's got jaws like a dinosaur.
(Enter PEGGY *with box of flowers)*

PEGGY Hello, Edith.

EDITH *(In a faint voice)* Hello, Peggy.

PEGGY *(Putting flowers on bed)* Here—

EDITH How thoughtful! Nurse, will you ask this damn hospital if they're equipped with a decent vase?
*(*NURSE *takes box, opens flowers and arranges them, with others, in window)*

PEGGY *(Leans over baby)* Oh, let me see. Oh, Edith, isn't he divine!

EDITH I hate that milky smell.

PEGGY *(Alarmed)* What's that on his nose?

EDITH What nose? Oh, that's an ash. *(Blows away ash. Hands* PEGGY *a letter from bedside table)*

PEGGY It's from Mary?

158

EDITH *(Nodding)* All about how healthy Reno is. Not a word about how she feels. I thought she cared more about Stephen than that. She sends her love to you and John. (PEGGY *reads. The wail of a new-born is heard outside)* Nurse, close that door. (NURSE *closes door)* I can't tell you what that new-born yodel does to my nerves. *(To* PEGGY*)* What're you so down in the mouth about? I feel as badly about it as you do, but it was the thing Mary wanted to do, or she wouldn't have done it. Judging by that, she's reconciled to the whole idea.

PEGGY She's just being brave!

EDITH Brave? Why should she bother to be brave with her friends? Here, Nurse, he's through. (NURSE *takes bundle from her)* I told Phelps to be sure to tell Stephen that Mary's perfectly happy. It will cheer Stephen up. He's been going around like a whipped dog.

PEGGY Oh, Edith, please let me hold him!
         (NURSE *gives* PEGGY *the baby)*

NURSE *(Smiling)* Careful of his back, Mrs. Day.

PEGGY *(Goes to window, hugging bundle)* Oh, I like the feeling so!

EDITH You wouldn't like it so much if you'd just had it. *(Whimpering)* I had a terrible time, didn't I, Nurse?

NURSE Oh, no, Mrs. Potter. You had a very easy time. *(She is suddenly angry)* Why, women like you don't know what a terrible time is. Try bearing a baby and scrubbing floors. Try having one in a cold filthy kitchen, without ether, without a change of linen, without decent food, without a cent to bring it up—and try getting up the next day with your insides falling out, to cook your husband's—! *(Controls herself)* No, Mrs. Potter, you didn't have a terrible time at all.—I'll take the baby, please. *(Sees reluctant expression on* PEGGY'S *face)* I hope some day you'll have one of your own, Mrs. Day.
         (NURSE *exits with baby.* PEGGY *breaks into tears)*

EDITH Well, for God's sake, Peggy, that old battle-axe didn't hurt my feelings a bit! They're all the same. If you don't get peritonitis or have quintuplets, they think you've had a picnic—*(PEGGY sits beside bed, crying)* What's the matter?

PEGGY Oh, Edith—John and I are getting a divorce!

EDITH *(Patting her hand)* Well, darling, that's what I heard.

PEGGY *(Surprised)* But—but we didn't decide to until last night.

EDITH *(Cheerfully)* Oh, darling, everybody could see it was in the cards. Money, I suppose?

PEGGY *(Nodding)* Oh, dear! I wish Mary were here—

EDITH Well, she'll be there. *(Laughs)* Oh, forgive me, dear. I do feel sorry for you. But it is funny.

PEGGY What's funny?

EDITH It's gonna be quite a gathering of the clan. *(Sitting up in bed, full of energy to break the news)* Howard Fowler's bounced Sylvia out right on her ear! He's threatened to divorce her right here in New York if she doesn't go to Reno. And named her young customer's man—

PEGGY But—Howard's always known—

EDITH Certainly. Howard hired him, so he'd have plenty of time for his own affairs. Howard's got some girl he wants to marry. But nobody, not even Winchell, knows who she is! Howard's a coony cuss. *(Laughing)* I do think it's screaming. When you remember how Sylvia always thought she was putting something over on us girls! *(She laughs so hard, she gives herself a stitch. She falls back among her pillows, limp and martyred)*

PEGGY *(Bitterly)* Life's awfully unattractive, isn't it?

EDITH *(Yawning)* Oh, I wouldn't complain if that damned stork would take the Indian sign off me.

CURTAIN

SCENE 2

A few weeks later. MARY'S *living room in a Reno hotel. In
rear wall, a bay window showing a view of Reno's squat
roof-tops and distant Nevada ranges.* L., *doors to kitchenette,
bedroom.* R., *a door to corridor. A plush armchair, a sofa. In
corner,* MARY'S *half-packed trunks and bags. It is all very
drab and ugly. As curtain rises,* LUCY, *a slatternly middle-
aged, husky woman in a housedress, is packing clothes that
are strewn on armchair and table. She is singing in a nasal
falsetto.*

LUCY

> Down on ole Smokey, all covered with snow,
> I lost my true lov-ver, from courtin' too slow.
> Courtin' is pul-leasure, partin' is grief,
> Anna false-hearted lov-ver is worse thanna thief—

> (PEGGY *enters,* R. *She wears a polo-coat and a wool
> tam. She is on the verge of tears*)

PEGGY Lucy, where's Mrs. Haines?
LUCY Down waiting for the mail. You'll miss her a lot when
she goes tomorrow? (PEGGY *nods, sinks, dejected, on sofa*)
Mrs. Haines is about the nicest ever came here.
PEGGY I hate Reno.
LUCY You didn't come for fun. (*Goes on with her packing
and singing*)

> The grave'll de-cay you, an' change you tuh dust,
> Ain't one boy outta twenty, a poor gal kin trust—

PEGGY You've seen lots of divorcees, haven't you, Lucy?
LUCY Been cookin' for 'em for ten years.
PEGGY You feel sorry for us?
LUCY Well, ma'am, I don't. You feel plenty sorry enough for
yourselves. (*Kindly*) Lord, you ain't got much else to do.

161

PEGGY *(Resentfully)* You've never been married, Lucy.

LUCY *(Indignant)* I've had three—

PEGGY Husbands?

LUCY Kids!

PEGGY Oh, then you're probably very happy—

LUCY Lord, ma'am, I stopped thinking about being happy years ago.

PEGGY You don't think about being happy?

LUCY Ain't had the time. With the kids and all. And the old man such a demon when he's drinking—Them big, strong, red-headed men. They're fierce.

PEGGY Oh, Lucy, he beats you? How terrible!

LUCY Ain't it? When you think what a lot of women in this hotel need a beating worse than me.

PEGGY But you live in Reno. You could get a divorce overnight.

LUCY Lord, a woman can't get herself worked up to a thing like that overnight. I had a mind to do it once. I had the money, too. But I had to call it off.

PEGGY Why?

LUCY I found out I was in a family way. *(A rap on door)*

PEGGY *(Going to her)* Lucy, tell Mrs. Haines I must talk to her—alone—before supper—

 (Enter COUNTESS DE LAGE, L. *She wears a gaudily checked riding habit, carries an enormous new sombrero and a jug of corn liquor)*

COUNTESS Ah, Peggy, how are you, dear child?

PEGGY All right, Countess de Lage.

COUNTESS I've been galloping madly over the desert all day. Lucy, here's a wee juggie. We must celebrate Mrs. Haines' divorce.

PEGGY Oh, Countess de Lage, I don't think a divorce is anything to celebrate.

COUNTESS Wait till you've lost as many husbands as I have, Peggy. *(Wistfully)* Married, divorced, married, divorced! But where Love leads I always follow. So here I am, in Reno.

PEGGY   Oh, I wish I were anywhere else on earth.

COUNTESS   My dear, you've got the Reno jumpy-wumpies. Did you go to the doctor? What did he say?

PEGGY   He said it was—the altitude.

COUNTESS   Well, la, la, you'll get used to that. My third husband, Gustav, was a ski instructor. If one lives in Switzerland, Peggy, one has simply got to accept the Alps. As I used to say to myself, Flora, there those damn Alps are, and there's very little even you can do about it.

PEGGY   Yes, Countess de Lage. *(Exits, hurriedly,* L.*)*

COUNTESS   Oh, I wish she hadn't brought up the Alps, Lucy. It always reminds me of that nasty moment I had the day Gustav made me climb to the top of one of them. *(Sits in armchair)* Lucy, pull off my boots. *(*LUCY *kneels, tugs at her boots)* Anyhow, there we were. And suddenly it struck me that Gustav had pushed me. *(Tragically)* I slid halfway down the mountain before I realized that Gustav didn't love me any more. *(Gaily)* But Love takes care of its own, Lucy. I slid right into the arms of my fourth husband, the Count.

LUCY   *(Rises, with boots)*   Ain't that the one you're divorcing now?

COUNTESS   But of course, Lucy. *(Plaintively)* What could I do when I found out he was putting arsenic in my Bromo Seltzer? Ah! L'amour! L'amour! Lucy, were you ever in love?

LUCY   Yes, ma'am.

COUNTESS   Tell me about it, Lucy.

LUCY   Well, ma'am, ain't much to tell. I was kinda enjoyin' the courtin' time. It was as purty a sight as you ever saw, to see him come lopin' across them hills. The sky so big and blue and that hair of his blazing like the be-jesuss in the sun. Then we'd sit on my back fence and spark. But, ma'am, you know how them big, strong, red-headed men are. They just got to get to the point. So we got married, ma'am. And natcherly, I ain't had no chance to think about love since—

COUNTESS *(She has not been listening)* The trouble with me, Lucy, is I've been marrying too many foreigners. I think I'll go back to marrying Americans.

> *(Enter* MIRIAM, R. *without a mudmask. She is a breezy, flashy red-head, about 28, wearing a theatrical pair of lounging pajamas)*

MIRIAM Hya, Lucy?

LUCY 'Evening, Mrs. Aarons. *(Exits* R.*)*

MIRIAM Hya, Countess, how's rhythm on the range? *(Sees jug on table, pours* COUNTESS *and herself drinks)*

COUNTESS Gallop, gallop, gallop, madly over the sagebrush! But now, Miriam, I'm having an emotional relapse. In two weeks I'll be free, free as a bird from that little French bastard. But whither, oh, whither shall I fly?

MIRIAM To the arms of that cowboy up at the dude ranch?

COUNTESS *(Modestly)* Miriam Aarons!

MIRIAM Why, he's nuts for you, Countess. He likes you better than his horse, and it's such a damn big horse.

COUNTESS *(Rises, and pads in her stocking-feet to sofa)* Well, Buck Winston is nice. So young. So strong. Have you noticed the play of his muscles? *(Reclining)* Musical. Musical.

MIRIAM He could crack a cocoanut with those knees. If he could get them together. Say, Countess, that guy hasn't been arousing your honorable intentions in you, has he?

COUNTESS Yes, Miriam, but I'm different from the rest of you. I've always put my faith in love. Still, I've had three divorces. Dare I risk a fourth?

MIRIAM What are you risking, Countess, or maybe I shouldn't ask?

COUNTESS I mean, Miriam, I could never make a success of Buck Winston at Newport.

MIRIAM Even Mrs. Astor would have to admit Buck's handsome. If I had your dough, I'd take him to Hollywood first, then Newport.

COUNTESS Hollywood? Why *not?* I might turn him into a picture star. After all, my second husband was a gondolier, and a month after I married him, a Duchess eloped with him. Ah! L'amour!

(*Enter* SYLVIA, R., *wearing smart dinner dress. Her trip to Reno has embittered but not subdued her*)

MIRIAM Hya, Sylvia? Going to a ball?

SYLVIA (*Pours drink*) Doing the town with a boy friend.

MIRIAM Where'd you pick him up?

SYLVIA The Silver State Bar. I'm not going to sit around moping, like Mary.

COUNTESS Poor Mary. If her husband gave her the flimsiest excuse, she'd take him back.

SYLVIA She has no pride. I'd roast in hell before I'd take Howard Fowler back. Kicking me out like that! After all I sacrificed!

MIRIAM Such as what?

SYLVIA I gave him my *youth!*

COUNTESS (*Dreamily*) Hélas, what else can a woman do with her youth but give it to a man?

MIRIAM Hélas, she can't preserve it in alcohol.

COUNTESS (*Practical*) But, Sylvia, how could your husband kick you out, if you were a femme fidèle?

SYLVIA Of course, I was a faithful wife. (*Miriam snorts*) What are you laughing at?

MIRIAM Two kinds of women, Sylvia, owls and ostriches. (*Raises her glass*) To the feathered sisterhood! To the girls who *get* paid and paid. (*Parenthetically*) And you got paid *plenty!*

SYLVIA You bet I got plenty! The skunk! And I'd have got plenty more, if only I could have pinned something on him.

MIRIAM Didn't you try?

SYLVIA Certainly not. To put it mildly, Howard has been impotent for years!

COUNTESS I never got a sou from any of my husbands except my first husband, Mr. Straus. He said the most touching thing in his will. I remember every word of it. "To my beloved wife, Flora, I leave all my estate in trust to be

administered by executors, because she is an A No. 1
schlemiel." (Touched anew) Wasn't that sweet?

    (Enter MARY, R. *She is subdued. She is carrying some
letters)*

MIRIAM Hya, queen?

MARY Fine.

MIRIAM Ya lie.

COUNTESS Mary, I'm starved.

    *(*LUCY *enters,* L., *takes* MARY'S *hat)*

MARY Supper's nearly ready. As my last official act in Reno,
I cooked the whole thing with my hands, didn't I, Lucy?

LUCY All but the steak and tomatoes and dessert, Mrs.
Haines. *(Exits,* L.*)*

MARY *(Gives letter to Sylvia, glancing, as she does so, at
inscription)* For you, Sylvia. From Edith?

SYLVIA You couldn't miss that infantile scrawl. *(Pointedly)*
You didn't hear from anyone?

MARY No.

SYLVIA Well, darling, Stephen's hardly worth a broken
heart.

MARY The less you have to say about me and Stephen the
better I like it!

SYLVIA I'm only trying to cheer you up. That's more than
you do for me.

MARY I'm doing enough, just being pleasant to you.

SYLVIA My, you have got the jitters, dear.

MIRIAM Hey, Sylvia, we're all out here in the same boat.
Mary's laid off you. Why don't you lay off her?

SYLVIA Oh, I'm just trying to make her see life isn't over
just because Stephen let her down. *(Opens her letter. A
batch of press-clippings falls out.* COUNTESS *picks them
up, reads them idly, as* SYLVIA *goes on with letter)*

COUNTESS You see, Miriam? What else is there for a woman
but l'amour?

MIRIAM There's a little corn whiskey left. *(She pours another drink)*

COUNTESS Cynic, you don't believe in Cupid.

MIRIAM That double-crossing little squirt! Give me Donald

Duck. *(To MARY)* Have a drink? *(MARY shakes head)* Listen, Babe, why not—relax? You'd feel better—

MARY *(Laughing)*   Miriam, you're not very chatty about your own affairs.

COUNTESS *(Suddenly engrossed by clippings from SYLVIA'S letter)* Miriam, you sly puss, you never even breathed that you knew Sylvia's husband.

SYLVIA *(Looking up from letter)* What?

COUNTESS *(Rises)* Sylvia, listen to this from Winchell: "Miriam Vanities Aarons is being Renovated. Three guesses, Mrs. Fowler, for whose Ostermoor?" *(SYLVIA snatches clippings from her)*

MIRIAM   Why can't those lousy columnists leave a successful divorce alone?

COUNTESS   *(Reading   another   clipping)* "Prominent stockbroker and ex-chorine to marry."

SYLVIA *(To MIRIAM)*   Why, you dirty little hypocrite!
> *(During this, PEGGY has entered and goes back of sofa. She listens but does not join group)*

MARY *(Going to her)*   Now, Sylvia—

SYLVIA   Did you know this?

MARY   No, But, Sylvia, why do you care? You don't love Howard—

SYLVIA *(Brushing her aside)*   Love has nothing to do with it. She just wants Howard for his money!

MIRIAM   And what did you want him for? I made Howard pay for what he wants; you made him pay for what he doesn't want.

COUNTESS   Why Sylvia, I thought you said Howard was impotent? What a lovely surprise! Besides I'll stay bought. That's more than you did, Sylvia.

MIRIAM   If Howard's impotent, so is Ali Kahn.

SYLVIA   Why, you dirty little trollop!

MIRIAM   Don't start calling names, you Park Avenue pushover!
> *(SYLVIA gives MIRIAM a terrific smack. In the twinkling of an eye, they are pulling hair. MARY seizes SYLVIA'S arm, SYLVIA breaks loose. COUNTESS tugs at*

MIRIAM'S *belt, as* LUCY *comes in, looks at fight with a rather professional eye, and exits for smelling-salts)*

COUNTESS Girls, girls, calmez-vous!

(Her interference enables SYLVIA *to slap* MIRIAM *unimpeded)*

MIRIAM *(Shoving the* COUNTESS *on sofa)* Out of the way, you fat old—! *(*SYLVIA *grabs* MIRIAM'S *hair)* Ouch, let go!

*(*SYLVIA *is about to use her nails.* MARY *takes a hand)*

MARY I won't have this, you hear!

*(*MARY'S *interference allows* MIRIAM *to give* SYLVIA *a terrific kick in the shins)*

SYLVIA *(Routed, in sobs)* Ouch! You bitch, you!

(As she turns away, MIRIAM *gives her another well-placed kick, which straightens* SYLVIA *up)*

MIRIAM Take that!

*(*SYLVIA, *shrieking with rage and humiliation, grabs* MIRIAM *again, sinks her white teeth into* MIRIAM'S *arm. At this mayhem,* MARY *seizes her, shakes her violently, pushes her sobbing into armchair)*

MARY *(To* MIRIAM) That's enough.

MIRIAM She's drawn blood!

MARY There's iodine in the bathroom.

MIRIAM Iodine? I need a rabies shot. *(Exits* R.)

SYLVIA *(Blubbering, nursing her wounds)* Oh, Mary, how could you let her do that to me!

MARY *(Coldly)* I'm terribly sorry, Sylvia.

SYLVIA The humiliation! You're on her side. After all I've done for you!

MARY What have you done for me?

SYLVIA I warned *you!*

MARY *(Bitterly)* I'm not exactly grateful for that.

SYLVIA *(Hysterical)* Oh, aren't you? Listen to me, you ball of conceit. You're not the object of pity you suppose. Plenty of the girls are tickled to death you got what was coming to you. You deserved to lose Stephen, the stupid way you acted. But I always stood up for you, like a loyal friend. What thanks do I get? You knew about that woman, and you stood by gloating, while she—

MARY   Get out of here!
(LUCY enters from bedroom, with spirits of ammonia, as SYLVIA gives way completely to hysteria, and, screaming with rage, picks up ash trays, glasses, and cigarette boxes, and hurls them violently against wall, while LUCY tries to get bottle under her nose)

SYLVIA *(At top of her lungs)* I hate you! I hate you! I hate everybody—

LUCY *(Takes SYLVIA firmly by shoulders, forces bottle under her nose)* Listen, Mrs. Fowler! You got the hy-strikes! *(Rushes her gasping, sobbing, to door)*

SYLVIA   You wait. Some day you'll need a woman friend. Then you'll think of me—
(Exit LUCY and SYLVIA, struggling helplessly, R.)

COUNTESS *(Rising from sofa)* Poor creatures. They've lost their equilibrium because they've lost their faith in love. *(Philosophically)* L'amour. Remember the song Buck made up, just for me? *(Pours herself a drink, sings a cowboy song:)* "Oh, a man can ride a horse to the range above, But a woman's got to ride on the wings of love, Coma a ti-yi-yippi a yippi yi-yay." *(Throws jug over her shoulder, and exits R., still singing, as MIRIAM enters, the ravages of her fight repaired with a handkerchief)*

MIRIAM   The coast clear?

PEGGY   Oh, that was the most disgusting thing I ever saw.

MIRIAM   Right, kid, we're a pair of alley cats—

MARY   You should not be here, Peggy, to see it all. *(She picks up ash trays, etc.)*

MIRIAM   What the hell are you doing here?

MARY   John wanted to buy a car.

PEGGY   With my money! John couldn't afford a car.

MARY   But *you* could. What was his—is yours. What is yours —is your own. Very fair.

PEGGY   A woman's best protection is to keep a little money of her own.

MARY   A woman's best protection is—the right man. *(With gentle sarcasm)* Obviously, John isn't the right man and Peggy will forget all about him in another month.

PEGGY   No, I won't. I can't. Because—because—*(Bursts into tears)* Oh, Mary, I'm going to have a baby. Oh, Mary, what shall I do?

MARY   Peggy, what's his telephone number?

PEGGY *(Quickly)*   Eldorado 5–2075. *(MIRIAM goes at once to phone. Gets operator, gives number)* But oh, Mary, I can't tell him!

MIRIAM   Why? Isn't it his?

PEGGY   Oh, of course!

MIRIAM   And make it snappy, operator.

PEGGY   I always wanted it. But what can I do with it now?

MIRIAM   Land it with the Marines—

MARY   Peggy, you've shared you love with him. Your baby will share your blood, your eyes, your hair, your virtues—and your faults—But your little pin-money, that, of course, you could not share.

PEGGY   Oh, Mary, I know I'm wrong. But it's no use—you don't know the things he said to me. I have my pride.

MARY *(Bitterly)*   Reno's full of women who all have their pride.

PEGGY   You think I'm like them.

MIRIAM   You've got the makings, dear.

MARY   Love has pride in nothing—but its own humility.

MIRIAM *(At phone)*   Mr. Day, please. Reno calling—Mr. Day? My God, he must live by the phone. Just hold the—
     (PEGGY leaps to phone)

PEGGY   Hello, John. *(Clears her throat of a sob)* No, I'm not sick. That is, I am sick! That is, I'm sick to my stomach. Oh, John! I'm going to have a baby—Oh, darling, are you?—Oh, darling, do you?—Oh, darling, so am I! So do I! 'Course, I forgive you—Yes, precious. Yes, lamb. On the very next train! John? *(A kiss into phone. It is returned)* Oh, Johnny, when I get back, things are going to be so different—! John, do you mind if I reverse the charges? *(Hangs up)* I can't stay for supper. I've got to pack.

MARY   When you get back—don't see too much of your girl friends for a while.

PEGGY   Oh, I won't, Mary. It's all their fault we're here.

MARY Not—entirely.

PEGGY Good-bye! Oh, I'm so happy, I could cry. *(exits* R.*)*

MIRIAM Getting wise, aren't you?

MARY Know all the answers.

MIRIAM Then, why're you here?

MARY I had plenty of advice, Miriam.
        (Phone rings. MIRIAM *goes to it)*

MIRIAM Hello. No, we completed that call, operator.
  (Hangs up)

MARY Cigarette?

MIRIAM *(Suddenly)* Listen.

MARY There's nothing you can say I haven't heard.

MIRIAM Sure? I come from a world where a woman's got to
  come out on top—or it's just too damned bad. Maybe I got
  a new slant.

MARY *(Wearily)* All right, Miriam. Talk to me about my—
  legal rights. Talk to me about security—What does it all
  come to? Compromise.

MIRIAM What the hell? A woman's compromised the day
  she's born.

MARY You can't compromise with utter defeat. He doesn't
  want me.

MIRIAM How do you know?

MARY How do I know—why else am I here?

MIRIAM *(A pause. Then, mock-tragically)* Because you've
  got no guts, Mary Haines. It happened to me—I lost my
  man, too.

MARY *(Smiling)* You?

MIRIAM Oh, it only happened once. Got wise to myself after
  that. Look, how did I lose him? We didn't have enough
  dough to get married. I wouldn't sleep with him until we
  did. I had ideals—God knows where I got 'em. I held out
  on him—*(Sighs)* Can you beat it? I liked him a lot better
  than I've ever liked anybody since. What'd my Romeo do?
  Got himself another girl. I made a terrible stink. Why
  shouldn't I? I should. But what I ought not to have done
  was say—good-bye. I was like you.

MARY I don't understand.

MIRIAM Then get a load of this. I should of licked that girl where she licked me—in the hay.

MARY Miriam!

MIRIAM That's where you win the first round. And if I know men, that's still Custer's Last Stand. (MARY *walks away from her*) Shocked you? You're too modest. You're ashamed. O.K., sister. But my idea of love is that love isn't ashamed of anything.

MARY (*Turning to her*) A good argument, Miriam. So modern. So simple. Sex the cause, sex the cure. It's too simple, Miriam. Your love battles are for—lovers—or professionals. (*Gently*) Not for a man and woman who've been married twelve quiet years! Oh, I don't mean I wouldn't love Stephen's arms around me again. But I wouldn't recapture, if I could, our—young passion. That was the wonderful young thing we had. That was part of our youth, like the —babies. But not the thing that made him my husband, that made me his wife—Stephen *needed* me. He *needed* me for twelve years. Stephen doesn't need me any more.

MIRIAM I get it. (*Phone rings*) That's why I'm marrying this guy Fowler. He sure needs me. If I don't marry him he'll drink himself to death in a month, the poor dope.

MARY (*At phone*) Yes? No, operator, we completed—you say New York is calling Mrs. Haines? She'll take that call— (*To* MIRIAM) Stephen!

MIRIAM Listen, make him that speech you just made me!

MARY (*Radiant*) I knew he'd call. I knew when the last moment came, he'd realize he needed me.

MIRIAM For God's sake, tell him that *you* need him!

MARY Hello-hello? Stephen? Mary. Yes. I'm very cheerful. It's so good to hear your voice, Stephen. I—Why, yes, the final decree is granted tomorrow at 12—but, Stephen, I can —(*Frightened*) But, Stephen! No—of course—I haven't seen the papers. How could I, out here? (*Long pause*) Yes, I'd rather *you* told me. Of course I understand the position you're both in. No, I'm not bitter, not bitter at all—I—I hope you'll both be very happy. No, I have no plans, no plans at all—Stephen, do you mind if I hang up? Good-bye, Stephen.—Good-bye—

MIRIAM   He's marrying her?

MARY   Tomorrow! Oh, God, why did I let this happen? We were married, We were one person. We had a good life. Oh, God, I've been a *fool!*

MIRIAM   Sure you have. Haven't we all, sister?

CURTAIN

SCENE 3

Early evening, two years later. CRYSTAL'S *bathroom.* L., *a black marbleized tub with frilled shower-curtains. In a niche, back of tub, a gilded French phone.* R., *a satin-skirted dressing table, covered with glittering toilet bottles and cosmetic jars. Towel-racks piled with embroidered bath-towels.* C., *a door to* CRYSTAL'S *bedroom. As curtain rises,* CRYSTAL *is lolling in the bath, reading a magazine, smoking, as* HELENE, *a chic French maid, enters.*

HELENE   Madame has been soaking an hour.

CRYSTAL   *(Rudely)*   So what?

HELENE   But monsieur—

CRYSTAL   Monsieur is going out with me and my friends, whether he likes it or not. Has that kid gone home yet?

HELENE   Mademoiselle Mary has just finished the supper with her daddy. Madame, monsieur is so anxious that you say good night to her.

CRYSTAL   Listen, that kid doesn't want to bid me beddy-bye any more than I do. He's tried for two years to cram us down each other's throats. Let her go home to her mommer. *(Passes* HELENE *a brush)* Here—scrub—Some day I'm going to slap that kid down. She's too—*(As* HELENE *scrubs too hard)* Ow! You're taking my skin off—Oh, I'm so bored I could—*(Hurls the soap across the room)* Helene, never marry a man who's deserted a "good woman." He's as cheerful as a man who's murdered his poor old mother. *(Telephone rings)* Get out! And, Helene, when Mrs. Fowler comes, keep her downstairs, if you have to sit on her. *(Exit* HELENE. CRYSTAL *picks up the telephone. Her voice melts)* Hello, darling, I'm in the tub. I'm shrivelled to a peanut waiting for this call. No, I'm not afraid of a shock. You ought to know—Oh, Buck, I'm going to miss you like nobody's business. I can't tell you what it did to

174

me, locking the door on our little apartment—I'll say we
had fun! Coma ti-yi-yippy, what? Oh, no, say anything you
like. This is the one place where I have some privacy.
*(CRYSTAL's back is to the door. She does not hear a brief
rap)* Listen, baby, must you really go to the coast? Oh, the
hell with Mr. Goldwyn. *(Enter LITTLE MARY. She stands
hesitantly against the door)* Listen, you don't have to tell
me what you sacrificed to have a movie career. I've seen
that cartoon you married. If Flora was ever a Countess, I'm
the Duchess of Windsor. Well, Buck, maybe she's not such
a half-wit, but—*(Sees LITTLE MARY)* Oh—call me back in
two minutes. I've had a small interruption. *(Hangs up)*
Who told you to come in here?

LITTLE MARY *(Politely)* Daddy. Good night. *(Turns to go)*

CRYSTAL *(Sweetly)* Oh, don't go, darling. Hand me that
brush.

LITTLE MARY *(Gently)* Please?

CRYSTAL Please.

    (LITTLE MARY gives her brush)

LITTLE MARY Good night. *(Goes to door)*

CRYSTAL My, you're in a hurry to tell Daddy about it.

LITTLE MARY About what?

CRYSTAL My talk on the telephone.

LITTLE MARY I don't understand grown-ups on the telephone. They all sound silly. Good night.

CRYSTAL Good night, who? *(A pause)* You've been told to
call me Aunty Crystal. *(A pause)* Why don't you do it?

LITTLE MARY *(Still edging to door)* Yes.

CRYSTAL Yes, what?

LITTLE MARY *(Lamely)* Yes, good night.

CRYSTAL *(Angry)* You sit down!

LITTLE MARY Oh, it's awfully hot in here. I've got my coat
on.

CRYSTAL You heard me! *(LITTLE MARY sits on stool before
dressing table, squirms)* We're going to have this out. I've
done my damn—my level best to be friends with you, but
you refuse to co-operate.

LITTLE MARY What?

CRYSTAL   Co-operate.

LITTLE MARY *(Nodding mechanically)*   Co-operate.

CRYSTAL *(Exasperated)*   Answer my question. You don't like me. Why?

LITTLE MARY *(Rising)*   Well, good night, Crystal—

CRYSTAL   I said, why?

LITTLE MARY *(Very patiently)*   Listen, Crystal, my mother told me I wasn't to be rude to you.

CRYSTAL   For the last time, young lady, you give me one good reason why you don't like me.

LITTLE MARY   I never said I didn't like you, Crystal.

CRYSTAL   But you don't like me, do you?

LITTLE MARY   No, but I never *said* so. I've been very polite, Crystal, considering you're something awful!

CRYSTAL   Wait till your father hears this!

LITTLE MARY *(Suddenly defiant)*   Listen—Daddy doesn't think you're so wonderful any more!

CRYSTAL   Did he tell you that?

LITTLE MARY   No. Daddy always pretends you're all right, but he's just ashamed to have Mother know what a mean, silly wife he's got. And I don't tell Mother what *we* think, because you've made her cry enough, Crystal. So I'm not going to co-operate *ever!*

CRYSTAL   Get out!

LITTLE MARY *(Goes to door, then turns, rather superior)*   And *another* thing, I think this bathroom is perfectly ridiculous! Good night, Crystal! *(Exits. Phone rings.* CRYSTAL *grabs it, irritable)*

CRYSTAL   Yes, darling—That Haines brat. God, she gets under my skin!—No, she didn't hear anything. What good would it do her, anyhow? You're off in the morning, and Lord knows we've been discreet—What? You are? *(Giggling)* Dining with the first Mrs. Haines?—Well, darling, lay off the gin. It makes you talk too much.—Well, just be careful, darling.

> *(Enter* SYLVIA, *without knocking. She wears elaborate evening gown, and carries a cocktail. These two years*

have had no appreciable effect on SYLVIA. *She is her old Act I self again)*

SYLVIA Yoohoo! May I come in?

CRYSTAL *(In phone)* No, this is not the Aquarium. It's Grand Central Station. *(Hangs up)*

SYLVIA Who was that?

CRYSTAL A wrong number.

SYLVIA You were talking to a man.

CRYSTAL Pass me that sponge.—Please.

SYLVIA *(Waiting on CRYSTAL)* Oh, Crystal, you know you can trust me.

CRYSTAL And that eye cup.

SYLVIA There must be someone. After all, I've known Stephen for years. He's really not your type. I often wonder how you two got together. I was telling my psychoanalyst about it. You know, I've got to tell him everything.

CRYSTAL That must be an awful effort.

SYLVIA I don't mind discussing myself. But talking about my friends does make me feel disloyal. He says Stephen has a Guilt Complex.

CRYSTAL What?

SYLVIA *(Cheerfully)* He says men of Stephen's generation were brought up to believe that infidelity is a sin. That's why he allowed Mary to divorce him, and that's why he married you, Crystal. He had to marry you just to convince himself he was not a sexual monster.

CRYSTAL Yes? Well, if Stephen is a sexual monster, psychoanalysis is through.

SYLVIA And he says you've got a Cinderella Complex. He says most American women have. They're all brought up to believe that marriage to a rich man should be their aim in life. He says we neither please the men nor function as child-bearing animals—

CRYSTAL *(Bored and angry)* Will you function yourself into the bedroom?

SYLVIA *(Hurt)* I don't think that's the way to talk to me, after all I've done for you. When you married Stephen you didn't know a soul. It wasn't easy to put *you* over. Everybody was on Mary's side.

CRYSTAL   They still are. They never miss a chance to remind me what a noble, useful woman Mary has become since she left Stephen.

SYLVIA   *(Comforting)* My dear, she's miserable! Why, she never sees a soul.

CRYSTAL   She's having a dinner party tonight.

SYLVIA   Edith told me. She's going. And Flora.

CRYSTAL   Flora?

SYLVIA   The Countess de Lage. Mrs. Buck Winston? My God, I have to laugh when I think of Flora actually turning that cowboy into a movie star. Of course he's not my type, but he's positively the Chambermaid's Delight—

CRYSTAL   *(Fiercely)* Will you shut up?

SYLVIA   But, Crystal—

CRYSTAL   I said shut up—*(Calling)* Helene!

SYLVIA   Well, I think you're very ungrateful.

CRYSTAL   Well, take it up with your psychoanalyst. *(HELENE enters)* Helene, draw the curtains. I want to take a shower. *(SYLVIA goes to door as HELENE draws curtains)* That's right, Sylvia—wait in the bedroom.

SYLVIA   *(Sees scales, decides to weigh herself)* Oh, dear, I've lost another pound. I must remember to tell my analyst. You know, everything means something. *(Shower goes on. HELENE exits. SYLVIA gets off scales. During the following monologue, she goes to CRYSTAL'S dressing table, where she examines all the bottles and jars)* But even my analyst says no woman should try to do as much as I do. He says I attach too much value to my feminine friendships. He says I have a Damon and Pythias Complex. I guess I have given too much of myself to other women. He says women are natural enemies—*(Picks up bottle)* Why, Crystal, I thought you didn't touch up your hair—*(Sniffing perfume)* My dear, I wouldn't use this. You smell it on every tart in New York. That reminds me—*(Going to shower-curtains)* If you do have an affair, Crystal, for heaven's sake, be discreet. Remember what Howard did to me, the skunk. *(Peeking in)* My, you're putting on weight. *(Going back to dressing table, she sits down, and begins to pry in all the drawers)* But men are so mercenary. They think they own you body and soul, just because they pay the bills—I tried this cream. It brought out pimples—Of course, Crystal, if you were smart, you'd have a baby. It's the only real hold a woman has—*(HELENE enters)*

HELENE Monsieur says will madame be long?

SYLVIA Can't you see she's rushing?—*(HELENE exits. Shower goes off)* Men are so selfish! When you're only making yourself beautiful for them. *(Opens another drawer)* I wish I could find a man who would understand my need for a companion—*(finds a key, examines it)* Why, Crystal, what are *you* doing with a key to the Gothic Apartments? *(CRYSTAL's head pops from behind curtain)*

CRYSTAL What?—Oh—*(Nervously)* Oh, that! *(Playing for time)* Throw me a towel, Sylvia!

SYLVIA *(Bringing her towel)* That's where Howard had me followed. The doorman there is a professional blackmailer! *(Crystal has wrapped herself in a big towel, now steps from behind shower-curtain and sits on rim of tub to dry her legs)* I asked my psychoanalyst about him, and he said blackmailers are really perverts who can't think of a good perversion. So they blackmail people instead.

CRYSTAL *(Going to dressing table)* Really? Well, he can't blackmail me now. *(As she passes SYLVIA, she lightly snatches key from her)* The Gothic Apartments are where Stephen and I had to go, before the divorce. I keep it for sentimental reasons. *(Smiling, she drops key back in drawer, locks it)*

SYLVIA Poor Stephen! My dear, I thought tonight how tired he looked, and old. Crystal, I've told you everything. Tell me: how long do you think you can be faithful to Stephen?

CRYSTAL *(Making up her face)* Well, life plays funny tricks. The urge might hit me tomorrow.

SYLVIA   I doubt it, pet. You're a typical blonde.

CRYSTAL   So what?

SYLVIA *(Loftily)*   Most *blondes* are frigid.

CRYSTAL   Really? Well, maybe that's just a dirty piece of *brunette* propaganda!

CURTAIN

SCENE 4

11 o'clock the same night. MARY'S *bedroom. A charming, simple room.* L., *a door to dressing-room.* R., *a door to hall. As curtain rises,* JANE *is arranging a number of evening wraps on the bed.* MIRIAM, MARY *and* NANCY *are entering.*

MIRIAM   Thanks, baby, a lot! I never was at a wetter dinner.

MARY   It was a success. I left Reno two years ago today. This was a memorial dinner for you old Renoites, and your new husbands.

MIRIAM   I get it. Listen, there's no soap eating out your heart, sister!

NANCY   Mary, if I had a heroine in one of my books who behaved the way you do, my two readers would never believe it. No one man is worth it.

MIRIAM   Say, the whole Racquet Club's not worth it— Speaking of my dear husband Howard—the skunk—can I have a whiskey and soda?

NANCY   Make it two. *(JANE exits* R.*)*

MIRIAM   I lay off when Howard's around. I'm weaning him from the bottle by easy stages. He's in the secondary stage now.

NANCY   What stage is that?

MIRIAM   He puts ice in.

MARY   How's matrimony, Miriam? Making a go of it?

MIRIAM   I'm doing a reconstruction job that makes Boulder Dam look like an egg-cup.
          (Enter PEGGY, R.*)*

PEGGY   Oh, Mary, can't we get off to the party? I have to get home early. Little John always wakes up. Little John said the cutest thing the other day. *(A dramatic pause)* He said da-da—!

NANCY   When does he enter Columbia?
          (Enter JANE *with tray and highballs)*

MARY Jane, tell Mrs. Winston the ladies are ready to go.

JANE Mrs. Winston, ma'am, is drinking with the gentlemen.

MARY Well, tell her to come up.

> (*Exit* JANE)

MIRIAM What's the hurry? Two more snootfuls, and Flora will float up on her own breath.

> (*Enter* EDITH, R.)

EDITH (*Petulantly*) Mary, I wish you had an elevator in this house. It's so difficult to walk upstairs in my condition.

MARY Edith, are you Catholic or just careless?

EDITH Mary, isn't this your old furniture?

MARY Yes.

EDITH I think you should get rid of it. There's nothing that keeps a woman so in the dumps as sleeping in a bed with old associations. Mary, you're carrying this nunnery business too far. How do you expect to find anyone else, if you don't make an effort?

MARY I don't want anyone, Edith. (*Mock cynical*) I hate men! Men are awful—

EDITH Oh, they're not all like Stephen, dear.

MARY I saw plenty of men when I came back from Reno. They're all alike. They never leave you at your own front door without a wrestling-match.

MIRIAM It beats me how, in a taxi, the nicest guy turns into Harpo Marx.

EDITH You know I asked Phelps about that once. I said, "Why does a man always act like a Don Juan in a taxi?" And he said it was a hang-over from their bachelor days when a man's sex life was conditioned by the click of the meter. Mary, want to hear something about Sylvia? (MARY, MIRIAM, NANCY *and* PEGGY: *chorus, "No!"*) Well, Sylvia's going to a psychoanalyst. She says you destroyed all her faith in friendship.

MARY As if any woman needed to go to a psychoanalyst to find out she can't trust women.

EDITH Mary, you've grown awfully cynical.

MARY Isn't "wise" the word? I'm beginning to understand women.

NANCY Too bad! That's the beginning of woman's in-humanity to woman.

EDITH *(Moving to door, L.)* Oh, they're going to talk phi-losophy, Peggy. Come on in here while I powder my nose.

PEGGY Edith, did I tell you how little John said *(A breath-less pause)* da-da?

EDITH Listen, I wouldn't care if *this* one was born reading Shakespeare!

> *(They exit, as enter MRS. MOREHEAD, in street clothes, R.)*

MRS. MOREHEAD Oh, hello, girls! Hello, dear. Party over?

MARY Enjoy the movies, Mother?

MRS. MOREHEAD I wish I could make up my mind whether or not I like the Beatles.

> *(Enter COUNTESS DE LAGE, R. She is a tangle of tulle and jewels. She has a slight "edge" on)*

COUNTESS Such a lovely dinner! It's so wonderful to see all our lives temporarily settled!

MARY My mother, Mrs. Morehead, Mrs. Winston. Mrs. Buck Winston.

MRS. MOREHEAD *(Trying to place the name)* Buck Win-ston?

MARY The movie star.

MRS. MOREHEAD Ah, yes! *(Pleasantly)* My granddaughter adores your son on the screen.

COUNTESS *(Good-naturedly)* I daresay the public does see Buck as just a boy. And it is a trifle absurd *me* being mar-ried to a movie star. But, Mrs. Morehead, you wouldn't believe how many of my Newport friends who ridiculed Buck when I married him positively claw for invitations to Hollywood. Mais là, East is East and West is West, but I always say Le Cinema is the Great Leveler!

MRS. MOREHEAD You don't say! *(Edges to hall door)*

COUNTESS Mrs. Morehead, do whip into something and come along with Mary to my party. The Casino Roof. Everyone's clamored to come. I have no idea who's going to be there.

MRS. MOREHEAD Well, you're sure to know somebody. *(To* MARY*)* Later, dear?

(MARY *nods,* MRS. MOREHEAD *escapes,* R.*)*

COUNTESS *(Gathering her wrap)* Mary, you're not coming?

MARY I'm very tired, Flora.

COUNTESS Oh, you're cross because Buck's had a wee droppie.

MIRIAM Don't be modest, Flora. Your groom is stinko.

COUNTESS I do wish he wouldn't drink straight gin. You know, he's not allowed to. Mr. Zanuck put that in the new contract.

MIRIAM Countess, you should have all your marriage contracts drawn up by Mr. Zanuck.

COUNTESS Mary, do come. This is *really* our farewell party. I'm never coming back to New York.

MARY What's wrong with New York, Flora?

COUNTESS *(Whispering)* Mary, can I trust you?

MARY Of course, Flora!

COUNTESS *(To others)* You will keep this just between the four of us?

MIRIAM Shoot, Flora, it's a nationwide hookup!

COUNTESS *(Settling herself beside* MARY *on foot of bed)* Well, you know how Buck was? *(Wistfully)* So—so impassioné?

MIRIAM That boy had something.

COUNTESS *(Tartly)* Well, he hasn't got it any more, Miriam! First, I thought it was just gin, interfering with his libido — *(Tearfully)* But now I think Buck is deceiving me—

NANCY How incredible!

COUNTESS Well, I have no proof. Except he comes home every afternoon smelling of a strange perfume.

MARY Where does he say he's been?

COUNTESS Visiting his horse. But Trixie was shipped to Hollywood last week. You remember, I was photographed with her in the baggage-car? Now he says he's been going to the Grand Central Gymnasium. But I telephoned today. Some great oaf answered. I said: "Is Buck Winston there?" He said: "Who? No." So I said: "My dear good man, he comes every day." So he said: "My mistake, lady, he's inside now boxing with James Bond."

MARY Poor Flora!

COUNTESS *(Practical)* That's why I think it's safer just to keep floating around.

MARY I understand—l'amour.

COUNTESS L'amour, yes, but jamais *(She has her lucid moments)* jamais *lopsided* amour!

MARY *(Laughing)* Lopsided amour is better than no amour at all. Flora, let him make a fool of you. Let him do anything he wants, as long as he stays. He's taking the trouble to deceive you. *(Half to herself)* And if he took the trouble, he really must have cared—

NANCY The Voice of Experience.

MIRIAM *(To Countess)* Come on, chin up.

NANCY That's right. Both of them! *(Enter PEGGY and EDITH)*

COUNTESS *(Rising)* Oh, cheries, you missed it! I was just saying—now you will keep this just among the six of us?— I suspect Buck of being unfaithful. Of course, it's my own fault. I should have had him watched. The way I did all the others. I wish I'd found out where he's had the apartment!

PEGGY An apartment—?

COUNTESS Where would you expect him to go? Central Park? Why, it's winter.

PEGGY Oh, I've always heard people went to hotels.

COUNTESS But, cherie, *Buck* couldn't go to a hotel. You know what would happen. At the most inopportune moment someone would say: "Mr. Winston, may I have your autograph?" It happened to us on our wedding night. I would have sent for the manager, but it was the manager asking for the autograph. *(Exits R.)*

EDITH *(Getting her wrap)* Darling, you really won't come to Flora's party?

MARY No, Edith!

EDITH Then I can tell you. Of course, I know how you feel about your Ex—and his New Deal—though I think you'd be glad he's so happy.

MARY I am.

EDITH Sylvia telephoned tonight. She and Crystal and Stephen are going on to the Roof with a theatre party. Well, darling, I don't feel much like going myself. I loathe this dress. My husband says I look as though I were going to sing Wagner in it. (*Exits R.*)

NANCY Think I'll go, too, Mary! It's a good chance to study Park Avenue's flora and fauna. And I'm writing a new book. It's called "Gone with the Ice-man," or "Sex Has No Place in the Home."

    (*Exits with* PEGGY)

MIRIAM (*To* MARY) Listen, Queen, change your mind! Let's go on to the party!

MARY No, Miriam.

MIRIAM Well, I'm going. Wish you could see the cooing-fest Howard and I put on for Sylvia—Shall I spit in Crystal's eye for you? (MARY *shakes her head*) You're passing up a swell chance, sister! Where I spit no grass grows ever!

    (*Exits.* JANE *enters,* R. MARY *begins to unfasten her dress, takes off her jewels, lays them on dresser*)

MARY Jane, turn down my bed.

JANE Yes, ma'am. (MARY *goes into boudoir,* L.)

MARY (*Off stage*) Did Mary have a nice time with her father?

JANE (*Turning down bed*) Well, ma'am, you know how she is when she comes home.

MARY (*Off stage*) I'm afraid she's never going to get used to it.

JANE She takes after you, ma'am, if you'll pardon me. Always brooding. Sometimes, ma'am, I think it would be better if she didn't see her father. Or maybe, ma'am— though it's none of my busines—if you could find some nice man—

    (*Enter* MRS. MOREHEAD, R., *in wrapper and slippers*)

MRS. MOREHEAD Going to bed, darling?

MARY (*Off stage*) Yes, Mother.

MRS. MOREHEAD Shall we chat for a moment? Jane, I'll have a cigarette.

JANE *(Surprised)* Mrs. Morehead!

MRS. MOREHEAD Those dreadful women made me nervous.
Why Mrs. Haines tolerates them even once a year is
beyond me!

MARY *(Entering, in a nightgown)* An object lesson. Smoking, Mother?

MRS. MOREHEAD Oh, you, too?

MARY Me too?

MRS. MOREHEAD I just felt your father give me a spooky
pinch. You'd think after ten years his ghost might have
grown more tolerant.

JANE Good night, ma'am. *(Switches off side-lights)*

MARY and MRS. MOREHEAD Good night, Jane. *(Exit JANE.
MARY gets into bed opens book, flips through it)*

MRS. MOREHEAD *(Sitting on bed)* Good book?

MARY Don't know. Nancy just gave it to me. It's about—
love. Poetry. All about love. *(Reads)* "When love beckons
to you, follow him, though his ways are hard and steep.
And when his wings enfold you, yield to him—Though his
voice may shatter your dreams as the North Wind lays
waste the garden."

MRS. MOREHEAD Well, all I can say is, that's very tactless of
Nancy. *(Suddenly)* Oh, Mary, I wish you could find—

MARY *(Slams book shut)* Some nice man. We've been all
over that before, Mother. I had the only one I ever wanted,
I lost him—

MRS. MOREHEAD It wasn't entirely your fault.

MARY If I hadn't listened to everyone, everything but my
own heart!

MRS. MOREHEAD He loved her.

MARY He still does. Though you know, Mother, I'm just
beginning to doubt it.

MRS. MOREHEAD Why?

MARY Because so many people, like Edith, make a point of
telling me how much he loves her. Oh, Mother, I'm terribly tired.

MRS. MOREHEAD Well, do cheer up, darling. Living alone
has its compensations. You can go where you please, wear

what you please and eat what you please. I had to wait
twenty years to order the kind of meal I liked! Your father
called it bird-food—And, heaven knows, it's marvelous to
be able to sprawl out in bed, like a swastika. Good night,
darling.

MARY Good night, Mother.

MRS. MOREHEAD Don't read by that light. You'll hurt your
eyes.

> (*Exits.* MARY *props herself against pillows, begins to
> read. Enter* LITTLE MARY, *in nightgown, barefooted,
> very sleepy*)

LITTLE MARY Mother?

MARY Darling, what's the matter?

LITTLE MARY (*Goes to bed*) I had a bad dream!

MARY Darling, what was it?

LITTLE MARY I forget. Let me crawl in with you, Mother.

MARY (*Helping her in*) I'm so restless.

LITTLE MARY I don't mind if you kick me. You know, that's
the only good thing about divorce; you get to sleep with
your mother. (*She kisses her. A pause*) I taste lipstick.

MARY I haven't washed yet. Good night, darling.

LITTLE MARY You know, you're a very sympathetic
mother.

MARY Am I?

LITTLE MARY Oh, yes. So would you just tickle my back?

MARY All right. But go to sleep—(*A pause*)

LITTLE MARY She's so silly!

MARY Who?

LITTLE MARY Crystal.

MARY Ssh—

LITTLE MARY I told Daddy so tonight.

MARY Oh, you mustn't hurt Daddy's feelings.

LITTLE MARY Mother?

MARY Sssh!

LITTLE MARY I think Daddy doesn't love her as much as
you any more.

MARY What makes you think so, Mary?

LITTLE MARY He told me so after I saw Crystal.

MARY What?

LITTLE MARY But he said I mustn't tell you because, naturally, why do you care how he feels. *(A pause)* Oh, don't stop tickling, Mother. *(A pause)* Mother?

MARY Yes?

LITTLE MARY What's anyone want with a telephone in the bathroom?

MARY I don't know. Sssh!

LITTLE MARY Crystal has one. She was awful mad when I walked in on her while she was talking.

MARY Sleep, Mary!

LITTLE MARY Mother, who's the Duchess of Windsor?

MARY What a question!

LITTLE MARY Well, Crystal said on the telephone if somebody else was a Countess, she was the Duchess of Windsor!

MARY Really!

LITTLE MARY Good night, Mother.

MARY Good night, baby. *(A pause)*

LITTLE MARY I wonder if it was the same man you had for dinner.

MARY Maybe, ssh!

LITTLE MARY I thought so.

MARY *(Curiously)* If who was the same man?

LITTLE MARY Crystal was talking to, so lovey-dovey.

MARY *(Protestingly)* Oh, Mary!

LITTLE MARY Well, the front part was the same, Mother.

MARY *(A pause)* The front part of what?

LITTLE MARY His name, Mother!

MARY *(Taking her by shoulders)* What are you talking about?

LITTLE MARY That man Crystal was talking to in the bathtub.

MARY *(Half shaking her)* Mary, what do you mean?

LITTLE MARY I mean his front name was *Buck*, Mother! (MARY *gets quickly out of bed, rings bell on table)* Oh, Mother, what are you doing?

MARY Go to sleep, darling. *(Begins to pull on her stockings)*

LITTLE MARY Grown-ups are so sudden. Are you dressing?

MARY   Yes, Mary.

LITTLE MARY   You forgot you were invited to a party?

MARY   Almost, Mary.

LITTLE MARY   What are you going to do when you get there, Mother?

MARY   I don't know yet. But I'm going to do something.

LITTLE MARY   Well, have a good time! *(Rolls over. Then suddenly sits up)* Mother!

MARY   Yes?

LITTLE MARY   I remember now I had something to tell you!

MARY *(Eagerly)*   Yes?

LITTLE MARY *(Dolefully)*   I was awfully rude to Crystal.

MARY   I'll forgive you this time.
      (Enter JANE*)*

JANE   You ring, ma'am?

MARY   Yes. My evening dress, Jane, and a taxi—and don't stand there gaping! Hurry! Hurry!

CURTAIN

SCENE 5

*Later, the same night. Powder Room at the Casino Roof.
The decoration is rich, tawdry and modernistic. R., a swinging door from lobby. L., another to the washrooms. The rest
of the wall-space, L. and R., is taken up by counter-like
dressing tables and mirrors. Rear wall is a great window
overlooking the glitter of midnight Manhattan. An over-
stuffed sofa and an armchair upholstered in modernistic
fabric. Near the door, R., a screen hides the coat-rack. By this,
a chair for* SADIE, *a little old woman in black maid's uniform
and apron. As curtain rises,* SADIE *is reading a tabloid,
which she puts down when two flashily dressed girls enter
from lobby. They check their wraps.*

1ST GIRL   It's jammed.

2ND GIRL   Oh, my boy-friend'll get a table.

> *(Enter two society women. They move directly across
> stage to washroom.)*

1ST WOMAN   My dear, won't he let you?

2ND WOMAN   No, he won't.

1ST WOMAN   How incredibly foul!

2ND WOMAN   I'm heartbroken. But I have to be philosoph-
ical; after all, missing one winter in Palm Beach really
won't kill me.

> *(Enter "Cigarettes," a pretty girl in white satin blouse
> and short black skirt. Carries tray of cigarettes)*

1ST GIRL *(Moving L.)*   Thought you and the boy friend had
a row?

2ND GIRL   We did.

1ST GIRL   What about?

2ND GIRL   His wife.

1ST GIRL   His wife? What right has she got to butt in?

2ND GIRL   He's got some cockeyed idea that after twenty
years he can't kick her out. *(They exit L.)*

CIGARETTES Jeepers, why don't they get sick of this joint night after night! Same music, same act, same faces.

SADIE They like familiarity. It gives them confidence.

CIGARETTES I'll say they like familiarity. Most of them shoving around that floor would be more comfortable with each other in bed.

SADIE In bed? If they was to get that over, what would they use for conversation?

> (*Enter a* DOWAGER *and a* DEBUTANTE, R. *They move directly across stage*)

DOWAGER —dancing like that! What can those boys think of you?

DEBUTANTE (*Wearily*) Oh, Mother.

DOWAGER Guzzling champagne like that! After all I spent on your education!

DEBUTANTE Oh, Mother.

DOWAGER It's one thing to come out. It's quite another to go under the table! (*They exit,* L.)

SADIE —Getting married, dearie?

CIGARETTES (*Sinking, very tired, on arm of a chair*) As soon as Mike gets a job. It ain't fair! Why, we could get married and have a family on that coat—Sadie, wh'd'ya say if I was to tell you I'm a Commyanist?

SADIE I'd say ya was bats. I was a Norman Thomas fan. Where'd it get me?

> (*Enter* COUNTESS, *piloted by* NANCY *and* MIRIAM. *She is tight and tearful.* MIRIAM *and* NANCY *get her, with some difficulty, to the sofa*)

COUNTESS (*Tacking*) How could Buck do such a thing to me! Oh, the Dr. Jekyll! The Mr. Hyde! Which was which?

MIRIAM Pipe down or you'll put an awful dent in his career, Flora.

COUNTESS What of my career? I've had five husbands. Buck's the first one who ever told me what he really thought of me—in public.

NANCY It takes all kinds of husbands to round out a career like yours, Flora.

COUNTESS He told me he'd been deceiving me for months.

Right in the middle of "Smoke Gets in Your Eyes." *(Kicks off shoes)* Oh, I feel so—superfluous!

MIRIAM *(To* SADIE*)* A bromo-seltzer.

COUNTESS Bromo-seltzer? Qu'-est-que c'est que ca?

NANCY It will settle your—superfluity. Flora, did he tell you the lady's name?

COUNTESS *(Indignant)* Unfortunately, Nancy, he's not that drunk.

MIRIAM *(As* SADIE *exits,* R.*)* And another drink for Mr. Winston!

COUNTESS No, Miriam. He wouldn't tell me her name, because she's a married woman. Buck is very proletarian. He just said *she* was a natural blonde.

NANCY That ought to narrow down the field.

COUNTESS He said she was pretty as a painted wagon.

MIRIAM Oh, you're a pretty damned colorful Calliope yourself. Snap out of it, Flora. You know, you're going to forgive him.

COUNTESS *(Firmly)* I'd forgive unfaithfulness, but not base ingratitude. I rescued him from those prairies. I married him. What thanks do I get? *(Wailing)* He says he'll be a cockeyed coyote if he'll herd an old beef like me back to the coast!

NANCY Let this be your lesson. Don't let your next husband become financially independent of you.

COUNTESS Now, don't lecture me, Nancy. Every time I marry I learn something. This has taught me once and for all—you can't expect *noblesse oblige* from a cowboy—*(Sitting up)* Ohhh, my eyes! They're full of mascara.

NANCY *(Helping her off couch. To* MIRIAM*)* We've got to get her home. I'll get Buck and meet us in the lobby. We're headin' for the last round-up!

　　*(*NANCY *exits* R.*)*

COUNTESS No. There's a telephone in there. And I'm going to call up Mr. Zanuck.

MIRIAM Now, Flora, what can he do?

COUNTESS I just want to remind him he can't make a picture with Buck until I say so.

MIRIAM   Why not?

COUNTESS   I own Buck's horse!

>   (MIRIAM *gives a cowboy yell, slaps* COUNTESS *on back.*
>   *They exit to Ladies' Room as* SADIE, *with a bromo-*
>   *seltzer enters* R., *followed by* CIGARETTES)

CIGARETTES   What's it all about?

SADIE *(Picks up* COUNTESS' *shoes, as she crosses* L.)   One gets you ten—some man.

CIGARETTES   Bet he isn't worth it.

SADIE   You can always collect on that one. *(Exits* L., *as re-enter,* L., DOWAGER *and* DEBUTANTE)

DOWAGER   —Laughing and joking with those boys like that!

DEBUTANTE   Yes, Mother.

DOWAGER   What can they think of you?

DEBUTANTE   Yes, Mother.

DOWAGER   And don't think I didn't overhear that Princeton boy call me an old drizzle-puss, either! *(Exits* R.)

SADIE *(Enters,* L., *to* CIGARETTES)   She wants gin in her bromo-seltzer.

>   (*Enter* MARY R. *and* MIRIAM L.)

MIRIAM *(Protesting)*   Crystal's not in there. I don't think she's in the joint.

MARY   She's coming. I know it.

MIRIAM   So what are you going to do when you find her?

>   (SADIE *takes* MARY'S *wrap)*

MARY   I don't know. But I've got to find her tonight. Buck's going to Hollywood in the morning.

MIRIAM   Say, why don't you settle this matter with Stephen?

MARY   I have no proof, I tell you! But if Buck is as drunk as you say, he'll give away something.

MIRIAM   Listen, he's been trying all night to give Flora away to the doorman. Got a twenty-dollar bill?

MARY   Yes.

MIRIAM   That'll get Buck locked in the men's room till we need him. *(Exits,* R., *with* MARY, *as enter,* L., *the two society women. They cross the stage)*

1ST WOMAN   Not three pounds?

2ND WOMAN   Three pounds!

1ST WOMAN How divine! Aren't you ecstatic?

2ND WOMAN Yes, but it's the moral satisfaction. Just bananas and milk for one whole week! That called for enormous character! *(They exit, R.)*

CIGARETTES *(To* SADIE*)* Comes the Revolution, she'll diet plenty.

> *(Enter* PEGGY *and* EDITH, R. *They powder, at mirror, R.)*

PEGGY I wish I hadn't come.

EDITH Well, your husband didn't want you to.

PEGGY *(Goes for her wrap)* Flora was disgusting!

EDITH But it was funny. Even the kettle drummer was laughing.

> *(*SADIE *gives* EDITH *and* PEGGY *their wraps)*

EDITH My dear, who could stand the life we lead without a sense of humor? But Flora is a fool. Always remember, Peggy, it's matrimonial suicide to be jealous when you have a really good reason.

PEGGY Edith, don't you ever get tired of giving advice?

EDITH Listen, Peggy, I'm the only happy woman you know. Why? I don't ask Phelps or any man to understand me. How could he? I'm a woman. *(Pulls down her corset)* And I don't try to understand them. They're just animals. Who am I to quarrel with the way God made them? I've got security. And I say: "What the hell?" And let nature take its course—it's going to, anyway. *(They exit, R., as enter the* 2 GIRLS, L.*)*

2ND GIRL *(Powdering at mirror, L.)* —So there we were on Sattiday night and it's Atlantic City. And he says: "I gotta go home tomorrow, baby!" And I says: *(Pulls up her stockings)* "Why dja got to?" And he says: "My wife always expects me home on Easter Sunday." So I says: "What's she expect ya to do? Lay an egg?"

1ST GIRL They got no sentiment.

> *(Enter, R., a girl, in distress. The shoulder strap of her very low décolletage has broken)*

GIRL IN DISTRESS *(To Sadie)* Have you got a safety pin? I was never so embarrassed!

(SADIE *gets pin*)

2ND GIRL *(Crossing, R.)* So I told him, "I had a great career until you made me give up the stage, you lunkhead. For what? A couple of cheesy diamond bracelets? A lousy car, which every time it breaks down you got to have the parts shipped over from Italy." *(Girls exit)*

GIRL IN DISTRESS *(Clutching right breast)* It practically popped out into the soup. So my escort says, "Don't look now, you've just dropped something!" If only it had been the left one. It's so much better.

> *(Enter* CRYSTAL *and* SYLVIA, R. *They move to check their wraps with* SADIE*)*

SADIE Just a minute, please. *(They go to mirror, L.)*

SYLVIA Stephen is in a mood.

CRYSTAL He can take it and like it.

GIRL IN DISTRESS *(To Sadie)* Does it show now?

SADIE Not what it did before, miss.

GIRL IN DISTRESS Thank you. *(She exits, R.* SADIE *takes* CRYSTAL'S *and* SYLVIA'S *wraps)*

CRYSTAL Is my mouth on straight?

SYLVIA Crystal, you didn't come here to see somebody, did you?

CRYSTAL Oh, Sylvia, can't you lay off that for a minute? *(Enter* MARY *and* MIRIAM, L.*)*

MARY *(Moving forward resolutely)* Mrs. Haines, this is a great pleasure!

CRYSTAL *(Turning)* I beg your pardon?

MARY Such a lovely party! I was afraid you weren't coming. *(Introducing* CRYSTAL *and* MIRIAM *and* SYLVIA*)* Mrs. Fowler, Mrs. Haines, Mrs. Fowler, Mrs. Fowler.

MIRIAM *(Graciously)* Chawmed. Chawmed.

SYLVIA *(Bridling)* This is absurd.

MARY Modern life is complicated. When you came in I was just telling Miriam—

CRYSTAL Oh, come along, Sylvia. The lady is tight.

SYLVIA Mary, when did you begin drinking?

MARY *(To Crystal)* Early in the evening, with Mr. Winston. You *know* Mr. Winston, don't you?

CRYSTAL *(At door)* I'm afraid I don't.

SYLVIA Of course you do, Crystal. I introduced you to him. Don't you remember?

CRYSTAL Oh, yes, at a cocktail party.

MARY Well, he's in the lobby now, waiting for someone, Mrs. Haines, and drunker than you can possibly imagine. You'd find him very difficult to handle, in front of Stephen.
> (CRYSTAL *suddenly changes her mind about going into lobby, moves toward washroom)*

SYLVIA Crystal, where are you going?

CRYSTAL I won't stand here and listen to drivel!

MARY I wouldn't go in there, either, Mrs. Haines. Buck's wife's in there now, having hysterics. She's found out that Buck has been deceiving her.

CRYSTAL Really! What has that to do with me?

MARY A good deal, I'm afraid. You seem to be the woman.

SYLVIA *(Delighted)* Why, Crystal!—*Are* you?

CRYSTAL If he used my name, it's a lie! He's just the cheap sort—

MARY Tomorrow it will be common gossip. I don't think Stephen's going to like it.

SYLVIA Oh, Crystal, he's going to loathe it! But my psychoanalyst is going to adore it.

CRYSTAL *(Going to her)* What are you trying to do? Pin something on me, in front of witnesses?

SYLVIA Whatever she's driving at, Crystal—*(Pointing to* MIRIAM) that little tramp put her up to it!

CRYSTAL *(To* SYLVIA) Keep out of this!

MIRIAM Yeah, check it, Sylvia, we're minor league this evening.

CRYSTAL All right, Mrs. Haines, you've been listening to the ravings of a conceited fool. What did he tell you?

MARY *(Playing for time, or inspiration)* Really, Mrs. Haines, this is very embarrassing.

CRYSTAL *(Brazening it out)* Yes, Mrs. Haines, isn't it? Exactly what do you think you know about me?

MARY Everything! *(A pause.* CRYSTAL *laughs)*

CRYSTAL Then why are you standing here talking to me?

You ought to be outside spilling it to Stephen. You're bluffing. Come along, Sylvia!

MARY *(Also moving to door.* CRYSTAL *stops)* That's very good advice. I will tell Stephen.

CRYSTAL Oh, he wouldn't believe you.

SYLVIA Oh, you can't tell, Crystal! He's terribly fond of Mary.

CRYSTAL Now get this straight, Mrs. Haines. You handed me your husband on a silver platter. *(Enter* NANCY, L.) But I'm not returning the compliment. I like what I've got and I'm going to keep it. I can't be stampeded by gossip. What you believe and what Stephen believes will cut no ice in a divorce court. You need proof and you haven't got it. When Mr. Winston comes to his senses, he'll apologize. And Stephen will have no choice but to accept my explanations. Now that's that! Good night!

MARY *(Desperately)* I hope Mrs. Winston will accept your explanations.

CRYSTAL What have I got to explain to her?

MARY *(With a conviction she does not feel)* What about the apartment?

CRYSTAL What apartment?

MARY You know as well as I do.

CRYSTAL Oh, stop trying to put two and two together—

MARY Oh, Mrs. Winston did that. She had you watched— she's seen you both.

CRYSTAL *(Defiantly)* Seen us both? Doing what?

MARY Going in, and coming out!

CRYSTAL Going in and coming out of *where?* *(A pause)* You're lying!

SYLVIA *(Warningly)* I wouldn't be so sure, Crystal!

MIRIAM Sounds like the McCoy to me, Crystal.

CRYSTAL Shut up!

SYLVIA Oh, Crystal, why didn't you confide in me?
(CRYSTAL turns to door again, triumphant)

MARY *(Dismayed)* Sylvia, didn't she?

SYLVIA Certainly *not!* (CRYSTAL *smiles, very pleased with herself)* She's the cat that walks alone. *(Goes to* CRYSTAL)

Why, Crystal, I could have told you some place *much safer* than the Gothic Apartments.

CRYSTAL *(Exploding)* Why, you big, loud-mouthed idiot!

SYLVIA How dare you!

CRYSTAL I'd like to slap your stupid face.

SYLVIA *(Backing up)* How dare you! Oh, Mary, how dare she?

MIRIAM Oh, I've got a job to do on Flora. *(She pats SYLVIA affectionately)* Kiss you when I get back, Sylvia. *(Exits L.)*

NANCY And I'll explain the facts of life to Stephen. *(NANCY exits R.)*

CRYSTAL *(To MARY, fiercely)* You're trying to break up my marriage!

SYLVIA The way you did hers, you floosie!

CRYSTAL *(Nasty)* Well, maybe you're welcome to my—leftovers.

MARY *(Calmly)* I'll take them, thank you.

SYLVIA Why, Mary, haven't you any *pride?*

MARY That's right. No, no pride; that's a luxury a woman in love can't afford.

    (Enter COUNTESS and MIRIAM, L. MIRIAM goes to SADIE, gets COUNTESS' and her own wraps)

COUNTESS *(Rushing for CRYSTAL)* Oh, you—you horse thief!

MARY *(Stopping her)* Flora, it's really too bad—

COUNTESS *(To CRYSTAL)* You—you painted wagon!

CRYSTAL So you're determined to have a scandal, Mrs. Haines.

COUNTESS I'm the one who's going to have the scandal. Why, Mary, she's no more a blonde naturelle than I am. What's the creature's name? Miriam forgot to tell me.

MARY Mrs. Stephen Haines, currently.

COUNTESS Is that the thing Stephen left you for? Well, cherie, all I can say is, you're an idiot! I hope I never live to see the day when an obvious piece like that conquers *me* on the champs d'amour! *(She exits R. followed by MIRIAM)*

CRYSTAL *(To* MARY*)* You were lying. That old fool didn't know about us.

    *(*SADIE *gives* MARY *her wrap)*

MARY I'm afraid she didn't. *(Enter* NANCY R.*)*

NANCY There's a gentleman called Mr. Haines. He says he's been waiting a long time for his wife—

    *(*CRYSTAL *moves to get her wrap)*

MARY *(Stepping between her and* SADIE*) I* am coming.

    (Exit NANCY *quickly)*

SYLVIA Mary, what a dirty female trick you played!

CRYSTAL Yes! From the great, noble little woman! You're just a cat, like all the rest of us!

MARY Well, I've had two years to sharpen my claws. *(Waves her hand gaily to* SYLVIA*)* Jungle Red, Sylvia! Good night, ladies!

    (Exits leaving CRYSTAL *and* SYLVIA *alone. As curtain falls* CRYSTAL *raises her bag to belt* SYLVIA *and* SYLVIA *backs fearfully away)*

OR

CURTAIN FALLS—*Then rises to find* CRYSTAL *and* SYLVIA *pulling hair.*

Play
with a Tiger

BY DORIS LESSING

CHARACTERS

ANNA FREEMAN   A woman of thirty-five, or so, who earns her living on the artistic fringes

DAVE MILLER   An American, about thirty-three, who is rootless on principle

MARY JACKSON   About ten years older than Anna: a widow with a grown-up son

TOM LATTIMER   Who is on the point of taking a job as business manager of a woman's magazine. About thirty-five, a middle-class Englishman

HARRY PAYNE   Fifty-ish. A journalist

JANET STEVENS   In her early twenties, the daughter of an insurance agent—American

Author's Notes
on Directing This Play

When I wrote *Play with a Tiger* in 1958 I set myself an artistic problem which resulted from my decision that naturalism, or, if you like, realism, is the greatest enemy of the theatre; and that I never wanted to write a naturalistic play again.

Now this play is about the rootless, declassed people who live in bed-sitting-rooms or small flats or the cheaper hotel rooms, and such people are usually presented on the stage in a detailed squalor of realism which to my mind distracts attention from what is interesting about them.

I wrote *Play with a Tiger* with an apparently conventional opening designed to make the audience expect a naturalistic play so that when the walls vanished towards the end of Act I they would be surprised (and I hope pleasantly shocked) to find they were not going to see this kind of play at all.

But there had to be a bridge between the opening of the play, and the long section where Anna and Dave are alone on the stage, and this bridge is one of style. This is why Anna's room is tall, bare, formal; why it has practically no furniture, save for the bed and the small clutter around it; and why there are no soft chairs or settees where the actors might lounge or sprawl. This stark set forces a certain formality of movement, stance and confrontation so that even when Dave and Anna are not alone on the stage creating their private world, there is a simplicity of style which links the two moods of the play together.

It is my intention that when the curtain comes down at the end, the audience will think: Of course! In this play no one lit cigarettes, drank tea or coffee, read newspapers, squirted soda into Scotch, or indulged in little bits of "business" which indicated "character." They will realize, I hope, that they have been seeing a play which relies upon its style and its language for its effect.

Act One

The action of this play takes place in ANNA FREEMAN'S
room on the first floor of MARY JACKSON'S house on a street
in London with heavy traffic. ANNA has lived here for some
years. There is another room, behind this one, used by her
son, now at school; but ANNA sleeps and lives in this room.
It is very large and looks formal because it is underfur-
nished. There are double doors at left-back. When they are
open the landing can be seen, and part of the stairway leading up. The house was originally built for rich people and
still shows signs of it. The landing and stairs are spacious
and carpeted in dark red; the banisters are elegant and
painted white. The upper part of the doors are of glass, and
therefore the doorway has a dark red curtain, usually drawn
back. The room is painted white, walls and ceilings. There is
a low wide divan, covered in rough black material, in the
right back corner; a window, with dark red curtains, in the
right wall; a large, round, ornate mirror, on the left wall; a
low shelf of books under the window. The floor is painted
black and has in the centre of it a round crimson carpet.
There are two stiff-looking chairs on either side of the mirror,
of dark wood, and seated in dark red. The life of the room
is concentrated around the divan. A low table by its head has
a telephone, and is loaded with books and papers and a small
reading light. At the foot of the divan is another low table,
with a typewriter, at which ANNA works by kneeling, or
squatting, on the divan. This table has another reading light,
and a record player. Around the divan is a surf of books,
magazines, newspapers, records, cushions. There is a built-in
cupboard, hardly noticeable until opened, in the right wall.
Two paraffin heaters, of the cheap black cylindrical kind, are
both lit. It is winter. The year is 1958. At the opening of the
play the time is about nine in the evening, at its close it is
four in the morning.

(ANNA *is standing at the window, which is open at the top, her back to the room. She is wearing slacks and a sweater: these are pretty, even fashionable; the reason for the trousers is that it is hard to play Act Two in a skirt.*

TOM *is standing behind* ANNA, *waiting, extremely exasperated. This scene between them has been going on for some time. They are both tense, irritated, miserable.*

TOM'S *sarcasm and pomposity is his way of protecting himself from his hurt at how he has been treated.*

ANNA'S *apparent casualness is how she wards off a hysteria that is only just under control. She is guilty about* TOM, *unhappy about* DAVE—*and this tension in her underlies everything she says or does until that moment towards the end of Act One when* DAVE, *because of his moral ascendancy over her, forces her to relax and smile.*

A moment's silence. Then a scream and a roar of traffic, which sounds as if it is almost in the room. TOM *loses patience, goes past* ANNA *to window, slams it shut, loudly.)*

TOM Now say: "I could repeat every word you've said."
ANNA *(In quotes)* I've scarcely seen you during the last two weeks. You always have some excuse. Mary answers the telephone and says you are out. I was under the impression we were going to be married. If I'm wrong please correct me. I simply cannot account for the change in your attitude . . . how's that?

(TOM *looks at her, gives her a small sardonic bow, goes past her to a chair which is set so he is facing half away from her. He sits in it in a pose which he has clearly been occupying previously—for* ANNA *looks at him, equally sardonic. Since the chair is hard and upright, not designed for comfort, he is almost lying in a straight line from his crossed ankles to his chin, which is upturned because he is looking with weary patience at the ceiling. His fingertips are held lightly together.*

ANNA, *having registered the fact that his pose is*

*designed to annoy, goes back to the window and
stands looking down)*

ANNA That man is still down there. Do you know, he comes
every night and just stands there, hour after hour after
hour. And it's so cold.

TOM Yes, it is ... Anna, I was under the impression that my
attraction for you, such as it is, of course, was that I'm
rather more reliable, more responsible? than the usual run
of your friends?

ANNA Do you realize that man hasn't so much as moved a
muscle since he arrived at six? There he stands, gazing up
at that window. And the top half of that house is a brothel.
He must have seen one of the girls in the street and fallen
in love. Imagine it, I've been living here all these years and
I never knew that house was a brothel. There are four
Lesbians living together, and that poor sap's in love with
one of them. Well, isn't it frightening?

TOM When you walked into my flat that evening—if I may
remind you of it—you said you were in search of a nice
solid shoulder to weep on. You said you couldn't stand
another minute of living like this. Well?

ANNA I asked the policeman at the corner. Why yes, miss,
he said, all fatherly and protective, they've been there for
years and years. But don't you worry your pretty little head
about a thing, we have our eyes on them all the time.

TOM I suppose what all this amounts to is that your fascinating American is around again.

ANNA I told you, no. I haven't seen Dave for weeks. Perhaps I should go down and tell that poor moon-struck idiot
—look, you poor sap, all you've got to do is to go upstairs
with fifty shillings in your hand and your goddess is yours?

TOM And while you're about it, you could take him off for
a nice cup of tea, listen to his troubles and tell him yours.

ANNA Yes I could. Why not?

TOM You're going to go on like this I suppose until the next
time Dave or some similarly fascinating character plays
you up and you decide that good old Tom will do for a
month or so?

ANNA   Tom, it's nine-fifteen. You're expected at the Jeffries at nine-thirty.

TOM   I did accept for you too.

ANNA   Yes you did, and you didn't even ask me first.

TOM   I see.

ANNA   No, you don't see. Tom, until two weeks ago you said you couldn't stand either of the Jeffries, you said, quote, they were boring, phoney and stupid. But now he's going to be your boss it's different?

TOM   No, they're still boring, phoney and stupid, but he is going to be my boss.

ANNA   You said if you took Jeffries' job, you'd be in the rat-race, stuck in the rut, and bound hand and foot to the grindstone.

TOM   I finally took that job because we were going to be married—so I thought.

ANNA   But now we're not going to be married you'll turn down the job? *(As he does not reply)* I thought not. So don't use me to justify yourself.

TOM   You really do rub things in, Anna. All right then. For a number of years I've been seeing myself as a sort of a rolling stone, a fascinating free-lance, a man of infinite possibilities. It turns out that I'm just another good middle-class citizen after all—I'm comfort-loving, conventionally unconventional, I'm not even the Don Juan I thought I was. It turns out that I'm everything I dislike most. I owe this salutary discovery to you, Anna. Thank you very much.

ANNA   Oh, not at all.

TOM   *(He now gets up from the chair, and faces her, attacking hard)* Oh my God, you stupid little romantic. Yes, that's what you are, and a prig into the bargain. Very pleased with yourself because you won't soil your hands. Writing a little review here, a little article there, an odd poem or two, a reflection on the aspect of a sidelight on the backwash of some bloody movement or other—reading tuppenny-halfpenny novels for publishers, Mr. Bloody Black's new book is or is not an advance on his last. Well, Anna, is it really worth it?

ANNA Yes it is. I'm free to live as I like. You won't be, ever again.

TOM And worrying all the time how you're going to find the money for what your kid wants. Do you think he's going to thank you for living like this?

ANNA: That's right. Always stick the knife in, as hard as you can, into a person's weakest spot.

TOM An art you are not exactly a stranger to? You live here, hand to mouth, never knowing what's going to happen next, surrounding yourself with bums and neurotics and failures. As far as you're concerned anyone who has succeeded at anything at all is corrupt. *(She says nothing)* Nothing to say, Anna? That's not like you.

ANNA I was thinking, not for the first time, unfortunately, how sad it is that the exquisite understanding and intimacy of the bed doesn't last into the cold light of day.

TOM So that's all we had in common. Thank you, Anna, you've now defined me.

ANNA All right, all right, all right. I'm sorry. What else can I say—I'm sorry.

> *(There is a knock on the door)*

ANNA Come in.

TOM Oh my God, Mary.

MARY *(Outside the door)* Pussy, pussy, pussy.

> *(A knock on the door)*

ANNA Come in.

TOM She's getting very deaf, isn't she?

ANNA She doesn't know it. *(As the door opens)* For the Lord's sake don't say ... *(she imitates him)* ... I was under the impression we had said come in, if I'm wrong please correct me.

TOM Just because you've decided to give me the boot, there's no need to knock me down and start jumping on me.

> *(MARY comes in, backwards, shutting the door to keep the cat out)*

MARY No pussy, you stay there. Anna doesn't really like you, although she pretends she does. *(To ANNA)* That cat is more like a dog, really, he comes when I call. And he waits for me outside a door. *(Peeping around the edge of the door)* No, puss, wait. I won't be a minute. *(To* ANNA*)* I don't know why I bothered to christen that cat Methuselah, it never gets called anything but puss. *(Sprightly with an exaggerated sigh)* Really, I'm getting quite an old maid, fussing over a cat . . . If you can call a widow with a grown up son an old maid, but who'd have believed I'd have come to fussing over a cat. *(Seeing* TOM*)* Oh, I didn't know you were here.

TOM Didn't you see me? I said hullo.

MARY Sometimes I think I'm getting a bit deaf. Well, what a surprise. You're quite a stranger, aren't you?

TOM Hardly a stranger, I should have said.

MARY Dropped in for old times' sake. *(*TOM *is annoyed.* MARY *says to* ANNA*)* I thought we might go out to the pub. I'm sick of sitting and brooding. *(As* ANNA *does not respond —quick and defensive)* Oh I see, you and Tom are going out, two's company and three's none.

ANNA Tom's going to the Jeffries.

MARY *(Derisive)* Not the Jeffries—you must be hard up for somewhere to go.

ANNA And I think I'll stay and work.

TOM Anna is too good for the Jeffries.

MARY Who isn't?

> *(*ANNA *has gone back to the window, is looking down into the street)*

TOM *(Angrily)* Perhaps you'd like to come with me, since Anna won't.

MARY *(Half aggressive, half coy)* You and me going out together—that'd be a change. Oh, I see, you're joking. *(Genuinely)* Besides, they really are so awful.

TOM Better than going to the pub with Methuselah, perhaps?

MARY *(With spirit)* No, I prefer Methuselah. You don't want to bore yourself at the Jeffries. Stay and have some coffee with us.

ANNA *(Her back still turned)* It's the Royal Command.

MARY   Oh. You mean you've taken the job after all? I told Anna you would, months ago. There, Anna, I told you he would. Anna said when it actually came to the point, you'd never bring yourself to do it.

TOM   I like the idea of you and Anna laying bets as to whether the forces of good or evil would claim my soul.

MARY   Well, I mean, that's what it amounts to, doesn't it? But I always said Anna was wrong about you. Didn't I, Anna? Anna always does this. *(Awkwardly)* I mean, it's not the first time, I mean to say. And I've always been right. Ah, well, as Anna says, don't you, Anna, if a man marries, he marries a woman, but if a woman marries, she marries a way of life.

TOM   Strange, but as it happens I too have been the lucky recipient of that little aphorism.

MARY   Well, you were bound to be, weren't you? *(She sees* TOM *is furious and stops)* Harry telephoned you, Anna.

ANNA   What for?

MARY   Well, I suppose now you're free he thinks he'll have another try.

TOM   May I ask—how did he know Anna was free. After all, I didn't.

MARY   Oh don't be silly. I mean, you and Anna might not have known, but it was quite obvious to everyone else . . . well, I met Harry in the street some days ago, and he said . . .

TOM   I see.

MARY   Well, there's no need to be so stuffy about it, Tom— *(A bell rings downstairs)*

MARY   Was that the bell? Are you expecting someone, Anna?

TOM   Of course she's expecting someone.

ANNA   No.

MARY   *(Who hasn't heard)*   Who are you expecting?

ANNA   Nobody.

MARY   Well, I'll go for you, I have to go down anyway. Are you in or out, Anna?

ANNA   I'm out.

MARY It's often difficult to say, whether you are in or out, because after all, one never knows who it might be.

ANNA *(Patiently)* Mary, I really don't mind answering my bell you know.

MARY *(Hastily going to the door)* Sometimes I'm running up and down the stairs half the day, answering Anna's bell. *(As she goes out and shuts the door)* Pussy, pussy, where are you, puss, puss, puss.

TOM She's deteriorating fast, isn't she? *(ANNA patiently says nothing)* That's what you're going to be like in ten years' time if you're not careful.

ANNA I'd rather be like Mary in ten years' time than what you're going to be like when you're all settled down and respectable.

TOM A self-pitying old bore.

ANNA She is also a kind warm-hearted woman with endless time for people in trouble . . . Tom, you're late, the boss waits, and you can't afford to offend him.

TOM I remember Mary, and not so long ago either—she was quite a dish, wasn't she? If I were you I'd be scared stiff.

ANNA Sometimes I am scared stiff. *(Seriously)* Tom, her son's getting married next week.

TOM Oh, so that's it.

ANNA No, that's not it. She's very pleased he's getting married. And she's given them half the money she's saved—not that there's much of it. You surely must see it's going to make quite a difference to her, her son getting married?

TOM Well, he was bound to get married some time.

ANNA Yes he was bound to get married, time marches on, every dog must have its day, one generation makes way for another, today's kittens are tomorrow's cats, life's like that.

TOM I don't know why it is, most people think I'm quite a harmless sort of man. After ten minutes with you I feel I ought to crawl into the nearest worm-hole and die.

ANNA We're just conforming to the well-known rule that when an affair ends, the amount of violence and unpleasantness is in direct ratio to its heat.

(*Loud laughter and voices outside*—HARRY *and* MARY)

TOM   I thought you said you were out. Mary really is quite impossible.

ANNA   It's Harry who's impossible. He always takes it for granted one doesn't mean him.

TOM   (*Angry*) And perhaps one doesn't.

ANNA   Perhaps one doesn't.

TOM   Anna! Do let's try and be a bit more . . .

ANNA   Civilized? Is that the word you're looking for?
      (HARRY *and* MARY *come in*)

HARRY   (*As he kisses* ANNA)   Civilized, she says. There's our Anna. I knew I'd come in and she'd be saying civilized. (*Coolly, to* TOM) Oh, hullo.

TOM   (*Coolly*)   Well, Harry.

MARY   (*Who has been flirted by* HARRY *into an over-responsive state*)   Oh, Harry, you are funny sometimes. (*She laughs*) It's not what you say, when you come to think of it, it's the way you say it.

HARRY   Surely, it's what I say as well?

ANNA   Harry, I'm not in. I told Mary. I don't want to see anybody.

HARRY   Don't be silly, darling, of course you do. You don't want to see anybody, but you want to see me.

TOM   (*Huffy*)   Anna and I were talking.

HARRY   Of course you are, you clots. And it's high time you stopped. Look at you both. And now we should all have a drink.

TOM   Oh damn. You and Mary go and have a drink.

HARRY   That's not the way at all. Anna will come to the pub with me and weep on my shoulder, and Tom will stay and weep on Mary's.

TOM   (*Rallying into his smooth sarcasm*)   Harry, I yield to no one in my admiration of your tact but I really must say . . .

HARRY   Don't be silly. I got a clear picture from Mary here, of you and Anna, snarling and snapping on the verge of tears—it doesn't do at all. When a thing's finished it's finished. I know, from my sins I'm an expert.

TOM Forgive me if I make an over-obvious point, but this really isn't one of the delightful little affairs you specialize in.

HARRY Of course it was. You two really aren't in a position to judge. Now if you weren't Tom and Anna, you'd take one look at yourselves and laugh your heads off at the idea of your getting married.

ANNA *(She goes to the window and looks down)* Harry, come and see me next week and I'll probably laugh my head off.

HARRY Next week's no good at all. You won't need me then, you'll have recovered.

TOM *(Immensely sarcastic)* Surely, Harry, if Anna asks you to leave her flat, the least you can do is to . . .
      (ANNA suddenly giggles)

HARRY There, you see? How could you possibly marry such a pompous idiot, Anna. *(To* TOM *affectionately)* Anna can't possibly marry such an idiot, Tom. Anna doesn't like well-ordered citizens, like you, anyway.

MARY I don't know how you can say well-ordered. He was just another lame duck until now.

HARRY But he's not a lame duck any more. He's going to work for Jeffries, and he'll be administering to the spiritual needs of the women of the nation through the "Ladies Own."

TOM I'm only going to be on the business side. I won't be responsible for the rubbish they—
      (He stops, annoyed with himself. HARRY *and* MARY *laugh at him)*

HARRY There you are, he's a solid respectable citizen already.

TOM *(To* HARRY*)* It's not any worse than the rag you work for is it?

HARRY *(Reacts to* TOM *with a grimace that says touche! and turns to* ANNA*)* When are you going to get some comfortable furniture into this room?

ANNA *(Irritated almost to tears)* Oh sit on the floor, go away, stop nagging.

HARRY Don't be so touchy. The point I'm trying to make is, Tom'd never put up with a woman like you, he's going to have a house with every modern convenience and everything just so . . . Anna, what've you done with Dave?

ANNA I haven't seen him for weeks.

HARRY That's silly, isn't it now?

ANNA No.

HARRY Now I'm going to give you a lot of good advice, Anna and . . .

TOM Fascinating, isn't it? Harry giving people advice.

MARY Harry may not know how to get his own life into order, but actually he's rather good at other people.

HARRY What do you mean, my life is in perfect order.

TOM Indeed? May I ask how your wife is?

HARRY *(In a much used formula)* Helen is wonderful, delightful, she is very happy and she loves me dearly.

TOM *(With a sneer)* How nice.

HARRY Yes, it is. And that's what I'm going to explain to you, Anna. Look at Helen. She's like you, she likes interesting weak men like me, and . . .

TOM Weak is not the word I'd have chosen, I must say.

MARY Surely not weak, Harry?

ANNA Weak is new, Harry. Since when, weak?

HARRY I'll explain. It came to me in a flash, one night when I was driving home very late—it was dawn, to be precise, you see, weak men like me . . .

ANNA *(Suddenly serious)* Harry, I'm not in the mood.

HARRY Of course you are. We are always in the mood to talk about ourselves. I'm talking about you, Anna. You're like Helen. Now what does Helen say? She says, she doesn't mind who I have affairs with provided they are women she'd like herself.

TOM Charming.

MARY But Harry, Helen's got to say something . . . well, I mean to say.

ANNA I simply can't stand your damned alibis.

HARRY Tom must have been bad for you, Anna, if you're going to get all pompous. Helen and I . . .

ANNA *(Snapping)* Harry, you forget I know Helen very well.

HARRY *(Not realizing her mood)* Of course you do. And so do I. And you ought to take on Dave the way Helen's taken me on . . .

ANNA Harry, go away.

HARRY *(Still blithe)* No, Anna, I've been thinking. You've got to marry Dave. He needs you. *(MARY makes a warning gesture at HARRY, indicating ANNA) (To MARY)* Don't be silly, darling. *(To ANNA again)* Helen knows I'll always come back to her. Anna, Dave needs you. Have a heart. What'll Dave do?

ANNA *(Snapping into hysterical resentment)* I'll tell you what he'll do. He'll do what you did. You married Helen who was very much in love with you. When she had turned into just another boring housewife and mother you began philandering. She had no alternative but to stay put.

HARRY Anna, Anna, Anna!

ANNA Oh shut up. I know Helen, I know exactly what sort of hell she's had with you.

HARRY Tom, you really have been bad for Anna, you've made her all bitchy.

ANNA Dave will marry some girl who's in love with him. Oh, he'll fight every inch of the way, of course. Then there'll be children and he'll be free to do as he likes. He'll have a succession of girls, and in between each one he'll go back and weep on his wife's shoulder because of his unfortunately weak character. Weak like hell. She'll forgive him all right. He'll even use her compliance as an additional attraction for the little girls, just as you do. My wife understands me, he'll say, with a sloppy look on his wife. She knows what I'm like. She'll always be there to take me back. God almighty, what a man.

HARRY Anna, you little bitch.

ANNA That's right. But there's just one thing, Dave shouldn't have picked on me. I'm economically independent. I have no urge for security so I don't have to sell myself out. And I have a child already, so there's no way of making me helpless, is there, dear weak, helpless Harry?

HARRY Mary, you should have told me Anna was in such a bitchy mood and I wouldn't have come up.

MARY But I did tell you, and you said, 'Well, Anna won't be bitchy with me.'

    (The door bell, downstairs)

MARY I'll go.

ANNA Mary, I'm out.

MARY Well, don't blame me for Harry, he insisted. *(As she goes out)* Pussy, pussy, puss, puss.

HARRY I can't think what Mary would do if Anna did get married.

TOM *(Spitefully)* They are rather like an old married couple, aren't they?

    (ANNA pulls down the window with a crash and turns her back on them)

HARRY But so nice to drop in on for aid and comfort when in trouble. *(To ANNA's back)* Anna, I'm in trouble.

ANNA Don't worry, you'll be in love with someone else in a few weeks.

HARRY *(Humorous but serious)* But I won't. This girl, my poppet, she's getting married. *(As ANNA shrugs)* For God's sake woman, shut the window, it's freezing. *(ANNA shuts it, but remains looking down)* She met some swine at a party—actually he's very nice. A handsome young swine— he really is nice. She's marrying him—actually, I advised her to. Anna!

ANNA Did you expect her to hang round for the rest of her life in a state of single blessedness because you didn't want to break up your happy home with Helen? *(She turns, sees his face, which is genuinely miserable)* Oh all right. I'm sorry. I'm very sorry. *(She puts her arms around him)*

HARRY There's my Anna. *(To TOM)* I'm sure you've never seen this side of her, but she is a sweet girl, at heart.

TOM Well, now you've gained your little meed of sympathy

from Anna, perhaps I may be permitted to say a word or two?

HARRY   No. You two should just kiss and say goodbye and stop tormenting each other.

TOM   Anna, I know that what goes on in the street is a hundred times more interesting than I am, but . . .

HARRY   Of course it is, she's waiting for Dave.

ANNA   I'm not waiting for Dave.
(She comes away from the window. Sits on the bed, her head in her hands)

TOM   I want to talk to Anna.

MARY *(From downstairs)*   Puss, puss, puss, puss.

TOM *(Mocking her)*   Puss, puss, puss, puss.

HARRY   Mary should get married. Anna, you should make Mary get married before it's too late.

TOM   Before it's too late!

ANNA   Mary could marry if she wanted.

TOM *(Derisively)*   Then why doesn't she?

ANNA   Strange as it might seem to you, she doesn't want to get married just for the sake of getting married.

HARRY   Yes, but that's all very well, Anna. It's all right for you—you're such a self-contained little thing. But not for Mary. You should get her married regardless to the first clot who comes along.

ANNA   I—self-contained!

TOM   Yes, it's true—self-contained!

MARY *(From downstairs)*   Pussy, pussy, yes come here, puss, puss, puss, puss.

TOM *(To HARRY)*   She's getting worse. *(As ANNA stiffens up)* Yes, all right, Anna, but it's true. *(To HARRY)* She's man-crazy . . .

HARRY   Oh you silly ass.

TOM   Well she is. She's crazy for a man, wide open, if you so much as smile at her, she responds. And Anna says she doesn't want to marry. Who are you fooling, Anna?

ANNA *(Sweetly)*   Perhaps she prefers to be sex-starved than to marry an idiot. Which is more than can be said about most men.

HARRY Now Anna, don't start. Anna, Tom's a nice man, but he's pompous. *(To* TOM*)* You're a pompous ass, admit it, Tom.

TOM All I said was, Mary's man-crazy.

ANNA *(On the warpath)* Do you know how Tom was living before he started with me?

HARRY Yes, of course. Anna, don't make speeches at us!

TOM Well, how was I living before I started with you?

HARRY Oh, my God.

ANNA What is known as a bachelor's life—Tom's own nice inimitable version of it. He sat in his nice little flat, and round about ten at night, if he felt woman-crazy enough, he rang up one of three girls, all of whom were in love with him.

HARRY Christ knows why.

ANNA Imagine it, the telephone call at bedtime—are you free tonight, Elspeth, Penelope, Jessica? One of them came over, a drink or a cup of coffee, a couple of hours of bed, and then a radio-taxi home.

HARRY Anna!

ANNA Oh from time to time he explained to them that they mustn't think his kind attentions to them meant anything.

HARRY Anna, you're a bore when you get like this.

TOM Yes, you are.

ANNA Then don't call Mary names.

(MARY *comes in*)

MARY *(Suspicious)* You were talking about me?

ANNA No, about me.

MARY Oh I thought it was about me. *(To* ANNA*)* There's a girl wants to see you. She says it's important. She wouldn't give her name.

ANNA *(She is thinking)* I see.

MARY But she's an American girl. It's the wrong time of the year—summer's for Americans.

ANNA An American girl.

MARY One of those nice bright neat clean American girls, how they do it, I don't know, all I know is that you can tell from a hundred yards off they'd rather be seen dead than with their legs or their armpits unshaved, ever so antiseptic, she looked rather sweet really.

HARRY   Tell her to go away and we'll all wait for you. Come on, Tom.

TOM   I'm staying.

HARRY   Come on, Mary, give me a nice cup of coffee.

MARY   It's a long time since you and I had a good gossip.
(HARRY *and* MARY *go out, arm in arm*)

TOM   Well, who is she?

ANNA   I don't know.

TOM   I don't believe you.

ANNA   You never do.
(MARY'S *voice, and the voice of an American girl, outside on the stairs.*
JANET STEVENS *comes in. She is a neat attractive girl of about 22. She is desperately anxious and trying to hide it*)

JANET   Are you Anna Freeman?

ANNA   Yes. And this is Tom Lattimer.

JANET   I am Janet Stevens. (*She has expected* ANNA *to know the name*) Janet Stevens.

ANNA   How do you do?

JANET   Janet Stevens from Philadelphia. (*As* ANNA *still does not react*) I hope you will excuse me for calling on you like this.

ANNA   Not at all.
(JANET *looks at* TOM. ANNA *looks at* TOM. TOM *goes to the window, turns his back*)

JANET   (*Still disbelieving* ANNA) I thought you would know my name.

ANNA   No.

TOM   But she has been expecting you all afternoon.

JANET   (*At sea*) All afternoon?

ANNA   (*Angry*) No, it's not true.

JANET   I don't understand, you were expecting me this afternoon?

ANNA   No. But may I ask how you know me?

JANET   Well, we have a friend in common. Dave Miller.

TOM *(Turning, furious)* You could have said so, couldn't you, Anna?

ANNA But I didn't know.

TOM You didn't know. Well, I'm going. You've behaved disgracefully.

ANNA Very likely. However just regard me as an unfortunate lapse from the straight and narrow on your journey to respectability.

(TOM goes out, slamming the door)

ANNA *(Politely)* That was my—fiancé.

JANET Oh, Dave didn't say you were engaged.

ANNA He didn't know. And besides, I'm not 'engaged' any longer.

(A silence. ANNA looks with enquiry at JANET, who tries to speak and fails)

ANNA Please sit down, Miss Stevens.

(JANET looks around for somewhere to sit, sits on a chair, smiles socially. Being a well brought up young lady, and in a situation she does not understand, she is using her good manners as a last-ditch defence against breaking down.

ANNA *looks at her, waiting)*

JANET It's this way, you see Dave and I . . . *(At ANNA's ironical look she stops)* . . . What a pretty room, I do so love these old English houses, they have such . . .

(ANNA looks at her: do get a move on)

JANET My father gave me a vacation in Europe for passing my college examinations. Yes, even when I was a little girl he used to promise me—if you do well at college I'll give you a vacation in Europe. Well, I've seen France and Italy now, but I really feel most at home in England than anywhere. I do love England. Of course our family was English, way back of course, and I feel that roots are important, don't you?

ANNA Miss Stevens, what did you come to see me for?

JANET Dave always says he thinks women should have careers. I suppose that's why he admires you so much. Though of course, you do wear well. But I say to him, Dave, if you *work* at marriage then it *is* a career . . . sometimes he makes fun because I took domestic science and home care and child care as my subjects in college, but I say to him, Dave, marriage is important, Dave, I believe that marriage and the family is the most rewarding career a woman can have, that's why I took home care as my first subject because I believe a healthy and well-adjusted marriage is the basis for a healthy nation.

ANNA You're making me feel deficient in patriotism.

JANET Oh, Dave said that too . . . *(She almost breaks down, pulls herself together: Fiercely)* You're patronizing me. I don't think you should patronize me.

ANNA Miss Stevens, do let's stop this. Listen to me. I haven't seen Dave for weeks. Is that what you came here to find out?

JANET I know that you are such old friends. He talks about you a great deal.

ANNA I've no doubt he does. *(She waits for* JANET *to go on, then goes on herself)* There's a hoary psychological joke— if I can use the word joke for a situation like this—about the way the betrayed women of the heartless libertine get together to lick their wounds—have you come here to make common cause with me over Dave? Because forgive me for saying so, but I don't think you and I have anything in common but the fact we've both slept with Dave. And that is not enough for the basis of a beautiful friendship.

JANET No! It wasn't that at all, I came because . . . *(She stops)*

ANNA I see. Then you've come because you're pregnant. Well, how far have you got?

JANET Five months.

ANNA I see. And you haven't told him.

JANET I knew if I told him he'd give me money and . . . well I love him. It would be good for him to have some responsibility wouldn't it?

ANNA I see.

JANET Yes, I know how it looks, trapping a man. But when I was pregnant I was so happy, and only afterwards I thought—yes, I know how it looks, trapping a man, but he said he loved me, he said he loved me.

ANNA But why come and tell me? *(As* JANET *doesn't answer)* He's ditched you, is that it?

JANET No! Of course he hasn't. *(Cracking)* I haven't seen him in days. I haven't seen him. Where is he, you've got to tell me where he is. I've got to tell him about the baby.

ANNA But I don't know where he is.

JANET You have to tell me. When he knows about the baby he'll . . . *(As* ANNA *shrugs)* Ah come on now, who do you think you're kidding. Well, I've got his baby, you haven't. You can't do anything about that, can you. I've got his baby, I've got him.

ANNA Very likely

JANET But what can I do? I want to be married. I'm just an ordinary girl and I want to be married, what's wrong with that?

ANNA There's nothing wrong with that. But I haven't seen Dave, and I don't know where he is, and so there's nothing I can do. *(Finally)* And you shouldn't have come to me.

(JANET goes out)

ANNA *(Almost in tears)* Oh Christ. *(Stopping the tears, angrily)* Damn. Damn.

(She goes to window. At once MARY *comes in)*

MARY Well, who was she? *(ANNA turns her back to hide her face from* MARY*)* Was she one of Dave's girls? *(ANNA nods.* MARY *moves so that she can see* ANNA'S *face)* Well, you knew there was one, didn't you? *(ANNA nods)* Well, then? *(ANNA nods)*

ANNA All right, Mary.

(MARY is in a jubilant mood. She has been flirting with HARRY. *Now, seeing* ANNA *is apparently all right, she says what she came in to say)*

MARY Harry and I are going out. There's a place he knows we can get drinks. I told him you wouldn't be interested. *(The telephone starts ringing)* Aren't you going to answer it? *(As* ANNA *shakes her head)* Odd, we've known each other all these years. He's really sweet, Harry. You can say what you like, but it's nice to have a man to talk to for a change—after all, how many men are there you can really talk to? *(The telephone stops)* Anna, what are you in this state for?

ANNA What I can't stand is, the way he makes use of me. Do you know, Mary, all this time he's been letting her know I'm in the background?

MARY Well, you are, aren't you?

ANNA "But Janet, you must understand this doesn't mean anything, because the woman I really love is Anna." He's not even married to me, but he uses me as Harry uses Helen.

MARY *(Not wanting to hear anything against* HARRY *at this moment)* Oh I don't know. After all, perhaps Helen doesn't mind. They've been married so long.

ANNA It really is remarkable how all Dave's young ladies turn up here sooner or later. He talks about me—oh, quite casually, of course, until they go round the bend with frustration and curiosity, and they just have to come up to see what the enemy looks like. Well, I can't be such a bitch as all that, because I didn't say, "My dear Miss Stevens, you're the fifth to pay me a social call in three years."

MARY But you have been engaged to Tom.

ANNA Yes. All right.

MARY It's funny, me and Harry knowing each other for so long and then suddenly . . .

ANNA Mary! the mood Harry's in somebody's going to get hurt.

MARY It's better to get hurt than to live shut up.

ANNA After losing that little poppet of his to matrimony he'll be looking for solace.

MARY *(Offended)* Why don't you concern yourself with Tom? Or with Dave? Harry's not your affair. I'm just going out with him. *(As she goes out)* Nice to have a night out for a change, say what you like.

    (The telephone rings. ANNA *snatches off the receiver, wraps it in a blanket, throws it on the bed)*

ANNA I'm not talking to you, Dave Miller, you can rot first.
(She goes to the record player, puts on Mahalia Jackson's "I'm on my Way," goes to mirror, looks into it. This is a long antagonistic look)

ANNA *(To her reflection)* All right then, I do wear well.
(She goes deliberately to a drawer, takes out a large piece of black cloth, unfolds it, drapes it over mirror)

ANNA *(To the black cloth)* And a fat lot of good that does me.

(She now switches out the light. The room is tall, shadowy, with two patterns of light from the paraffin heaters reflected on the ceiling. She goes to the window, flings it up)

ANNA *(To the man on the pavement)* You poor fool, why don't you go upstairs, the worst can happen is that the door will be shut in your face.

(A knock on the door—a confident knock)

ANNA If you come in here, Dave Miller . . .
(DAVE comes in. He is crew cut, wears a sloppy sweater and jeans. Carries a small duffle-bag. ANNA turns her back and looks out of the window. DAVE stops the record player. He puts the telephone receiver back on the rest. Turns on the light)

DAVE Why didn't you answer the telephone?

ANNA Because I have nothing to say.

DAVE *(In a parody of an English upper-middle-class voice)* I see no point at all in discussing it.

ANNA *(In the same voice)* I see no point at all in discussing it.

(DAVE stands beside ANNA at the window)

DAVE *(In the easy voice of their intimacy)* I've been in the telephone box around the corner ringing you.

ANNA Did you see my visitor?

DAVE No.

ANNA What a pity.

DAVE I've been standing in the telephone box ringing you and watching that poor bastard on the pavement.

ANNA He's there every night. He comes on his great black

dangerous motor bike. He wears a black leather jacket and big black boots. He looks like an outrider for death in a Cocteau film—and he has the face of a frightened little boy.

DAVE   It's lurve, it's lurve, it's lurve.

ANNA   It's love.

> *(Now they stare at each other, antagonists, and neither gives way.* DAVE *suddenly grins and does a mocking little dance step. He stands grinning at her.* ANNA *hits him as hard as she can. He staggers. He goes to the other side of the carpet, where he sits cross-legged, his face in his hands)*

DAVE   Jesus, Anna.

ANNA   *(Mocking)* Oh, quite so.

DAVE   You still love me, that's something.

ANNA   It's lurve, it's lurve, it's lurve.

DAVE   Yes. I had a friend once. He cheated on his wife, he came in and she laid his cheek open with the flat-iron.

ANNA   *(Quoting him)* "That I can understand"—a great country, America.

DAVE   *(In appeal)* Anna.

ANNA   No.

DAVE   I've been so lonely for you.

ANNA   Where have you been the last week?

DAVE   *(Suspicious)* Why the last *week?*

ANNA   I'm interested.

DAVE   Why the last week? *(A pause)* Ringing you and getting no reply.

ANNA   Why ringing *me?*

DAVE   Who else? Anna, I will not be treated like this.

ANNA   Then, go away.

DAVE   We've been through this before. Can't we get it over quickly.

ANNA   No.

DAVE   Come and sit down. And turn out the lights.

ANNA   No.

DAVE   I didn't know it was as bad as that this time.

ANNA   How long did you think you could go on—you think

you can make havoc as you like, and nothing to pay for it, ever?

DAVE Pay? What for? You've got it all wrong, as usual.

ANNA I'm not discussing it then.

DAVE "I'm not discussing it." Well, I'm saying nothing to you while you've got your bloody middle-class English act on, it drives me mad.

ANNA Middle-class English. I'm Australian.

DAVE You've assimilated so well.

ANNA *(In an Australian accent)* I'll say it like this then—I'll say it any way you like—I'm not discussing it. I'm discussing nothing with you when you're in your role of tuppence a dozen street corner Romeo. *(In English)* It's the same in any accent.

DAVE *(Getting up and doing his blithe dance step)* It's the same in any accent. *(Sitting down again)* Baby, you've got it wrong. *(ANNA laughs)* I tell you, you've got it wrong, baby.

ANNA *(In American)* But baby, it doesn't mean anything, let's have a little fun together, baby, just you and me—just a little fun, baby . . . *(In Australian)* Ah, damn your guts, you stupid, irresponsible little . . . *(In English)* Baby, baby, baby—the anonymous baby. Every woman is baby, for fear you'd whisper the wrong name into the wrong ear in the dark.

DAVE In the dark with you I use your name, Anna.

ANNA You *used* my name.

DAVE Ah, hell, man, well. Anna, beat me up and be done with it and get it over. *(A pause)* O.K., I know it. I don't know what gets into me: O.K. I'm still a twelve-year-old slum kid standing on a street corner in Chicago, watching the expensive broads go by and wishing I had the dough to buy them all. O.K., I know it. You know it. *(A pause)* O.K. and I'm an American God help me, and it's no secret to the world that there's bad man-woman trouble in America. *(A pause)* And everywhere else, if it comes to that. O.K., I do my best. But how any man can be faithful to one woman beats me. O.K., so one day I'll grow up. Maybe.

ANNA Maybe.

DAVE *(Switching to black aggression)* God, how I hate your smug female guts. All of you—there's never anything free —everything to be paid for. Every time, an account rendered. Every time, when you're swinging free there's a moment when the check lies on the table—pay up, pay up, baby.

ANNA Have you come here to get on to one of your anti-woman kicks?

DAVE Well, I'm not being any woman's pet, and that's what you all want. *(Leaping up and doing his mocking dance-step)* I've kept out of all the traps so far, and I'm going to keep out.

ANNA So you've kept out of all the traps.

DAVE That's right. And I'm not going to stand for you either —mother of the world, the great womb, the eternal conscience. I like women, but I'm going to like them my way and not according to the rules laid down by the incorporated mothers of the universe.

ANNA Stop it, stop it, stop boasting.

DAVE But Anna, you're as bad. There's always a moment when you become a sort of flaming sword of retribution.

ANNA At which moment—have you asked yourself? You and I are so close we know everything about each other— and then suddenly, out of the clear blue sky, you start telling me lies like—lies out of a corner-boy's jest book. I can't stand it.

DAVE *(Shouting at her)* Lies—I never tell you lies.

ANNA Oh hell, Dave.

DAVE Well, you're not going to be my conscience. I will not let you be my conscience.

ANNA Amen and hear hear. But why do you make me your conscience?

DAVE *(Deflating)* I don't know. *(With grim humour)* I'm an American. I'm in thrall to the great mother.

ANNA Well, I'm not an American.

DAVE *(Shouting)* No, but you're a woman, and at bottom you're the same as the whole lousy lot of . . .

ANNA   Get out of here then. Get out.

DAVE *(He sits cross-legged, on the edge of the carpet, his head in his hands)* Jesus.

ANNA   You're feeling guilty so you beat me up. I won't let you.

DAVE   Come here. (ANNA *goes to him, kneels opposite him, lays her two hands on his diaphragm)* Yes, like that. *(He suddenly relaxes, head back, eyes closed)* Anna, when I'm away from you I'm cut off from something—I don't know what it is. When you put your hands on me, I begin to breathe.

ANNA   Oh. *(She lets her hands drop and stands up)*

DAVE   Where are you going?
       (ANNA *goes back to the window. A silence. A wolf-whistle from the street. Another)*

ANNA   He's broken his silence. He's calling her. Deep calls to deep.
       (Another whistle. ANNA *winces)*

DAVE   You've missed me?

ANNA   All the time.

DAVE   What have you been doing?

ANNA   Working a little.

DAVE   What else?

ANNA   I said I'd marry Tom, then I said I wouldn't.

DAVE *(Dismissing it)* I should think not.

ANNA *(Furious)* O-h-h-h.

DAVE   Seriously, what?

ANNA   I've been coping with Mary—her son's marrying.

DAVE *(Heartily)* Good for him. Well, it's about time.

ANNA   Oh quite so.

DAVE *(Mimicking her)* Oh quite so.

ANNA *(Dead angry)* I've also spent hours of every day with Helen, Harry's ever-loving wife.

DAVE   Harry's my favourite person in London.

ANNA   And you are his. Strange, isn't it?

DAVE   We understand each other.

ANNA   And Helen and I understand each other.

DAVE *(Hastily)* Now, Anna.

ANNA   Helen's cracking up. Do you know what Harry did? He came to her, because he knew this girl of his was thinking of getting married, and he said: Helen, you know I love you, but I can't live without her. He suggested they should all live together in the same house—he, Helen and his girl. Regularizing things, he called it.

DAVE *(Deliberately provocative)*   Yeah? Sounds very attractive to me.

ANNA   Yes, I thought it might. Helen said to him—who's going to share your bed? Harry said, well, obviously they couldn't all sleep in the same bed, but . . .

DAVE   Anna, stop it.

ANNA   Helen said it was just possible that the children might be upset by the arrangement.

DAVE   I was waiting for that—the trump card—you can't do that, it might upset the kiddies. Well, not for me, I'm out.

ANNA *(Laughing)*   Oh are you?

DAVE   Yes. *(ANNA laughs)* Have you finished?

ANNA   No. Harry and Helen. Helen said she was going to leave him. Harry said: "But darling, you're too old to get another man now and . . ."

DAVE *(Mocking)*   Women always have to pay—and may it long remain that way.

ANNA   Admittedly there's one advantage to men like you and Harry. You are honest.

DAVE   Anna, listen, whenever I cheat on you it takes you about two weeks to settle into a good temper again. Couldn't we just speed it up and get it over with?

ANNA   Get it over with. *(She laughs)*

DAVE   The laugh is new. What's so funny?
      (A wolf-whistle from the street. Then a sound like a wolf howling. ANNA *slams the window up)*

DAVE   Open that window.

ANNA   No, I can't stand it.

DAVE   Anna, I will not have you shutting yourself up. I won't have you spitting out venom and getting all bitter and vengeful. Open that window. *(ANNA opens it. Stands by it passive)* Come and sit down. And turn the lights out.

(As she does not move, he turns out the light. The room as before: two patterned circles of light on the ceiling from the paraffin lamps)

ANNA   Dave, it's no point starting all over again.

DAVE   But baby, you and I will always be together, one way or another.

ANNA   You're crazy.

DAVE   In a good cause. *(He sits cross-legged on the edge of the carpet and waits)* Come and sit.

(ANNA slowly sits opposite him. He smiles at her. She slowly smiles back. As she smiles, the walls fade out. They are two small people in the city, the big, ugly, baleful city all around them, overshadowing them)

DAVE   There baby, that's better.

ANNA   O.K.

DAVE   I don't care what you do—you can crack up if you like, or you can turn Lesbian. You can take to drink. You can even get married. But I won't have you shutting yourself up.

(A lorry roars. A long wolf whistle. Shrill female voices from the street)

ANNA   Those girls opposite quarrel. I hate it. Last night they were rolling in the street and pulling each other's hair and screaming.

DAVE   O.K. But you're not to shut it out. You're not to shut anything out.

ANNA   I'll try.

(She very slowly gets to her feet, stands concentrating)

DAVE   That's right. Now, who are you?

END OF ACT ONE

Act Two

ANNA *and* DAVE, *in the same positions as at the end of Act One. No time has passed. The lights are out. The walls seem to have vanished, so that the room seems part of the street. There is a silence. A lorry roars.*

DAVE   Who are you?

ANNA *(In English)*   Anna Freeman.

DAVE   O.K. Go, then.
       (A silence)

ANNA   I can't. I'm all in pieces.

DAVE   Then go back. Who are you now?

ANNA *(She slowly stands up, at the edge of the carpet)* Anna.

DAVE   Anna who?

ANNA *(In Australian)*   Anna MacClure from Brisbane. *(In English)* The trouble is, she gets further and further away. She's someone else. I know if she goes altogether then I'm done for. *(A pause. In Australian)* The smell of petrol. In a broken-down old jalopy—six of us. It's night. There's a great shining moon. We've been dancing. I'm with Jack. We've stopped at the edge of the road by a petrol pump. All the others are singing and shouting and the petrol pump attendant's angry as a cross cat. Jack says, "Anna, let's get married." *(Speaking to* JACK*)* "No, Jack, what's all this about getting married. I want to live, Jack, I want to travel, I want to see the world. . . . Yes, I know, but I don't want kids yet. I don't want . . ." *(To* DAVE*)* He says, "Anna, you'll be unhappy. I feel it in my bones, you'll be unhappy." *(She talks back to* JACK*)* "I don't care, I tell you. I know if I marry you, you'll be for the rest of my life. You aren't the world, Jack . . . All right, then I'll be unhappy. But I want a choice. Don't you see, I want a choice."*(She*

232

crouches down, her hands over her face) Let's have the lights, Dave.

DAVE   Wait. Go back some more—that's not Anna Mac-Clure the Australian. That's Anna MacClure who's already half in Europe.

ANNA   But it's so hard.

DAVE   Breathe slowly and go. Who are you?

ANNA   *(Slowly standing. In a child's voice, Australian)* Anna MacClure.

DAVE   Where?

ANNA   On the porch of our house. I've quarrelled with my mother. *(She stands talking to her mother)* I'm not going to be like you, ma, I'm not, I'm not. You're stuck here, you never think of anything but me and my brother and the house. You're old, ma, you're stupid. *(Listening while her mother lectures her)* Yah, I don't care. When I grow up I'm never going to be married, I'm not going to get old and dull. I'm going to live with my brother on an island and swim and catch fish and . . . *(She sings)* The moon is in my windowpane, the moon is in my bed, I'll race the moon across the sky and eat it for my bread. I don't care, ma, I don't care . . . *(She dances a blithe, defiant dance. In English)* Dave, Dave, did you see? That was just like you.

> *(*DAVE *gets up and does his blithe defiant dance beside her on the carpet. He mocks her.* ANNA, *furious, leaps over and smacks him)*

ANNA   "There, stupid child, you're wicked and stupid, you're not going to defy me, so you think you'll defy me . . ."

> *(They both at the same moment crouch down in their former positions on either side of the carpet)*

ANNA   Let me have the light on now, please Dave.

> *(*DAVE *switches it on, the room becomes the room again.* DAVE *returns to where he was)*

DAVE   *(Patting the carpet beside him)* Anna.

ANNA   No.

DAVE   Let me love you.

ANNA No.

DAVE *(Laughing and confident)* You will, Anna, so why not now.

ANNA You'll never love me again, never, never, never.

DAVE *(Suddenly scared)* Why not? Why not?

ANNA You know why.

DAVE I swear I don't.

ANNA What am I going to be without you, what shall I do?

DAVE But baby, I'm here.

ANNA And what are you going to do with Janet?

DAVE Janet?

ANNA Janet Stevens, from Philadelphia.

DAVE What about her?

ANNA You don't know her, of course.

DAVE She's a friend of mine, that's all.

ANNA Do you know, Dave, if I walked into your room and found you in bed with a girl and said Dave, who is that girl, you'd say what girl? I don't see any girl, it's just your sordid imagination.

DAVE Some time you've got to learn to trust me.

ANNA What you mean by trust is, you tell me some bloody silly lie and I just nod my head and smile.

DAVE *(Inside the wild man)* That's right, baby, you should just nod your head and smile.

ANNA You mean, it's got nothing to do with me.

DAVE That's right, it's got nothing to do with you.

(ANNA withdraws from him into herself)

DAVE Ah, hell, Anna, she means nothing to me.

ANNA Then it's terrible.

(A pause)

DAVE I don't understand why I do the things I do. I go moseying along, paying my way and liking myself pretty well, then I'm sounding off like something, and people start looking at me in a certain way, and I think, Hey, man is that you? Is that you there, Dave Miller? He's taken over again, the wild man, the mad man. And I even stand on one side and watch pretty awed when you come to think of it. Yes, awed, that's the word. You should be awed too,

Anna, instead of getting scared. I can't stand it when you're scared of me.

ANNA   I simply want to run out of the way.

DAVE   The way of what? Go on, tell, I want to know.

ANNA   I want to hide from the flick-knives, from the toma-hawks.

DAVE   *(With a loud, cruel laugh—he is momentarily inside the wild man)* Jesus. Bloody Englishwoman, middle-class lady, that's what you are. *(Mimicking her)* Flick-knives and tomahawks—how refined.

ANNA   *(In the voice of* ANNA MACCLURE*)* Dave, man, stand up and let it go, let it go.

> *(*DAVE *slowly stands. He switches off the light—the walls vanish, the city comes up. Back on the carpet, stands relaxed)*

ANNA   Who are you?

DAVE   Dave Miller, the boss of the gang, South Street, Al Capone's territory . . . Chicago.

ANNA   What's your name?

DAVE   Dave Miller.

ANNA   No, in your fantasy.

DAVE   Baby Face Nelson. No, but the way I dreamed him up, he was a sort of Robin Hood, stealing from the rich to give to the poor.

ANNA   Oh, don't be so childish.

DAVE   That was the point of this exercise I thought.

ANNA   Sorry. Go ahead.

DAVE   I'm fifteen years old. I'm wearing a sharp hat, such a sweet sharp hat—pork-pie, cleft in the middle, set on side. The hat is in dark green. My jacket is two yards wide across the shoulders, nipped in at the waist, and skirted. In a fine, sweet cinnamon brown. Trousers in forest green, very fancy. My shirt is the finest money can buy, one dollar fifty, at Holy Moses Cut Price Emporium. In deciduous mauve. My tie is orange and black in lightning stripes. I wear velveteen spats, buttoned sweetly up the side, in hearth-rug white. I have a key-chain with a key on it, probably about six feet long, which could sweep the pavement if it

hung free, but it never does, because we stand, lounging
on the street corner, our home, men of the world, twirling
the chain between our fingers, hour after hour through the
afternoons and evenings. That year I'm a shoe-shine boy,
a news-boy and a drug-store assistant. But my life, my real
sweet life is on the pavement. *(Speaking to someone)* Jedd,
see that broad? *(Waits for an answer)* Gee, some dish, bet
she's hot. *(Waits again)* See that dame there, Jesus Christ.
*(He wolf-whistles) (ANNA swanks, bottom wagging in
front of him. DAVE whistles after her. He is echoed by a
wolf-whistle from the street. ANNA wheels at the window
to shut it)* I told you, keep it open.

 (ANNA returns, squatting on the edge of the carpet)

DAVE   Jesus, Anna, when I think of that kid, of all us kids, it
makes me want to cry.

ANNA   Then cry.

DAVE   The year of our Lord, 1936, all our parents out of
work, and World War II on top of us and we didn't know
it.

ANNA   Did you carry a knife?

DAVE   We all did.

ANNA   Ever use it?

DAVE   Hell no, I told you, we were fine idealistic kids. That
was my anarchist period. We stood twirling our keychains
on the corner of the street, eyeing the broads and I quoted
great chunks of Kropotkin to the guys. Anyone who joined
my gang had to be an anarchist. When I had my socialist
period, they had to be socialists.

ANNA   Go on.

DAVE   Isn't it enough?

ANNA   I'm waiting for the tomahawk. You're seven years old
and you scalp all the nasty adults who don't understand
you.

DAVE   O.K. I was a red Indian nine-tenths of my childhood.
O.K. *(In his parody of an English upper-class accent)*
There is no point whatever in discussing it . . . O.K. Some-
where in my psyche is a tomahawk-twirling Red Indian
. . Anna? Do you know what's wrong with America?

ANNA Yes.

DAVE At the street corners now the kids are not prepared to fight the world. They fight each other. Everyone of us, we were prepared to take on the whole world single-handed. Not any longer, they know better, they're scared. A healthy country has kids, every John Doe of them knowing he can lick the whole world, single-handed. Not any more.

ANNA I know.

DAVE You know. But you're scared to talk. Everyone knows but they're scared to talk. There's a great dream dead in America. You look at us and see prosperity—and loneliness. Prosperity and men and women in trouble with each other. Prosperity and people wondering what life is for. Prosperity—and conformity. You look at us and you know it's your turn now. We've pioneered the golden road for you . . .

ANNA Who are you lecturing, Anna MacClure?

DAVE O.K., O.K., O.K.

(He flops down on the carpet. ANNA *puts her arms around his shoulders)*

DAVE If you think I'm any safer to touch when I'm flat than when I'm mobile you're wrong. *(He tries to pull her down. She pulls away)* O.K. *(Pause)* Did I tell you I went to a psycho-analyst? Yeah, I'm a good American after all, I went to a psycho-analyst.

ANNA *(Mocking him)* Do tell me about your psycho-analysis.

DAVE Yeah, now I refer, throwing it away, to "when I was under psycho-analysis."

ANNA The way you refer, throwing it away, to "when I was a car salesman," which you were for a week.

DAVE Why do you always have to cut me down to size?

ANNA So, how many times did you go?

DAVE Twice. *(*ANNA *laughs)* The first interview was already not a success. Now, doc, I said, I have no wish to discuss my childhood. There is no point whatever in discussing it. I want to know how to live my life, doc. I don't want you to sit there, nodding while I talk. I want your advice, I said. After all, doc, I said, you're an educated man, Eton and Oxford, so you told me—throwing it away, of course. So pass on the message, doc, pass it on. (ANNA *rolls on the carpet, laughing*) It was no laughing matter. I talked for one hour by the clock, begging and pleading for the favour of one constructive word from him. But he merely sat like this, and then he said: "I'll see you next Thursday, at five o'clock precisely." I said, it was no laughing matter—For a whole week I was in a trance, waiting for the ultimate revelation—you know how we all live, waiting for that revelation? Then I danced up to his room and lay on to his couch and lay waiting. He said not a word. Finally I said don't think I'm resisting you, doc, please don't think it. Talk doc, I said. Give. Let yourself go. Then the hour was nearly up. I may say, I'd given him a thumbnail sketch of my life previously. He spoke at last: "Tell me, Mr. Miller, how many jobs did you say you had had?" My God, doc, I said, nearly falling over myself in my eagerness to oblige, if I knew, I'd tell you. "You would admit," he said at last, "that the pattern of your life shows, ho, hum, ha, a certain instability?" My God, yes, doc, I said, panting at his feet, that's it, you're on to it, hold fast to it doc, that's the word, instability. Now give, doc, give. Tell me, why is it that a fine upstanding American boy like me, with all the advantages our rich country gives its citizens, why should I be in such trouble. And why should so many of us be in such trouble—I'm not an American for nothing, I'm socially minded, doc. Why are there so many of us in such trouble. Tell me, doc. Give. And why should you, Dr. Melville Cooper-Anstey, citizen of England, be sitting in that chair, in a position to dish out advice and comfort? Of course I know that you got all wrapped up in this thing because you, uh, kind of like people, doc, but after all, to kinda like people, doc, puts you in a pretty privileged class for a start—so few citizens can afford to really kinda like people. So tell me doc, tell me . . .

ANNA Well, don't shout at me, I'm not Doctor Melville Cooper-Anstey.

DAVE You listen just like him—judging. In possession of some truth that's denied to me.

ANNA I've always got to be the enemy. You've got to have an enemy . . .

DAVE You're right. I've got to have an enemy. Why not? I'm not going to love my brother as myself if he's not worth it. Nor my sister, if it comes to that—where was I?

ANNA Kinda liking people.

DAVE There was a sort of thoughtful pause. I waited, biting my nails. Then he said, or drawled, "Tell me, just at random now, is there any thing or event or happening that has seemed to you significant. Just to give us something to get our teeth into, Mr. Miller?" Well, doc, I said, just at random, and picking a significant moment from a life full of significant moments, and on principle at that—latch on to that, doc, it's important in our case, that my life has been uninterruptedly full of significant moments . . . but has yours, doc? I want to know? We should talk as equals, doc, has your life been as full as mine of significant moments?

ANNA Dave, stop boasting.

DAVE Hell, Anna. If you love me, it's because I lived that way. Well? And so. But to pull just one little cat or kitten out of the bag, doc, I would say it was the moment I woke beside a waitress in Minnesota, and she said to me in her sweet measured voice: "Honey, you're nuts. Did you know that?" . . . Well, to tell the truth no, I hadn't known it. Light flooded in on me. I've been living with it ever since. And so. I was all fixed up to see one of your opposite numbers in the States, my great country, that was in L.A., California, where I happened to be at the time, writing scripts for our film industry. Then I heard he was a stool pigeon for the FBI. No, don't look like that, doc, don't—very distasteful, I'll admit, but the world's a rough place. Half his patients were int-ell-ectuals, and Reds and Pinks, since intellectuals so often tend to be, and after every couch session, he was moseying off to the FBI with information. Now, doc, here's an American and essentially socially-minded, I want an answer, in this great country, England, I can come to you with perfect confidence that you won't go trotting off to MI5, to inform them that during my communist period I was a communist. That is, before I was expelled from that institution for hinting that Stalin had his weak moments. I tend to shoot off my mouth, doc. A weakness, I know, but I know that you won't, and that gives me a profound feeling of security.

ANNA Dave, you're nuts.

DAVE So said the waitress in Minnesota. Say it often enough and I'll believe it.

ANNA So what did Doctor Cooper-Anstey say?

DAVE He lightly, oh so lightly, touched his fingertips together, and he drawled: "Tell me, Mr. Miller, how many women have you had?" (ANNA *laughs*) Hey doc, I said, I was talking seriously. I was talking about the comparative states of liberty in my country and in yours. He said: "Mr. Miller, don't evade my question."

    (ANNA *laughs*)

DAVE O.K. doc, if you're going to be small-minded . . . but let's leave the statistics, doc. I'm pretty well schooled in this psycho-analysis bit, I said, all my fine stable well integrated friends have been through your mill. And so I know that if I pulled out a notebook full of statistics, you'd think I was pretty sick—you may think it careless of me, doc, but I don't know how many women I've had. "But Mr. Miller," he drawled, "you must have some idea?" Well, at this point I see that this particular morale-builder is not for me. Tell me, Dr. Melville Cooper-Anstey, I said, how many women have *you* had? (ANNA *rolls, laughing*) Hey, Anna, this is serious, girl. A serious matter . . . hey, ho, he was mad, was Dr. Melville Cooper-Anstey sore. He sat himself up to his full height, and he told me in tones of severe displeasure, that I was an adolescent. Yeah, doc, I said, we Americans are all children, we're all adolescent, we know that. But I wanted to know—how many women have you had, doc?

Because we have to talk man to man, doc, adolescent or not. There's got to be some sort of equality around this place, I said. After all, I said, one woman is not like another, doc, believe me, if you've slept with one woman you've not slept with them all and don't you think it. And besides, doc, I said, you're an Englishman. That is not without relevance. Because, judging from my researches into this field, Englishmen don't like women very much. So Englishwomen complain. So they murmur in the dark night watches with their arms gratefully around the stranger's neck. Now I like women, doc, I like them. The point is, do you? He laughed. Like this: (DAVE *gives a high whinnying laugh*) But I persisted. I said, doc, do you like your wife? And what is more important, does she like you? Does she, doc? And so.

ANNA   And so?

DAVE   And so he kicked me out, with all the dignity an upper-class Englishman brings to such matters. In tones frozen with good taste, he said, "Mr. Miller, you know how to find your own way out, I think."

ANNA   It's all very well.

DAVE   *(Mimicking her)* It's all very well, don't freeze up on me, Anna, I won't have it. *(A pause)* Anna, he did vouchsafe me with two little bits of information from the heights of integration. One. He said I couldn't go on like this. I said, that's right, that's why I've come to you. And two. He said I should get married, have two well-spaced children and a settled job. Ah, doc, now you're at the hub of the thing. What job, I said? Because I'll let you into a secret. What's wrong with all of us is not that our mummies and daddies weren't nice to us, it's that we don't believe the work we do is important. Oh, I know I'm earnest, doc, I'm pompous and earnest—but I need work that makes me feel I'm contributing. So doc, give—I'm a man of a hundred talents, none of them outstanding. But I have one thing, doc, just one important thing—if I spend eight hours a day working, I need to know that men, women and children are benefiting by my work. So . . . What job shall I do. Tell me.

ANNA So?

DAVE He said I should get any job that would enable me to keep a wife and two children, and in this way I would be integrated into society. *(He flings himself down on the carpet)* Anna, for God's sake, Anna.

ANNA Don't ask me.

DAVE Why not? I can't ask Dr. Anstey. Because the significant moment I keep coming back to he wouldn't see at all. It wasn't the moment I decided to leave America. I drove right across the States, looking up all my friends, the kids who'd been world-challengers with me. They were all married. Some of them were divorced, of course, but that's merely an incident in the process of being married. They all had houses, cars, jobs, families. They were not pleased to see me—they knew I was still unintegrated. I asked each one a simple question. Hey, man, I said, this great country of ours, it's in no too healthy a state. What are we going to do about it? And do you know what they said?

ANNA Don't rock the boat.

DAVE You've got it in one, kid. But I had one ace up my sleeve. There was my old buddy, Jedd. He'll still be right in there, fighting. So I walked into his apartment where he was sitting with his brand new second wife. There was a nervous silence. Then he said: "Are you successful yet, Dave?" And so I took the first boat over.

ANNA And the wife and the two well-spaced kids?

DAVE You know I can't get married. You know that if I could I'd marry you. And perhaps I should marry you. How about it?

ANNA No. The wedding would be the last I'd see of you— you'd be off across the world like a dog with a firecracker tied to its tail.

DAVE I know. So I can't get married. *(A pause)* Why don't you just trap me into it? Perhaps I need simply to be tied down?

ANNA No.

DAVE Why not?

ANNA Any man I have stays with me, voluntarily, because he wants to, without ties.

DAVE Your bloody pride is more important to you than what I need.

ANNA Don't beat me up.

DAVE I will if I want. You're my woman so if I feel like beating you up I will. And you can fight back . . . Anna, what are you being enigmatic about? All the time, there's something in the air, that's not being said. What is it?

ANNA Not being said, I keep trying. Don't you really know?

DAVE *(In a panic)* No. What?

ANNA If I told you, you'd say I was just imagining it. All right, I'll try again, Janet Stevens.

DAVE *(Furious)* You're a monomaniac. Janet Stevens. Do you imagine that a nice little middle-class girl, whose poppa's sort of sub-manager for an insurance company, do you imagine she can mean anything to me?

ANNA Oh my God, Dave

DAVE You're crazy. It's you that's crazy.

ANNA Dave, while you're hanging and crashing about the world, playing this role and that role, filling your life full of significant moments—there are other people in the world . . . hell, what's the use of talking to you. *(A pause)* As a matter of interest, and this is a purely abstract question, suppose you married Janet Stevens, what would you have to do?

DAVE Anna, are you crazy? Can you see me? God help me, I'm a member of that ever-increasing and honourable company, the world's ex-patriates. Like you, Anna.

ANNA Oh, all right.

DAVE How the hell could I marry her? She wouldn't understand a word I ever said, for a start.

ANNA Oh, all *right*.

DAVE "There's no point at all in discussing it."

ANNA None at all.

DAVE I said to Dr. Melville Cooper-Anstey: This society you want me to be integrated with, do you approve of it? If you don't, what are you doing, sitting there with those big black scissors cutting people into shapes to fit it? Well, doc, I'll tell you something, I don't approve of society, it stinks. I don't want to fit into it, I want society to fit itself to me —I'll make a deal with you, doc, I'll come and lie on this comfortable couch of yours, Tuesdays and Fridays from 2 to 3 for seven years, on condition that at the end of that time society is a place fit for Dave Miller to live in. How's that for a proposition, doc? Because of course that means you'll have to join the Dave Miller fraternity for changing the world. You join my organization and I'll join yours. *(He turns on* ANNA*)* Hey, Anna, don't just lie there, reserving judgment.

ANNA I didn't say a word.

DAVE You never have to. You're like Doctor Melville Cooper-Anstey—you put your spiritual finger-tips together and purse your lips.

ANNA *(Furious)* Dave, do you know something—when you need an enemy, you turn me into a kind of—lady welfare worker. Who was the great enemy of your childhood? The lady welfare worker. *(Jumping up—in Australian)* I'm Anna MacClure the daughter of a second-hand car dealer. My grand-father was a horse-doctor. My great-grand-father was a stock farmer. And my great-great-grand-father was a convict, shipped from this our mother country God bless her to populate the outback. I'm the great-great-grand-daughter of a convict, I'm the aristocracy so don't get at me, Dave Miller, corner-boy, street-gang-leader— I'm as good as you are, any day. *(He pulls her down on the carpet, she pushes his hands away)* No. I told you no.

DAVE *(Swinging her round to sit by him. His arms round her)* O.K. then baby, we don't have to make love. Like hell we don't. O.K. sit quiet and hold my hand. Do you love me, Anna?

ANNA Love you? You are me. *(Mocking)* You are the flame, the promise and the enchantment. You are for me—what Janet Stevens is for you. *(She laughs)* Imagine it, Dave Miller, for you the flame is embodied in a succession of

well-conducted young ladies, each one more banal than
the last. For me—it's you. *(Suddenly serious)* You are my
soul.

DAVE *(Holding her down beside him)* If I'm your soul, then
surely it's in order to sit beside me?

    (They sit, arms round each other, ANNA'S *head on his
shoulder)*

ANNA   I only breathe freely when I'm with you.

DAVE *(Complacent)* I know.

ANNA *(Furious)* What do you mean? I was on the point of
getting married.

DAVE   Don't be absurd.

ANNA   What's going to become of us?

DAVE   Perhaps I shall go back to Doctor Melville Cooper-
Anstey—like hell.

ANNA   It's not fair to take it out on Dr. Melville Cooper-
Anstey just because he isn't God.

DAVE   Of course it's fair. If God wasn't dead I wouldn't be
going to Dr. Melville Cooper-Anstey. Perhaps I should
wrestle with him—after all, these people have what's the
word?

ANNA   Stability.

DAVE   You were born with one skin more than I have.

ANNA *(Mocking)* But *I* come from a stable home.

DAVE   Doctor Melville Cooper-Anstey said to me: "Mr.
Miller, your trouble is, you come from a broken home."
But doc, I said, my home wasn't broken—my parents were
both union organizers. He winced. A look of distaste settled around his long sensitive nose. He fought for the right
comment. At last it came: "Really?" he said. Yeah, really,
I said. My parents were professional union organizers.

ANNA *(Being* DOCTOR MELVILLE COOPER ANSTEY*)* Union
organizers, Mr. Miller.

DAVE   That's right, doc, it's true that my childhood was
spent hither and thither as you might say, but it was in a
good cause. My mother was usually organizing a picket line
in Detroit while my father was organizing a strike in Pittsburgh.

ANNA Really, Mr. Miller.

DAVE But doc, it was the late 'twenties and early 'thirties—people were hungry, they were out of work.

ANNA You must stick to the point, Mr. Miller.

DAVE But if I spent my time hither and thither it was not because my parents quarrelled. They loved each other.

ANNA Were you, or were you not, a disturbed child, Mr. Miller?

DAVE The truth compels me to state, I was a disturbed child. But in a good cause. My parents thought the state of the world was more important than me, and they were right, I am on their side. But I never really saw either of them. We scarcely met. So my mother was whichever lady welfare worker that happened to be dealing with the local delinquents at the time, and my father was, the anarchists, the Jewish socialist youth, the communists and the Trotskyists. In a word, the radical tradition—oh, don't laugh, doc. I don't expect they'll have taught you about the radical tradition in Oxford, England, but it stood for something. And it will again—it stood for the great dream—that life can be noble and beautiful and dignified.

ANNA And what did he say?

DAVE He said I was an adolescent. Doc, I said, my childhood was disturbed—by the great dream—and if yours was not, perhaps after all you had the worst of it.

ANNA You are evading the issue, Mr. Miller.

DAVE But you're all right, you have stability—Anna, you didn't come from a broken home.

ANNA No, I come from a well-integrated, typical stable marriage.

DAVE Then tell me, Anna, tell me about stable and well-integrated marriage.

ANNA *(Standing up and remembering. She shudders)* My mother wanted to be a great pianist. Oh she was not without talent. She played at a concert in Brisbane once—that was the high point of her life. That night she met my father. They married. She never opened the piano after I was born. My father never earned as much money as he thought life owed him—for some reason, the second-hand cars had a spite on him. My mother got more and more garrulous. In a word, she was a nag. My father got more and more silent. But he used to confide in me. He used to tell me what his dreams had been when he was a young man. Oh yes, he was a world-changer too, before he married.

DAVE All young men are world-changers, before they marry.

ANNA O.K.—It's not my fault . . .

(They look at each other. DAVE leaps up, switches out the light. DAVE stands across from ANNA, in a hunched, defeated pose. ANNA has her hands on her hips, a scold)

ANNA Yes, Mr. MacClure, you said that last month—but how am I going to pay the bill from the store, tell me that?

DAVE *(In Australian)* A man came in today, he said he might buy that Ford.

ANNA Might buy! Might buy! And I promised Anna a new coat, I promised her, this month, a new coat.

DAVE Then Anna can do without, it won't hurt her.

ANNA That's just like you—you always say next month, next month things will be better—and how about the boy, how can we pay his fees, we promised him this year . . .

DAVE Ah, shut up. *(Shouting)* Shut up. I said. Shut up . . .

(He turns away, hunched up)

ANNA *(Speaking aloud the monologue of her mother's thoughts)* Yes, that's how I spend my life, pinching and saving—all day, cooking and preserving, and making clothes for the kids, that's all I ever do, I never even get a holiday. And it's for a man who doesn't even know I'm here—well, if he had to do without me, he'd know what I've done for him. He'd value me if he had to do without me—if I left him, he'd know, soon enough there's Mr. Jones from the store; he's a soft spot for me, trying to kiss me when there's no one there but us two, yes, I'd just have to lift my finger and Mr. Jones would take me away—I didn't lack for men before I married—they came running when I smiled. Ah God in heaven, if I hadn't married this good-for-nothing here, I'd be a great pianist, I'd know all the golden cities of the world—Paris, Rome, London, I'd know the great world, and here I am, stuck in a dump like this, with two ungrateful kids and a no-good husband . . .

DAVE *(Speaking aloud* MR. MACCLURE'S *thoughts)* Well, what the hell does she want—I wouldn't be here in this dump at all if it wasn't for her; does she think that's all I'm fit for, selling old cars, to keep food and clothes in the home? Why, if I hadn't married her, I'd be free to go where I liked—she sees me as a convenience to get money to keep her and her kids, that's all she cares about, the kids, she doesn't care for me. Without her I'd be off across the world —the world's a big place, I'd be free to do what I liked— and the women, yes, the women, why, she doesn't regard me, but only last week, Mrs. Jones was giving me the glad eye from behind the counter when her old man wasn't looking—yes, she'd better watch out, she'd miss me right enough if I left her . . .

ANNA *(As* ANNA*)* A typical well-integrated marriage. *(As her* MOTHER*)* Mr. MacClure, are you listening to me?

DAVE *(As* MR. MACCLURE*)* Yes, dear.

ANNA *(Going to him, wistful)* You're not sorry you married me?

DAVE No dear, I'm not sorry I married you.
(They smile at each other, ironical)

ANNA *(As* ANNA*)* The highest emotion they ever knew was a kind of ironical compassion—the compassion of one prisoner for another . . . *(As her* MOTHER*)* There's the children, dear. They are both fine kids, both of them.

DAVE Yes, dear, they're both fine kids. *(Patting her)* There, there dear, it's all right, don't worry, dear.

ANNA *(As* ANNA*)* That's how it was. And when I was nine years old I looked at that good fine stable marriage and at the marriages of our friends and neighbours and I swore, I swore to the God I already did not believe in, God, I said, God, if I go down in loneliness and misery, if I die alone somewhere in a furnished room in a lonely city that doesn't know me—I'll do that sooner than marry as my father and mother were married. I'll have the truth with the man I'm with or I'll have nothing. *(Shuddering)* Nothing.

DAVE Hey—Anna!
(He switches on the lights, fast. Goes to her)

DAVE *(Gently)* Perhaps the irony was the truth.

ANNA No, no, no. It was *not*.

DAVE *(Laughing at her, but gently)* You're a romantic, Anna Freeman. You're an adolescent.

ANNA Yes, I'm an adolescent. And that's how I'm going to stay. Anything, anything rather than the man and woman, the jailed and the jailer, living together, talking to themselves, and wondering what happened that made them strangers. I won't, I'll die alone first. And I shall. I shall.

DAVE *(Holding her)* Hey, Anna, Anna. *(Gently laughing)* You know what Doctor Melville Cooper-Anstey would say to that?

ANNA Yes.

DAVE And what all the welfare workers would say?

ANNA Yes.

DAVE And what all the priests would say?

ANNA Yes.

DAVE And what the politicians would say?

ANNA Yes. *(She tears herself from him)* Don't rock the boat.

DAVE *(Taking her up)* Don't rock the boat. *(He switches off the lights)*
(They look at each other, beginning to laugh. The following sequence, while they throw slogans, or newspaper headlines at each other should be played with enjoyment, on the move, trying to out-cap each other)

ANNA Don't rock the boat—work.

DAVE Produce goods and children for the State.

ANNA Marry young.

DAVE The unit of society is a stable marriage.

ANNA The unit of a healthy society is a well-integrated family.

DAVE Earn money.

ANNA   Remember the first and worst sin is poverty.

DAVE   The first and best virtue is to own a comfortable home full of labour-saving devices.

ANNA   If you have too much leisure, there are football matches, the pools and television.

DAVE   If you still have too much leisure be careful not to spend it in ways that might rock the boat.

ANNA   Don't rock the boat—society might have its minor imperfections, but they are nothing very serious.

DAVE   Don't dream of anything better—dreams are by definition neurotic.

ANNA   If you are dissatisfied with society, you are by definition unstable.

DAVE   If your soul doesn't fit into the patterns laid down for you—

ANNA   Kill yourself, but don't rock the boat.

DAVE   Be integrated.

ANNA   Be stable.

DAVE   Be secure.

ANNA   Be integrated or—

DAVE and ANNA   Die! Die! Die!

DAVE   The trouble with you, Anna, is that you exaggerate everything.

ANNA   The trouble with you, Dave, is that you have no sense of proportion.

DAVE   Proportion. I have no sense of proportion. I must scale myself down . . . I have spent my whole life on the move . . . I've spent my youth on the move across the continent and back again—from New York to Pittsburgh, from Pittsburgh to Chicago, from Chicago . . . *(By now he is almost dancing his remembering)* . . . across the great plains of the Middle West to Salt Lake City and the Rocky Mountains, and down to the sea again at San Francisco. Then back again, again, again, from West to East, from North to South, from Dakota to Mexico and back again . . . and sometimes, just sometimes, when I've driven twelve hours at a stretch with the road rolling up behind me like a carpet, sometimes I've reached it, sometimes I've

reached what I'm needing—my head rests on the Golden
Gates, with one hand I touch Phoenix, Arizona, and with
the other I hold Minneapolis, and my feet straddle from
Maine to the Florida Keys. And under me America rocks,
America rocks—like a woman.

ANNA Or like the waitress from Minnesota.

DAVE Ah, Jesus!

ANNA You are maladjusted, Mr. Miller!

DAVE But you aren't, do tell me how you do it!

ANNA Now when I can't breathe any more I shut my eyes
and I walk out into the sun—I stand on a ridge of high
country and look out over leagues and leagues of—empti-
ness. Then I bend down and pick up a handful of red dust,
a handful of red dust and I smell it. It smells of sunlight.

DAVE Of sunlight.

ANND I tell you, if I lived in the bloody mildewed little
country for seven times seven years, my flesh would be
sunlight. From here to here, sunlight.

DAVE You're neurotic, Anna, you've got to face up to it.

ANNA But you're all right, you're going to settle in a split-
level house with a stable wife and two children.

DAVE *(Pulling* ANNA *to the front of the stage and pointing
over and down into the house)* Poke that little nose of
yours over your safe white cliffs and look down—see all
those strange coloured fish down there—not cod, and halibut and Dover sole and good British herring, but the poisonous coloured fish of Paradise.

ANNA Cod. Halibut. Dover sole. Good British herring.

DAVE Ah, Jesus, you've got the soul of a little housewife
from Brixton.

ANNA *(Leaping up and switching on the lights)* Or from
Philadelphia. Well, let me tell you, Dave Miller, any little
housewife from Brixton or Philadelphia could tell you
what's wrong with you.

DAVE *(Mocking)* Tell me, baby.

ANNA You are America, the America you've sold your soul
to—do you know what she is?

DAVE *(Mocking)* No, baby, tell me what she is?

ANNA She's that terrible woman in your comic papers—a great masculine broad-shouldered narrow-hipped black-booted blonde beastess, with a whip in one hand and a revolver in the other. And that's why you're running, she's after you, Dave Miller, as she's after every male American I've ever met. I bet you even see the Statue of Liberty with great black thigh-boots and a pencilled moustache—the frigid tyrant, the frigid goddess.

DAVE *(Mocking)* But she's never frigid for me, baby. *(He does his little mocking dance)*

ANNA God's gift to women, Dave Miller.

DAVE That's right, that's right, baby.

ANNA And have you ever thought what happens to them—the waitress in Minnesota, the farmer's wife in Nebraska, the club-hostess in Detroit? Dave Miller descends for one night, a gift from God, and leaves the next day. "Boo-hoo, boo-hoo," she cries, "stay with me, baby." "I can't, baby, my destiny waits"—your destiny being the waitress in the next drive-in café. *(She is now dancing around him)* And why don't you stay, or don't you know? It's because you're scared. Because if you stay, she might turn into the jack-booted whip-handling tyrant.

DAVE No. I'm not going to take the responsibility for you. That's what you want, like every woman I've ever known. That I should say, I love you baby and . . .

ANNA I love you, Anna Freeman.

DAVE I love you, honey.

ANNA I love you, Anna Freeman.

DAVE I love you, doll.

ANNA I love you, Anna Freeman.

DAVE I love you—but that's the signal for you to curl up and resign your soul to me. You want me to be responsible for you.

ANNA You'll never be responsible for anyone. *(Flat)* One day you'll learn that when you say I love you baby it means something.

DAVE Well, everything's running true to form—I haven't

been back a couple of hours but the knives are out and the tom-toms beating for the sex-war.

ANNA It's the only clean war left. It's the only war that won't destroy us all. That's why we are fighting it.

DAVE Sometimes I think you really hate me, Anna.

ANNA *(Mocking)* Really? Sometimes I think I've never hated anyone so much in all my life. A good clean emotion hate is. I hate you.

DAVE Good, then I hate you.

ANNA Good, then get out, go away. *(She wheels to the window, looks out. He goes to where his duffle bag is, picks it up, drops it, and in the same circling movement turns to face her as she says)* I hate you because you never let me rest.

DAVE So love is rest? The cosy corner, the little nook?

ANNA Sometimes it ought to be.

DAVE Sometimes it is.

ANNA Ha! With you! You exhaust me. You take me to every extreme, all the time. I'm never allowed any half-measures.

DAVE You haven't got any.

ANNA Ah, hell.

(She flings her shoes at him, one after the other. He dodges them, jumps to the bed, crouches on it, patting it)

DAVE Truce, baby, truce . . .

ANNA *(Mocking him)* You're going to love me, baby, warm-hearted and sweet? Oh you're a good lay, baby, I'd never say you weren't.

(The sound of screechings and fighting from the street. ANNA is about to slam window down, stops on a look from DAVE)

ANNA Last night the four of them were scratching each other and pulling each other's hair while a group of fly-by-night men stood and watched and laughed their heads off. Nothing funnier, is there, than women fighting?

DAVE Sure, breaks up the trade union for a bit . . . *(This is*

black and aggressive—she reacts away from him. He looks
at her grimaces) Hell, Anna.

(He goes fast to the mirror, studies the black cloth)

DAVE What's the pall for?

ANNA I don't like my face.

DAVE Why not?

ANNA It wears too well.

DAVE You must be hard-up for complaints against life . . .
(Looking closely at her) You really are in pieces, aren't
you? You mean you went out and bought this specially?

ANNA That's right.

DAVE Uh-huh—when?

ANNA When we quarrelled last time—finally, if you
remember?

DAVE Uh-huh. Why really, come clean?

ANNA It would seem to suit my situation.

DAVE Uh-huh . . . *(He suddenly whips off the cloth and
drapes it round his shoulders like a kind of jaunty cloak,
or cape. Talking into mirror, in angry, mocking self-
parody)* Hey there, Dave Miller, is that you, man? *(In a
Southern accent)* Yes, ma'am, and you have a pretty place
around here. Mind if I stay a-while? Yeah, I sure do like
your way of doing things . . . *(Accent of the Mid-West)* Hi,
babe, and what've you got fixed for tonight? Yes, this is the
prettiest place I've seen for many a day . . . *(In English)*
Why, hullo, how are you? *(He crashes his fist into the mirror)*

(ANNA, watching him, slowly comes from window as
he talks, first crouches on the carpet, then collapses
face down—she puts her hands over her ears, then
takes them away)

DAVE *(Into mirror)* Dave Miller? David Abraham Miller?
No reply. No one at home. Anna, do you know what I'm
scared of? One of these fine days I'll look in the glass,
expecting to see a fine earnest ethical young . . . and
there'll be nothing there. Then, slowly, a small dark stain
will appear on the glass, it will slowly take form and . . .
Anna, I want to be a good man. I want to be a good man.

ANNA *(For herself)* I know.
     (But he has already recovered. He comes to her, pulls her up to sit by him)

DAVE If that God of theirs ever dishes out any medals to us, what'll it be for?

ANNA No medals for us.

DAVE Yes, for trying. For going on. For keeping the doors open.

ANNA Open for *what?*

DAVE You know. Because if there's anything new in the world anywhere, any new thought, or new way of living, we'll be ready to hear the first whisper of it. When Doctor Melville Cooper-Anstey imagines God, how does he imagine him?

ANNA As Dr. Melville Cooper-Anstey, two sizes larger.

DAVE But we've got to do better. Anna, look—the walls are down, and anyone or anything can come in. Now imagine off the street comes an entirely new and beautiful phenomenon, a new human being.

ANNA Jewish boy—you're a good Jewish boy after all waiting for the Messiah.

DAVE That's what everyone's waiting for, even if they don't know it—something new to be born. Anna, supposing superman walked in now off the street, how would you imagine him?

ANNA Superwoman.

DAVE Oh O.K.

ANNA *(In despair)* Me.

DAVE I know. I know it. Me too. I sit and think and think —because if we don't know what we want to grow into, how can we shape ourselves better? So I concentrate until my brain is sizzling, and who comes in through the door —me!

ANNA Just once it wasn't me.

DAVE *(Excited)* Who?

ANNA I was sitting here, like this. I was thinking—if we can't breed something better than we are, we've had it, the human race has had it. And then, suddenly . . .

DAVE What?

ANNA He walked in, twitching his tail. An enormous glossy padding tiger. The thing was, I wasn't at all surprised. Well, tiger, I said, and who do you belong to?

DAVE *(Furious)* Anna, a tiger walks in here, and all you can say is, wild beast, whose label is around your neck?

ANNA I thought you wanted to *know*.

DAVE Go on.

ANNA The tiger came straight towards me. Hullo tiger, I said, have you escaped from the zoo?

DAVE *(Mocking)* Of *course* he's escaped from the zoo. He couldn't be a wild tiger, could he?

ANNA *(She kneels, talking to the tiger)* Tiger, tiger, come here. *(She fondles the tiger)* Tiger, tiger—The tiger purred so loud that the sound drowned the noise of the traffic. And then suddenly—(ANNA *starts back, clutching at her arms)* He lashed out, I was covered with blood. Tiger, I said, what's that for . . . he backed away, snarling.

    (ANNA is now on her feet, after the tiger)

DAVE *(Very excited)* Yeah. That's it. That's it. That's it.

ANNA He jumped on to my bed and crouched there, lashing his tail. But tiger, I said, I haven't done anything to you, have I?

DAVE *(Furious)* Why didn't you offer him a saucer of milk? Kitty, kitty, have a nice saucer of milk?

ANNA *(Beside the bed, trying to hold the tiger)* Tiger, don't go away. But he stared and he glared, and then he was off —down he leaped and out into the street, and off he padded with his yellow eyes gleaming into the shadows of Earls Court. Then I heard the keepers shouting after him and wheeling along a great cage . . . *(She comes back opposite* DAVE*)* That was the best I could do. I tried hard, but that was the best—a tiger. And I'm covered with scars.

DAVE *(Gently)* Anna.

    (They kneel, foreheads touching, hands together. The telephone starts ringing)

DAVE Answer it.

ANNA No.

DAVE Is it Tom?

ANNA Of course it isn't Tom.

DAVE Then who?

ANNA Don't you really know?
 (She goes to answer telephone, it stops ringing. She stands a moment. Then turns to him, fast)

ANNA Love me, Dave. Love me, Dave. Now.
 *(*DAVE* rolls her on to the carpet. They roll over and over together. Suddenly she breaks free and begins to laugh)*

DAVE What's so funny?

ANNA *(Kneeling up, mocking)* I'll tell you what's funny, Dave Miller. We sit here, tearing ourselves to bits trying to imagine something beautiful and new—but suppose the future is a nice little American college girl all hygienic and virginal and respectable with a baby in her arms. Suppose the baby is what we're waiting for—a nice, well-fed, well-educated, psycho-analysed superman . . .

DAVE Anna, please stop it.

ANNA But imagine. Anything can come in—tigers, unicorns, monsters, the human being so beautiful he will send all of us into the dust-can. But what does come in is a nice, anxious little girl from Philadelphia.

DAVE Well, Anna?

ANNA Well, Dave?
 (A fresh burst of fighting from the street. ANNA *moves to shut the window,* DAVE *holds her)*

DAVE I'm surprised I have to tell you that anything you shut out because you're scared of it becomes more dangerous.

ANNA Yes, but I've lived longer than you, and I'm tired.

DAVE That's a terrible thing to say.

ANNA I daresay it is.

END OF ACT TWO

Act Three

ANNA *and* DAVE *in the same positions as at the end of Act Two—no time has passed.*

ANNA Yes, I daresay it is.
(She goes to the light, switches it on, the room is closed in)

ANNA *(As she switches on the light)* I must be mad. I keep trying to forget it's all over. But it is.
(From the moment ANNA *says "It's all over" it is as if she has turned a switch inside herself. She is going inside herself: she has in fact "frozen-up on him." This is from self-protection, and* DAVE *knows it. Of course he knows by now, or half-knows, and still won't admit to himself, about* JANET. *But he is trying to get through to* ANNA. *He really can't stand it when she freezes up on him. From now until when Mary comes in should be played fast, wild, angry, mocking: they circle around each other, they do not touch each other.*

ANNA *goes straight from the light switch to the record-player, puts on "I'm on My Way," goes to the bottom of her bed, where she kneels, and shuts* DAVE *out by pretending to work on something)*

DAVE *(Shouting across music)* Anna. I could kill you. *(As she ignores him)* . . . come clean, what have you been really doing in the last weeks to get yourself into such a state?

ANNA *(Shouting)* I've been unhappy, I've been so unhappy I could have died.

DAVE Ah come on, baby.

ANNA But I can't say that, can I? To say, You made me unhappy, is to unfairly curtail your freedom?

DAVE But why the hell do you have to be unhappy?

ANNA Oh quite so. But I didn't say it. I've been sitting here, calm as a rock, playing *I'm on My Way.*

258

DAVE   Why?

ANNA   It would seem I have the soul of a Negro singer.

DAVE   Oh Christ. *(He turns off the record-player)*

ANNA   *(Too late)* Leave it on.

DAVE   No, I want to talk.

ANNA   All right, talk. *(He bangs his fist against the wall)* Or shall I ask you what you've been doing in the last few weeks to get yourself into such a state?

   (A silence)

ANNA   Well, talk. *(Conversational)* Strange, isn't it, how the soul of Western man—what may be referred to, loosely, as the soul of Western man, is expressed by Negro folk music and the dark rhythms of the ... *(DAVE leaps up, he begins banging with his fists against the wall)* I'm thinking of writing a very profound article about the soul of Western man as expressed by ...

DAVE   *(Banging with his fists)* Shut up.

ANNA   I'm *talking.* Looked at objectively—yes objectively is certainly the word I'm looking for—what could be more remarkable than the fact that the soul of Western man ...

DAVE   *(Turning on her)* You have also, since I saw you last, been engaged to marry Tom Lattimer.

ANNA   Don't tell me you suddenly care?

DAVE   I'm curious

ANNA   *(Mocking)* I was in lurve. Like you were.

DAVE   You were going to settle down?

ANNA   That's right, I decided it was time to settle *down.*

DAVE   If you're going to get married you might at least get married on some sort of a level.

ANNA   But Dave, the phrase is, settle *down.* *(She bends over, hold her hand a few inches from the floor)* It is no accident, surely, that the phrase is settle *down.* *(DAVE stands watching her, banging the side of his fist against the wall)* I'm thinking of writing a short, pithy, but nevertheless profoundly profound article on the unconscious attitude to marriage revealed in our culture by the phrase settle *down.*

(DAVE *lets his fist drop. Leans casually against the wall, watches her ironically*)

DAVE   Anna, I know you too well.

ANNA   An article summing up—how shall I put it—the contemporary *reality*.

DAVE   I know you too well.

ANNA   But it seems, not well enough . . . We're through, Dave Miller. We're washed up. We're broken off. We're finished.

DAVE *(With simplicity)*   But Anna, you love me.

ANNA   It would seem there are more important things than love.

DAVE *(Angry)*   Lust?

ANNA   Lust? What's that? Why is it I can say anything complicated to you but never anything simple? I can't say you made me unhappy. I can't say—are you sure you're not making someone else unhappy. So how shall I put it? Well, it has just occurred to me in the last five minutes that when Prometheus was in his cradle it was probably rocked by the well-manicured hand of some stupid little goose whose highest thought was that the thatch on her hut should be better plaited than the thatch on her neighbour's hut. Well? Is that indirect enough? After all, it is the essence of the myth that the miraculous baby should not be recognized. And so we are both playing our parts nicely. You because you're convinced it can't happen to *you*. Me because I can't bear to think about it.

DAVE   Anna, you haven't let that oaf Tom Lattimer make you pregnant.

ANNA   Oh my God. No. I haven't. No dear Dave, I'm not pregnant. But perhaps I should be?

DAVE   O.K. Anna, I'm sorry. I'm sorry I made you unhappy. But—well, here I am, Anna.

ANNA   Yes, here you are. *(In pain)* Dave, you have no right, you have no right . . . you're a very careless person, Dave . . . *(She gets off the bed and goes to the window)* What's the use of talking of rights and wrongs? Or of right or wrong? O.K., it's a jungle. Anything goes. I should have let myself get pregnant. One catches a man by getting pregnant. People like you and me make life too complicated. Back to reality. *(Looking down)* My God, that poor fool is still down there.

DAVE Anna, don't freeze up on me.

ANNA You want to know what I've been doing? Well, I've been standing here at night looking into the street and trying not to think about what you've been doing. I've been standing here. At about eleven at night the law and the order dissolve. The girls stand at their window there, kissing or quarrelling as the case might be, in between customers. The wolves prowl along the street. Gangs of kids rush by, living in some frightened lonely violent world that they think we don't understand—ha! So they think we don't understand what's driving them crazy? Old people living alone go creeping home, alone. The women who live alone, after an hour of talking to strangers in a pub, go home, alone. And sometimes a married couple or lovers— and they can't wait to get inside, behind the walls, they can't wait to lock the doors against this terrible city. And they're right.

DAVE They're not right.

ANNA Put your arms around one other human being, and let the rest of the world go hang—the world is terrifying, so shut it out. That's what people are doing everywhere, and perhaps they are right.

DAVE Anna, say it!

ANNA All right. You're an egotist, and egotists can never bear the thought of a new generation. That's all. And I'm an egotist and what I call my self-respect is more important to me than anything else. And that's all. There's nothing new in it. There's nothing new anywhere. I shall die of boredom. Sometimes at night I look out into a street and I imagine that somewhere is a quiet room, and in the room is a man or a woman, thinking. And quite soon there will be a small new book—a book of one page perhaps, and on the page one small new thought. And we'll all read it and shout: Yes, yes, that's it.

DAVE Such as?

ANNA *(Mocking)* We must love one another or die, something new like that.

DAVE Something new like that.

ANNA But of course it wouldn't be that at all. It would probably turn out to be a new manifesto headed: Six new rules for egotists, or How to eat your cake and have it.

DAVE Anna, stop beating us up.

ANNA Ah *hell*.

(DAVE *puts out a hand to her, drops it on her look*)

DAVE O.K., Anna, have it your way . . . You're not even interested in what I've been doing since I saw you? You haven't even asked.

ANNA The subject, I thought, had been touched on.

DAVE No, honey, I was being serious. Work, I mean work. I've been working. *(Mocking himself)* I've been writing a sociological-type article about Britain.

ANNA So that is what you've been doing for the last week. *We* were wondering.

DAVE *(Acknowledging the "we")* O.K. Anna, O.K., O.K.

ANNA What am I going to be without you? I get so lonely without you.

DAVE But baby, I'm here. *(At her look)* O.K. Anna. O.K.

ANNA All right, Dave. But all the same . . . I sometimes think if my skin were taken off I'd be just one enormous bruise. Yes, that's all I am, just a bruise.

DAVE Uh-huh.

ANNA However, comforting myself with my usual sociological-type thought, I don't see how there can be such pain everywhere without something new growing out of it.

DAVE Uh-huh.

ANNA *(Fierce)* Yes!

DAVE All the same, you're tough. At a conservative estimate, a hundred times tougher than I am. Why?

ANNA *(Mocking)* Obviously, I'm a woman, everyone knows we are tough.

DAVE Uh-huh . . . I was thinking, when I was away from you, every time I take a beating it gets harder to stand up afterwards. You take punishment and up you get smiling.

ANNA Oh quite so. Lucky, isn't it?

DAVE Tell me, when your husband was killed, did it knock you down?

ANNA Oh of course not, why should it?

DAVE O.K., Anna.

ANNA Everyone knows that when a marriage ends because the husband is killed fighting heroically for his country the marriage is by definition romantic and beautiful. *(At his look)* All right, I don't choose to remember. *(At his look)* O.K., it was a long time ago.

DAVE Well then, is it because you've got that kid?

ANNA *(Irritated)* Is *what* because I've got that kid. That kid, that kid . . . You talk about him as if he were a plant in a pot on the windowsill, or a parcel I've left lying about somewhere, instead of what my life has been about.

DAVE Why take men seriously when you've got a child?

ANNA *(Ironic)* Ho-ho, I see.

DAVE All right then, tell me truthfully, tell me straight, baby, none of the propaganda now, what does it really mean to you to have that kid?

ANNA But why should you be interested, you're not going to have children . . .

DAVE Come on, Anna, you can't have it both ways.

ANNA No.

DAVE Why not?

ANNA *(Angry)* Because I can never say anything I think, I feel—it always ends up with what you think, you feel. My God, Dave, sometimes I *feel* you like a great black shadow over me I've got to get away from . . . oh all right, all right . . .

(She stands, slowly smiles)

DAVE Don't give me that Mona Lisa stuff, I want to know.

ANNA Well. He sets me free. Yes, that's it, he sets me free.

DAVE Why, for God's sake, you spend your time in savage domesticity whenever he's within twenty miles of you.

ANNA Don't you see? He's *there*. I go into his room when
he's asleep to take a good long look at him, because he's too
old now to look at when he's awake, that's already an
interference. So I look at him. He's *there*.

DAVE He's there.

ANNA There he is. He's something new. A kind of ray of
light that shoots off into any direction. Or blaze up like a
comet or go off like a rocket.

DAVE *(Angry)* Oh don't tell me, you mean it gives you a
sense of power—you look at him and you think—I made
that.

ANNA No, that's not it. Well, that's what I said would happen. You asked, I told you, and you don't believe me.
      *(She turns her back on him, goes to window. A long
      wolf-whistle from outside. Another)*

ANNA Let's ask him up and tell him the facts of life.

DAVE Not much point if he hasn't got fifty shillings.

ANNA The State is prosperous. He will have fifty shillings.

DAVE No, let us preserve romance. Let him dream.
      (Shouting and quarrelling from the street)

DAVE *(At window with her)* There's the police.

ANNA They're picking up the star-struck hero as well.

DAVE No mixing of the sexes at the police station so he can
go on dreaming of his loved one from afar even now.
      *(A noise of something falling on the stairs. Voices.
      Giggling)*

DAVE What the hell's that?

ANNA It's Mary.

DAVE She's got herself a man? Good for her.

ANNA *(Distressed and irritable)* No, but she's going to get
herself laid. Well, that's O.K. with you isn't it? Nothing
wrong with getting oneself laid, according to you.

DAVE It might be the beginning of something serious for
her.

ANNA Oh quite so. And when you get yourself laid. *(Conversationally and with malice)* It's odd the way the American male talks of getting himself laid. In the passive. "I
went out and got myself laid" what a picture—the poor

helpless creature, pursuing his own pure concerns, while
the predatory female creeps up behind him and lays him
on his back . . .

DAVE   Don't get at me because you're worried about Mary.
(*He goes over and puts his arm about her. For a moment, she accepts it*) Who is it?

ANNA   Harry. (MARY *and* HARRY *have arrived outside*
ANNA'S *door. Can be seen as two shadows. One shadow
goes upstairs. One shadow remains*) I hope she doesn't
come in.

DAVE   But he shouldn't be here if Helen's in a bad
way . . . (*As* ANNA *looks at him*) Hell.
(*He goes across to the mirror, where he stands grimac-
ing at himself.* MARY *knocks and comes in. She is
rather drunk and aggressive*)

MARY   You're up late, aren't you?

ANNA   Have a good time?

MARY   He's quite amusing, Harry. (*She affects a yawn*) I'm
dead. Well, I think I'll pop off to bed. (*Looking suspiciously
at* ANNA) You weren't waiting up for me, were you?

ANNA   (*Looking across at* DAVE) No.
(MARY *sees* DAVE, *who is draping the black cloth
across the mirror*)

MARY   Well, what a stranger. What are you doing? Don't
you like the look of yourself?

DAVE   Not very much. Do you?

MARY   I've been talking over old times with Harry.

DAVE   Yes, Anna said.

MARY   I expect you two have been talking over old times
too. I must go to bed, I'm dead on my feet. (*There is a noise
upstairs. Quickly*) That must be the cat. Have you seen the
cat?

ANNA   Yes, I suppose it must.

MARY   I was saying to Anna, only today, I'm getting a proper
old maid—if a widow can be an old maid, fussing over a cat,
well you'd never believe when you were young what you'll
come to.

DAVE You an old maid—you've got enough spunk for a twenty-year-old.

MARY Yes, Harry was saying, I wouldn't think you were a day over twenty-five, he said. *(To* DAVE*)* Did you know my boy was getting married next week?

DAVE Yes, I heard.

MARY He's got himself a nice girl. But I can't believe it. It seems only the other day . . . *(There is a bang upstairs. A moment later, a loud miaow outside* ANNA'S *door)* Why, there's my pussy cat. *(Another crash upstairs)* I must go and see . . . *(She scuttles out.* HARRY'S *shadow on the stairs. Putting her head around the door)* Isn't it nice, Harry's decided to pop back for a cup of coffee.

> *(She shuts the door.* ANNA *and* DAVE, *in silence, opposite each other on the carpet. Dance music starts, soft, upstairs)*

ANNA A good lay, with music.

DAVE Don't, baby. If I was fool enough to marry I'd be like Harry.

ANNA Yes.

DAVE Don't hate him.

ANNA I can make out Harry's case as well as you. He wanted to be a serious writer, but like a thousand others he's got high standards and no talent. So he works on a newspaper he despises. He goes home to a wife who doesn't respect him. So he has to have the little girls to flatter him and make him feel good. O.K., Dave—but what more do you want? I'll be back on duty by this evening, pouring out sympathy in great wet gobs and I'll go on doing it until he finds another little girl who looks at him with gooey eyes and says: oh Harry, oh Dave, you're so wonderful.

DAVE It wouldn't do you any harm to indulge in a bit of flattery from time to time.

ANNA Oh yes it would. I told you, I'm having the truth with a man or nothing. I watch women buttering up their men, anything for a quiet life and despising them while they do it. It makes me sick.

DAVE Baby, I pray for the day when you flatter me for just ten seconds.

ANNA Oh go and get it from—Janet.

(MARY comes in fast, without knocking)

MARY *(She is very aggressive)* Anna, I didn't like your manner just now. Sometimes there is something in your way I don't like at all.

(ANNA turns away)

ANNA Mary, you're a little high.

MARY I'm not. I'm not tight at all. I've had practically nothing to drink. And you don't even listen. I'm serious and you're not listening. *(Taking hold of Anna)* I'm not going to have it. I'm simply not going to have it.

(HARRY comes in. He is half drunk)

HARRY Come on, Mary. I thought you were going to make me some coffee. (MARY *bangs ineffectually at* ANNA'S *shoulder with her fist*) Hey, girls, don't brawl at this time of night.

MARY I'm not brawling. *(To DAVE)* He's smug too, isn't he. Like Anna. *(To ANNA)* And what about you? This afternoon you were still with Tom and now it's Dave.

HARRY You're a pair of great girls.

(ANNA looks in appeal at DAVE)

DAVE *(Coming gently to support MARY)* Hey, Mary, come on now.

MARY *(Clinging to him)* I like you, Dave. I always did. When people say to me, that crazy Dave, I always say, I like Dave. I mean, it's only the crazy people who understand life when you get down to it . . .

DAVE That's right, Mary. *(He supports her)*

(HARRY comes and attempts to take MARY'S arm. MARY shakes him off and confronts ANNA)

MARY Well, Anna, that's what I wanted to say and I've said it.

(HARRY is leading MARY out)

MARY The point is, what I mean is.

HARRY You've made your point, come on.

ANNA   See you in the morning, Mary.

MARY   Well, I've been meaning to say it and I have.

    (HARRY and MARY go out, HARRY with a nod and a smile at the other two)

DAVE   Anna, she'll have forgotten all about it in the morning.

    (He goes to her. She clings to him)

DAVE   And if she hasn't, you'll have to.

ANNA   Oh, hell, hell, hell.

DAVE   Yes, I know, baby, I know.

ANNA   She's going to wish she were dead tomorrow morning.

DAVE   Well, it's not so terrible. You'll be here and you can pick up the pieces. *(He leads her to the bed, and sits by her, his arm around her)* That's better. I like looking after you. Let's have six months' peace and quiet. Let's have a truce —what do you say?

    (The telephone rings. They are both tense, listening. HARRY comes in)

HARRY   Don't you answer your telephone, Anna? What's the matter with you two? *(He goes to the telephone to answer it. Sees their faces, stops)* I'm a clod. Of course, it's Tom.

ANNA   It isn't Tom.

HARRY   Of course it is. Poor bastard, he's breaking his heart and here you are dallying with Dave.

ANNA   I know it isn't.

DAVE   Never argue with Anna when she's got one of her fits of intuition.

ANNA   Intuition!

HARRY   Mary's passed clean out. Mary's in a bad way tonight. Just my luck. I need someone to be nice to me, and all Mary wants is someone to be nice to her.

ANNA   I hope you were.

HARRY   Of course I was.

ANNA   Why don't you go home to Helen?

HARRY   *(Bluff)* It's four in the morning. Did you two fools know it's four in the morning? I'll tell Helen my troubles tomorrow. Anna, don't tell me you're miserable too. *(Going to her)* Is that silly bastard Dave playing you up? It's a hell of a life. Now I'll tell you what. I'll pick you up for lunch tomorrow, I mean today, and I'll tell you my troubles and you can tell me yours. *(To* DAVE*)* You've made Anna unhappy, you clod, you idiot.

ANNA Oh damn it, if you want to play big Daddy why don't you go home and mop up some of Helen's tears?

HARRY *(Bluff)* I don't have to worry about Helen, I keep telling you.

ANNA Harry!

HARRY *(To* DAVE, *shouting it)* Clod. Fool . . . all right, I suppose I've got to go home. But it's not right, Anna. God in his wisdom has ordained that there should be a certain number of understanding women in the world whose task it is to bind up the wounds of warriors like Dave and me. Yes, I'll admit it, it's hard on you but—you're a man's woman, Anna, and that means that when we're in trouble you can't be.

ANNA Thank you, I did understand my role.
    (The telephone rings)

HARRY He's a persistent bugger isn't he? *(He picks up telephone, shouts into it)* Well, you're not to marry him, Anna. Or anyone. Dave and I won't let you.
    (He slams receiver back)

ANNA Go home. Please go home.

HARRY *(For the first time serious)* Anna, you know something? I'm kind Uncle Harry, the world's soft shoulder for about a thousand people. I make marriages, I patch them up. I give good advice. I dish out aid and comfort. But there's just one person in the world I can't be kind to.

ANNA Helen's ill.

HARRY I know she is. I know it. But every time it's the same thing. I go in, full of good intentions—and then something happens. I don't know what gets into me . . . I was looking into the shaving glass this morning, a pretty sight I looked, I was up all last night drinking myself silly because my poppet's getting married. I looked at myself. You silly sod,

I said. You're fifty this year, and you're ready to die because of a little girl who . . . you know, Anna, if she wanted me to cut myself into pieces for her I'd do it? And she looked at me yesterday with those pretty little eyes of hers and she said—primly, she said it, though not without kindness—Harry, do you know what's wrong with you? You're at the dangerous age, she said. All men go through it. Oh Christ, Anna, let me take you out and give you a drink tonight. I've got to weep on someone's shoulder. I'd have wept on Mary's, only all she could say was: "Harry, what's the meaning of life?" She asks me.

ANNA Anything you like but for God's sake go home now.

HARRY I'm going. Helen will pretend to be asleep. She never says anything. Well, I suppose she's learned there's not much point in her saying anything, poor bitch.

(He goes. DAVE *and* ANNA *look at each other)*

DAVE O.K., Anna. Now let's have it.

ANNA *(In cruel parody)* I'm just a little ordinary girl, what's wrong with that? I want to be married, what's wrong with that? I never loved anyone as I loved Dave . . .

DAVE No, Anna, not like that.

ANNA *(In* JANET'S *voice, wild with anxiety)* When I knew I was pregnant I was so happy. Yes I know how it looks, trapping a man, but he said he loved me, he said he loved me. I'm five months pregnant.

(She stands waiting. DAVE *looks at her)*

ANNA Well, haven't you got anything to say?

DAVE Did you expect me to fall down at your feet and start grovelling? God, Anna, look at you, the mothers of the universe have triumphed, the check's on the table and Dave Miller's got to pay the bill, that's it, isn't it?

(She says nothing. DAVE *laughs)*

ANNA Funny?

DAVE *(With affection)* You're funny, Anna.

ANNA It's not my baby. I'm sorry it isn't. I wasn't so intelligent.

DAVE That's right. You've never got the manacles on me, but Janet has. Now I marry Janet and settle down in the insurance business and live happily ever after, is it that? Is that how you see it? If not, this cat and mouse business all evening doesn't make sense.

ANNA   And the baby? Just another little casualty in the sex war? She's a nice respectable middle-class girl, you can't say to her, have an illegitimate baby, it will be an interesting experience for you—you could have said it to me.

DAVE   Very nice, and very respectable.

ANNA   You said you loved her.

DAVE   Extraordinary. You're not at all shocked that she lied to me all along the line?

ANNA   You told her you loved her.

DAVE   I'll admit it's time I learned to define my terms . . . you're worried about Janet's respectability? If the marriage certificate is what is important to her I'll give her one. No problems.

ANNA   No problems!

DAVE   I'll fix it. Anna, you know what? You've been using Janet to break off with me because you haven't the guts to do it for yourself? I don't come through for you so you punish me by marrying me off to Janet Stevens?

ANNA   O.K., then why don't you come through for me? Here you are, Dave Miller, lecturing women all the time about how they should live—women should be free, they should be independent, etc, etc. None of these dishonest female ruses. But if that's what you really want what are you doing with Janet Stevens—and all the other Janets? Well? The truth is you can't take us, you can't take me. I go through every kind of bloody misery trying to be what you say you want, but . . .

DAVE   O.K., some of the time I can't take you.

ANNA   And what am I supposed to do when you're off with the Janets?

DAVE   (*With confidence*) Well, you can always finally kick me out.

ANNA   And in a few months' time when you've got tired of yourself in the role of a father, there'll be a knock on the door . . . "Hi, Anna, do you love me? Let's have six months' peace and quiet, let's have a truce . . ." and so on, and so on, and so on, and so on . . .

> *(The telephone rings)*

DAVE *(At telephone)* Hi, Janet, Yeah. O.K., baby. O.K., I'm on my way. Don't cry baby.

> *(He puts down receiver. They look at each other)*

DAVE Well, baby?

ANNA Well?

> *(He goes out. Now* ANNA *has a few moments of indecision, of unco-ordination. She begins to cry, but at once stops herself. She goes to cupboard, brings out Scotch and a glass. She nearly fills the glass with Scotch. With this in her hand she goes to the mirror, carefully drapes the black cloth over it. Goes to carpet, where she sits as if she were still sitting opposite Dave. The Scotch is on the carpet beside her. She has not drunk any yet.* ANNA *sits holding herself together, because if she cracked up now, it would be too terrible. She rocks herself a little, perhaps, picks bit of fluff off her trousers, makes restless, unco-ordinated movements.*
> MARY *comes in)*

MARY I must have fallen asleep. I don't know what Harry thought, me falling asleep like that . . .what did you say? I don't usually . . . Where's Dave?

ANNA He's gone to get married.

MARY Oh. Well, he was bound to get married some time, wasn't he?

> *(Now she looks closely at* ANNA *for the first time)*

MARY I must have been pretty drunk. I still am if it comes to that.

> *(She looks at the glass of Scotch beside Anna, then at the black cloth over the mirror)*

MARY Hadn't you better get up?

> *(*MARY *goes to the mirror, takes off the black cloth and begins to fold it up. She should do this like a housewife folding a tablecloth, very practical)*

MARY I suppose some people will never have any more sense than they were born with.

(She lays down the cloth, folded neatly. Now she comes to Anna, takes up the glass of Scotch, and pours it back into the bottle)

MARY God only knows how I'm going to get myself to work today, but I suppose I shall.

(She comes and stands over ANNA. ANNA *slowly picks herself off the floor and goes to the window)*

MARY That's right. Anna, have you forgotten your boy'll be home in a few days? *(As* ANNA *responds)* That's right. Well, we always say we shouldn't live like this, but we do, don't we, so what's the point . . . *(She is now on her way to the door)* I was talking to my boy this morning. Twenty-four. He knows everything. What I wouldn't give to be back at twenty-four, knowing everything . . .

*(*MARY *goes out. Now* ANNA *slowly goes towards the bed. As she does so, the city comes up around her, and the curtain comes down)*

Calm Down Mother

A Transformation for Three Women

BY MEGAN TERRY

CHARACTERS

WOMAN ONE

WOMAN TWO

WOMAN THREE

SCENE: *An open stage. Four chairs are in view. Lights dim up during following speech on tape. Three* WOMEN *are clustered together to suggest a plant form.*

WOMAN'S VOICE *(To be read with the attitude of an amused gentlewoman)* Three one-celled creatures float with currents under the sea. They are propelled at different rates of speed depending upon which current surrounds them. From time to time they reach a byway in the current and float aimlessly. They engulf food whenever they can. When the current changes they are swept into one water force. They come near the shore: the waves push them against the sand: they fall back. Again they are swept up the beach, and again the water pulls them back. Before the next wave hits, they are swept into a small whirlpool where they join together and again are swept up the beach. This time they are not swept back, but take root: one of the first plants to come out of the sea.

A tornado uproots and splits the plant. Two parts fall away. One stretches toward the sun.

> *(The middle* WOMAN *walks toward the audience and smiles at them in joyous wonder)*

WOMAN ONE   I'm Margaret Fuller. I know I am because . . . "From the time I could speak and go alone, my father addressed me not as a plaything, but as a living mind." I am Margaret Fuller. I am Margaret Fuller and I accept the universe!

TWO WOMEN *(Assuming superior postures)* You had better. You had better. Carlyle said that you had better. You had better. You had better. You bet your butter, Carlyle said that you had better.

WOMAN ONE   I accept. I accept, not as a furry animal play-

279

thing, but as a mind, as a living loving blinding mind. My father said . . .

TWO WOMEN   If you know what's good for you, you had better. Better grab that universe, little daughter. Grab it while you can. You had better, you had better. You had better grab it before you melt.

> *(A brief freeze. Then* WOMAN ONE *moves to a store counter. She becomes* SOPHIE. WOMAN THREE *becomes* ESTHER. WOMAN TWO *is a nineteen-year-old* GIRL. *Scene is a delicatessen in Brooklyn)*

GIRL   *(Entering store)*   Six packa Ballantine Ale, please.

SOPHIE   *(At counter. She stares at* GIRL)   Six pack?
> *(But she doesn't move)*

GIRL   *(At first impatient, but then she smiles)*   Make it two six packs.

SOPHIE   Six packs?

ESTHER   She wants ale, Sophie.

SOPHIE   I heard her, Esther,

GIRL   Of Ballantine's. Ballantine Ale.

SOPHIE   Esther, see? Her hair.

ESTHER   So—her hair? What about it? All girls got hairs.

SOPHIE   But it's *her* hair. *(To the* GIRL)   Your hair.

GIRL   I'm in a hurry and I'd . . .

SOPHIE   *(Smiling)*   It's just like . . . you see, your hair . . . it's just like Mother's was. Just like it. Same color even.

ESTHER   She ain't got all day. Sophie, you get; I can't reach the 'frigerator.

SOPHIE   *(Reaching toward the* GIRL's *hair)*   My hair was like yours . . . but now? *(She shrugs)* Surgery. *(She nods)* Major operations.

ESTHER   *Oy Vey!*

SOPHIE   Every time . . . major operations . . . every time I go . . .

ESTHER   Twenty years it was ago!

SOPHIE   Something about the anesthesia. Every time I go under I come out with less hair. *(She shakes her head and smiles)* Your hair—it's like hers was. Like mine was, like hers was. Even more though.

ESTHER Selfish! Always washing and combing herself. Could never get ready to go out myself. Some sister!

SOPHIE She had something to be proud of. She used to say that boys waited up to eight hours just to take her out.

GIRL Uh, I'd really like those two six packs of Ballantine's.

SOPHIE *(Moving to GIRL)* I know. I got them for you nearly. Let me just touch your hair. It's so like . . . Something about the anesthetic made mine go and get straight. See, feel me.

GIRL Couldn't they uh make tests . . . allergies . . . you should have tested . . . well you know you may a been allergic to whatever they knocked you out with . . . Your hair fell out fer God's sake. It's important to a girl for God's sake. Her hair. You know what I mean.

SOPHIE *(Nodding sadly)* Well they're interested in pulling you . . . Yes, sure they want to bring you through. Open heart surgery ain't the simplest thing in the world.

ESTHER *(In union with SOPHIE on last line)* Open heart surgery ain't the simplest thing in the world.

SOPHIE But your hair! My mother's hair went in points from here. One point right here and then back and so wavy. Wavy here and here and here. And then it came to a little point in the back. I used to comb it for her when she took her bath. Here, give me the comb, let me do it for you. That's right. Oh Esther you should feel this, so like Momma's. And her skin like milk. And her skin . . . you should . . .

ESTHER *(Talking to God)* Her skin wasn't so hot. My skin's the same. So what's so wrong with my skin? Only sixty years older that's only . . .

SOPHIE Her skin . . . and then I'd wash her back.

(ESTHER *and* GIRL *begin a mournful hum that builds to a lament by the end of the speech*)

I had skin like her, too, till the blood pressure . . . And then I'd wash her back. And . . . I did. I did it for the last time. Her skin and her hair. I'll never forget the last time, before they put her in her silk . . . before they laid her out you know . . . and everyone came from all over the neighborhood . . . her hair . . . wavy like yours . . . points . . . from here . . . to . . .

> *(When* SOPHIE *joins the lament, the three women are stroking and combing each other's hair. The* GIRL *goes with the grief until it arrives at fever pitch—then she feels suffocated and flings the other two women away)*

WOMAN TWO *(To audience)* I want to get to the point in my life where the anger that people send me, the disapproval they show me, the criticism they yell at me can be absorbed by me and sent right on through me into the ground all the way down to China and out the other side. *(She pins her hair back up)* I can't stand going into these tailspins. I hate the discomfort of it. *(She walks back and leans against* WOMAN THREE. *As she walks she throws her feeling to* WOMAN ONE*)*

WOMAN ONE *(During this speech the other women rub their hands together and hiss)* I want to hit. *(She doubles her fist)* I want to hit! *(She brings her fist up and shows it to audience)* I want to hit! I WANT TO HIT! *(She paces back and forth slamming her fist into the other open palm)* Hit, hit, hit, hit, hit, hit! Bang, Screw! Screw this hitting. All this side of me is aching to hit. It's like a stroke. My left side has nothing more to say. *(She strokes the right side of her head.* WOMEN TWO *and* THREE *freeze)* This whole part of this side of my head is one red rage and it all adds up to—HIT! I can't sleep any more. When I'm out with people, I have to sit on this hand. I'm so afraid I'll hit someone.

> *(Her hitting hand comes up across her chest, arcs under her throat and she opens her mouth as her hand and fingers splay open toward the audience.* WOMEN TWO *and* THREE *duplicate her gesture. There is a short freeze)*

WOMAN THREE *(Steps toward audience)* Talk . . . Talk . . . talk . . . lay bare every part of your limited life. Maybe you could force your life to grow into lives. Facts. Add up all the desperate facts, pitiful few facts as they are—add them all up to enter on the human record, short as it is.

Keep writing. Maybe if I keep talking and writing, listing all the facts of my life, I won't seem so small, at least not so small to me. When I get scared I can pick up all the lists —all the long lists of the facts of my life and read them out loud to myself, and maybe then I won't feel so crippled, so unconnected—at least not to myself . . . A lot of people must start writing with the absurd conviction they are talking to or will contact someone. SOMEONE! SOME-ONE! SOMEONE!

WOMEN ONE AND TWO (*Laugh operatically and menace* WOMAN THREE, *and beat her down to the floor. Where she lies prone during the next scene.* WOMEN ONE *and* TWO *jump up and down, landing flat, making loud thumping noises. Suddenly they change into New Yorkers in a charming flat*)

NANCY (*A hearty Oklahoma accent. She's had about ten drinks. Pacing with relish*) So this is your new apart-ment. (*Her eyes try to glow*) Why it's very . . . it's really very charming. It really is. Downright Greenwich Village, the clean West Side, that is. (*She throws down a heavy leather bag and continues her inspection tour of the small apart-ment*) Look at this table. It's perfect. (*If the actress can play this with the gusto of a robust outdoor woman it would be best. However, it's also possible for her to play the entire scene in a semi-catatonic state gripping the back of a chair*)

SALLY Authentic Goodwill—stripped down by human hands. (*She gets glasses, little snacks*)

NANCY Has he bothered you since? Did you have to get out a restraining order? How do you feel? (*She throws her arms around* SALLY *and smiles*)

SALLY Relieved. He hasn't come near since the suit was filed.

NANCY Good, good, I was worried. You're so soft. I was afraid you'd take him back.

SALLY I'd rather live with King Farouk and three Bengal tigers.

NANCY You'd be happier with the tigers. This place is damn

cute. *(She winks broadly at* SALLY*)* Hey, here we go, ducks. *(She brings a bottle out of her giant bag)* Scotch. Housewarming! I should have brought champagne to break over your head. Don't get into any more impossible marriages for a few weeks. I need a rest.

SALLY   You old party gal! *(Pouring the drinks)* It's just great to see you, Nan. It's been too too long.

NANCY   It doesn't matter . . . I'm back on the scene now. Back to stay. I hope there'll be enough scenes . . . to make . . . too bad we got you straightened out so fast. *(Reaching for her hand, she says grimly)* Sal, I'm going to fall apart.

SALLY   *(Laughing)* Hey, Nan, don't talk like that. Hey, Stella Dallas—snap to!

NANCY   Yeah, yeah, Lolly baby—old Stell will come through —old bulwark of the family. The fight settler. Held Sister together through divorce. Settled Granddaddy's estate. Got Jorgensen into State Assembly. Oh, Christ, Sal . . . hold on to me . . . I can't any more . . . *(She downs her drink)*

SALLY   Nancy, what . . . what is it? What can I do?

NANCY   I wish someone could do . . . what? But there's nothing. I've done everything possible. Brought her up to Harkness Pavilion . . . Every expert in the East. Then last night . . . got the corroborative diagnosis.

SALLY   Nancy, Nan . . . for you. . . ?

NANCY   Mother . . . it's "terminal bone cancer." Sal, it's not fair. It is *not* fair. She's such a fighter. My God, she began a whole new career when Dad retired to his bottle of booze. No training, only her guts . . . good taste. Do you know she knows as much about fashion as I do? She always knew. She knew how to see. She *knows* how to see. So what happens, does this snap him back to reality? No. She's dying, so Dad fakes a heart attack. I've been on the phone with Sister all night. Who's in the hospital. Who's getting all the attention? He is!

SALLY   But Nan, maybe he really . . . needs . . .

NANCY   Such a fighter. Like me. No, I'm like her. Give me a light, will you . . . I can't make these matches work. Thanks, I'm fond of you, you know that?

SALLY Nan, I never could have made it through the breakup without you.

NANCY Men, you can't live with them and all that jazz . . .

SALLY Nancy, how long?

NANCY Six months, 180 days. I can't accept it.

SALLY When are you leaving for Tulsa?

NANCY I was going to take the next plane, but the doctor talked me out of it. You see, if I suddenly appear—you see —she'll think it's the end. If the children all swoop home and stand around the bed, it means, in her mind, she only has hours left. . . . I can't go to her until it really *is* the end. Oh God, Sal, how am I going to stand it? I'll be dying for her every day, every goddamned day from now till . . . till . . .

> (SALLY *and* NANCY *embrace and freeze*)

WOMAN THREE (*Comes up from her floor bed and moves downstage with exuberant motion. Kneels and speaks to audience*)

> Once upon a green time . . .
> Once upon a green time . . .
> My girlhood was still all flowers
>   all flowers
>   all flowers . . .

> (*She freezes for an instant, then rises. She walks upstage and turns her back on the other two.* WOMEN ONE *and* TWO *sit in two chairs facing audience. They are two chairs in a nursing home*)

MRS. TWEED Ah, yes, Mrs. Watermellon, and the days go by and the days go by and the days go by and the days go by, and by and by the days go by. My God, how the days go by!

MRS. WATERMELLON From where I sit . . . I have to agree with you. But they don't go fast enough by, Mrs. Tweed, not by a half sight, not by a full sight. The world is waiting for the sunrise, and I'm the only one who knows where it begins.

MRS. TWEED Why do you keep it a secret?

MRS. WATERMELLON No secret. I've told everyone. I've told and told and told everyone.

MRS. TWEED Where *does* it begin then?

MRS. WATERMELLON *(Clasping her breast)* Here, right here, right here it starts. From the old ticker it starts and pumps and pumps around and thumps around, coagulates in my belly and once a month bursts out onto the ground . . . but all the color's gone . . . all but one . . . all but one . . .

MRS. TWEED You shouldn't think of such things. Woman a' yore age.

MRS. WATERMELLON You're so much! You three-minute egg! You runny, puny, twelve-weeks-old, three-minute egg. You're underdone and overripe. What do you know? You only learned to speak when you got mad enough. I'm going to sleep. I'd as soon live in the mud with the turtles as have to converse with the likes of you.

MRS. TWEED I'm going to call your mother. I'll fly her here on a plane and have her commit you. I'm going to phone your son. I'm going to fly him here on a plane and have you committed. I am. I will. You'll be committed.

MRS. WATERMELLON Dry up, you old fart. I already am.

NURSE *(Entering with tray)* Time for cream of wheat. *(She smiles as she says this, but her voice is flat and mechanical)* Time for your creamy wheat. Time for your wheat. Your cream's all gone. Time for the heap the wheat's all dry. Sit up like good wrinkled girls and dribble it down your chins. Time for your cream of wheat, the sugar's all gone.

MRS. WATERMELLON I'm tired of being a middleman for that pap. Flush it down the nearest john!

NURSE I'll eat it myself. I'll eat it all up.

MRS. TWEED *(Standing and whirling to face nurse)* It's worms. Look at her eat the pail of wiggly worms.

MRS. WATERMELLON *(Joining TWEED)* You got it all wrong, you three-eyed egg. That's the worm, and she's eating herself. *(The NURSE tries to get through to them but the*

TWO WOMEN *become a subway door. They open and close
and chant the while)*

TWO WOMEN Please keep your hands off the doors.
Please keep your hands off the doors.
Please keep your hands off the doors.
Please keep your hands off the doors.
Please keep your hands off the doors.
Please keep your hands off the doors.
Please keep your hands off the doors.
Please keep your hands off the doors.
Please keep your hands off the doors.
Please keep your hands off the doors.
Please keep your hands off the doors.

(One WOMAN *breaks through—goes to the chairs and
sits. They are now call-girls in a lush apartment. Each
is dressing and applying make-up)*

MOMO What are you smirking for. You walk around here
like you had the biggest prick in the world.

FELICIA And you're jealous.

MOMO I do all right.

FELICIA Don't open your yap if you can't back it up.

MOMO I could back it up to you.

FELICIA Not any more you couldn't. I could take anyone
away from you.

INEZ Shut up, you two. We'll never be ready for the first
party.

MOMO Well make her get off my back.

FELICIA With spikes.

MOMO She turns on me. Why you get so nervous whenever
we have to ball a gang? It isn't as if you never did it before.

FELICIA I'll stick holes in your diaphragm. Let me see in the
mirror.

INEZ Felicia, come over here. There's plenty of room.

FELICIA I can't see in that mirror. The light's no good.

MOMO You can't see, period. You've got your mascara half
way down your navel.

FELICIA Bugger off, you—or I'll put alum on your tits.

INEZ Dry up, Felicia! We've got to get ready for work.

FELICIA   Make her stop.

INEZ   I'm going to call Ricky. I'm gonna throw you both out. She can't saddle me with inexperienced bums!

MOMO AND FELICIA   Who's inexperienced?

INEZ   You are!

MOMO AND FELICIA   We've turned more tricks in the last year than . . .

INEZ   Balls! You don't know how to handle yourselves. You don't know how to even get ready to work. What you burning up all your good working energy yapping at each other? You don't stop fighting, I'll boil both you bitches in oil and circumcise your snatches!

FELICIA   Calm down, mother. I can keep Momo in line by telling Ricky . . .

MOMO   You can't tell Ricky any . . .

FELICIA   *(Pulls out a roll of bills)* Oh no? What's this? Looks like money—looks like you've been stashing your tips in the bathtub water spout.

MOMO   I never . . .

FELICIA   You forgot to clean out your hiding place last night, but I didn't.

MOMO   You took it . . . you crosseyed sonofa—

INEZ   *(Coming between them and grabbing money)* I'll take that. Ricky gets that. What's the matter with you, Momo? Girls have drowned in acid for less than that. You want to ruin your nest?

MOMO   It wasn't a regular lay, it was a piece of cake. He just wanted to look at me. All I had to do was take off my clothes and climb the furniture and spread my fur . . . it wasn't work. I'm saving up for . . .

INEZ   Saving up for what?

MOMO   My vacation. I never been south of Jersey.

INEZ   If Ricky ever found out, we'd all get bumped. I'm responsible for us. It takes us five nights to knock down the rent of this place, we work another week to pay off the fuzz, that leaves two weeks to split with Ricky and the three of us. What if we had to pay income tax, too? For Christ's sakes we couldn't afford to put out!

MOMO Don't tell Ricky, for God's sake don't tell . . .

INEZ I'll give you one more chance. One. You get that? One. One don't mean two! All right? All right.

FELICIA Move it. I need this mirror to finish my make-up. I'm near-sighted and you shouldn't hold it against me.

MOMO I wouldn't hold anything against . . .

INEZ That's enough, that's *enough!*

MOMO I'm sick of you two ganging up on me!

INEZ I think you'll turn into a real swinger, kid, but you got a lot to learn. You're still on probation.

MOMO All right. I'm sorry. What should I do—tear out my ovaries?

INEZ Keep your nose clean, and sweeten that sour mouth. The both of yez!

FELICIA *(Throws herself in INEZ's arms)* Oh, Momma baby, mommie, mommie. We won't fight. We won't do it any more. We didn't mean to get you mad.

INEZ I should blister you till you couldn't sit down.

FELICIA *(Turns her bottom up for spanking)* Do it. We're bad. Bad, bad girls.

MOMO *(Nearly on her knees—she does the same)* Bad, bad, bad, we should have a spanking.

INEZ Stop pawing me. Stop that now. You're spoiling my makeup.

> *(They are in physical contact at this moment. Two are touching, one resisting. They freeze and—*
>
> *The WOMEN form a triangle and throw sentences to each other. The one who receives repeats before she sends on the next new sentence)*

WOMAN ONE Have confidence.

WOMAN TWO Have confidence. You've been found.

WOMAN THREE You've been found. Have confidence.

WOMAN ONE Have confidence. You've been found.

WOMAN TWO You've been found. Have confidence.

WOMAN THREE Have confidence.

TOGETHER You've been found!

> *(They break the formal attitude and tease and walk about. Asking it as a question "You've been found?*

I've been found. Oh, you've been found? No, I've been found." They assume positions of co-operative dish washing at a tenement sink. SUE *who puts dishes away tries to read a magazine at the same time)*

SUE *(Slapping down the magazine)* All this birth control jazz. Who're they kidding? Being mad if you don't let a baby happen? That old dame Mother Nature does it every month—and look, Ma, no rubber!

SAK What're you talking about, no rubber?

SUE No rubber, stupid. Tampax!

SAK Moron, that's for your period.

SUE And it puts a period to the egg, too, don't it, stupid?

MA I want you girls should stop arguing and fighting all the time.

SUE She's too stupid to argue and fight with me.

MA The Bible says you shouldn't cast thy seed upon the ground.

SAK That applies to the fellas, Ma.

SUE You see, you see how dumb you are? What you think grows up in your belly every month—cotton candy?

SAK Make her stop.

MA You should stop, Sue.

(MA and SAK sit on chairs side by side)

SUE I never started it, Ma. That old boy you fall down on your knees and talk to every night—he started it. And he started it here. *(She slaps her belly)* Guys got seeds and girls got seeds, and if that old old old garden planter planted all the damn seeds in the first place, he fixed it so's they wouldn't all grow. They fall on the ground of their own accord, so then? So then, who the hell, then, then who the holy hell are all these priests and magazine writers to say it's wrong? Who the hell are all these guys on platforms to say you can't take pills, you can't use rubbers, down with vaseline, out with diaphragms, who the hell then are they? For God's sake. They're all preventing life!

SAK Make her stop talking like that, Ma. It's just you, Sue, you feeling guilty. You, 'cause you're taking them pills, and you know you shouldn't ought.

SUE Get off my back and get some brains, for God's sake. Listen to me. If you can focus your dirty ears. I'm twenty years old, right?

SAK Twenty and three months.

SUE Je-sus!

SAK Well you are.

SUE Christ. I'm twenty, see, and I'm good till I'm fifty, see. Judging from Ma.

MA Sue!

SUE For God's sake, Ma. You're a female ain't you? You didn't have your period now for three years, right? (*MA counts on her fingers and nods*) So I figure I'm good fer as long as you, so—that makes thirty years still, see?

SAK All you think about is one thing, all you think about is . . .

SUE All I'm trying to prove to you is a proven scientific fact, that is all I'm trying to do to you.

SAK You're disseminating, that's what you're doing.

SUE In your eye! Oh, God. I can't believe you're my sister. Ma, tell me you chose, and only her out of thousands of upturned faces at the orphanage. Please, please?

MA Stop it, the both of you.

SUE Well, I didn't. See, I got enough eggs in me for thirty years, see. That's one a month for thirty years. Twelve times thirty is—360 eggs. Three hundred and sixty possibilities. Three hundred and sixty babies could be born out of my womb. So, if I don't produce each and every one of them, which is a mathematical impossibility, should I go to hell for that? So what should I do—pray and moan on beans? So what should I do, catch eggs and save them in a test tube for when after the BOMB comes? And I'm only one bearer of the eggs. You sitting on yours, you're nineteen. You got a whole year's eggs on me still. So if God sees fit to flush them down the pipe every month if they don't meet up with an electric male shock, then who the hell are these priests and all to scream about pills and controls? Tell me that! Who the hell are they? They want to save my eggs till they can get around to making them into babies, they can line up and screw the test tubes. Yeah! That's a sight. They're welcome. But they can't shoot twins into my test tubes. And you two! You sit there in the church every Sunday, kneeling and mumbling and believing all that crap that those men tell you, and they don't even know what the hell they are talking about. And I'll bet you don't know what I'm talking about. Because I'm the only one in this whole carton of eggs what's got any brains. And I'm taking my pills and I ain't kneeling on any beans or babies' brains to make up for it.

(*The three resume dish washing*)

SAK   You'll burn in the fire for what you just said. . . .

SUE   They'll make me a saint! A thousand years from now they'll award me a medal for not contributing to the population!

SAK   All the candles in the world lit like the stars couldn't get you into Purgatory even.

SUE   Good, then I won't have to be with you.

SAK   You know why she's talking that way, Ma. You know what she's been doing and why she's taking them pills? Where's her husband, Ma? Where's the guy? When's the marriage, Ma? Look at her. She never comes home till four in the morning, Ma. And me, I never stay out past ten.

SUE   Cause nobody asks you that's why.

MA   Pack your things.

SUE   Ah, Ma.

MA   You're no daughter of mine. You pack your things!

SUE   I was only trying to prove . . .

MA   You proved what you are to me all right . . . you pack your things.

SUE   But Ma?

MA   Pack your things.

SUE   I'm proving.

MA   Pack . . . you!

SUE   Ma! I been born out of my time. Or you never left yours. That's right—three hundred years old—that's what you are. You two escapees from Shangri-la. You wrinkle brains, you vegetables, you empty bottles of holy water. I'll go, all right! I don't need any bags. I got everything I need right here in my belly. I got everything I need for the next thirty years, and how!

(The three stand together and smile at the audience. They then speak to it slowly, sweetly, like amused gentlewomen)

TOGETHER *(They place their hands on bellies)*   Our bellies
WOMAN TWO *(On sides)*   Our bodies
TOGETHER *(Back on bellies)*   Our bellies
TOGETHER *(On bellies)*   Our bellies
WOMAN THREE *(On sides)*   Our bodies
TOGETHER *(On bellies)*   Our bellies
WOMAN ONE *(On breasts)*   Our funnies
TOGETHER *(Bellies)*   Our bellies
WOMAN TWO *(Sides)*   Bodies
WOMAN ONE *(Bellies)*   Our eggies
WOMAN THREE *(Bellies)*   Our eggies
WOMAN TWO *(Bellies)*   The eggies in our beggies
WOMAN ONE *(Sides)*   Are enough
WOMAN TWO *(Sides)*   Are enough.
WOMAN THREE *(Sides)*   Are enough
TOGETHER *(Turn their backs on audience)*   ARE THEY?

CURTAIN

The Advertisement

BY NATALIA GINZBURG
Translated by Henry Reed

CHARACTERS

TERESA

ELENA

LORENZO

GIOVANNA

[BOY*]

*TRANSLATOR'S NOTE: This text of *The Advertisement*, though substantially the same as the one used by the BBC and the National Theatre, has been revised in the light of the printed Italian text published by Einaudi. It therefore includes a few changes made by Signora Ginzburg herself. The largest of these is a brief scene near the end of the first act, between Teresa and a grocer's boy. Since Signora Ginzburg regards this scene as optional, and leaves it to the producer to decide whether to include it or to omit it, I have put it in parentheses. (The "boy" may, I suppose, be of any age up to about eighteen.) I have taken the opportunity to correct a number of my own original errors, to rephrase certain remarks, and to restore three sentences I had carelessly omitted.—H.R.

Act One

SCENE: *A doorbell rings.* TERESA *opens the door. Enter* ELENA.

TERESA   Good afternoon.

ELENA   Good afternoon. I telephoned this morning. I've come about the advertisement in the paper. My name's Elena Tesei.

TERESA   Which advertisement was it? I put in three advertisements.

ELENA   The one for the room.

TERESA   Ah, yes, the room. You're looking for a room? Well, I'll show you the room. It faces west. It gets the sun the whole of the afternoon. There's a view of Saint Peter's. Do sit down a moment. Can I get you a cup of coffee?

ELENA   No, thank you.

TERESA   There are five rooms in the flat, so it's really too big for me; but I don't want to leave it: I can't bear moving . . . It's always so sad, I think. So I want to let one room to a university girl in exchange for a little light housework and so on. I loathe housework. Don't you?

ELENA   No, some housework I quite enjoy. And I can't afford to pay for a room. That was why I answered your advertisement.

TERESA   As I said, I put in three advertisements. One was for the sideboard. You don't know anyone who wants to buy a genuine nineteenth-century inlaid rosewood sideboard, I suppose? That's it, over there. I don't keep dishes in it; it's full of old magazines at the moment. In fact, I really haven't any use for a sideboard. I have all my meals in the kitchen. The third advertisement I put in was for my house in the country at Rocca di Papa. I want to sell it. It has ten rooms and an English garden. Well, I say garden: it's more of a park actually. I never go there. The few times

299

I *have* been, I nearly died of depression. I can't bear the country. The minute I smell hay, or cows, it makes me want to cry. It may be because I lived in the country when I was little. I began to hate the country even when I was a little girl. I had a horrible childhood.

ELENA Did you get any replies?

TERESA To the advertisements? Yes, a woman rang up about the sideboard. I was very rude to her, I'm afraid. She said, "How much are you asking?" I said, "Two million lire, or nearest offer." Nearest offer means I'm willing to discuss it, doesn't it? She said, "It's too much." Too much . . . for a genuine nineteenth-century inlaid rosewood sideboard! And she'd never even seen it . . . I've had no replies so far about the house at Rocca di Papa.

ELENA And the room?

TERESA I've had four applications for the room—including yourself, that is. The first was an unmarried mother with a three-months-old baby. No, thank you. The next was a girl who was studying the violin. No. Mind you, I like music, and I'm very fond of little children. I unfortunately can't have a baby myself. But I suffer dreadfully from headaches these days, I must have a little peace and quiet. A third woman came this morning, but she was too old. I expressly put "student" in the advertisement, and this woman was an old-age pensioner. She must have been at least sixty. I must have someone young. Besides she was common, and I do want someone refined about the place, someone with a bit of education. I mean someone you feel you can have a little chat and a cup of tea with from time to time. Or play some records. Living alone, you see, I feel the need for a bit of company every now and then. What use would an old woman's company be to me? Don't you agree?

ELENA Why, of course!

TERESA Would you like to see the room then? *(She opens a door back-stage, and they look at the room)* You can't see Saint Peter's today, because of the mist. But ordinarily you can see it. It's nice and cool here: we're under the

Gianicolo. . . . You're a student, then? What are you studying?

ELENA Philosophy. I'm in my second year. Last year I stayed with my uncle and aunt, but I don't want to stay there any longer, because it's so noisy. I share a room with two of my cousins, and when I have to stay up working late, they grumble about the light. My parents live in the country, just outside Pistoia. They run a little *pension* for foreign tourists. They can't give me much money, they haven't enough for themselves; and they say I can stay at uncle's. It doesn't cost me anything to stay there. But I don't like it there; well, it's not exactly that I don't like it: it's the noise.

TERESA I'm not asking anything for the room. Just a little company occasionally, and a little light housework, that's all. I'm here by myself.

ELENA You're not married?

TERESA I am married. We separated. We're still on good terms; he often drops in to see me. He actually telephoned me a little while ago. He said to me: "You're quite right, get yourself a young student, then you won't be alone the whole time." Because you see, I get so frightened all alone here at night. I did have a maid, to begin with, but she stole, so I got rid of her. Besides, she was old. I don't get on with old people. Perhaps because I grew up at my grandparents'—my father's people. They didn't like me. They preferred my brother. I had the most horrible childhood! What I mean is I can't bear to be with my mother, because she's so old. I can't stand her. It isn't that I don't get on with her. You couldn't *not* get on with my mother, because she never says anything. I don't suppose she's uttered more than a hundred words since the day she was born. But it's no good, I can't bear her. Do you get on with your mother?

ELENA Oh, yes. But my mother isn't old. She's very young. People take us for sisters. And she doesn't try to *make* herself look young, either. She washes her face with kitchen soap. She's up at six every morning, in her tartan skirt, and her red stockings, and her climbing boots. She always wears climbing boots, so that she can prowl round the country-side and slop about in the streams, up to her ankles in mud. She potters about the garden, and the hen-house, and the woodshed. She goes shopping in the village with a sack on her back. She's never still for a moment, and she's always cheerful. My mother's a remarkable woman.

TERESA   She runs a *pension*, you were saying? What sort?

ELENA   For foreign tourists. It's quite a small *pension*. But the house was too large for us, and as there's a lot of country all round it, some years ago my parents got the idea of starting a *pension*. It's a very beautiful house, but it's old-fashioned and cold and uncomfortable. But of course, that's what the foreign tourists like. It was all Mother's idea really. Father never had ideas. Poor Mother, she works herself to death over that *pension*. You can't get servant girls to stay, because it's so far away from anywhere: she's always without a maid, or without a cook. She even has to light the fires herself quite often; wood fires. My father's no help. All he does is play tennis with the guests, and talk English to them. He speaks English very well: he has the most beautiful Oxford accent. At the time I left, we had six guests staying. Sometimes we have as many as eleven. But as Mother charges them so little, we never make any money out of it. It's just hard labour and nothing else. For Mother, I mean: Father's quite happy talking English, or playing tennis and ping-pong.

TERESA   I wonder if *I* could start a *pension* in my house at Rocca di Papa? There are ten rooms there. But then I'd have to stay at Rocca di Papa. I hate the place.

ELENA   Why did you take a house there, if you hated the place?

TERESA   That was Lorenzo. My husband. Lorenzo loves the country. He wanted us to settle at Rocca di Papa. So he built the house there. We used to go over every day, to see how the work was getting on: as a matter of fact, the house is very carefully designed, down to the tiniest detail. We spent so much money on it. . . . Then when it was finished we spent one night there. Just the one. In the morning, my husband said he had things to do in Rome and that he'd be back that evening. He took his car, and went. I stayed behind. I looked out of the window. I looked at the trees and the hills in the mist, and the fields and the city. Dear me, the city did seem a long way away! And then I heard cow-bells. And there was a great smell of cows and milk: oh, it was so depressing! So I took my car, the *seicento*—I had a *seicento*, and Lorenzo had a Flavia, we each had a car. So I ran into Rome. We still had a flat in Rome: not this one, it was one in the Via dei Banchi Nuovi. But of course there was no furniture in it, because we'd taken all the furniture to Rocca di Papa. The place was completely empty. So I went out and bought two bedsteads, two mattresses, two blankets, and four sheets, and we camped in the flat. My husband said, "All right, we'll sleep here tonight, and tomorrow we'll start living at Rocca di Papa." But he's never set foot in the house at Rocca di Papa since. I did go back there once or twice, to fetch pillow-cases and sheets. We slept for months in the empty flat, with just the beds. When they brought us coffee up from the bar, we had to stand the cups on the floor. We had all our meals in restaurants. All so as not to go back to Rocca di Papa.

ELENA   But couldn't you have told your husband you didn't like being at Rocca di Papa? I mean, couldn't you have told him before he built the house?

TERESA   Well, I didn't know I wouldn't like being there. I thought I'd like it. And in those days, I still thought we were going to have seven or eight children. I expected to work in the garden, and keep rabbits and hens. Like your mother. Your mother works in the garden, I suppose?

ELENA   She does, yes.

TERESA   And does she keep rabbits and hens?

ELENA   Yes.

TERESA   Yes, well, I found I hated hens as well. It wasn't just cows. And that day, in that big, lovely, empty house, with all those trees round it, I suddenly felt the most appalling depression. I could smell the countryside; and it brought back my childhood. I mentioned what a very unhappy childhood I had, didn't I? We lived with my father's parents: there was Mother, and my brother, and me. My grandparents were peasants. Poor peasants. My father was there as well, at the beginning; and I was frightened of my father. He used to hit my mother. He didn't hit me, but whenever he saw me playing in the kitchen, he used to pick me up by one arm, and put me out of doors. He always said I wasn't his. He said my brother was his, but I wasn't. He said I was Uncle Giacomo's. Whether I actually was Uncle Giacomo's I don't know, I've never known. Uncle Giacomo lived at the other end of the village, and I used to see him sometimes in the street: he was a little man, with a pipe and riding-boots. He had a huge dog; it followed him everywhere. He used to look at me, and fumble in his pockets, and give me a few sweets. Then he'd whistle the dog, and go on. I used to think, "Why doesn't he take me away, if I'm his? Why doesn't he take me home with him?" He had a lovely house, with a verandah all round it, and a huge front door. I used to play by the fire in the kitchen at home, and my father used to pick me by one arm, and put me outside in the street. I used to cry, and Granny would fetch me inside again. She'd say to my father, "What are you? A dog?" And he'd say, "You shut up. You know nothing. She isn't mine, she's Giacomo's." Giacomo was my father's brother, but he'd quarrelled with my grandparents over a wood, and they weren't on speaking terms. Granny used to say, "Well, even if she is Giacomo's, it isn't her fault." And father would say, "I know it isn't, but I can't bear the sight of her; and one of these days I'm going to America, so I shan't have to see her again." And my father used to wake up in the middle of the night, and hit my mother, and make her nose and mouth bleed. Then my father did go away to America, and we stayed behind with my grandparents. And *they* were very unkind to my mother too, always shouting at her. And my mother got more and more gloomy, and untidy, and frightened, and crippled. My father used to write to my brother, from

America, and send him parcels of clothes. So my brother was always nicely dressed: he used to have coloured sweaters with zips, and leather gloves, and fur-lined jackets. Then, when he was fourteen, my father sent him the money to get to America. So my brother left, too.

ELENA And your mother let him go?

TERESA Of course she let him go! We were so poor! Then my grandfather had a stroke, and my mother looked after him. She dressed him and fed him; she used to pick him up in her arms as if he were a baby, and sit him by the fire. And he was always swearing at her, and scolding her. And Granny used to scold her too; she was always shouting at her, and saying it was her fault father had gone away and left no one to work in the fields. My mother was almost killing herself working in the fields, and looking after Grandpa, and getting the food ready for the animals. Mother never said anything. She always kept her mouth shut. And one of her legs got swollen, so that she always had to drag this leg after her, with her foot in a slipper. I still met Uncle Giacomo in the village, but he'd stopped giving me sweets: he just used to look at me, and go straight on. And I always thought, "Why doesn't he come and fetch me, if I'm his?" And then gradually we sold all the land, and the animals, and there was a mortgage on the house. My grandparents died, and we gave the house away, and went to live at Aunt Amata's. She had a small drapery business. Mother became Aunt Amata's servant. It was her nature to be a servant, she'd never been anything else all her life. And as soon as I was twenty, I ran away from the village. I didn't want to be stuck there for ever in the drapery, selling buttons. I didn't want to end up like Mother.

ELENA So you came to Rome?

TERESA Yes, I came to Rome. I worked in a wine-and-oil shop. I was very pretty, so of course there were always a lot of men after me. And one of them said to me one day: "Come and let me get you a walk-on part in a film!" He was something or other in the movies, and he took me to Cinecittà. I had to take all my clothes off, and just wear a gold lamé brassière and slip, and a veil down to my ankles. I looked marvellous, and I thought, "Everything will be fine now, I'm going to be a film-star." I even wrote and told Mother I was all fixed up, and asked her to come to Rome and live with me. But she didn't, and actually I was glad she didn't, because I really can't bear the way she drags that leg of hers after her the whole time. Whenever she comes near me, I somehow feel angry and humiliated. It always makes me think of all those years of poverty at Reggiano Alto.

ELENA And did you really become a film-star?

TERESA Far from it. They did use me from time to time, but I was never more than an extra. After that time with the gold bra, they took me on for another film, and this time the bra and slip were violet velvet, and I had to lie stretched out on a tiger-skin. Actually I was a bit more than an extra that time, because at one point I had to get up, and take a bunch of grapes off a fruit-dish, and eat them; and while I was eating them, I had to waggle my hips and smile at a sailor who came up and started to eat them with me. I think that must have been the time when they realized I wasn't much good at smiling, *or* at waggling my hips. They kept telling me: "More voluptuous! More languid! Waggle those hips! Waggle them!" And so on. I had to go over it again and again. By the time I finished, I'd waggled my hips so much I'd strained the muscles of my stomach. Then they had me for a nun, escaping from a burning hospital. I was always at Cinecittà, waiting at the gates in case they wanted me. I hardly earned a penny, but I was always full of hope. And it was there, at Cinecittà, that I met Lorenzo. My husband. I was there one day, sitting on the ruins of Troy—a lot of old burnt stones, and so on. I was sitting there, eating chicken sandwiches: you see, they always handed out packets of food at lunchtime, and that day it was chicken, and I love chicken, so of course I was enjoying myself. I was dressed as a Trojan girl, with a big sheet wrapped all round me, and Lorenzo came and sat down

beside me, and said: "You know, you *are* a lovely girl.
What's that you're eating? Chicken? Got a bit for me?" I
just shrugged my shoulders. I thought he was too small, and
I've never liked small men. He was wearing a crumpled
old white raincoat, and a black beret, and a grey turtle-
neck sweater. And he hadn't shaved. He looked just like a
poor university student. And then suddenly the most awful
north wind began to blow; and there was his raincoat bil-
lowing out behind him, and there was my sheet flapping
about so that I had to press my legs together to keep it on.
We were on a little sandy piazza sort of place; and I was
eating chicken and sand. I said to him: "Who are you? A
student?" He said: "No, I'm not a student. I finished at the
university a long while ago. I'm thirty. I'm an engineer."
And I said: "What are you doing here?" He told me he was
just there by chance; he was with a German friend who was
doing the music for a film. I looked at him, and the only
thing I liked about him was his eyes. I mean Lorenzo has
got the most beautiful eyes: big, and blue, and bright, with
long lashes. Too beautiful, really: rather wasted on a man.
I said to him: "Why haven't you shaved today?" And he
rubbed his chin, and said: "Oh, yes, so I haven't. Look, I tell
you what: I'll go and get a shave and see you later." And
there he was, that evening, waiting at the gates, leaning up
against a lamp-post, smoking. So we all went out to dinner
—Lorenzo, and I, and his friend, the German composer.
He was called Gunther. So after a time, we dropped the
German composer, and Lorenzo came back to my place to
sleep. I had a frightful room in the Via del Lavatore: I paid
twelve thousand lire a month for it. For three whole days,
we never went out; in those three days, we did nothing but
make love, sleep, smoke and eat tins of corned beef which
I used to keep on the window-ledge. We hardly even
spoke; as a rule Lorenzo carries on like a windmill, but in
those three days we hardly said a thing: we were both of
us so sleepy; we just wanted to make love and sleep, and
that was all. And then, eventually, he said he had to run
down to get some cigarettes. He never came back. I didn't

see him again for six months. Every now and then I used
to think: "Whatever happened to him? Was he frightened?
Did he think I'd expect him to pay me, the silly fool?" I felt
so mortified I couldn't bear to go back to Cinecittà, I
thought what queer types you bump into there, I thought,
they go to bed with you, eat every scrap of corned beef in
the place, and then disappear without a word. So I got a job
at a hairdresser's. I decided I wanted to be an artistic hair-
stylist. They never gave me anything to do. I just looked
after the hairpins, and did an occasional shampoo; and the
pay was dreadful. It was a lovely shop in the Piazza di
Spagna. And then, one day, I saw him come into the place:
Lorenzo, with a tall beautiful woman in a mink coat. He
was the same as ever: beret, raincoat, sweater. And he
hadn't shaved. He said: "Oh! You're *here*? Just as if we'd
seen each other the day before. The woman had come to
have her streaks touched up. She was American; she
couldn't speak a word of Italian. I whispered to him: "What
are you doing with a girl-friend like this?" He said: "She
isn't my girl-friend. She's Gunther's girl-friend." So I said,
"How is Gunther?" And he said: "Fine!" Is all this boring
you?

ELENA No, no, I'm enjoying it. Do go on.

TERESA He introduced me to the American girl, but she
couldn't understand a word I said; all she could do was
point to her streaks, and say, "Bad, bad." She thought they
looked awful. He kept talking to her very fast in English.
I think he was trying to tell her her streaks didn't look too
bad. But after a time he must have got fed up: he simply
went away across the Piazza di Spagna, with his raincoat
flapping about behind him, and I thought: "There, I've lost
him again." The American woman gave us all a good tick-
ing-off about her streaks, bought a small cart-load of soaps
and perfumes, and then *she* went away too. That evening
Lorenzo was waiting for me at the door of the shop. He
took me out to dinner.

ELENA With the American girl?

TERESA Good heavens, no. In fact he told me he didn't like

the American girl; he was just walking her about a bit to oblige Gunther. You see, the American girl was a bit noisy and exhausting, so poor Gunther had to ask for a breathing-spell every now and then. I said to Lorenzo, "What about the cigarettes?" He said: "What cigarettes?" I said: "Yes, didn't you manage to get any cigarettes? Is that why you didn't come back?" And then he told me that that morning, in the tobacconist's, he'd run into a friend of his, and they'd started to talk, and he completely forgot about me. When he remembered he was supposed to be coming back to me, it was late at night, and he thought I'd be asleep. The next day his mother wanted him to fetch some dogs up from the country. Coming back with the dogs, he had an accident with the car, and dislocated his shoulder. They had to put it in plaster. He couldn't remember my number in Via del Lavatore, that was why he couldn't write to me. In any case he never wrote letters. He hadn't written a letter since he was eight. The last letter he'd written, when he was eight, was to Father Christmas, to ask for a fire-man's helmet. The fireman's helmet never arrived, so he'd never written any letters since. That was what he told me. How that man talked! He went on like a windmill. I sat there spellbound, just listening to him. But I did say: "I have the feeling you're just telling me a pack of lies." He said: "No, I never tell lies, never. I really have been in hospital with my shoulder in plaster. But all these months I've preserved a very favourable memory of you." I said: "What an awful way to talk." I said: "You talk as if I was a thing, not a person." Then he said: "You're not a person yet—not to me at any rate. You may perhaps become one; it's quite possible you may become one. But so far you haven't. And I'm quite certain I'm not a person to you either: I'm just a vague, indefinite shadow." I said to him: "No, no, no! When I've made love with a man, he isn't a shadow to me, not at all. I don't make love with shadows, I make love with people; and I want you to realize that *I'm* a person. I want you to be considerate to me, and treat me with respect; otherwise you'd better go away and leave me alone." And I started to cry. He gave me his hankerchief! You should have seen that handkerchief! It was so dirty I flung it on the floor. I said: "I'm not going to use a filthy rag like that!" Is this boring you?

ELENA No.

TERESA I said to him: "I've had lots of men, the first one I had was when I was fifteen; it was the chemist at Reggiano Alto. I've often been treated badly, but I've never had a man tell me I wasn't a *person* before. As if I was something people leave behind them—a ghost. And no one's ever dropped me, I've always dropped *them*, when I've been fed up with them, and I get fed up very quickly!" I said. And there I was, crying like a fool. Do you know why? It was because I was in love. It was the very first time I'd ever been in love, and I thought, "Well, there you are," I thought, "you have to fall in love with this thing: a dirty, penniless little engineer who never shaves, and goes on like a windmill and tells you goodness knows how many lies; and before I know where I am, he'll probably be off round the corner, and disappear for another six months!" And all the time I was crying, he sat there looking at me, and rubbing his chin. Then all of a sudden he got up and paid the bill, and went out. I ran after him. I caught up with him at the car-park in the Piazza del Popolo, just as he was getting into his car. He had an Anglia in those days. I slipped into the car beside him (I was still crying) and I said to him: "Don't leave me like this!" And he said: "What do you want me for? Why don't you look for someone else, someone who can make you happy? What have you and I got in common?" And I said: "No, I want to stay with you! I don't know why, but I want to stay with you!" So he came back with me to the Via del Lavatore. I asked him: "How do you come to have a car? I thought you were very poor?" And he said: "Poor? Why, no, I've got lots of money!" And that was how I first found out how rich he was. He lived with his mother in a huge place on the Via Venti Settembre; he owned the whole house. They even had a butler. . . . Well, we lived together for a little while before we got married, in my room to begin with, then in an apartment on the Via dei Banchi Nuovi. And every now and then Lorenzo used to say: "If you're really keen on it, I'll marry you. I can see we get along well together. Very well indeed. From every point of view." And I said to him: "I've become a person for you at last, then?" And he said: "I almost believe you have." So he lived with me; but every now and then, he'd go back to his mother's; he'd be away for several days, and I was always afraid he was never coming back. Because with him, you could never be sure. Whenever he went to see his mother, she always made terrible scenes about me. She threatened to disinherit him if he married me—which in fact she never did, though I can't think why. In the meantime I'd given up working; I used to stay at home, reading books, because Lorenzo said I was as ignorant as a cook. So I read. But, you know, everything I read, it was like water off a duck's back, I forgot everything the minute I'd read it: perhaps because I could never stop thinking about him. There he was, stuck bang in the middle of my life: it was just the same, whether he was sitting beside me in his sweater, sharpening pencils, and filling little notebooks with numbers . . . or out with his friends in town, talking, waving his arms about the way he did. . . . And eventually, he married me, because we thought I was expecting a baby. Then it turned out I wasn't expecting a baby, but anyway we got married, at Reggiano Alto, my own village. We spent our honeymoon at Reggiano Alto, at the Hotel Italia, and in the evenings we used to sit in the back room at my Aunt Amata's drapery-shop, and play lottery with my aunt and my mother. My mother literally worshipped Lorenzo. So did Aunt Amata. She said to me: "You never deserved such a husband! Mind you hold on to him, you might easily go and lose him, a stupid crazy girl like you, after the dreadful life you've been living!" Aunt Amata's never forgiven me for running away from the village; and she also knew I used to have men in Rome, and appear almost naked in the movies. But now she was proud of me, because I'd married an engineer, and she knew he was well-educated and wealthy, with a great big house in Rome. And though he was so rich, he was simple, and ready to play lottery in the little back room; and he was always kind and attentive to her and mother. So she liked him.

ELENA Is that your husband? In the photograph?

TERESA Yes. We'd only just got married, it was taken just after we got back from Reggiano Alto. He took me to see his mother, and of course she already hated me without ever having seen me, and when she did see me she hated me even more, and I cordially disliked her too. We kept giving one another polite little smiles. I sat there with my hands in my lap. She was very jumpy: she kept patting her blue-washed fringe the whole time. She did try to be kind, just a little. She gave me a ring, but the minute I was out of the room, she told Lorenzo she couldn't understand what he saw in me: I wasn't the least bit refined, she said, and I had hands and feet like a cook. Lorenzo used to enjoy repeating to me every thing his mother said about me. It made him laugh like crazy. So I told him I'd never go to see his mother again. I did, though; because every now and then he wanted us to go there together. So I obeyed; I always ended up doing whatever he wanted.

ELENA But why?

TERESA Why? Because he bullied me; he was able to bully me because I loved him. He ordered me to read, and I read. He ordered me to go out with him and his friends, and I went. He ordered me to stop eating spaghetti and beans, because I was putting on weight, and he couldn't bear women being fat; and I obeyed. I used to cook spaghetti and beans for him, and while he ate them I used to sit looking out of the window, and nibbling a bit of lettuce. I *obeyed* him. I no longer had any will of my own left. He ordered me to go with him to his mother's, and I went. He forced me to be nice to her; and she even forced herself to be nice to me. It was always Lorenzo she quarrelled with; she didn't want to waste her breath quarrelling with me. They used to have business discussions about the es-

tates they owned down in Apulia, at a place called La
Pavona. They were always quarrelling. In the end I always
fell asleep in an armchair, because I'd eaten so much; the
one thing I liked at my mother-in-law's was the food, and
I always used to stuff myself as full as I could, partly because Lorenzo used to let me eat there without comment-
ing on how fat I was getting; or perhaps he let me eat as
a reward for going there: he knew how boring it was for
me. And then my mother-in-law used to say that when a
young woman fell asleep after lunch, it was a sign her liver
wasn't working properly. She had a perfect liver herself.
She never stopped talking about her liver, and her kidneys,
and her circulation, and her spleen; everything was always
in perfect condition. It was the same with her daughter
Paola, who was married, and living down in Apulia: she
had marvellous health too, and a complexion like a baby,
insides like clockwork, and perfect teeth. Lorenzo had
once enjoyed perfect health too, she said. He'd ruined it by
leaving home. His complexion was muddy, she said, and his
eyes were bloodshot, and he was losing his hair. Because he
was drinking hard liquor, and staying up all night in the
bars, and eating meat cooked in cheap fat. I said: "It's not
true! I don't cook with cheap fat! I have olive oil sent from
Reggiano Alto!" But she wouldn't believe in the olive oil
from Reggiano Alto. She only believed in her own olive oil
from her own estates. That was the only good olive oil
there was. Not that she ever gave us a drop of it. She was
always promising to, but she never did. In all the five years
we were married, I never saw a single drop of it. Whenever
Lorenzo went down to La Pavona, I always asked him to
sneak a few bottles and bring them home with him: after
all, it was his olive oil too; but he always forgot, and I always
lost my temper; and I lost my temper about his sister too;
she was living down there, with no expenses: there were
she and her husband and nine children, all consuming
olive oil and wine and cheese which were just as much ours
as they were theirs. But Lorenzo said I had a vulgar mind.
At first we lived as though we were poor, not for any

particular reason, but because it never occurred to us to want a better life, and we were happy. He had just that one sweater, two shirts with the cuffs all frayed, and no tie at all. I had a three-year-old skirt, and the heels of my shoes were all broken down. Then we remembered we had money, and began to pour it down the drain. I don't know how I spent so much money; I just used to go out and buy everything in sight. Lorenzo was mad about pictures. So he started buying pictures; he bought them right and left; he collected an immense number of them. They filled the flat; every wall was covered with pictures, there were pictures in the bathroom, pictures in the kitchen. If they weren't on the walls, they were stacked on the floor. Then he began buying motor-cycles and cars. Whenever a new model of a motor-cycle came out, he immediately gave the old one away, and bought himself the new one. He was just the same about cars. He used to ride his motor-cycle like a madman: he'd already had four motor-cycle accidents, and two serious car accidents, and he was continually getting summonses for speeding. Whenever he went out in a car or on his motor-cycle, I used to almost die with anxiety. He never used to pay the summonses, because he always went out without any money; he used to tell *me* to go and pay them, but I used to forget, and I was for ever finding these summonses all over the place—in his desk, in his pockets, on the seat of the car, on the floor of the car: I can't tell you the anxiety these summonses gave me, but I wouldn't go and pay them, because I felt that *he* ought to go.

ELENA   He must have been a very disorganized person.

TERESA   Yes. He was disorganized, and *I* was disorganized, and the disorganization we managed to get into between us was unbelievable. He said that what he'd really needed was an orderly wife who'd keep his desk tidy, and pay his summonses. He was always telling me what I ought to have been like, how happy he'd have been if I'd been a *wife*. And I did nothing but tell him how I'd have liked him to be a *husband*. What I'd really have liked would have been a husband who didn't spend so much; I'd have liked him to be gentle and simple and understanding, and not to keep muddling my brain with all those long, hard lectures. I'd have liked him to have brought me a little present or something now and then . . . a few flowers, or a box of chocolates. I'd have liked a bit of attention. I got no attention. If ever he met a friend in the street, he'd forget to come home for dinner. I'd wait for hours, with dinner cooked and ready, half-dead with worry that something had happened to him.

ELENA Couldn't he have telephoned you?

TERESA He never telephoned. He never telephoned, because he never thought of me. When he was busy talking to his friends, I never crossed his mind.

ELENA What an odd person!

TERESA So then we began to quarrel, not just once in a while, but every day, and things between us began to go to pieces. We used to have frightful scenes; he'd slap me, and I'd bite him and scratch him. Sometimes we stayed awake all night quarrelling, and at five in the morning he'd go off on his motor-cycle, and I'd stay in bed crying.

ELENA What did you quarrel about?

TERESA What about? I can't even remember now. About him always being late; and the summonses; and the money; and the pictures he kept on buying; and his family; about a word, even. He'd pounce on to some word I'd used without thinking: and he'd dissect it; he'd drag out all the possible hidden meanings, so that word would grow and grow till it was like a monster. And after a time I wouldn't be able to tell what he was talking about, my mind would be all confused, and I'd start to sob, and then he'd hit me, and I'd bite his hands and wrists, and all the time I was biting and scratching, I kept thinking: look what we've come to, how low we've sunk! The disgrace and the hell of it!

ELENA Yes, it must really have been a hell.

TERESA It *was* a hell. Then somehow or other we'd make peace, and the hell would disappear. He'd slap me and punch me, and then he'd suddenly become very gentle and kind. He'd say he loved me, and wouldn't change me for any other woman in the world. So then we'd make love, and then he'd say he was a bit hungry, and I'd get up and cook him some *pasta*. Then we'd both go to sleep, and sleep till three in the afternoon. We both loved sleeping. Sometimes we'd sleep so long you'd think we were never going to wake up.

ELENA But didn't he work?

TERESA No, he didn't work. He had that degree in engineering, but he never did anything with it. He never wanted to take any kind of a job at all. He said if he had a job it would make him depressed. He was working for another degree, in pure physics. He was mad about pure physics. He had a lot of squared notebooks he kept filling with sums; then he'd get fed up, and tear the pages out. And I'd find these pages, covered with numbers all over the place, mixed up with the bills and the summonses. Of course, he didn't need to take a job, because we had enough to live on. *He* used to say we had too much. We both spent money like water. Sometimes we'd go out dancing in the night-clubs with our friends. There'd be eight or ten of us, and he'd pay for everyone. Then he got the idea of the villa at Rocca di Papa. It was the same there: I can't tell you how much money we threw away on that. There was something about the arrangement of the rooms he didn't like, after it was finished. So he had several of the walls pulled down. He went backwards and forwards between Rome and Rocca di Papa, on his motor-cycle or in the car, driving like mad the whole way. Then he'd go round the antique shops, buying old furniture. We have some very valuable furniture and pictures there.

ELENA And isn't anyone staying in the villa at the moment?

TERESA Not a soul. Who do you think would want to stay there? It's frightening to go inside it, even. Empty houses always are. It smells all shut up, and damp—because after all it *is* a damp spot, with all those trees round it. I could let it, of course. But you see, it upsets me to think of anyone else living there where *we* ought to be. I'd rather sell it, with everything in it. Then it'd be all over and done with.

It wouldn't be mine any more, I'd never see it again. It's registered in my name. Lorenzo registered it in my name.

ELENA But won't it be broken into, staying empty like that?

TERESA I don't know. And after all, what's it matter to me? Oh, I know there are some valuable pictures there. I'm always telling him to go and fetch them away, but he never does. He puts it off, and puts it off—he's a man who spends his whole life putting things off, as if he had unlimited time in front of him. Besides, he doesn't care a damn about the pictures now. The picture-craze is all over.... Even before the villa was properly finished, he used to spend whole days there, hanging pictures. He put up all the pictures we had, plus some others he bought on purpose. We gradually stripped the flat in the Via dei Banchi Nuovi, till it was completely empty. He could never talk of anything else but the villa, and the life we were going to lead there, with so many friends, and animals, and children. I wanted children too; I used to think of all the children we were going to have, and what I was going to call them, and the clothes and toys I'd buy for them. The doctors had told me I couldn't have children. But I was sure they were wrong, and I was going to have lots of them.... Well, as I told you, we spent one night at Rocca di Papa. A single night.

ELENA And afterwards?

TERESA Afterwards, I told you, we went on living in the flat in the Via dei Banchi Nuovi: but all the furniture had gone, by then, and it was very uncomfortable, because there wasn't even a table to put a glass down on. As we'd spent so much on the house at Rocca di Papa, we found we were short of money. So we quarrelled: either about the money, or because it was so uncomfortable in the flat; but when we weren't actually quarrelling, we kept saying that this was all just temporary, and in a short time we'd be settled in Rocca di Papa. As a matter of fact, neither of us wanted to go there, but we each kept pretending it was the other who didn't want to go; he said it was I who didn't want to, because I was too fond of going out to night-clubs with our friends. Then he started saying I'd ruined him, because I'd "deprived him of the wish to read and study". He used to say that the minute he settled down to study, I used to call him to come and sit with me, or make love. He never managed to concentrate on anything, he said. And as the flat was so uncomfortable, he took to spending every afternoon at his mother's.

ELENA   Did he study, at his mother's?

TERESA   Never. He did nothing there either. He'd settle down there with his books, and then his friends would come and call, and start him talking. And how he talked! My God, how he talked with those friends of his! They were my friends too, and sometimes they'd come and see me, and tell me how badly I was behaving to him. They used to say he was unhappy with me because I didn't understand him; I tormented him and oppressed him with my anxiety and jealousy, they said. And it's true: I was very jealous, and in those days every time he came home, I made scenes, and accused him of going with other women. They told me I ought to let him study, because he was working at something very important, and the only thing I ought to do was to provide him with an ordered, peaceful life, and a home that was a *home*. I was wild at these friends of his, because *I* believed *they* were the ones who wasted his time, talking and arguing. But I was very unhappy too: I felt so lonely. And then something happened. I was unfaithful to him. I'd never been unfaithful to him. I'd often been on the verge of being unfaithful to him, but I'd always stopped in time.

ELENA   Unfaithful with whom?

TERESA   It was with a friend of his, a man named Mario, a newspaperman who was always dropping in. He and Lorenzo had been great friends ever since schooldays. I was unfaithful to him with Mario.

ELENA   Did Lorenzo know?

TERESA   Yes. He found us in bed together. He'd gone down to La Pavona; he'd been away a fortnight, and came back unexpectedly one night. I was in bed with Mario. I heard the key turn in the lock. Mario was asleep. I shook him; and at that moment Lorenzo came in, with his suitcase and his beret and his crumpled raincoat. And, of course, he hadn't shaved. He stood there for a minute in the doorway, small, and pale, with no expression on his face, just looking blank and cold. . . . Mario had woken up, and they stared at each other. Lorenzo . . . just went away again. I heard the door bang to, I slipped into my dressing-gown—I was trembling and crying—I ran down the stairs after him, and saw him get into the car, the Flavia. He slammed the car door to, and drove off. And there I was in my dressing-gown, in the street, in the middle of the night, shivering and crying and desperate, because I knew at once that everything was over. I went back upstairs. Mario had dressed, and he said, "I'll go after him." He was upset too. And he also went away. I didn't mean a thing to him, it had all been so silly, it was one of those things you don't know how they happen. . . . You feel a sort of curiosity . . . and anxiety. I went with Mario in the hope of getting rid of my anxiety about Lorenzo. I grabbed at him the way you might grab at a tree on a winter night. But he didn't matter to me, not one bit. And so I started to write to Lorenzo, I wrote letter after letter to his mother's; and I kept trying to phone him, but the butler always said he wasn't in. So I went and called on his mother. I didn't see *him* anywhere. His mother was in her armchair in the drawing-room, with her blue-washed fringe and her feather boa. His sister was there too. I could never bear his sister, though we were always very polite to one another. I used to send her Christmas presents for her nine children, and she always sent me a crochet bed-jacket. They told me Lorenzo wasn't there; they didn't know where he was, they said. They told me we must start proceedings for legal separation right away because we obviously couldn't go on living together. We were destroying one another, they said. I started to cry, and I said they were wrong, we were very happy together. I said they couldn't realize how much we loved one another. Talk, talk, talk; there we were, talking, and I felt I hated them so much I just couldn't keep it in. I started to shout. I said they were the ones who'd turned Lorenzo against me, and they were all against me because I was poor. I shouted rude things about their money, and at one point I used the word "arse." It made my mother-in-law faint, or pretend to, and my sister-in-law pushed me to the door, saying I was killing her mother. "You're killing Mamma, you're killing her," she kept saying. And I went downstairs, shouting and crying; and there was that butler, helping me on with my coat, and handing me my scarf, as if nothing had happened.

ELENA And you've never seen Lorenzo since?

TERESA Of course I've seen him. I saw him a few days later. I told you, I'm always seeing him, he's always here, he may be here any minute. You'll meet him if you stay on a little longer.

ELENA No. It's late, and I must be getting along. I have to go to the university for a lesson.

  [*(The doorbell rings.* TERESA *opens the door. A* BOY *comes in with a package)*

TERESA Ah, yes. The groceries.

BOY Shall I just put them down here?

TERESA Yes, leave them there. *(To* ELENA*)* It's just a few tinned things I ordered. Corned beef. Tinned fruit. I always eat out of tins, now I'm by myself. I'm a very good cook, as a matter of fact, but I can't bear just cooking for myself.

BOY About the cat. Dad says he'll send her round later. He hasn't got her at the shop, she's at home. He says he'll go and get her tonight, and bring her round to you. She's a *lovely* little cat. And pure-bred too.

TERESA Yes, all right. *(To* ELENA*)* They're giving me a little Siamese cat.

BOY Dad did say as well . . . Perhaps you wouldn't mind settling the bill?

TERESA Of course I'll settle it.

BOY Dad says . . . He's very sorry, but could you pay it by tonight? He has to do his accounts.

TERESA Of course I'll pay it. Don't bother me now. Can't you see I'm busy?

(Exit BOY*)*]

TERESA So you'd like the room?

ELENA Oh, certainly, yes please. Could I move in tomorrow?

TERESA Yes, come tomorrow. I'll be expecting you. I won't disturb you when you have work to do, of course, but if you ever do stop working for a minute or two, we could see a little of each other, perhaps. I need company, I'm very lonely. I've become like a lonely dog. And I'm not very good at being alone. I get anxious.

ELENA Haven't you any women friends?

TERESA No. I did have, when I was younger, but I've lost sight of them. You see, I was always with Lorenzo, and when I was with him, I didn't need anyone else. We had friends—men *and* women—the ones we used to go out with in the evening; but I never see them now. I don't even want to: they remind me of the time when I had Lorenzo, and was his wife, and everything was marvellous: and we were happy and carefree, like two children, full of hope.

ELENA But didn't you say that living with him was a hell?

TERESA Yes. It was a hell. But I was happy in that hell. I'd give my life to have it back again, and be like we were a year ago. We've only been separated a year. Separation by mutual consent. His mother wanted to insist on separation with guilt, so that he wouldn't have to pay me alimony. But Lorenzo didn't want that. After we'd separated, he helped me to find this flat, and gave me the money to furnish it. I bought some furniture. The sideboard.

ELENA The rosewood sideboard? The one you want to sell?

TERESA Yes. What should I want a sideboard for? I haven't any dishes. I never ask anyone in for a meal. I eat in the kitchen. I'm all alone.

ELENA Why did you buy it then?

TERESA I don't know. I think I bought it with the idea that Lorenzo might come back to live with me. And of course, if he did, I would have to make a proper home for him.

ELENA But he won't come back?

TERESA He'll never come back. It's all over. He says since

he left me, he's found peace again; and balance, he says. He says with me it was always like living in a sandstorm. He says with me he always felt he was sinking into a well full of black, muddy, stinking water; he was gradually losing himself, bit by bit, he says. Ah, the things he says! He's never at a loss for words. He says he left me, because he'd have slapped me hard enough to kill me. Or I'd have killed him. He says he gets on very well, when I'm not there. I don't know whether it's true. He doesn't look at all happy to *me*. He hasn't a girl, or a woman. He just goes with prostitutes. He spends the evenings in night-clubs, with his friends, exactly like he used to with me. I don't think he studies. He says he does, he says he studies, but I don't believe him. He just talks, talks, talks, with his friends. The other day I saw him in the street. He was with Mario. I hadn't seen Mario since that dreadful night; and I felt a sort of pang seeing them both together. There they were; talking. I went up to them, and we all went and had an ice, the three of us. Mario was slightly embarrassed. But *he* wasn't. He went on talking as if nothing had ever happened. They were talking about Spinoza. A philosopher.

ELENA I'm working on Spinoza at the moment, for my exam. I have an exam in February.

TERESA I see, you have an exam in February. Good. I shall leave you to study, I won't disturb you. I'll sometimes bring you some coffee, or a zabaione even, to keep your strength up. I shall be like a mother to you. You're so much younger than I am. How old are you? Eighteen?

ELENA Heavens, no! I'm twenty-two.

TERESA How old do you think I am?

ELENA I . . . don't know.

TERESA Well, there'd be no point in telling you how old I am. Of course, I'm a bit run down at the moment, because I can't sleep. I'm run down, and I've put on weight. Horrible, isn't it? It's because I'm unhappy: that makes me put on weight. I eat for consolation. Do you think I'm fat?

ELENA No. Just right.

TERESA Don't you think I look run down?

ELENA A little bit pale, perhaps. . . .

TERESA That's my insomnia. I take things for it, but they're no help. Ah, how I used to sleep when Lorenzo was with me! Deep, deep sleep! Now I sleep for a bit, and wake up again: it's like that all night. And sometimes I have a dream, a horrible dream. I wake up soaked in sweat.

ELENA What do you dream about?

TERESA It's horrible, and I don't know why it *is* horrible, but I know I wake up in an icy-cold sweat, and I can't breathe. What happens is I dream I'm in a courtyard, and at the far end of it there's this wall, a very high, blank wall. . . . And I know what's on the other side of it.

ELENA What is it?

(The telephone rings. TERESA *answers it)*

TERESA Hullo? Who's that? The advertisement? Yes. The one for the sideboard? It's a genuine nineteenth-century inlaid rosewood sideboard. Would you care to come and look at it? . . . M'm? Two million lire, or nearest offer. . . . What? Nearest offer. I said nearest offer! *(*ELENA *makes signs of departure)* One moment, please. *(Covers telephone)*

ELENA I must go. I'll come tomorrow.

TERESA I'll expect you. We'll both be very happy: you'll see. The room gets the sun the whole afternoon. Because it faces west, you see: it's exposed to the west. I shan't give you the slightest trouble, I shan't interrupt your work at all . . . except to bring you coffee, or tea, or a zabaione. . . . As if I were your mother.

ELENA Thank you. Good-bye for now.

(Exit ELENA*)*

TERESA Good-bye. *(To the telephone)* I was saying two million, or nearest offer. Come and see the sideboard. Come today, I'm in all day. What do you mean, too much? But I said, "or nearest offer." But you've not even seen it. Why, how much did you want to spend? What do you mean a sideboard couldn't cost two million lire? An antique sideboard? Wherever were you brought up? Do you think I'm going to give it away for a crust of bread? This is a genuine nineteenth-century inlaid rosewood sideboard with three winged cherubs, supporting vines . . . ! But come and look at it! I said come and look at it, never mind about the price, I've said, "or nearest offer"! Don't you understand? I said, *"nearest offer!"*

Act Two

SCENE: *The doorbell rings.* ELENA *opens the door. Enter* LORENZO.

LORENZO   Oh . . . excuse me. . . . The lady isn't in?
ELENA   She's out. She'll be back very shortly.
LORENZO   Where's she gone?
ELENA   Are you Lorenzo?
LORENZO   I'm Lorenzo, yes. You must be the student?
ELENA   Yes, I'm the student. My name's Elena Tesei.
LORENZO   I'm Lorenzo Del Monte. How d'you do?
ELENA   How d'you do?
LORENZO   Where's Teresa gone?
ELENA   She's gone to Rocca di Papa, with some people who may buy the villa. She put an advertisement in the paper. The people telephoned early this morning. They seemed quite keen on buying it. Teresa was very pleased.
LORENZO   Have you seen the villa?
ELENA   No.
LORENZO   That's a pity. It's very beautiful. We spent thousands on it. I designed it myself. I sometimes think I took up the wrong profession: I ought to have been an architect. The trouble with me is I can do too many things well, but none of them thoroughly. And I'm always wavering between pure science and applied. I can't make up my mind: I'm attracted to both of them at the same time. Can you understand that?
ELENA   Yes.
LORENZO   The trouble is, I'm an amateur. In this world there are the amateurs and the professionals. I'm only an amateur, unfortunately. Well, well, I'd better be going. Will you tell Teresa I'll drop in again?
ELENA   No, don't go. Teresa's sure to be back in a little while. She's been expecting to see you day after day, but

325

you never came! She wouldn't leave the place. Sometimes I wanted to take her to a movie, but she wouldn't hear of it. She never left the flat in case you might come and find no one here. She's phoned you again and again, but there was never any answer.

LORENZO   I've been down in Apulia. I've been in Apulia the whole month. My phone didn't answer because I'm on my own now. I stayed at my mother's to begin with, but now I've taken a little flat just below her. I was in Apulia. Seeing about the estate.

ELENA   You might perhaps have dropped Teresa a line.

LORENZO   What, write? I never write letters. I doubt if I've written a single letter since I was eight.

ELENA   I know: you haven't written a letter since the time you wrote to Father Christmas asking him to bring you a guardsman's helmet; and he never brought it.

LORENZO   Not a guardsman's helmet. A fireman's.

ELENA   A fireman's. I'm sorry.

LORENZO   He never brought it. Instead he brought me a damn silly kaleidoscope, which fell to pieces the day I had it. Is that the sort of joke to play on a child?

ELENA   Certainly not!

LORENZO   I gather Teresa must have told you quite a lot about me?

ELENA   Teresa's always talking about you. She never mentions anyone else.

LORENZO   How is she?

ELENA   Quite well. She says she sleeps better, now I'm here. She isn't frightened at night any more. She's stopped having those nightmares.

LORENZO   What about you? How do you get on here?

ELENA   Oh, I'm very happy here. Teresa and I keep each other company. In the evenings, when I really ought to be working, we play cards, or talk, or listen to records. Then we go off to bed and in the mornings, while Teresa is still asleep, I get up and go out and do the shopping, and tidy up, and then I go off to the university. We have almost all our meals together. We've become great friends. . . . A week or so ago I had a touch of 'flu and Teresa looked after me. She wouldn't let me get up, she brought all my meals to me in bed, on a tray.

LORENZO I'm glad you've made friends. Teresa's very lonely. About a month ago, the day before I went down to the country, she phoned me and said: "I'm so pleased, I've got a very nice girl coming to live with me. She's studying philosophy." I said: "Really? Good, I'll come and meet her." But unfortunately I had to go away.

ELENA Yes, we're very good friends. And to think I came here just by chance, because of an advertisement! If I hadn't happened to look in the paper that day, I'd never have met Teresa.

LORENZO Why does that strike you as odd? All human relationships are a matter of chance. We go where the wind takes us. I met Teresa because a friend of mine took me to Cinecittà one day. I'd never been there before, and I don't suppose I'll ever go there again. There was a north wind blowing, and Teresa was sitting on the ruins of Troy. It was a dry, sandy wind. The ruins of Troy were in a sort of clearing in the sand. The wind kept whipping the sand up into our eyes and mouth. It was really quite difficult to stand up. I've always had the feeling that I first met Teresa in a sandstorm.

ELENA I know. Teresa told me about it. She's told me everything.

LORENZO Teresa's still hoping I'll come back and live with her again. But I can't. It would never work.

ELENA No, she doesn't hope that. Not any more.

LORENZO She's told you she doesn't? It's not true. She's always hoping it. I'm still bang in the centre of everything she thinks. I wish she could find some other man and begin life over again.

ELENA She never sees anyone.

LORENZO She never sees anyone because she doesn't want to see anyone; because she's still thinking about me. She hopes for *me*. She thinks I left her because of something that happened. But it wasn't that. That wasn't why I left her. That was merely a pretext. I'd have left her in any case a very few days later. The truth is I left her because I no longer loved her. I felt no jealousy. When that happened, I was already a million light-years away from her. I no longer loved her. I've tried to explain that to her a hundred times. But she doesn't understand. She doesn't want to understand.

ELENA Poor Teresa!

LORENZO In fact, I think I fell out of love with her quite early on, a short time after we started living together. But I didn't tell myself that, *frankly*, so soon. The feelings I had for her were complex . . . undecipherable. It took me some time to figure them out. I came to live with her because I was sorry for her. She was suffering from nightmares . . . from fears and anxieties. I came to live with her because I wanted to annoy my mother. Because of that, I came to live with a girl who was lonely, and poor, and bewildered . . . a girl who came from a completely different world from the world of my family. I came to live with her because I *wanted* to live with a girl who was crazy and disorganized and confused. I wanted to cure her anxieties and throw light on her confusion. But in fact I was anxious and confused myself: I couldn't in any way give a sense of security to someone who was in so many ways exactly like myself. That was my mistake. Coming to live with someone who was like I was, when in fact we're only happy with people who aren't like us at all; we're only happy with our opposites, people who have something that's missing in ourselves. Instead of curing her anxiety I felt myself involved in it; I felt I was gradually sinking into a black, muddy well. I was losing my breath, my reason . . . a horrible sensation.

ELENA But why?

LORENZO What do you mean, why? Why did I feel like that? Don't you understand? Perhaps you're too young to understand? I felt as if I was drowning. Haven't you ever felt as if you were drowning?

ELENA I did nearly get drowned once when I was a child.

LORENZO You're not much more than a child now. I

oughtn't to be talking to you about my troubles. In any case, I'm sure Teresa will already have told you what went on. You need fresh air. It's stifling here.

ELENA Oh, no. I'm very happy here.

LORENZO In this place? Happy? You poor girl. God knows how Teresa must depress you with the tale of our misfortunes. And you see, I'm just like Teresa. I too feel the need of someone to pour out my troubles to . . . but neither she nor I ever bother to see if whoever listens to us is able to bear the burden of our troubles.

ELENA I don't know if I'm any help to Teresa. When she talks I sit and listen. I don't give her advice, or not much. What could I advise her to do? I tell her to stop brooding about *you*.

LORENZO That's good advice. But useless. Advice always is useless anyway. The only real help we can give people is to listen to them in silence.

ELENA You're quite different from how I thought you'd be.

LORENZO Really? How did you think I'd be? Teresa never describes me as I am. She's never understood me. I'm just like her, but she's never understood me.

(The doorbell rings. ELENA opens the door. Enter TERESA)

TERESA Hullo. Kind of you to call. I haven't heard a word from you for over a month.

LORENZO I've been down in Apulia. Well? I hear there's someone wants to buy our villa.

TERESA *Our* villa? It isn't our villa. It's my villa. If I sell it, the money's mine. Isn't it registered in my name?

LORENZO Have I ever said I wanted the money for it?

TERESA Someone just thought of buying it. I've just come from Rocca di Papa. I went with him. He's a bank manager.

LORENZO Which bank?

TERESA I don't know. I never asked him.

LORENZO That was the first thing you should have asked him.

TERESA Well, *you* look after it then, if I don't ask the right questions.

LORENZO   Why should I look after it, if the house is yours?

TERESA   You say I don't ask the right questions.

LORENZO   I haven't the time.

TERESA   I haven't the time either.

LORENZO   Why? What have *you* got to do all day?

TERESA   And what have *you* got to do?

LORENZO   More than you.

TERESA   I have plenty to do.

LORENZO   Such as what?

TERESA   It's none of your business.

LORENZO   Well, is this bank manager of yours buying it? Does he like it?

TERESA   No. He says the layout of the rooms is crazy. He says you have to walk along three miles of corridor to get to the bathroom. And the terrace faces north. And the kitchen's too dark. I said to him: "The layout of the rooms wasn't my responsibility. The plans for the villa were drawn up by my ex."

LORENZO   You really said that: by my ex? *(He laughs)*

TERESA   Yes. When you talk about me, you refer to me as "my ex."

LORENZO   I never say "my ex."

TERESA   I've heard you.

LORENZO   When?

TERESA   Anyway, he wouldn't even think of buying it.

LORENZO   He's an idiot. The terrace faces north so that there's somewhere cool in the summer. And the bathroom isn't all that far away from the bedrooms.

TERESA   He may be an idiot. But he isn't buying.

LORENZO   *(To* ELENA*)* You ought to see it. Go and take a look at it one day. If you like, I could come with you. It's really a most beautiful house.

TERESA   What's the use of Elena seeing it? You surely don't expect her to buy it?

LORENZO   Why not?

TERESA   She hasn't a penny.

LORENZO   All the same I'd like her to see it. Then she'd see that I do know how a house ought to be built.

TERESA Why don't you go and live there if you like it so much?

LORENZO What, me? At Rocca di Papa?

TERESA Why not?

LORENZO I'm perfectly all right where I am.

TERESA At your mother's?

LORENZO I've already told you I'm no longer at my mother's. I have a small place of my own.

TERESA Somewhere you can take your whores to, every night.

LORENZO Now we're separated, I can take who I like there.

ELENA Teresa: I've put the chicken on. We are having chicken soup, aren't we?

TERESA Yes, darling.

LORENZO Are you going to ask me to stay for lunch?

ELENA We'd love you to. Wouldn't we, Teresa?

TERESA He doesn't like chicken soup.

LORENZO That's quite untrue; I like it very much.

TERESA Your tastes must have changed in the last twelve months.

LORENZO My mother makes it for me regularly.

TERESA So you've been down to Apulia?

LORENZO I've been down to Apulia, yes. *(To* ELENA*)* I have an estate down there. It's doing well. We have olives, and corn, and vines: about seventy-five acres all told. My sister and her husband live there. They have nine children. I do envy them. They're very fond of each other; they're never apart. My brother-in-law looks after the estate, and paints in his spare time. I have to admit the paintings are pretty dreadful. . . . My sister rides a little. The children go to school at Torcia, which is the nearest village. My brother-in-law hunts. . . . A most delightful life.

ELENA I grew up in the country. Teresa gets depressed there. I don't. My parents run a small *pension* for foreign tourists outside Pistoia. *We* have olives and vines too. But not corn. We haven't any corn.

LORENZO Yes, Teresa gets depressed in the country. It reminds her of her childhood. She didn't have a very happy childhood. She'll have told you about it.

ELENA   Yes. She's told me everything. I know all about her. And I've told her everything about me too. It's true there wasn't much to tell about me. I lived in the country till I was twenty; and nothing ever happened there. My last years there, I began to get a bit bored. A pleasant sort of boredom in a way, because I could read a lot, and daydream, and think. When I left, I could hardly stop crying: I was so upset at leaving my mother and my little sisters. It was perhaps the first real unhappiness I've ever known.

LORENZO   And what about here? Did nothing happen here?

ELENA   In Rome? Not much. Last year I stayed with my uncle and aunt. But it was too noisy. Then I saw an advertisement in the paper; I answered it and came here. Teresa and I got on very well from the very first day. She's my best friend now. I wrote and told my mother so. We're very happy together, aren't we, Teresa?

TERESA   Yes, darling.

LORENZO   You women make friends very quickly. Give you a month and you're bosom friends. With men, friendship develops gradually, slowly. I only know one feeling that's sudden and overwhelming: love.

TERESA   That's not true! Just after you first met me you disappeared for six months. There wasn't a sign from you. So *that* can't have been very overwhelming.

LORENZO   When I met you, do you mean? On the ruins of Troy?

TERESA   Yes.

LORENZO   How do you know I haven't been overwhelmed on other occasions? Do you think you've been the only person in my life?

TERESA   Well, who else has there been? That girl you had when you were twenty-two? The one who threw you over?

LORENZO   Look: is that soup ready?

ELENA   Nearly: the chicken has to cook a bit longer. I'll go and grate the cheese. Are you feeling depressed, Teresa?

TERESA   No. I have a headache.

(*Exit* ELENA)

LORENZO You have a headache?

TERESA A bit.

LORENZO Are you depressed?

TERESA Perhaps.

LORENZO That girl's very pretty. Very charming, very simple.

TERESA Yes.

LORENZO It was a good idea putting in that advertisement. I feel happier myself, now you're no longer alone in the place. I worried about that, especially at night. Are you sleeping well now? The girl told me you were.

TERESA What's the girl know about it?

LORENZO Do you still have nightmares?

TERESA I keep having that horrible dream.

LORENZO What dream?

TERESA I've told you about it hundreds of times. You don't remember anything. . . . No, it's not that you don't remember anything: you just don't remember anything about me. Like that time you went out to get cigarettes and never came back: you'd forgotten I existed.

LORENZO Oh, for God's sake, stop dragging up ancient history! What's the use of being separated if we have to go on ferreting about in the past?

TERESA It was a very bad beginning. I might have known. In the tobacconist's you met a friend, and started to talk; and you forgot all about me. I might have been a common tart.

LORENZO Oh, shut up! I knew nothing about you in those days!

TERESA No. We'd been together for three days and nights. For three days and nights we'd made love. To me those three days meant something. *I* wouldn't have forgotten *you* if *I'd* run down to the tobacconist's. Which friend was it you met at the tobacconist's anyway? Mario? Gunther?

LORENZO I don't remember. Anyway, what does it matter?

TERESA Perhaps it was Mario?

LORENZO Perhaps it was.

TERESA Do you see much of him?

LORENZO Who?

TERESA Mario.

LORENZO I see him every day.

TERESA And I suppose you never remember that you found him in bed with me that night? When you look him in the face, doesn't the thought ever cross your mind that he betrayed you? He was your closest friend and he betrayed you. Do you never think of that?

LORENZO Don't go on. *Please* don't go on. It's a thing I've got over. My friendship for Mario is something extremely delicate and pure and deep. I don't intend to let the memory of that incident poison it. It's a memory I've completely wiped away, and our friendship is just as it was before. I ask you not to meddle with it. There are some things you aren't capable of understanding.

TERESA Oh, you've wiped the memory of it away? Why? Because it was a dirty memory?

LORENZO Well, even you will perhaps realize that it's not exactly *pleasant* to find one's wife in bed with one's dearest childhood friend. But please forget it. Let's talk about something else.

TERESA And what about *me?* I'd betrayed you too. Your friendship with Mario has been washed and cleaned and rinsed, and now it's just as good as new. That's what you said. Your feelings about me can't be washed and cleaned, and rinsed, I suppose? Those feelings were dirtied for ever, I suppose, and you've chucked them away? You've forgiven Mario, you see him from morning till night; but you can't forgive me? I suppose your feelings for me weren't delicate and deep.

LORENZO Teresa: you still persist in believing I left you because you were unfaithful to me. No. I would have left you anyway, whatever happened. I went away that evening because I said to myself: "She's with Mario, I might as well clear out." But I wasn't, as you seem to think, furiously jealous. I felt slightly bitter; I felt vaguely astonished. But it was all over before that, can't you see that? It was all over, I was millions of light-years away from you; when I saw my sister down in Apulia, I'd already told her I was going to leave you, because I could no longer live with you. You were destroying me and I was destroying you.

TERESA   Were you in love with someone else?

LORENZO   No, no, no! Love isn't by any means the only thing in the world! I don't live just for love; at the present moment I'm not in love with anyone, and I go on living just the same, I talk to my friends, I go on with my studies, I still buy pictures! In your world nothing matters but sex! That's why I can't breathe in your world! I've had enough sex, I'm tired to death of it!

ELENA *(Entering)*   It's almost ready. The chicken's nearly done.

TERESA   You're tired of sex, are you?

LORENZO   Tired to death of it!

TERESA   What lies you tell! I know you by now! You always say you've never told a lie in your life, but the truth is you're made of lies from head to foot! Do you think I don't notice the way you look at women? The minute a woman comes near you you change colour, you brighten up, you switch on like an electric light. Do you think I don't notice?

LORENZO   Nevertheless I tell you, I'm perfectly happy without women. It's the ideal state, so far as I'm concerned.

ELENA   I've done some mashed potatoes as well.

LORENZO   Teresa mustn't eat potatoes. They make her put on weight.

TERESA   What's it to do with you if I put on weight? I don't have to please you any more. We're separated. I can eat all the potatoes I want.

ELENA   Oh, I haven't done a lot. I've mashed them. I mashed them in the liquidizer.

TERESA   Is the liquidizer working? It didn't seem to me to be working last night.

ELENA   Yes, it's working.

LORENZO   This'll be the first time I've eaten here.

TERESA   Yes, this'll be the first time he's eaten here. He's never once condescended to eat with me, ever since we separated. He comes in, stays a quarter of an hour, and disappears.

LORENZO You're determined to quarrel. But I don't feel like quarrelling today. *(To* ELENA*)* I was telling you a little while ago about my sister, and the enviable life she leads. I stayed there a whole month with them. The peace of it! My sister's house is in a lovely situation—it's up on a little hill, and in the distance you can see the sea. I used to go down to the beach first thing every morning on my motor-bike. There was never a soul on the beach except me. It was enormously peaceful; it steadied my nerves. That's why Teresa can't work up a quarrel with me today.

TERESA *I* don't envy your sister's life at all. Her husband's an imbecile.

LORENZO He's not exactly an Einstein, I agree. But he's a pleasant, decent sort of man.

TERESA Once when we went down to see them, he trapped me in the passages and kissed me. On the mouth.

LORENZO My brother-in-law?

TERESA Your brother-in-law, yes.

LORENZO I never heard about that before.

TERESA Well, I didn't tell you, because I didn't want you to be upset. He must give your sister quite a time of it. Though it's true she's as boring as a bottle of olive oil.

LORENZO I didn't know olive oil was boring?

TERESA And why couldn't you bring me a few bottles of olive oil from down there, I'd like to know? *(To* ELENA*)* I told you what quantities they have. You'd think someone might occasionally do me a little favour, for once in a while. His sister, I mean. Her husband's unfaithful to her right and left. Poor woman, *I* don't envy her—far from it. She's twenty-nine and looks forty. And she has the biggest arse you ever saw.

LORENZO *(To* ELENA*)* Actually, my sister's a very beautiful woman. She looks like a Botticelli.

TERESA She looks like a wine-barrel. She *is* a wine-barrel! Yes, and you haven't even brought me a drop of wine back,

I suppose, either? They've got so much wine they have to give it away. But of course *I've* never been favoured with a single drop. All his sister has ever sent me are those ghastly bed-jackets. And I was always sending her the most lovely parcels of things for all those kids.

LORENZO   Look, let's go and eat. Where are we eating? In the kitchen?

TERESA   Yes, in the kitchen. I haven't any china. I haven't any silver, even. If I had any decent plates and cutlery, I'd lay the table here in the dining-room, properly, with a table-cloth. As I've nothing but crockery plates, I eat in the kitchen. It's your fault. We were married for five years, and you were never even kind enough to buy me a dinner-service. Whenever I wanted to buy one, you always said it wasn't worth it. Your mother was always promising me a proper silver-service but I never caught sight of one. Your sister has a lovely silver-service. Your mother gave it to her.

LORENZO   Well, why don't you buy yourself some plates and cutlery?

TERESA   Where do you think the money's coming from? You think you give me so much money, but you hardly give me enough to live on. I'm going to put another advertisement in the paper, about the sideboard. I'm selling it. What use have I got for a sideboard? There's nothing in it but old magazines. And I want to put another advertisement in about the little cat.

LORENZO   Cat?

TERESA   My little Siamese cat. Haven't you see her? She must be out on the balcony. I was given it a week ago. I want to mate her with a pure Siamese. I don't want her crossed with a half-breed. She's in season. She keeps howling all night.

LORENZO   Who gave it to you?

TERESA   I was given it. You don't have to know who by.

ELENA   The grocer gave it to her. It strayed into his place. It must have got out through a window somewhere.

LORENZO   My sister has six dogs and five cats.

TERESA And nine children?

LORENZO Nine children.

ELENA My mother has three dogs. And no cats. She doesn't like cats.

LORENZO Didn't you say your people had a house in the country near Pistoia? I love the Tuscan countryside. Do you ever go and see them?

ELENA Of course, I'm always going there. I'm very fond of my mother.

LORENZO Perhaps I could come with you sometime? To see the country. I love it in Tuscany. It steadies my nerves.

ELENA Of course.

TERESA No. Don't take him with you. When your mother sees him, she'll think he's a criminal. Don't you think he looks like a criminal? Unshaven, as usual, and with that old sweater. He looks dirty, doesn't he? You know, he never washes. They don't go in for washing much in their family. You can smell his sister three feet away.

LORENZO Will you leave my sister alone, please? Are we going to eat?

ELENA Yes, let's go and eat.

TERESA What about the little cat? Has she eaten?

ELENA I gave her a chicken-bone.

TERESA Are you crazy? Cats mustn't be given bones to eat; they make them sick. Cats aren't the same as dogs.

Act Three

TERESA *(Yawning)* What time is it? Eleven? Is it eleven o'clock already? Shall we make some coffee?

ELENA I've already made it. I'll bring you some in. *(She goes out and returns with the coffee)*

TERESA You were very late coming in last night. I heard you. I couldn't sleep because of that damned cat. She did nothing but howl all night.

ELENA I went to the pictures.

TERESA With Lorenzo?

ELENA The others came too.

TERESA Who were the others? Mario and Gunther?

ELENA Yes. And after the pictures, we went and had an ice. That's why I was so late.

TERESA I put three more advertisements in the paper yesterday. One for the cat, one for the sideboard, and one for the room. I didn't put any advertisement in for the villa at Rocca di Papa. I don't want to sell it now. I'm thinking of turning it into a *pension,* like your mother's. Perhaps I shall make some money. I could go on living here, and put someone in charge of the *pension.* The main thing is to make some money. This is dreadful coffee this morning. It tastes of nuts.

ELENA It tastes all right to me. . . . This is the last time we shall be having our coffee together. Tomorrow morning I shall be at uncle's. I'm terribly sorry to be leaving. I'd grown so fond of the flat.

TERESA Only the flat?

ELENA Oh, don't, Teresa. You know how I hate leaving you. But really, I do have to study; and you know I've not been able to study here with you. We just talk the whole time. There's a lot more noise at uncle's; but I do get more done.

TERESA Yes, Lorenzo was always saying he could never work or concentrate when he lived with me. There must

339

be something about me that prevents other people from concentrating. But Lorenzo was lying, because even now he's no longer with me, he still never manages to get anything done. He talks. Strolls about the streets. God, how that man talks!

ELENA But he's just about to publish a book.

TERESA A book? What sort of book?

ELENA A book about atoms. Gunther says it's very good.

TERESA What does Gunther know about atoms? He's a composer, isn't he?

ELENA Another reason I was late last night is that after the ice, we walked about the town. I walked and walked. My legs are still stiff.

TERESA All four of you?

ELENA No, just Lorenzo and myself.

TERESA He never wanted to walk with me. He always took the car, with me. He could always walk with his friends, but never with me. He said I always got on his nerves because I couldn't take such long steps as he could. He said my steps were too short.

ELENA There's something I ought to tell you, Teresa.

TERESA What is it?

ELENA It's difficult.

TERESA Whatever can it be? I didn't close my eyes all last night. I've got a terrible headache. If I can't find a Siamese cat, I'll fix the little beast up with the porter's cat.

ELENA You used to be so fond of that cat, and now you call her a little beast!

TERESA Well, she won't let me sleep.

ELENA Teresa. The thing I have to tell you is this: Lorenzo and I are in love. Very much in love. That's the real reason I'm leaving. Not because I have to study. But because I love him. So obviously, I can't stay here any longer.

TERESA I knew it without being told.

ELENA You knew? You really knew? Is it so obvious?

TERESA Yes.

ELENA You knew, and said nothing? You didn't cry or make a fuss; you just felt cold, and silent, and calm?

TERESA   Why should I cry? He doesn't want *me* any more. So it's all the same to me whether he goes with you or anyone else.

ELENA   And can we still be friends? Can I still come and see you? Will you still be as fond of me—as you were before?

TERESA   Why not, darling?

ELENA   What a good person you are! Good, and generous. I know you still love him!

TERESA   It's true. I do still love him. I shall always love him. That's the trouble. If he were halfway across the world, and just lifted a finger, I'd run to him. I'd run to him on all fours. I'd always take him back, even if he was old, and lost, and starving; even if he was flea-ridden, and syphilitic, with holes in his trousers. That's the truth. Living with him was hell, but I'd give my life, my whole life, to have the time back when we were together. However, there's no question of that; you needn't worry. Do you think you'll marry him?

ELENA   How can I? He's married to you.

TERESA   I can give him an annulment.

ELENA   Oh, Teresa, how good you are! I'm so happy! He's such an extraordinary man! I fell in love with him the moment I saw him. And he with me.

TERESA   Yes. I knew.

ELENA   What a strange thing fate is! To think I came here by chance, by the merest chance, answering an advertisement! I might easily never have looked in the paper that day, and never have come here at all! And I'd never have known either of you!

TERESA   When people are happy, they never stop marvelling at the great intelligence of *chance;* because it's made them happy. And when they're unhappy, they're not at all surprised to discover how stupid chance is. Stupid and blind. It seems natural to them that chance should be stupid. Obviously, people regard unhappiness as a natural occurrence. It doesn't surprise anybody.

ELENA   You *are* in a strange mood today! You sit there, arguing so calmly and coldly and rationally!

TERESA About the advertisements: I told you I'd put an advertisement in for the room. The same as the one I put in for you.

ELENA The same?

TERESA Yes. Two or three people have rung up. That's why I'd like you to tidy the room up, and move your clothes off the chairs: so the room will look all right if anyone comes to see it.

ELENA The room is tidy. I've already packed. I'm leaving at midday.

TERESA Is Lorenzo bringing the car round for you?

ELENA Yes. . . . And you've put an advertisement in for the cat as well? And one for the sideboard?

TERESA Yes. But I'm not sure about the cat—whether to keep her or not. Would you like her?

ELENA I can't possibly have her at uncle's. They wouldn't want her. Even my mother wouldn't have her. She doesn't like cats. Why don't you want her any more? You used to be so fond of her! Once she's mated, she'll stop making so much noise.

TERESA I know. Last night she didn't let me sleep at all. It was morning before I dropped off. I had that awful dream.

ELENA The one about the wall?

TERESA Yes. A wall, a courtyard, old furniture . . . rags and broken glass. I'm wandering about the place, rummaging among the rags. Then I beat on the wall, and try to call out. I try to shout out, but I haven't any voice. I know that on the other side of the wall, there's something dreadful.

ELENA What is it?

TERESA Someone. A person very dear to me. And I can't reach whoever it is, because of the wall.

ELENA I have bad dreams, too, when I'm tired, or when I've got exams coming. It's because you're tired. Why don't you go down to the country, and see your mother?

TERESA Yes, perhaps I ought to go home for a bit. It's a long while since I saw my mother. I never write to her. Living with Lorenzo, I picked up his awful habit of never writing letters. I did occasionally write to my mother before then.

I was better in those days. How a man can ruin you! Ruin you, and then just drop you.

ELENA Forgive him. It isn't all his fault he behaved badly to you. After all, you behaved badly to him too. And that wasn't your fault either.

TERESA You're right. And *he* was better before, too. He wasn't so frivolous and cynical. Before the unfortunate day when we first met.

ELENA He's neither frivolous nor cynical. And you know he isn't.

TERESA I could have married someone else, if I hadn't met him that day. I was so young and pretty. There were lots of men after me. I could have picked a nice, quiet, simple man, and had a settled, orderly life. Instead, I fall in with *him*. That's my luck! He ruins me. Destroys me. And goes away, like somebody who's just trampled his way through a cornfield. "You're nothing," he told me. "You're not a person at all, so far as I'm concerned. You were unfaithful to me, but that doesn't bother me. I'm millions of light-years away from you," he said. What am I to do? Tell me what I should do next. The only thing for me to do is put a bullet through my heart. Did you know I have a small pistol? I've had it ever since we had the villa at Rocca di Papa. I thought I'd be frightened, being alone at night, when he was away. And then we only stayed for one night. A dreadful night. We quarrelled. I can't remember why. Some idiotic little reason. A lost key, perhaps. Or even just a word. A simple word, between him and me, could turn into a monster. He'd disembowel it. Vivisect it. He'd squeeze the very last possible bit of meaning out of it. I bit his hand. He slapped me. My ears were buzzing, my nose was bleeding. There were the marks of my teeth on his wrist, and on his forehead there was a wound I'd made with a pair of scissors. I even used scissors on him. He had to put a plaster on it. And I thought: "But I'll kill him now, now I've got a pistol!"

ELENA Where do you keep this pistol now?

TERESA What's it matter where I keep it? I keep it, that's

all. It's in my handbag. One day I shall shoot myself. Then you won't need the annulment. I'll make him a widower.

ELENA Give me that pistol.

TERESA Don't be silly.

ELENA Give me your bag.

TERESA Don't be silly.

ELENA Throw the pistol away! Please, Teresa, I do beg of you, throw it away!

TERESA All right. I'll throw it away.

ELENA I must dress. It's getting late. I must lock my bag. He'll be down below very soon, waiting for me. You won't be alone, Teresa! I'll always be coming to see you; he'll always be coming too! We shall always be fond of you, both of us! *(Embraces her)*

TERESA Yes.

ELENA I must go and dress. *(Exit)*

> *(TERESA goes into her own room. Then into ELENA'S room. The stage remains empty. Then a pistol shot is heard. TERESA runs to the telephone and dials a number)*

TERESA Hullo, Lorenzo! Lorenzo! Come round, for God's sake, come round, I've killed her! I didn't mean to, I didn't mean to, but I've killed her! She's dead, she died at once. For God's sake, Lorenzo, do come, do come! *(She collapses into sobs)*

> *(The doorbell rings. TERESA wipes her eyes on her hands. She opens the door. Enter GIOVANNA)*

GIOVANNA Good morning. I telephoned a short while ago. I've come about the advertisement in the paper. My name's Giovanna Ricciardi.

TERESA Which advertisement was it? I put in three advertisements.

GIOVANNA The one for the room.

CURTAIN

Rites

BY MAUREEN DUFFY

CHARACTERS

MEG

ADA

OLD WOMAN

FIRST OFFICE GIRL

SECOND OFFICE GIRL (NORMA)

THIRD OFFICE GIRL

NELLIE

DOT

GIRL

FIRST WOMAN

SECOND WOMAN

THIRD WOMAN

Introduction

"Would you like to see those women?" Dionysus asks Pentheus at the turning point of Euripides' *The Bacchae.* "I am not eager to see them drunk; that would be a painful sight," he answers, and Dionysus replies, "Yet you would be glad to see a sight that would pain you?" The answer is yes. To gratify his curiosity he is even prepared to dress as a woman. What Pentheus thinks he will see are people, women, particularly his own mother, making love. He will see something titillating, shocking, different. By the rules of Greek drama we never know what he sees except through the words of the messenger. At first the Bacchae seem innocent as a Mothers' Union picnic then suddenly they become frenzied furies who tear Pentheus to pieces.

There is a Peeping Tom in all of us. We should all like to be able to eavesdrop, to know how people behave alone or in groups when they can really be themselves. By watching them we can enjoy the vicarious pleasure of their "shameful behaviour" and the breaking of innumerable taboos. Like Pentheus we want to be shocked and pained. "There but for the grace of God go I," is a rationalizing moral cloak beneath which we may read of and undergo those unrealized and unacknowledged fantasies that are the staple nourishment of both "The News of the World" and Greek myth.

The Greek gods and heroes form a huge family encompassing every human emotion, every sexual combination and variation. There is no need for us to commit incest or murder: they have done it already. There is no need for us to feel guilty for homosexual or adulterous fantasies: Zeus will have Ganymede and Semele on our behalf. If we lust after our mother or an animal, Oedipus and Europa will be both gratified and punished for us. If we are puritanical or power-mad somewhere there will be a story to embody our hopes and terrors.

Aristotle himself saw that myth translated through the medium of tragedy did exactly this " . . . through pity and fear it effects relief (katharsis) to these and other emotions," is the famous quotation. It seems obvious to me that he is saying not what it *should* do but what it *does*. His is not a moralistic comment about the function or purpose of tragedy; it is an analysis of his own feelings at the end of Sophocles' *Oedipus*. He is describing that state, which we all recognize, of being drained, purged, purified by the emotions we have vicariously suffered in the organized dreamworld of art.

By Aristotle's definition *Rites* is a tragedy though he would probably have deplored the hybridization of the actions of gods and kings expressed in the idiom of low life. However when asked to pigeonhole the play, and to give actors an idea of how it should be played, I have called it black farce, a style of drama derived from the mediaeval morality where the devil and all his works were often funny at the same time as fearful.

Purposely it is pitched between fantasy and naturalism and here Aristotle will bail me out again. "For poetic (i.e., artistic) effect a convincing impossibility is preferable to that which is unconvincing though possible." My ladies' public lavatory is as real as in a vivid dream and it need be no more real than that. Its occupants speak in the cliches which in dreams often mask our meaning from ourselves. I would not have used a real child for Dionysus if I could have had one. A doll is at once more terrifying, more enigmatic and more appropriate, artistically to the dream idiom like the impossible crematorium/altar incinerator, and psychologically—little girls play with dolls, "women worship images."

The Bacchae is Pentheus' story; *Rites* is Agave's. Agave in Euripides is punished mercilessly for her denial by rejecting his pregnant mother, her sister, Semele of the life that Dionysus represents. She is driven temporarily demented and kills her own son, Pentheus, another life denier: a son for a mother. Ada has also denied life by translating sex and love into money and revenge. However she escapes. In a world of stereotypes and attitudes (men do this, women are like that; feminine reaction, masculine response) she is society's product if not victim. All reduction of people to objects, all imposition of labels and patterns to which they must conform, all segregation can lead only to destruction. In the very moment when the women have got their own back on men for their type-casting in an orgasm of violence they find they have destroyed themselves and in death there is certainly no difference.

I have talked about Greek myth and drama but *Rites* was not written as a version of *The Bacchae* and no attempt was made to make it conform to that play. It may be seen in its own right as Joyce's *Ulysses* may be read without reference to Homer's Odyssey or a piece of Titian flesh admired without our knowing it is Venus we are lusting for. Yet there is a pleasure in knowing, in adding another layer, in making the particular general, and to realize that it's distorted from a classic may make it more difficult for some people to dismiss as merely shocking goings-on in a ladies' loo and nothing to do with me thank you or as "no more yielding than a dream" (there are those who see "A wood near Athens" as the setting for just another fairy story). I would want you to take from this introduction only as much as is necessary for you to feel Aristotle's purging at work.

MAUREEN DUFFY

A procession of workmen bearing laminated plastic sheets for the walls of the cubicles and doors which they fit up and hang. A workman or perhaps two bring in a large mirror. Others put up the side wall with the incinerator opening. A foreman directs them silently. When six cubicles are erected down one side and the seventh, opposite number One, by itself, the workmen go out and return in solemn file with lavatory bowls which they place inside the cubicles. They come to the doors. The foreman bows, they bow and go off to return with sanitary bins. It must all be very stately and they are dressed in white overalls. The bowing is repeated. The third time they go off and return with cisterns, trailing their chains, and borne like coffers. This time there is a lot of banging and hammering, then a pause and simultaneous flushing sound. Once again they bow and go off. Finally there is a procession with two white painted chairs, large notice about VD clinics, sanitary towel machine, perfume spray which they position, turn to face the foreman and bow. All go out; a pause. A woman enters from the Right with a small holdall, looks round furtively and goes into number One.

MEG *enters from the Left and begins to go into the facing cubicles flushing them and wiping the seats.* ADA *enters from the Right, takes off her coat, puts on a white nylon overall, takes her handbag over to the mirror and begins an elaborate coiffure and make-up. It is clear that this is a daily ritual. It must be done with deliberate vulgarity in the knowledge that she isn't observed as are all the actions. When she puts on her mascara she takes out a little pot and brush, spits into the pot, mixes well with brush and little finger and then applies it with the brush. She constantly admires the effect she is creating.*

MEG   Number Three's awash again. Like the Sea of Galilee.
Anyone who goes in there'll have to be good at walking on
the water. One's out of paper. Dunno what they do with
it. Always number One. Monday they'd had a paper chase
and wrapped the cistern up in it. Tuesday it was all tore up
in little shreds, someone hadn't had no confetti to take to
the wedding I suppose, Wednesday was stuffing up the
plug hole night and now they've copped the whole roll.
Well as long as they took it home with 'em. I can't stand
it when they hide it in the cistern. As long as it ent that.
All soggy and breaking apart. Turns me up. As long as it ent
that.

ADA   *(Should be spitting in pot, etc.)*   Now look what you've
done. I've stuck me pencil in me eye. I've told you before.
Don't excite me when it comes to the eyes. Very delicate
work the eyes. You can't do nothing without them and
you've made the left one run.

MEG   Sorry I spoke. You do look lovely this morning. I don't
know how you do it. Up all night and then responsibility
for all this.

ADA   Wait till I get me promotion.

MEG   You'll take me with you, won't you? You wouldn't
leave me here. I'll ask for a transfer.

ADA   There'll be others.

MEG   Oh I know. I do understand. You'll have two or three
under you then. I won't expect no favours. But it wouldn't
be the same left here with someone new.

ADA   We'll have to see. You're getting on. It's a question of
whether you're up to it.

MEG   No one'd keep it as lovely as you do. And now we've
got the cremator. I wouldn't trust anyone to have charge
of that. *(They both turn and look at the steel flap)* Sometimes I think I can hear it roaring like a great furnace, a
wild beast.

ADA   It's an incinerator. I wish you'd get the word right.

MEG   Was he lovely?

ADA   Who?

MEG   Last night.

ADA *(Going back to her ritual)* I've had better. Not bad. All right for a weeknight. I like to keep it a bit quiet. Wouldn't do for a Saturday though. No dash. I like a bit of dash of a weekend. Not much staying power either. If they haven't got dash or staying power there's not much left except a Thursday. Getting over the hump of the week I call it.

    (A bundled-up FIGURE *shuffles in from the Right with an old leatherette shopping bag. She wears plimsolls)*

ADA You're too early. We're not open yet. Tell her we're not open.

MEG She's come for her breakfast. She's been coming every morning for a fortnight.

ADA So I've noticed. Used to be one of Tilly's regulars at Waterloo. Don't know why she's switched to us. If they offer me that I shall turn it down straight. They're not class the lot they get in there. All lay-abouts and soaks. Dirty too, like her. Tell her we're not open yet.

MEG *(As to the half-witted)* We're not open. Opening time's nine. Ten minutes to go. *(The* FIGURE *stares uncomprehendingly. Makes little gestures of pleading and despair.* MEG *points to her watch)* Ten minutes.

ADA Shoo! Out! *(The* FIGURE *finally turns and shuffles away.* ADA *shudders)* I dunno how they let themselves get like it. No pride. I dunno how they expect anyone to fancy them.

MEG But then we don't all start with your advantages.

ADA *(Returning to the mirror)* No, but that's no excuse for not making the best of what you've got. It's not much and you've got to tart it up a bit to sell it high. After all the goods are all the same when they get the wrapping off. You've got to make them pay for the wrapping off. It's the first law of finance.

MEG You're so clever Ada. I do admire you. You've got it all thought out.

ADA You have to have to live. Know your market it says. You want to read more. It's all on the back pages of the paper, just before the sport, if you know where to look. They think we don't read that far.

MEG I've never got farther than the headlines. All that small print.

ADA "How the market closed" it says. Gold's steady, rubbers are up, diamonds are still a girl's best friend. Better than the stars you follow.

MEG Read them to me. We've got a minute. (ADA *gets out a huge pair of glasses and a newspaper from her bag*) Why ever do you have such a huge pair?

ADA It's something else I read. "Think big," it said. You've got to put it in the shop window, it's no good under the counter. Now, do you want to hear?

MEG Read me, read me!

ADA Be quiet then. Let's see . . . Virgo.

MEG *(Lingeringly)* Virgo.

ADA A new figure will come into your life today who will completely change its course. Be careful with the pence.

MEG A new figure. What's yours? Go on, read yours.

ADA All right. But you know I don't believe in it. Scorpio. Something you have wanted for a long time is within your grasp. Be bold. The pounds will take care of themselves.

MEG Promotion! Charing Cross at least. *(The bundled up* FIGURE *shuffles in again and makes for a cubicle)* She can tell the time.

ADA Oh, shut her in number One and let her get on with it. But I don't want crumbs and greaseproof bags all over the floor. Tell her to eat tidy or we won't let her in.

MEG You hear what madam says: Eat tidy.
    (The FIGURE *goes into the first cubicle, bangs and locks the door. Sound of cistern flushing. Pause. The others listen. A loud rustling)*

ADA It's like having mice. Right. Are we ready for the first rush? *(She looks round)* Have you done number Five? There's bound to be writing. There always is. Brings them all out in a hot flush of words number Five.
    (Enter three OFFICE GIRLS *quickly, clattering and chattering)*

FIRST OFFICE GIRL He never!

SECOND OFFICE GIRL God's truth and cross me heart.

THIRD OFFICE GIRL   What in the pictures?

SECOND OFFICE GIRL   Right in the front row. I didn't know where to look.

FIRST OFFICE GIRL   You don't have to look.
>   *(They all burst into screams of laughter, rush into cubicles and bang the doors. Pause. Loud flushing.* ONE *and* THREE *come out.* TWO *is in number Five)*

THIRD OFFICE GIRL   Come on Norma. We'll be late. *(Bangs on door)*

FIRST OFFICE GIRL   She's always ages. *(Flushing noise.* NORMA *comes out)*

SECOND OFFICE GIRL *(To* ADA*)*   You want to clean them things off the walls. I've never been so disgusted!

FIRST OFFICE GIRL   What's it say?

NORMA   I couldn't repeat it. Couldn't bring me mouth to say it without washing it out with soap and water after.

THIRD OFFICE GIRL *(Goes into cubicle)*   Here Sheila, you want to see this.
>   *(*FIRST OFFICE GIRL *joins her. They come out)*

NORMA *(To* ADA*)*   I've got a good mind to report you.

FIRST OFFICE GIRL   No decent woman'd write things like that. You must've had a bloke in here.

ADA *(To* MEG*)*   I told you to make sure of number Five.

MEG   I never had time Ada.

ADA   You and the stars.

THIRD OFFICE GIRL   We could report you having blokes in here.

ADA   If you didn't know what they mean you wouldn't be disgusted.

FIRST OFFICE GIRL   Whatd'ya mean?

NORMA   I'll scratch her eyes out she says things like that to me.

THIRD OFFICE GIRL   Go on Norma.

ADA   Yes, go on Norma. *(A moment while they confront each other)*

NORMA   I wouldn't demean myself.

MEG   It's the night staff dear. When she goes off for her cup of tea.

NORMA Well, you want to get it cleaned up. Filth!

ADA We all do it, and so did our mothers and fathers.

FIRST OFFICE GIRL Yeah, but it's different reading about it. It's like . . .

NORMA Watching yourselves in the mirror . . .

THIRD OFFICE GIRL Dirty postcards . . .

FIRST OFFICE GIRL Blue films . . .

NORMA Stripteasing . . .

THIRD OFFICE GIRL French model . . .

NORMA French letters . . .

FIRST OFFICE GIRL House of correction . . .

ALL THREE *(Staccato)* Only men, only men, only men do that. *(Pause)*

THIRD OFFICE GIRL Do you like your Eddy?

NORMA He's all right. He'll go a long way.

FIRST OFFICE GIRL Yeah, if you push him.

> *(They scream with laughter.* NORMA *goes over to the mirror.* ADA *takes up her paper and sits on one of the white chairs.* MEG *takes the other and produces some knitting from a bag)*

NORMA I don't think I'm going in today.

ADA Haven't you finished that?

FIRST OFFICE GIRL What you gonna do?

MEG He'll have it for Christmas.

NORMA Fancy a day off.

ADA Anyone'd think it was your life's work.

THIRD OFFICE GIRL They won't pay you.

MEG I like to take me time.

NORMA I fancy a day by the sea, all waves and wind tossed hair like the adverts.

FIRST OFFICE GIRL I read a lovely story last week. There was this girl . . .

ADA There always is.

MEG What?

ADA Time if you take it.

THIRD OFFICE GIRL They're too quick to take it off.

NORMA What?

FIRST OFFICE GIRL The money.

NORMA Why don't we all . . . ?

MEG We're not all made like you.

THIRD OFFICE GIRL What?

NORMA Have the day off.

ADA Never shut the stable door till the horse has bolted. Gilts are holding well. Oils are smooth.

NORMA The smooth skin rippled as he flexed the tanned muscles of his . . .

FIRST AND THIRD OFFICE GIRLS Oh shut up Norma.

NORMA I learnt it.

ADA Don't take much learning.

NORMA Off by heart.

ADA Nor that neither.

NORMA You've got no romance.

ADA Unilever, Dunlop, Consols, Industrials; lead up, silver down.

FIRST OFFICE GIRL What's all that for?

MEG She's studying form.

ADA Taking stock. Strategy.

NORMA Sounds nasty to me. Mercenary.

ADA And you're a fool, green as little apples and the cradle marks still showing. Don't you think he'll study the assets before he makes a takeover bid. You've got to value your own stock or you'll undersell yourself. Dazzled by securities and the unit trust and not looking to your dividends that's you.

NORMA I suppose you do better playing the market?

ADA War bonds. They're the only really safe bet. Till death do us part, them and us. You can put your money on that.

FIRST OFFICE GIRL Like in the playground, boys against girls. Them onto us. He's onto me.

NORMA *(Longingly)* I wish he was.

THIRD OFFICE GIRL Dear Auntie Mabel, my boy is always begging me to do wrong. He says if I loved him I would be kind to him. What shall I do? I am frightened of losing him if I do not give in.

FIRST OFFICE GIRL Dear Worried Blue Eyes, on no account let him force you to anticipate the delights of the honeymoon. Two people should save themselves for each other. If this is all this boy wants from you he does not really love you and once he has had it he will quickly tire.

NORMA Eddy always falls dead asleep after.

MEG Men are made different.

FIRST OFFICE GIRL That's for sure.

(They scream with laughter)

THIRD OFFICE GIRL *(Singing)*

> She stood on the bridge at midnight
> Throwing snowballs at the moon
> Though she said she'd never had it
> Yet she spoke too bleeding soon.

(NELLIE and DOT come in Right walking together in step. They are in their sixties, respectably and identically hatted and coated, with large bags)

NELLIE I cleaned his shoes for him every day of our life and he'd put them on always of an evening to sit about in. Couldn't stand slippers. Said they were sloppy. Brown shoes; they shone like conkers. He was a lovely dresser.

(They trot forward and go straight into Three and Four, banging the doors simultaneously)

FIRST OFFICE GIRL You'd catch me cleaning anyone else's boots.

THIRD OFFICE GIRL It was different for them though.

NORMA How was it?

THIRD OFFICE GIRL They never went to work. All they did all day was sweep and tidy and wash.

FIRST OFFICE GIRL Make flour puddings: wrap in a piece of sheet and bubble in an iron pot overnight.

NORMA Something out of nothing.

THIRD OFFICE GIRL Take one sheep's head, remove the eyes, wash well in salted water. Boil with an onion stuck with cloves for six hours, removing the scum from time to time.

FIRST OFFICE GIRL When tender remove from the flame.

THIRD OFFICE GIRL Separate the meat from the bones. Chop and add brains and peeled tongue.

NORMA Put in a clean basin and cover with the liquor. Leave to set on the window sill.

FIRST OFFICE GIRL Then remove to the bottom of the garden . . .

THIRD OFFICE GIRL Dig large hole and bury . . .

NORMA And wait to see what comes up next Spring.

(NELLIE and DOT come out of their cubicles with a simultaneous flushing, opening and banging of doors)

ALL Now wash your hands please.

NELLIE I always got him a bit of fish of a Friday and steamed it between two plates and went through it for the bones. He couldn't bear to come across a bone. Put him right off it would.

(They go to the mirror and remove their hats. They begin to comb their hair)

FIRST OFFICE GIRL I'd flesh his bones for him.

MEG In my young day . . .

ADA You never had one.

MEG Oh Ada I did. I was a girl once with hair so long I could sit on it.

ADA And that's all you did: sit on it. *(The OFFICE GIRLS laugh)* You'll never get that done by Christmas.

NORMA If I went bald I'd shoot meself.

FIRST OFFICE GIRL You could always wear a wig like Queen Elizabeth.

THIRD OFFICE GIRL When I was little I had an uncle used to sing that song about after the ball. *(Singing)* After the ball is over, See her take out her glass eye, Put her false teeth in some water, Get out a bottle of dye, Put her cork leg in the corner, Hang up her wig on the wall, Then all the rest went to bye-byes, After the ball. Give me the nightmares it did. I used to lie and shudder.

NORMA It must be terrible to be old. *(There is a pause and loud rustling from number One)* Here, you got mice?

ADA There's a lady in there having her breakfast. I keep a very clean establishment. You could eat off our floors.

MEG That's right. I go over them twice and it's fresh water the second time.

NELLIE I never knew how much he earned but he give me my money regular as clockwork every Friday night, after he'd put his shoes on before he ate his fish. Without he so much as touched his knife and fork he'd pass it across the table. Always had a piece of bread and jam after to take the taste away. I couldn't go without a hat could you?

DOT They don't seem to wear them these days, the young-sters.

NELLIE It keeps you from blowing about.

NORMA All wind tossed hair like the adverts.

FIRST OFFICE GIRL When they chopped her head off and the executioner went to hold it up by the hair for everyone to see he dropped it cos her wig fell off.

THIRD OFFICE GIRL You're making it up.

FIRST OFFICE GIRL It's in the history books.

NORMA She never had her head off. She died in her bed.

THIRD OFFICE GIRL With her boots on. Imagine a bald head and big boots.

NELLIE When I was a little girl I had button boots for Sunday best.

ADA It was Mary Queen of Scots.

NORMA I said she never had her head off.

FIRST OFFICE GIRL What does it matter? All those old queens were the same.

ADA She was a raving beauty. Men went wild for her. She had three husbands and the pick of the world for her lov-ers.

FIRST OFFICE GIRL She was bald. And how do you know anyway?

MEG She reads a lot.

NELLIE When I was a girl I always had my nose stuck in a book. Lovely reading it was in those days.

THIRD OFFICE GIRL That's all they could do: read about it.

FIRST OFFICE GIRL Because they didn't have . . .

ALL THREE (Staccato) The marvels of modern science.

NELLIE Better than life it was.

DOT The children make it worth it.

FIRST OFFICE GIRL Ent you going in then Norma?

NORMA I'm sick of old Villars and his, "Type this Miss Smith, file that Miss Smith, take it down Miss Smith, lick it, stamp on it, post it. In tray, out tray."

THIRD OFFICE GIRL In out, in out.

NELLIE Can I try your hat Dot?

DOT Let me try yours.
(They solemnly exchange hats and try them on before the mirror)

NELLIE Doesn't suit me.

DOT It's not quite your style.

NELLIE Goes better with your colouring.

DOT I like yours best on you. *(They give the hats back and put them on)*

ADA At his beck and call. I wouldn't stand for it.

FIRST OFFICE GIRL It's better than the typing pool.

THIRD OFFICE GIRL Or the bench. I had six months on the production line.

ADA I work for no man.

NELLIE He wouldn't have me out to work. Said when he couldn't keep me at home he'd die.

MEG Don't leave me here alone when you go. Not with someone new. It wouldn't be the same.

NORMA I dunno how you can do a job like this.

MEG What's wrong with it?

FIRST OFFICE GIRL I wouldn't fancy it cooped up in here all day. In winter you mustn't never see the daylight.

ADA Who does in winter?

THIRD OFFICE GIRL We've got a big window we can look out of. We're high up. You can see right across to the river. There's four of us and when he goes out of the room we have a laugh and a chat.

FIRST OFFICE GIRL I wouldn't want to be on the switch-board with no one to talk to all day, nothing to say but, "Can I help you?"

NELLIE You get used to being alone. Thirty-six years I waited all day for him to come home in the evening except for popping out for a bit of shopping or when you came Dot.

ADA   And now?

DOT   We're both alone now.

NELLIE   We get about. We don't let it get us down. After all . . .

NELLIE and DOT   It's no good giving way, letting yourself go to pieces. Things are sent to try us. Time heals all.

DOT   We come up West and look at the shops.

ADA   Go West young man.

NELLIE   Or a day trip to Eastbourne.

DOT   Sometimes it's a show.

NELLIE   Wednesday night's bingo.

DOT   The time passes.

NELLIE   We don't let it get us down.

DOT   A regular pension. No financial worries.

NELLIE   No one can dock our money if it's a bad week.

DOT   Or ask where it's all gone.

NORMA   Sounds to me as if you're better off without them.

NELLIE AND DOT   What a terrible thing to say.

FIRST OFFICE GIRL   You can't talk to them. They're all the same.

THIRD OFFICE GIRL   Me mum won't look at the truth.

ADA   Truth!

NORMA

> I promised you and you promised me
> To be as true as I would be.
> But since I see your double heart
> Farewell my part.

FIRST OFFICE GIRL   Where'd you get that? Off a card?

THIRD OFFICE GIRL   Don't be silly, they don't have cards for that.

NORMA   I learned it at school

FIRST OFFICE GIRL   They never teach you anything you really want to know at school.

THIRD OFFICE GIRL   I wouldn't have been a teacher and had to deal with us lot.

FIRST OFFICE GIRL   You could talk to the married ones

though. You felt they knew what it was all about. Not dried
up. *(To* ADA*)* Are you married?

NELLIE   Don't be personal. They ask things today we
wouldn't even have thought of.

ADA   I am when I want to be. I don't like to be tied down.

NORMA   You'd rather sit here all day.

MEG   Madam's independent.

ADA   Down here what I say goes.

FIRST OFFICE GIRL   We don't have to come here you know.

THIRD OFFICE GIRL   Yeah, you're not indispensable.

ADA   Aren't I?

NORMA   What about a splash of perfume, a dab of scent
behind the ears. *(She goes to the perfume spray and works
it)* Smell me, I'm lovely.

FIRST OFFICE GIRL *(opening flap of incinerator)*   Look a
letter box. *(There is a roaring sound. She steps back quickly
letting the flap drop)* Here that's dangerous. People could
burn themselves on that. You shouldn't have a roaring
furnace loose in a place like this.

MEG   Tisn't loose. It's well under control. Caged like a wild
beast. Madam keeps it in order.

ADA   Supposing I said that goes straight down to hell.
  (A FIGURE *comes on Right, pushes its way through to
  the towel machine and buys one)*

MEG   That's right dear pull hard. It's a bugger for getting
stuck. *(The* FIGURE *goes along the cubicles and tries to get
into number One. There is a strangled cry)* Engaged dear!
There's someone in there. I don't know why they all go for
number One. *(The* FIGURE *goes for number Three)* Not
that one dear. We've got trouble with the water works in
there. Try number Two. That's nice and dry.
  (The FIGURE *goes into number Two)*

NELLIE   Likes the privacy I suppose. I don't like these flimsy
little cubby holes where everyone can hear everything.

ADA   They're cheaper than bricks and mortar and we're all
made the same.

NELLIE   No privacy. More like the gents. Not that I've ever
been in one.

DOT I have.

ALL except ADA and MEG You never!

DOT Yes I did. Once when me and my Frank was out I was caught very short. Must have had a chill or something cos I'm always very careful about that. I mean you don't know what you might pick up and I always sit on my hands like my mother taught me.

ADA You won't pick up anything in here.

MEG Eat off our floors you could and all the seats are done twice a day with disinfectant.

NELLIE What happened? What's it like?

DOT Frank stood guard for me, he'd been in first of course to make sure there was no one in there, and when I got in there was a long trough, like for animals to drink from, and a round basin in the corner. I didn't know what to do I was so nervous.

FIRST OFFICE GIRL Go on.

DOT Then, all of a sudden, there was this terrible rushing noise as if there was lots of people in there all pulling the chains at once and water poured down the trough. I thought I'd be washed away.

THIRD OFFICE GIRL What did you do?

DOT I waited till it stopped and then I used the little basin. I had to stand on tip-toe and sort of cock one leg.

NELLIE Men are taller than women.

FIRST OFFICE GIRL Besides they've got more aim in life.
     (They scream with laughter)

THIRD OFFICE GIRL We went to Spain last year. You should see them there. A hole in the ground and two concrete footprints.

NELLIE Disgusting! Foreigners.

THIRD OFFICE GIRL Men and women together.

DOT I never heard of such a thing.

THIRD OFFICE GIRL And a man attendant to look after them. *(To ADA)* You'd be out of a job.

NELLIE I see they've appointed the first man matron of a hospital.

ADA Nothing's sacred. They couldn't do it. Not as well. I

don't care what you say. It needs a special touch. Men aren't built for it. They haven't the capacity. *(Two* WOMEN *enter Right leading in a lifesize toddler boy doll between them. This must be as realistic as possible and dressed in real clothes)* Isn't he a little old to be still coming down here? Time he found his own way about in the world.

(The WOMEN *laugh)*

MEG   Madam asked you a question. *(They laugh again)* It's time he stuck to his own side of the fence.

(They stand still and then the FIRST WOMAN *picks him up in her arms)*

FIRST WOMAN   Come up then, Mummy's big boy, Mummy's little love. There's pretty curls.

NELLIE   Looks more like a girl. Half the time you can't tell the difference these days. They all wear trousers and they all have curls.

NORMA   I can tell the difference.

DOT   How old is he?

SECOND WOMAN   Oh he's tall for his age.

MEG   Grow like weeds they do now. It's all the free this and that.

NELLIE   They grow up too fast. You don't have them babies five minutes. We were glad to have them round us as long as we could. Now their mothers can't wait to get them off hand, packed away to the nursery school as soon as they can toddle while they're out bringing in the money. Miss all the pleasure of keeping them spotless and wheeling them out of an afternoon. I've sat there in the park in summer just waiting for someone to come up and sit down and say, "There's a lovely baby."

FIRST WOMAN   Mummy's lovely boy.

MEG   A pity they ever have to grow up.

ADA   Some of them never do.

SECOND WOMAN   All men are babies.

NORMA   You should see my Eddy, gambols around like a kid; bounces up the road till I'm ashamed of him, and then he cries.

FIRST OFFICE GIRL   Boys don't cry.

THIRD OFFICE GIRL When did he cry.

NORMA Never you mind. But he cried, great tears as if his heart was breaking.

FIRST OFFICE GIRL What did you do?

NORMA Kissed it and made it better. What do you think?

SECOND WOMAN Nothing but great babies.

ADA He's too big to be brought in here.

MEG How do you know it's a "he." Perhaps it's a little girl: a sweet clean little girl.

THIRD OFFICE GIRL What are little girls made of?

NELLIE and DOT Sugar and spice and all things nice That's what little girls are made of.

SECOND WOMAN What are little boys made of?

ADA Snaps and snails and puppy dogs' tails.

FIRST OFFICE GIRL That's how you can tell.

THIRD OFFICE GIRL How?

FIRST OFFICE GIRL See if he's got a puppy dog's tail. That's what we did when we were little. We'd catch a little boy and take his trousers down to see what he was made of.

ALL Snaps and snails and puppy dogs' tails.

FIRST WOMAN Oh he's all there.

SECOND WOMAN And half way back.

ADA Stand him on this chair and let's see.

> *(The white chair is put in the centre of the stage and the doll placed on it. One of the women supports it from behind. It has a cherubic and blandly smiling face)*

MEG Go on Ada.

> *(ADA undoes its shirt, takes down its short trousers. The OFFICE GIRLS giggle nervously. Underneath there are loose-legged pants which she also drops to its ankles. There is an audible sigh. Her actions must be deliberate and ritually slow)*

FIRST OFFICE GIRL Well, he's lifesize.

> *(They laugh loudly but forcedly)*

NORMA Made to measure I'd say.

THIRD OFFICE GIRL Tailored with you in mind.

NELLIE Just like my Willy.

FIRST WOMAN Mummy's big boy. *(She strokes its body)*

MEG I had a baby brother once.

ADA Looks so harmless all quiet there. A pity they ever have to grow up. Snaps and snails and puppy dogs' tails.

DOT Cause all the trouble in this world they do.

ADA Never still. Always have to be up and doing. *(She puts out a hand)*

FIRST WOMAN Don't touch!

ADA I was only seeing.

FIRST WOMAN He's my boy.

MEG What was you seeing Ada?

ADA It'd be so easy, and then nobody'd know the difference.

FIRST WOMAN Leave him alone. He's mine.

ADA Who wants him. I don't. I've got plenty.

MEG Madam's got plenty. Whatever she wants.

ADA And I don't have to nurse it and cosset it. Let them come to me. Let them pay me for looking after, with interest.

FIRST WOMAN Mummy's little prince.

SECOND WOMAN Cover him up.

ADA What are you so careful about. No one's going to hurt him.

FIRST OFFICE GIRL Yeah, we're only looking. There's no harm in looking.

THIRD OFFICE GIRL They can't stop you looking.

NORMA *(Lingeringly)* The first time I looked at Eddy I got the shock of me life.

NELLIE I never saw him undressed in thirty-six years until they came to lay him out. "You'd like to wash him yourself I expect," she said. I was so surprised.

FIRST OFFICE GIRL To hear my mum talk you'd wonder how you ever got born.

NORMA And then I thought, "I love you. You're beautiful."

ADA Love!

NORMA Yes, love.

ADA Pop songs, sugar and spice and all things nice that's what you're fed on. Cover him up. *(The TWO WOMEN dress*

the doll hastily and the FIRST WOMAN *moves the chair to
the side and sits down with it on her lap during the suc-
ceeding speech)* I'll tell you about your kind of love: a few
moments pleasure and then a lifetime kidding yourselves.
Caught, bound, even if you don't know it. Or a lifetime
looking, like Meg, and wailing what you've missed. Years
of ministering to a stranger like them— *(She indicates* NEL-
LIE *and* DOT*)*—or making heroes of your children only to
see them stride off and leave you. *(To the* WOMAN *with the
doll)*

> *(There is a loud crash from number Two)*

ADA *(To* MEG*)* What's that?

MEG That girl who went into number Two, she's never
come out.

ADA Knock on the door. See if she's all right.

> *(*MEG *goes obediently to number Two and knocks)*

MEG Are you all right dear? *(They all listen. Silence. The*
FIRST WOMAN *gets up, leaving the doll sitting on the chair
and joins the group)* She don't answer.

ADA So I heard. *(She goes up to the door and bangs)* Time
you was out of there.

NORMA Perhaps she's not well.

NELLIE Could have fainted.

FIRST OFFICE GIRL Can't you unlock it?

THIRD OFFICE GIRL Maybe she just likes it in there.

ADA *(Calling)* Are you all right?

> *(There is silence and then a loud rustling)*

MEG Perhaps she's having breakfast too.

ADA No, that was from number One.

FIRST WOMAN What're you going to do?

SECOND WOMAN You can't leave her in there.

DOT That's where the gents are easier. No doors.

ADA Be quiet. I'm thinking.

FIRST OFFICE GIRL You're in charge. Why don't you just
unlock it?

ADA Because it's bolted on the inside. They call it privacy.

NORMA You could die in there in private.

ADA *(to* MEG*)* Look under the door.

MEG   I couldn't get down there Ada and if I did I'd never get up again.

THIRD OFFICE GIRL   I'll get down. I used to be good at gym. *(She hitches up her miniskirt and gets down on her knees to peer under. The others all bend as if they could peer too)*

NORMA   What can you see?

THIRD OFFICE GIRL   She's got her head in the pan. I think she's fainted. Oh my gawd, it's blood.

ADA   Where?

THIRD OFFICE GIRL   Everywhere. You'll have to get her out. She'll bleed to death. *(She gets up)*

MEG   If she's not dead already.

NORMA   Break the door down.

ADA   It's too strong.

FIRST OFFICE GIRL   If two of us . . .

NELLIE   You'll have to get a man.

ADA   I'm not having any man down here.

FIRST WOMAN   Call a policeman.

DOT   Policemen are different.

NELLIE   He'd have had that down in a trice, put his shoulder to it and bang . . . torn the hinges right out of their sockets. You ought to get a man.

SECOND WOMAN   She might be dying in there. *(General buzz)*

ADA   Shut up all of you! No man's coming down here and that's that.

THIRD OFFICE GIRL   She's lying against the door.

ADA   *(Triumphant)* There. You couldn't push the door down anyway without doing her an injury.

FIRST OFFICE GIRL   Why not?

ADA   Because it opens inward so you can keep a hand against it when you're sitting there with a broken lock. Someone'll have to climb up.

THIRD OFFICE GIRL   You go Norma. Me and Sheila'll make a back.

NORMA   I couldn't. I can't stand the sight of blood.

FIRST WOMAN   Suppose she fainted in there too.

DOT   Imagine us all piled up on top of each other.

THIRD OFFICE GIRL   Oh I'll go. Come on you two. *(The other two make a back. She climbs up and lies over the top of the door reaching down for the bolt to murmurs of encouragement))*

ADA   Can you reach it?

THIRD OFFICE GIRL   No. It's too low. I'll have to get down inside somehow. *(She inches along the top, gets a leg over and finally disappears. There is a loud splash)* Sod!

ADA   Open the door.

THIRD OFFICE GIRL   I slipped. *(The door is opened)* I put me feet down the pan. It's all slithery.

ADA   Get her out. *(The FIRST OFFICE GIRL and one of the WOMEN haul the girl out. The THIRD OFFICE GIRL limps out behind)* She's cut her wrists the silly bitch!

NORMA   I don't feel well.

MEG   Look at my nice clean floor.

THIRD OFFICE GIRL   I've sprained my ankle.

ADA   Put her head between her knees, she's going to faint. *(NELLIE sits NORMA on a chair and puts her head down)*

DOT   You'll have to get someone now. She could bleed to death.

THIRD OFFICE GIRL   My shoe's all wet.

ADA *(Inspecting the cuts)* It looks worse than it is. Blood always does. Something for a bandage. Get a couple of towels out of the machine.

(FIRST OFFICE GIRL goes to the machine and pulls the handle)

FIRST OFFICE GIRL   Who's got six penn'orth of coppers.

(DOT finds her the money. She gets the towels in their little boxes and hands them to ADA)

ADA   Undo them then. They're no use like that. You can keep the pins.

NELLIE   I think she should have an ambulance.

ADA *(Busy strapping the girl up)* They can put you inside for this you know.

FIRST OFFICE GIRL   Prison?

ADA The nut house. She'd be grateful to wake up in there.

THIRD OFFICE GIRL My shoe's full of water.

ADA She's only nicked herself. Another faints at the sight of blood. Virgins!

NORMA I'm no bloody virgin.

ADA *(To* MEG*)* Clean up that mess. *(*MEG *goes for a mop)* She's coming round. *(The figure stirs and moans)*

GIRL Desmond!

ADA Another bleeding man!

FIRST OFFICE GIRL I'm shivered if I'd top meself for someone called Desmond.

GIRL Desmond!

DOT What did he do to you dear?
      (The GIRL *cries incoherently)*

ADA Bastard men! Get a man she says. I'll get him right where I want him. He thinks because I'm flat on my back he's got me but I've got him; caught, clenched as if I had my teeth in him. "Come in," I say all soft and I squeeze him tight, loving as a boa constrictor. And they're wild for it. They swoon and cry and die in my arms and come back for more. "Screw me," I whisper and they pound and pant in their pitiful climaxes they think so earth shaking. "That was a good one," they say and then I make them pay for it.

DOT It's only like a sneeze when all's said and done.

NELLIE I never once, not in thirty six years.

MEG No one ever wanted me except one night behind the gas works and he was a bit simple.

FIRST OFFICE GIRL You're all right till you're stuck with a kid then they don't want to know.

NORMA My Eddy's a Catholic. He says it's up to me.

FIRST WOMAN Why do they have to grow up?

THIRD OFFICE GIRL I've laddered me stocking.

FIRST OFFICE GIRL When we go to a dance they all stand up at the bar putting away jar after jar and you're left on your own.

THIRD OFFICE GIRL Then one of them'll come up as if he's

inspecting the cattle in the market, look you all over and
nod.

SECOND WOMAN   Tread all over your feet in the quick-step
while you say sorry.

NELLIE   Cos you mustn't hurt their pride.

DOT   Look after them, minister to them.

FIRST WOMAN   A pity they have to grow up. Mother's little
prince'll make someone else his queen.

MEG   I was better off without him. *(She puts a coat over the
figure)* There dear. You'll be all right.

ADA   We don't need them. We can do without them.

FIRST OFFICE GIRL   We can dance together. *(They begin to
dance with each other backwards and forwards in the
latest version of the shake)* Come on Norma.

    *(*NORMA *joins in and gradually the watchers, first the*
    TWO WOMEN *tentatively imitating, then* NELLIE *and*
    DOT, MEG *swaying with her mop until they are all
    moving except* ADA *and the figure on the floor)*

THIRD OFFICE GIRL   We don't need them. Don't need them.

ALL   Don't need them, don't need them.

    *(The door of number One is unbolted and the bundled
    up* FIGURE *shambles out)*

ADA *(Shouting)*   One day you'll be old like her. *(The dancing stops. They stand and stare at her)* Old Mother Brown
that's who she is. That's how we all end up. *(There is an
angry hiss)*

NELLIE   Knees up Mother Brown.

    *(They begin to sing it, in hissed whispers at first, very
    menacingly, encircling the* OLD WOMAN *who turns
    her scarfed head from side to side uncomprehend-
    ingly. Then they join hands round her and begin to
    quicken the pace and sing louder, meeting across her
    making her duck and cower. She holds up her bag to
    her head as if to protect herself as they dance on.)*

ALL

Knees up Mother Brown, knees up Mother Brown
Under the table you must go

Ee aye, ee aye, ee aye o!
If I catch you bending
I'll saw your legs right off
So knees up, knees up
Don't get the breeze up
Knees up Mother Brown.

(This is repeated until it reaches a frenzy of menace and the old woman cowers down making little noises of fear. Suddenly a figure appears from number seven and tries to get to the exit right. Head bent; it is suited and coated, short-haired and masculine)

ADA Look a bloody man. In here. Spying on us. *(They stop and all turn panting towards the figure which tries to back away)* He's trying to run for it. Don't let him out. *(Some of the women run behind him and edge him in)* You think you can get away with murder, that we've no place we can call our own. Coming down here to see what we get up to when we're alone. Bastard Men!

CHORUS *(Whispering menacingly)* Bastard men!

ADA We'll teach you to come spying.
(She leads them forward, the OLD WOMAN *joining in. They fall upon the figure and it goes under as if drowned. It disappears beneath the flailing crowd. There is frenzied activity and a scream. There is another cry and the crowd breaks apart leaving a tattered and broken figure wrapped in bloody clothing. Only* NORMA *is left crouching down)*

ADA Look at it! I've seen prettier in the butcher's shop. Animals! Bastard men.

NORMA *(Slowly standing up)* Christ! It was a woman.

NELLIE Oh my gawd!

ADA That?

NORMA Don't you think I know. It was a bloody woman.

ADA *(Going over she bends down and examines the figure. Then she straightens up)* She shouldn't have done it.

FIRST OFFICE GIRL I want to cry.

ADA   She shouldn't have done it. How could we tell; the mouth, the eyes . . . ?

DOT   It's all the same now.

MEG   Ada, what will you do? Your promotion.
   (ADA pauses for a moment and then goes forward and lifts the flap of the incinerator. There is a roar)

ADA   That's what we'll do. Down there. It's waiting. Ash is only ash; sift it fine enough and who can tell. It's hungry. Listen to it roar. We'll feed it. *(To the two OFFICE GIRLS)* Come on you two. Pick that up.

NELLIE   To die like that.

THIRD OFFICE GIRL   You have to pay extra for cremation.

FIRST OFFICE GIRL   She couldn't have been happy.

NORMA   *(Fiercely)* Why not, she was alive.
   (The two OFFICE GIRLS pick up the figure. ADA holds the slot open and it disappears into the hole)

ADA   Push.
   (There is a pause then they all come to the basin and wash their hands)

NORMA   She was really dead wasn't she? I mean . . .

ADA   We all did it. Every one of us.

MEG   *(Nodding at the girl still lying on the floor under her coat)* What about her?

ADA   She won't remember or if she does she'll think it was just a dream. *(To NORMA)* You look after her. Get her out of here.

NORMA   *(Goes over to the figure and shakes it)* Come on dear. We'll see you home. *(She and the other OFFICE GIRLS get her to her feet and help her off Right)*

NELLIE   *(Looking in the mirror)* Is my hat straight?

DOT   Oh it does suit you like that.

NELLIE and DOT   Well, we'd best be getting along. Can't spend all day here. *(They trot off Right)*

ADA   *(To the other TWO WOMEN)* Haven't you got something you should be doing? *(They look at each other and begin to move. She nods toward the doll still sitting on the chair)* And take that thing with you. He's too old to be down here. *(They lead him off)*

FIRST WOMAN Mummy's prince. Mummy's little love.

ADA *(To the* OLD WOMAN*)* Shoo! *(She scuttles away.* ADA *goes back to the mirror and begins to retouch her make-up.* MEG *gets her mop and cloth. She goes into number Five. There is a sound of flushing. She comes out)*

MEG When you get your promotion you won't leave me here will you? You'll let me come with you now, won't you? *(*ADA *goes on with her make-up.* MEG *sits down at the table)* What's he like your Friday feller?

CURTAIN

Wine in the Wilderness

BY ALICE CHILDRESS

CHARACTERS

BILL JAMESON   An artist aged thirty-three

OLDTIMER   An old roustabout character in his sixties

SONNY-MAN   A writer aged twenty-seven

CYNTHIA   A social worker aged twenty-five. She is Sonny-man's wife

TOMMY   A woman factory worker aged thirty

SCENE: *A one room apartment in a Harlem Tenement. It used to be a three room apartment but the tenant has broken out walls and is half finished with a redecorating job. The place is now only partly reminiscent of its past tawdry days, plaster broken away and lathing exposed right next to a new brick-faced portion of wall. The kitchen is not a part of the room. There is a three-quarter bed covered with an African throw, a screen is placed at the foot of the bed to insure privacy when needed. The room is obviously black dominated, pieces of sculpture, wall hangings, paintings. An artist's easel is standing with a drapery thrown across it so the empty canvas beneath it is hidden. Two other canvases the same size are next to it, they too are covered and conceal paintings. The place is in a beautiful, rather artistic state of disorder. The room also reflects an interest in other darker peoples of the world . . . A Chinese incense-burner Buddha, an American Indian feathered war helmet, a Mexican serape, a Japanese fan, a West Indian travel poster. There is a kitchen table, chairs, floor cushions, a couple of box crates, books, bookcases, plenty of artist's materials. There is a small raised platform for model posing. On the platform is a backless chair.*

The tail end of a riot is going on out in the street. Noise and screaming can be heard in the distance, . . . running feet, voices shouting over loudspeakers.

OFFSTAGE VOICES Offa the street! Into your homes! Clear the street! *(The whine of a bullet is heard)* Cover that roof! It's from the roof! (BILL *is seated on the floor with his back to the wall, drawing on a large sketch pad with charcoal pencil. He is very absorbed in his task but flinches as he hears the bullet sound, ducks and shields his head with upraised hand, . . then resumes sketching. The telephone*

383

rings, he reaches for phone with caution, pulls it toward
him by the cord in order to avoid going near window or
standing up)

BILL   Hello? Yeah, my phone is on. How the hell I'm gonna
be talkin' to you if it's not on? *(Sound of glass breaking in*
the distance) I could lose my damn life answerin' the
phone. Sonny-man, what the hell you callin' me up for! I
thought you and Cynthia might be downstairs dead. I
banged on the floor and hollered down the air-shaft, no
answer. No stuff! Thought yall was dead. I'm sittin' here
drawin' a picture in your memory. In a bar! Yall sittin' in
a bar? See there, you done blew the picture that's in your
memory . . . No kiddin', they wouldn't let you in the block?
Man, they can't keep you outta your own house. Found?
You found who? Model? What model? Yeah, yeah, thanks,
. . . but I like to find my own models. No! Don't bring
nobody up here in the middle of a riot . . . Hey, Sonny-man!
Hey!

   (Sound of yelling and rushing footsteps in the hall)

WOMAN'S VOICE *(Offstage)*   Dammit, Bernice! The riot is
over! What you hidin' in the hall for? I'm in the house, your
father's in the house, . . . and you out here hidin' in the hall!

GIRL'S VOICE *(Offstage)*   The house might burn down!

BILL   Sonny-man, I can't hear you!

WOMAN'S VOICE *(Offstage)*   If it do burn down, what the
hell you gon' do, run off and leave us to burn up by ourself?
The riot is over. The police say it's over! Get back in the
house!

   (Sound of running feet and a knock on the door)

BILL   They say it's over. Man, they oughta let you on your
own block, in your own house . . . Yeah, we still standing',
this seventy year old house got guts. Thank you, yeah,
thanks but I like to pick my own models. You drunk? Can't
you hear when I say not to . . . Okay, all right, bring her
. . . *(Frantic knocking at the door)* I gotta go. Yeah, yeah,
bring her. I gotta go . . . *(Hangs up phone and opens the*
door for OLDTIMER. *The old man is carrying a haul of loot*
. . . *two or three bottles of liquor, a ham, a salami and a*

suit with price tags attached) What's this! Oh, no, no, no, Oldtimer, not here. . . . *(Faint sound of a police whistle)* The police after you? What you bring that stuff in here for?

OLDTIMER *(Runs past* BILL *to* C. *as he looks for a place to hide the loot)* No, no, they not really after me but . . . I was in the basement so I could stash this stuff, . . . but a fella told me they pokin' round down there . . . in the back yard pokin' round . . . the police doin' a lotta pokin' round.

BILL If the cops are searchin' why you wanna dump your troubles on me?

OLDTIMER I don't wanta go to jail. I'm too old to go to jail. What we gonna do?

BILL We can throw it the hell outta the window. Didn't you think of just throwin it away and not worry 'bout jail?

OLDTIMER I can't do it. It's like . . . I'm Oldtimer but my hands and arms is somebody else that I don't know-a-tall. *(*BILL *pulls stuff out of* OLDTIMER'S *arms and places loot on the kitchen table.* OLDTIMER'S *arms fall to his sides)* Thank you, son.

BILL Stealin' ain't worth a bullet through your brain, is it? You wanna get shot down and drown in your own blood, . . . for what? A suit, a bottle of whiskey? Gonna throw your life away for a damn ham?

OLDTIMER But I ain' really stole nothin', Bill, cause I ain' no thief. Them others, . . . they smash the windows, they run in the stores and grab and all. Me, I pick up what they left scatter in the street. Things they drop . . . things they trample underfoot. What's in the street ain' like stealin'. This is leavin's. What I'm gon' do if the police come?

BILL *(Starts to gather the things in the tablecloth that is on the table)* I'll throw it out the air-shaft window.

OLDTIMER *(Places himself squarely in front of the air-shaft window)* I be damn. Uh-uh, can't let you do it, Billy-Boy. *(Grabs the liquor and holds on)*

BILL *(Wraps the suit, the ham and the salami in the table-cloth and ties the ends together in a knot)* Just for now, then you can go down and get it later.

OLDTIMER *(Getting belligerent)* I say I ain't gon' let you do it.

BILL Sonny-man calls this "The people's revolution." A revolution should not be looting and stealing. Revolutions are for liberation. *(Oldtimer won't budge from before the window)* Okay, man, you win, it's all yours. *(Walks away from* OLDTIMER *and prepares his easel for sketching)*

OLDTIMER Don't be mad with me, Billy-Boy, I couldn' help myself.

BILL *(At peace with the old man)* No hard feelin's.

OLDTIMER *(As he uncorks bottle)* I don't blame you for bein' fed up with us, . . . fella like you oughta be fed up with your people sometime. Hey, Billy, let's you and me have a little taste together.

BILL Yeah, why not.

OLDTIMER *(At table pouring drinks)* You mustn't be too hard on me. You see, you talented, you got somethin' on the ball, you gonna make it on past these white folk, . . . but not me, Billy-boy, it's too late in the day for that. Time, time, time, . . . time done put me down. Father Time is a bad white cat. Whatcha been paintin' and drawin' lately? You can paint me again if you wanta, . . . no charge. Paint me 'cause that might be the only way I get to stay in the world after I'm dead and gone. Somebody'll look up at your paintin' and say, . . . "Who's that?" And you say, . . . "That's Oldtimer." *(*BILL *joins* OLDTIMER *at table and takes one of the drinks)* Well, here's lookin' at you and goin' down me. *(Gulps drink down)*

BILL *(Raising his glass)* Your health, oldtimer.

OLDTIMER My day we didn't have all this grants and scholarship like now. Whatcha been doin!?

BILL I'm working on the third part of a triptych.

OLDTIMER A what tick?

BILL A triptych.

OLDTIMER Hot-damn, that call for another drink. Here's to the trip-tick. Down the hatch. What is one-a-those?

BILL It's three paintings that make one work . . . three paintings that make one subject.

OLDTIMER Goes together like a new outfit . . . hat, shoes and suit.

BILL Right. The title of my triptych is . . . "Wine In The Wilderness" . . . Three canvases on black womanhood . . .

OLDTIMER *(Eyes light up)* Are they naked pitchers?

BILL *(Crosses to paintings)* No, all fully clothed.

OLDTIMER *(Wishing it was a naked picture)* Man, ain' nothin' dirty 'bout naked pitchers. That's art. What you call artistic.

BILL Right, right, right, but these are with clothes. That can be artistic too. *(Uncovers one of the canvases and reveals painting of a charming little girl in Sunday dress and hair ribbon)* I call her . . . "Black girlhood."

OLDTIMER Awwwww, that's innocence! Don't know what it's all about. Ain't that the little child that live right down the street? Yeah. That call for another drink.

BILL Slow down, Oldtimer, wait till you see this. *(Covers the painting of the little girl, then uncovers another canvas and reveals a beautiful woman, deep mahogany complexion, she is cold but utter perfection, draped in startling colors of African material, very "Vogue" looking. She wears a golden head-dress sparkling with brilliants and sequins applied over the paint)* There she is . . . "Wine In The Wilderness" . . . Mother Africa, regal, black womanhood in her noblest form.

OLDTIMER Hot damn. I'd die for her, no stuff, . . . oh, man. "Wine In The Wilderness."

BILL Once, a long time ago, a poet named Omar told us what a paradise life could be if a man had a loaf of bread, a jug of wine and . . . a woman singing to him in the wilderness. She is the woman, she is the bread, she is the wine, she is the singing. This Abyssinian maiden is paradise, . . . perfect black womanhood.

OLDTIMER *(Pours for BILL and himself)* To our Abyssinian maiden.

BILL She's the Sudan, the Congo River, the Egyptian Pyramids . . . Her thighs are African Mahogany . . . she speaks and her words pour forth sparkling clear as the waters . . . Victoria Falls.

OLDTIMER Ow! Victoria Falls! She got a pretty name.

BILL *(Covers her up again)* Victoria Falls is a waterfall not her name. Now, here's the one that calls for a drink. *(Snatches cover from the empty canvas)*

OLDTIMER *(Stunned by the empty canvas)* Your . . . your pitcher is gone.

BILL Not gone, . . . she's not painted yet. This will be the third part of the triptych. This is the unfinished third of "Wine In The Wilderness." She's gonna be the kinda chick that is grass roots, . . . no, not grass roots, . . . I mean she's underneath the grass roots. The lost woman, . . . what the society has made out of our women. She's as far from my African queen as a woman can get and still be female, she's as close to the bottom as you can get without crackin' up . . . she's ignorant, unfeminine, coarse, rude . . . vulgar . . . a poor, dumb chick that's had her behind kicked until it's numb . . . and the sad part is . . . she ain't together, you know, . . . there's no hope for her.

OLDTIMER Oh, man, you talkin' 'bout my first wife.

BILL A chick that ain' fit for nothin' but to . . . to . . . just pass her by.

OLDTIMER Yeah, later for her. When you see her, cross over to the other side of the street.

BILL If you had to sum her up in one word it would be nothin'!

OLDTIMER *(Roars with laughter)* That call for a double!

BILL *(Beginning to slightly feel the drinks. He covers the canvas again)* Yeah, that's a double! The kinda woman that grates on your damn nerves. And Sonny-man just called to say he found her runnin' round in the middle-a this riot, Sonny-man say she's the real thing from underneath them grass roots. A back-country chick right outta the wilds of Mississippi, . . . but she ain' never been near there. Born in Harlem, raised right here in Harlem, . . . but back country. Got the picture?

OLDTIMER *(Full of laughter)* When ... when ... when she
get here let's us stomp her to death.

BILL Not till after I paint her. Gonna put her right here on
this canvas. *(Pats the canvas, walks in a strut around the
table)* When she gets put down on canvas, ... then triptych
will be finished.

OLDTIMER *(Joins him in the strut)* Trip-tick will be finish
... trip-tick will be finish ...

BILL Then "Wine In The Wilderness" will go up against the
wall to improve the view of some post office ... or some
library ... or maybe a bank ... and I'll win a prize ... and
the queen, my black queen will look down from the wall
so the messed up chicks in the neighborhood can see what
a woman oughta be ... and the innocent child on one side
of her and the messed up chick on the other side of her
... MY STATEMENT.

OLDTIMER *(Turning the strut into a dance)* Wine in the
wilderness ... up against the wall ... wine in the wilderness
... up against the wall ...

WOMAN FROM UPSTAIRS APT. *(Offstage)* What's the matter!
The house on fire?

BILL *(Calls upstairs through the air-shaft window)* No,
baby! We down here paintin' pictures!
     (Sound of police siren in distance)

WOMAN FROM UPSTAIRS APT. *(Offstage)* So much-a damn
noise! Cut out the noise! *(To her husband, hysterically)*
Percy! Percy! You hear a police siren! Percy! That a fire
engine?!

BILL Another messed up chick. *(Gets a rope and ties it to
OLDTIMER's bundle)* Got an idea. We'll tie the rope to the
bundle, ... then ... *(Lowers bundle out of window)* lower
the bundle outta the window ... and tie it to this nail here
behind the curtain. Now! Nobody can find it except you
and me ... Cops come, there's no loot. *(Ties rope to nail
under curtain)*

OLDTIMER Yeah, yeah, loot long gone 'til I want it. *(Makes
sure window knot is secure)* It'll be swingin' in the breeze
free and easy. *(There is knocking on the door)*

SONNY-MAN Open up! Open up! Sonny-man and company.

BILL *(Putting finishing touches on securing knot to nail)*
Wait, wait, hold on. . . .

SONNY-MAN And-a here we come!

> *(Pushes the door open. Enters room with his wife*
> CYNTHIA *and* TOMMY. SONNY-MAN *is in high spirits.*
> *He is in his late twenties, his wife* CYNTHIA *is a bit*
> *younger. She wears her hair in a natural style, her*
> *clothing is tweedy and in good, quiet taste.* SONNY-
> MAN *is wearing slacks and a dashiki over a shirt.*
> TOMMY *is dressed in a mis-matched skirt and sweater,*
> *wearing a wig that is not comical, but is wiggy look-*
> *ing. She has the habit of smoothing it every once in a*
> *while, patting to make sure it's in place. She wears*
> *sneakers and bobby sox, carries a brown paper sack)*

CYNTHIA You didn't think it was locked, did you?

BILL Door not locked? *(Looking over* TOMMY)

TOMMY You oughta run him outta town, pushin' open people's door.

BILL Come right on in.

SONNY-MAN *(Standing behind* TOMMY *and pointing down at*
her to draw BILL*'s attention)* Yes, sireeeeee.

CYNTHIA Bill, meet a friend-a ours . . . This is Miss Tommy
Fields. Tommy, meet a friend-a ours . . . this is Bill, Jameson
. . . Bill, Tommy.

BILL Tommy, if I may call you that . . .

TOMMY *(Likes him very much)* Help yourself, Bill. It's a
pleasure. Bill Jameson, well, all right.

BILL The pleasure is all mine. Another friend-a ours, Oldtimer.

TOMMY *(With respect and warmth)* How are you,
Mr. Timer?

BILL *(Laughs along with others,* OLDTIMER *included)*
What you call him, baby?

TOMMY Mr. Timer, . . . ain't that what you say? *(They all
laugh expansively)*

BILL No, sugar pie, that's not his name, . . . we just say
. . . "Oldtimer," that's what everybody call him. . . .

OLDTIMER   Yeah, they all call me that . . . everybody say that
. . . OLDTIMER.

TOMMY   That's cute, . . . but what's your name?

BILL   His name *is* . . . er . . . er . . . What *is* your name?

SONNY-MAN   Dog-bite, what's your name, man?

> *(There is a significant moment of self-consciousness as*
> CYNTHIA, SONNY *and* BILL *realize they don't know*
> OLDTIMER'S *name)*

OLDTIMER   Well, it's . . . Edmond L. Matthews.

TOMMY   Edmond *L.* Matthews. What's the L for?

OLDTIMER   Lorenzo, . . . Edmond Lorenzo Matthews.

BILL AND SONNY-MAN   Edmond Lorenzo Matthews.

TOMMY   Pleased to meetcha, Mr. Matthews.

OLDTIMER   Nobody call me that in a long, long time.

TOMMY   I'll call you Oldtimer like the rest but I like to know
who I'm meetin'. *(OLDTIMER gives her a chair)* There you
go. He's a gentleman too. Bet you can tell my feet hurt. I
got one corn, . . . and that one is enough. Oh, it'll ask you
for somethin'.

> *(General laughter.* BILL *indicates to* SONNY-MAN *that*
> TOMMY *seems right.* CYNTHIA *and* OLDTIMER *take*
> *seats near* TOMMY*)*

BILL   You rest yourself, baby, er . . . er . . . Tommy. You did
say Tommy.

TOMMY   I cut it to Tommy . . . Tommy-Marie, I use both of
'em sometime.

BILL   How 'bout some refreshment?

SONNY-MAN   Yeah, how 'bout that. *(Pouring drinks)*

TOMMY   Don't yall carry me too fast, now.

BILL *(Indicating liquor bottles)*   I got what you see and also
some wine . . . couple-a cans-a beer.

TOMMY   I'll take the wine.

BILL   Yeah, I knew it.

TOMMY   Don't wanta start nothin' I can't keep up.

> *(OLDTIMER slaps his thigh with pleasure)*

BILL   That's all right, baby, you just a wine-o.

TOMMY   You the one that's got the wine, not me.

BILL   I use this for cookin'.

TOMMY You like to get loaded while you cook?
        (OLDTIMER *is having a ball*)

BILL *(As he pours wine for* TOMMY*)* Oh, baby, you too much.

OLDTIMER *(Admiring* TOMMY*)* Oh, Lord, I wish, I wish, I wish I was young again.

TOMMY *(Flirtatiously)* Lively as you are, . . . I don't know what we'd do with you if you got any younger.

OLDTIMER Oh, hush now!

SONNY-MAN *(Whispering to* BILL *and pouring drinks)* Didn't I tell you! Know what I'm talking' about. You dig? All the elements, man.

TOMMY *(Worried about what the whispering means)* Let's get somethin' straight. I didn't come bustin' in on the party, . . . I was asked. If you married and any wives or girl-friends round here . . . I'm innocent. Don't wanta get shot at or jumped on. Cause I wasn't doin' a thing but mindin' my business! . . . *(Saying the last in loud tones to be heard in other rooms)*

OLDTIMER Jus' us here, that's all.

BILL I'm single, baby. Nobody wants a poor artist.

CYNTHIA Oh, honey, we wouldn't walk you into a jealous wife or girl friend.

TOMMY You paint all-a these pitchers?
        (BILL *and* SONNY-MAN *hand out drinks*)

BILL Just about. Your health, baby, to you.

TOMMY *(Lifts her wine glass)* All right, and I got one for you. . . . Like my grampaw used-ta say, . . . Here's to the men's collars and the women's skirts, . . . may they never meet. *(General laughter)*

OLDTIMER But they ain't got far to go before they do.

TOMMY *(Suddenly remembers her troubles)* Niggers, niggers . . . niggers, . . . I'm sick-a niggers, ain't you? A nigger will mess up everytime . . . Lemmie tell you what the niggers done . . .

BILL Tommy, baby, we don't use that word around here. We can talk about each other a little better than that.

CYNTHIA Oh, she doesn't mean it.

TOMMY What must I say?

BILL Try Afro-Americans.

TOMMY Well, . . . the Afro-Americans burnt down my house.

OLDTIMER Oh, no they didn't!

TOMMY Oh, yes they did . . . it's almost burn down. Then the firemen nailed up my door . . . the door to my room, nailed up shut tight with all I got in the world.

OLDTIMER Shame, what a shame.

TOMMY A *damn* shame. My clothes . . . Everything gone. This riot blew my life. All I got is gone like it never was.

OLDTIMER I know it.

TOMMY My transistor radio . . . that's gone.

CYNTHIA Ah, gee.

TOMMY The transistor . . . and a brand new pair-a shoes I never had on one time . . . *(Raises her right hand)* If I never move, that's the truth . . . new shoes gone.

OLDTIMER Child, when hard luck fall it just keep fallin'.

TOMMY And in my top dresser drawer I got a my-on-ase jar with forty-one dollars in it. The fireman would not let me in to get it . . . And it was a Afro-American fireman, don't-cha know.

OLDTIMER And you ain't got no place to stay. (BILL *is studying her for portrait possibilities*)

TOMMY *(Rises and walks around room)* That's a lie. I always got some place to go. I don't wanta boast but I ain't never been no place that I can't go back the second time. Woman I use to work for say . . . "Tommy, any time, any time you want a sleep-in place you come right here to me." . . . And that's Park Avenue, my own private bath and T.V. set . . . But I don't want that . . . so I make it on out here to the dress factory. I got friends . . . not a lot of 'em . . . but a few *good* ones. I call my friend—girl and her mother . . . they say . . . "Tommy, you come here, bring yourself over here." So Tommy got a roof with no sweat. *(Looks at torn walls)* Looks like the Afro-Americans got to you too. Breakin' up, breakin' down, . . . that's all they know.

BILL No, Tommy, . . . I'm re-decorating the place . . .

TOMMY You mean you did this yourself?

CYNTHIA It's gonna be wild . . . brick-face walls . . . wall to wall carpet.

SONNY-MAN She was breakin' up everybody in the bar . . . had us all laughin' . . . crackin' us up. In the middle of a riot . . . she's gassin' everybody!

TOMMY No need to cry, it's sad enough. They hollerin' whitey, whitey . . . but who they burn out? Me.

BILL The brothers and sisters are tired, weary of the endless get-no-where struggle.

TOMMY I'm standin' there in the bar . . . tellin' it like it is . . . next thing I know they talkin' bout bringing' me to meet you. But you know what I say? Can't nobody pick nobody for nobody else. It don't work. And I'm standin' there in a mis-match skirt and top and these sneaker-shoes. I just went to put my dresses in the cleaner . . . Oh, Lord, wonder if they burn down the cleaner. Well, no matter, when I got back it was all over . . . They went in the grocery store, rip out the shelves, pull out all the groceries . . . the hams . . . the. . . the . . . the can goods . . . everything . . . and then set fire . . . Now who you think live over the grocery? Me, that's who. I don't even go to the store lookin' this way . . . but this would be the time, when . . . folks got a fella they want me to meet.

BILL *(Suddenly self-conscious)* Tommy, they thought . . . they thought I'd like to paint you . . . that's why they asked you over.

TOMMY *(Pleased by the thought but she can't understand it)* Paint me? For what? If he was gonna paint somebody seems to me it'd be one of the pretty girls they show in the beer ads. They even got colored on television now, . . . brushin' their teeth and smokin' cigarettes, . . '. some of the prettiest girls in the world. He could get them, . . . couldn't you?

BILL Sonny-man and Cynthia were right. I want to paint you.

TOMMY *(Suspiciously)* Naked, with no clothes on?

BILL No, baby, dressed just as you are now.

OLDTIMER Wearin' clothes is also art.

TOMMY In the cleaner I got a white dress with a orlon sweater to match it, maybe I can get it out tomorrow and pose in that.

> (CYNTHIA, OLDTIMER *and* SONNY-MAN *are eager for her to agree*)

BILL No, I will paint you today, Tommy, just as you are, holding your brown paper bag.

TOMMY Mmmmmm, me holdin' the damn bag, I don' know 'bout that.

BILL Look at it this way, tonight has been a tragedy.

TOMMY Sure in hell has.

BILL And so I must paint you tonight, . . . Tommy in her moment of tragedy.

TOMMY I'm tired.

BILL Damn, baby, all you have to do is sit there and rest.

TOMMY I'm hongry.

SONNY-MAN While you're posin' Cynthia can run down to our house and fix you some eggs.

CYNTHIA *(Gives her husband a weary look)* Oh, Sonny, that's such a lovely idea.

SONNY-MAN Thank you, darlin', I'm in there, . . . on the beam.

TOMMY *(Ill at ease about posing)* I don't want no eggs. I'm goin' to find some Chinee food.

BILL I'll go. If you promise to stay here and let me paint you, . . . I'll get you anything you want.

TOMMY *(Brightening up)* Anything I want. Now, how he sound? All right, you comin' on mighty strong there. "Anything you want." When last you heard somebody say that? . . . I'm warnin' you, now, . . . I'm free, single and disengage, . . . so you better watch yourself.

BILL *(Keeping her away from ideas of romance)* Now this is the way the program will go down. First I'll feed you, then I'll paint you.

TOMMY Okay, I'm game, I'm a good sport. First off, I want me some Chinee food.

CYNTHIA Order up, Tommy, the treat's on him.

TOMMY How come it is you never been married? All these girls runnin' round Harlem lookin' for husbands. *(To Cynthia)* I don't blame 'em, 'cause I'm lookin' for somebody myself.

BILL I've been married, married and divorced, she divorced me, Tommy, so maybe I'm not much of a catch.

TOMMY Look at it this-a-way. Some folks got bad taste. That woman had bad taste. *(All laugh except BILL who pours another drink)* Watch it, Bill, you gonna rust the linin' of your stomach. Ain't this a shame? The riot done wipe me out and I'm sittin' here havin' me a ball. Sittin' here ballin'! *(As BILL refills her glass)* Hold it, that's enough. Likker ain' my problem.

OLDTIMER I'm havin' me a good time.

TOMMY Know what I say 'bout divorce. *(Slaps her hands together in a final gesture)* Anybody don' wantcha, . . . later, let em go. That's bad taste for you.

BILL Tommy, I don't wanta ever get married again. It's me and my work. I'm not gettin' serious about anybody. . . .

TOMMY He's spellin' at me, now. Nigger, . . . I mean Afro-American . . . I ain' ask you nothin'. You hinkty, I'm hinkty too. I'm independent as a hog on ice, . . . and a hog on ice is dead, cold, well-preserved . . . and don't need a mother-grabbin' thing. *(All laugh heartily except BILL and CYNTHIA)* I know models get paid. I ain't no square but this is a special night and so this one'll be on the house. Show you my heart's in the right place.

BILL I'll be glad to pay you, baby.

TOMMY You don't really like me, do you? That's all right, sometime it happen that way. You can't pick for *nobody*. Friends get to matchin' up friends and they mess up everytime. Cynthia and Sonny-man done messed up.

BILL I like you just fine and I'm glad and grateful that you came.

TOMMY Good enough. *(Extends her hand. They slap hands together)* You 'n me friends?

BILL Friends baby, friends. *(Putting rock record on)*

TOMMY *(Trying out the model stand)* Okay, Dad! Let's see

'bout this *anything I want* jive. Want me a bucket-a Egg
Foo Yong, and you get you a shrimp-fry rice, we split that
and each have some-a both. Make him give you the soy
sauce, the hot mustard and the duck sauce too.

BILL Anything else, baby?

TOMMY Since you ask, yes. If your money hold out, get me
a double order egg roll. And a half order of the sweet and
sour spare ribs.

BILL *(To* OLDTIMER *and* SONNY-MAN*)* Come on, come on.
I need some strong men to help me bring back your order,
baby.

TOMMY *(Going into her dance. . . simply standing and going
through some boo-ga-loo motions)* Better go get it 'fore
I think up some more to go 'long with it. *(The men laugh
and vanish out of the door. Steps heard descending stairs)*
Turn that off. *(Cynthia turns off record player)* How could
I forget your name, good as you been to me this day. Thank
you, Cynthia, thank you. I *like* him. Oh, I *like* him. But I
don't wanta push him too fast. Oh, I got to play these cards
right.

CYNTHIA *(A bit uncomfortable)* Oh, Honey, . . . Tommy,
you don't want a poor artist.

TOMMY Tommy's not lookin' for a meal ticket. I been doin'
for myself all my life. It takes two to make it in this high-
price world. A black man see a hard way to go. The both
of you gotta pull together. That way you accomplish.

CYNTHIA I'm a social worker . . . and I see so many broken
homes. Some of these men! Tommy, don't be in a rush
about the marriage thing.

TOMMY Keep it to yourself, . . . but I was thirty my last
birthday and haven't even been married. I coulda been.
Oh, yes, indeed, coulda been. But I don't want any and
everybody. What I want with a no-good piece-a nothin'?
I'll never forget what the Reverend Martin Luther King
said . . . "I have a dream." I like him sayin' it 'cause truer
words have never been spoke. *(Straightening the room)* I
have a dream, too. Mine is to find a man who'll treat me
just half-way decent . . . just to meet me half-way is all I ask,

to smile, be kind to me. Somebody in my corner. Not to wake up by myself in the mornin' and face this world all alone.

CYNTHIA About Bill, it's best not to ever count on anything, anything at all, Tommy.

TOMMY *(This remark bothers her for a split second but she shakes it off)* Of course, Cynthia, that's one of the foremost rules of life. Don't count on *nothin'!*

CYNTHIA Right, don't be too quick to put your trust in these men.

TOMMY You put your trust in one and got yourself a husband.

CYNTHIA Well, yes, but what I mean is . . . Oh, you know. A man is a man and Bill is also an artist and his work comes before all else and there are other factors . . .

TOMMY *(Sits facing CYNTHIA)* What's wrong with me?

CYNTHIA I don't know what you mean.

TOMMY Yes you do. You tryin' to tell me I'm aimin' too high by lookin' at Bill.

CYNTHIA Oh, no my dear.

TOMMY Out there in the street, in the bar, you and your husband were so sure that he'd *like* me and want to paint my picture.

CYNTHIA But he does want to paint you, he's very eager to . . .

TOMMY But why? Somethin' don't fit right.

CYNTHIA *(Feeling sorry for Tommy)* If you don't want to do it, just leave and that'll be that.

TOMMY Walk out while he's buyin' me what I ask for, spendin' his money on me? That'd be too dirty. *(Looks at books. Takes one from shelf)* Books, books, books everywhere. '"Afro-American History." I like that. What's wrong with me, Cynthia? Tell me, I won't get mad with you, I swear. If there's somethin' wrong that I can change, I'm ready to do it. Eighth grade, that's all I had of school. You a social worker, I know that mean college. I come from poor people. *(Examining the book in her hand)* Talkin' 'bout poverty this and poverty that and studyin' it. When you in it you don't be studyin' 'bout it. Cynthia, I remember my mother tyin' up her stockin's with strips-a rag 'cause she didn't have no garters. When I get home from school she'd say, . . . "Nothin' much here to eat." Nothin' much might be grits, or bread and coffee. I got sick-a all that, got me a job. Later for school.

CYNTHIA The Matriarchal Society.

TOMMY What's that?

CYNTHIA A Matriarchal Society is one in which the women rule . . . the women have the power . . . the women head the house.

TOMMY We didn't have nothin' to rule over, not a pot nor a window. And my papa picked hisself up and run off with some finger-poppin' woman and we never hear another word 'til ten, twelve years later when a undertaker call up and ask if Mama wanta come claim his body. And don'cha know, mama went on over and claim it. A woman need a man to claim, even if it's a dead one. What's wrong with me? Be honest.

CYNTHIA You're a fine person . . .

TOMMY Go on, I can take it.

CYNTHIA You're too brash. You're too used to looking out for yourself. It makes us lose our femininity . . . It makes us hard . . . it makes us seem very hard. We do for ourselves too much.

TOMMY If I don't, who's gonna do for me?

CYNTHIA You have to let the black man have his manhood again. You have to give it back, Tommy.

TOMMY I didn't take it from him, how I'm gonna give it back? What else is the matter with me? You had school, I didn't. I respect that.

CYNTHIA Yes, I've had it, the degree and the whole bit. For a time I thought I was about to move into another world, the so-called "integrated" world, a place where knowledge and knowhow could set you free and open all the doors, but that's a lie. I turned away from that idea. The first thing I did was give up dating white fellas.

TOMMY I never had none to give up. I'm not soundin' on

you. White folks, nothin' happens when I look at 'em. I don't hate 'em, don't love 'em, . . . just nothin' shakes a-tall. The dullest people in the world. The way they talk . . . "Oh, hooty, hooty, hoo" . . . break it down for me to A, B, C's. That Bill . . . I like him, with his black, uppity, high-handed ways. What do you do to get a man you want? A social worker oughta tell you things like that.

CYNTHIA Don't chase him . . . at least don't let it look that way. Let him pursue you.

TOMMY What if he won't? Men don't chase me much, not the kind I like.

CYNTHIA *(Rattles off instructions glibly)* Let him do the talking. Learn to listen. Stay in the background a little. Ask his opinion . . . "What do *you* think, Bill?"

TOMMY Mmmmm, "Oh, hooty, hooty, hoo."

CYNTHIA But why count on him? There are lots of other nice guys.

TOMMY You don't think he'd go for me, do you?

CYNTHIA *(Trying to be diplomatic)* Perhaps you're not really his type.

TOMMY Maybe not, but he's mine. I'm so lonesome . . . I'm *lonesome* . . . I want somebody to love. Somebody to say . . . "That's all right," when the World treats me mean.

CYNTHIA Tommy, I think you're too good for Bill.

TOMMY I don't wanta hear that. The last man that told me I was too good for him . . . was tryin' to get away. He's good enough for me. *(Straightening room)*

CYNTHIA Leave the room alone. What we need is a little more sex appeal and a little less washing, cooking and ironing. *(*TOMMY *puts down the room straightening)* One more thing, . . . do you have to wear that wig?

TOMMY *(A little sensitive)* I like how your hair looks. But some of the naturals I don't like. Can see all the lint caught up in the hair like it hasn't been combed since know not when. You a Muslim?

CYNTHIA No.

TOMMY I'm just sick-a hair, hair, hair. Do it this way, don't do it, leave it natural, straighten it, process, no process. I get sick-a hair and talkin' 'bout it and foolin' with it. That's why I wear the wig.

CYNTHIA I'm sure your own must be just as nice or nicer than that.

TOMMY It oughta be. I only paid nineteen ninety five for this.

CYNTHIA You ought to go back to usin' your own.

TOMMY *(Tensely)* I'll be givin' that some thought.

CYNTHIA You're pretty nice people just as you are. Soften up, Tommy. You might surprise yourself.

TOMMY I'm listenin'.

CYNTHIA Expect more. Learn to let men open doors for you . . .

TOMMY What if I'm standin' there and they don't open it?

CYNTHIA *(Trying to level with her)* You're a fine person. He wants to paint you, that's all. He's doing a kind of mural thing and we thought he would enjoy painting you. I'd hate to see you expecting more out of the situation than what's there.

TOMMY Forget it, sweetie-pie, don' nothin' happen that's not suppose to.

(Sound of laughter in the hall. BILL, OLDTIMER *and* SONNY-MAN *enter)*

BILL No Chinese restaurant left, baby! It's wiped out. Gone with the revolution.

SONNY-MAN *(To Cynthia)* Baby, let's move, split the scene, get on with it, time for home.

BILL The revolution is here. Whatta you do with her? You paint her!

SONNY-MAN You write her . . . you write the revolution. I'm gonna write the revolution into a novel nine hundred pages long.

BILL Dance it! Sing! "Down in the cornfield Hear dat mournful sound . . . *(*SONNY-MAN *and* OLDTIMER *harmonize)* Dear old Massa am-a sleepin' A-sleepin' in the cold, cold ground." Now for "Wine In The Wilderness!" Triptych will be finished.

CYNTHIA *(In* BILL'S *face)* "Wine In The Wilderness," huh? Exploitation!

SONNY-MAN Upstairs, all out, come on, Oldtimer. Folks can't create in a crowd. Cynthia, move it, baby.

OLDTIMER *(Starting toward the window)* My things! I got a package.

SONNY-MAN *(Heads him off)* Up and out. You don't have to go home, but you have to get outta here. Happy paintin', yall. *(One backward look and they are all gone)*

BILL Whatta night, whatta night, whatta night, baby. It will be painted, written, sung and discussed for generations.

TOMMY *(Notices nothing that looks like Chinese food. He is carrying a small bag and a container)* Where's the Foo-Yong?

BILL They blew the restaurant, baby. All I could get was a couple-a franks and a orange drink from the stand.

TOMMY *(Tensely)* You brought me a frank-footer? That's what you think-a me, a frank-footer?

BILL Nothin' to do with what I think. Place is closed.

TOMMY *(Quietly surly)* This is the damn City-a New York, any hour on the clock they sellin' the chicken in the basket, barbecue ribs, pizza pie, hot pastrami samitches; and you brought me a frank-footer?

BILL Baby, don't break bad over somethin' to eat. The smart set, the jet set, the beautiful people, kings and queens eat frankfurters.

TOMMY If a queen sent you out to buy her a bucket-a Foo-yung, you wouldn't come back with no lonely-ass frank-footer.

BILL Kill me 'bout it, baby! Go 'head and shoot me six times. That's the trouble with our women, yall always got your mind on food.

TOMMY Is that our trouble? *(Laughs)* Maybe you right. Only two things to do. Either eat the frankfooter or walk on outta here. You got any mustard?

BILL *(Gets mustard from the refrigerator)* Let's face it, our folks are not together. The brothers and sisters have busted up Harlem, . . . no plan, no nothin'. There's your black revolution, heads whipped, hospital full and we still in the same old bag.

TOMMY *(Seated at the kitchen table)* Maybe what everybody need is somebody like you, who know how things oughta go, to get on out there and start some action.

BILL You still mad about the frankfurter?

TOMMY No. I keep seein' pitchers of what was in my room and how it all must be spoiled now. *(Sips the orange drink)* A orange never been near this. Well, it's cold. *(Looking at an incense burner)* What's that?

BILL An incense burner, was given to me by the Chinese guy, Richard Lee. I'm sorry they blew his restaurant.

TOMMY Does it help you to catch the number?

BILL No, baby, I just burn incense sometime.

TOMMY For what?

BILL Just 'cause I feel like it. Baby, ain't you used to nothin'?

TOMMY Ain't used to burnin' incent for nothin'.

BILL *(Laughs)* Burnin' what?

TOMMY That stuff.

BILL What did you call it?

TOMMY Incent.

BILL It's not incent, baby. It's incense.

TOMMY Like the sense you got in your head. In-sense. Thank you. You're a very correctable person, aint you?

BILL Let's put you on canvas.

TOMMY *(Stubbornly)* I have to eat first.

BILL That's another thing 'bout black women, they wanta eat 'fore they do anything else. Tommy, . . . Tommy, . . . I bet your name is Thomasina. You look like a Thomasina.

TOMMY You could sit there and guess til your eyes pop out and you never would guess my first name. You might could guess the middle name but not the first one.

BILL Tell it to me.

TOMMY My name is Tomorrow.

BILL How's that?

TOMMY Tomorrow, . . . like yesterday and *tomorrow,* and the middle name is just plain Marie. That's what my father name me, Tomorrow Marie. My mother say he thought it had a pretty sound.

BILL   Crazy! I never met a girl named Tomorrow.

TOMMY   They got to callin' me Tommy for short, so I stick with that. Tomorrow Marie, . . . Sound like a promise that can never happen.

BILL   *(Straightens chair on stand. He is very eager to start painting)* That's what Shakespeare said, . . . "Tomorrow and tomorrow and tomorrow." Tomorrow, you will be on this canvas.

TOMMY   *(Still uneasy about being painted)* What's the hurry? Rome wasn't built in a day, . . . that's another saying.

BILL   If I finish in time, I'll enter you in an exhibition.

TOMMY   *(Loses interest in the food. Examines the room. Looks at portrait on the wall)* He looks like somebody I know or maybe saw before.

BILL   That's Frederick Douglass. A man who used to be a slave. He escaped and spent his life trying to make us all free. He was a great man.

TOMMY   Thank you, Mr. Douglass. Who's the light colored man? *(Indicates a frame next to the Douglass)*

BILL   He's white. That's John Brown. They killed him for tryin' to shoot the country outta the slavery bag. He dug us, you know. Old John said, "Hell no, slavery must go."

TOMMY   I heard all about him. Some folks say he was crazy.

BILL   If he had been shootin' at *us* they wouldn't have called him a nut.

TOMMY   School wasn't a great part-a my life.

BILL   If it was you wouldn't-a found out too much 'bout black history cause the books full-a nothin' but whitey, . . . all except the white ones who dug us, . . . they not there either. Tell me, . . . who was Elijah Lovejoy?

TOMMY   Elijah Lovejoy, . . . Mmmmmmm. I don't know. Have to do with the Bible?

BILL   No, that's another white fella, . . . Elijah had a printin' press and the main thing he printed was "Slavery got to go." Well the man moved in on him, smashed his press time after time . . . but he kept puttin' it back together and doin' his thing. So, one final day, they came in a mob and burned him to death.

TOMMY *(Blows her nose with sympathy as she fights tears)* That's dirty.

BILL *(As TOMMY glances at titles in book case)* Who was Monroe Trotter?

TOMMY Was he white?

BILL No, soul brother. Spent his years tryin' to make it all right. Who was Harriet Tubman?

TOMMY I heard-a her. But don't put me through no test, Billy. *(Moving around studying pictures and books)* This room is full-a things I don't know nothin' about. How'll I get to know?

BILL Read, go to the library, book stores, ask somebody.

TOMMY Okay, I'm askin'. Teach me things.

BILL Aw, baby, why torment yourself? Trouble with our women, . . . they all wanta be great brains. Leave somethin' for a man to do.

TOMMY *(Eager to impress him)* What you think-a Martin Luther King?

BILL A great guy. But it's too late in the day for the singin' and prayin' now.

TOMMY What about Malcolm X.?

BILL Great cat . . . but there again . . . Where's the program?

TOMMY What about Adam Powell? I voted for him. That's one thing 'bout me. I vote. Maybe if everybody vote for the right people . . .

BILL The ballot box. It would take me all my life to straighten you on that hype.

TOMMY I got the time.

BILL You gonna wind up with a king size headache. The Matriarchy gotta go. Yall throw them suppers together, keep your husband happy, raise the kids.

TOMMY I don't have a husband. Course, that could be fixed. *(Leaving the unspoken proposal hanging in the air)*

BILL You know the greatest thing you could do for your people? Sit up there and let me put you down on canvas.

TOMMY Bein' married and havin' a family might be good

for your people as a race, but I was thinkin' 'bout myself a little.

BILL Forget yourself sometime, sugar. On that canvas you'll be givin' and givin' and givin' . . . That's where you can do your thing best. What you stallin' for?

TOMMY (*Returns to table and sits in chair*) I . . . I don't want to pose in this outfit.

BILL (*Patience is wearing thin*) Why, baby, why?

TOMMY I don't feel proud-a myself in this.

BILL Art, baby, we talkin' art. Whatcha want . . . Ribbons? Lace? False eyelashes?

TOMMY No, just my white dress with the orlon sweater, . . . or anything but this what I'm wearin'. You oughta see me in that dress with my pink linen shoes. Oh, hell, the shoes are gone. I forgot 'bout the fire . . .

BILL Oh, stop fightin' me! Another thing . . . our women don't know a damn thing 'bout bein' feminine. *Give in* sometime. It won't kill you. You tellin' me how to paint? Maybe you oughta hang out your shingle and give art lessons! You too damn opinionated. You gonna pose or you not gonna pose? Say somethin'!

TOMMY You makin' me nervous! Hollerin' at me. My mama never holler at me. Hollerin'.

BILL I'll soon be too tired to pick up the brush, baby.

TOMMY (*Eye catches picture of white woman on the wall*) That's a white woman! Bet you never hollered at her and I bet she's your girlfriend . . . too, and when she posed for her pitcher I bet yall was laughin' . . . and you didn't buy her no frankfooter!

BILL (*Feels a bit smug about his male prowess*) Awww, come on, cut that out, baby. That's a little blonde, blue-eyed chick who used to pose for me. That ain't where it's at. This is a new day, the deal is goin' down different. This is the black moment, doll. Black, black, black is bee-yoo-tee-full. Got it? *Black is beautiful.*

TOMMY Then how come it is that I don't *feel* beautiful when you *talk* to me?!!

BILL That's your hang-up, not mine. You supposed to

stretch forth your wings like Ethiopia, shake off them chains that been holdin' you down. Langston Hughes said let 'em see how beautiful you are. But you determined not to ever be beautiful. Okay, that's what makes you Tommy.

TOMMY Do you *have* a girl friend? And who is she?

BILL *(Now enjoying himself to the utmost)* Naw, naw, naw, doll. I *know* people, but none-a this "tie-you-up-and-I-own-you" jive. I ain't mistreatin' nobody and there's enough-a me to go around. That's another thing with our women, . . . they wanta *latch* on. Learn to play it by ear, roll with the punches, cut down on some-a this "got-you-to-the-grave" kinda relationship. Was today all right? Good, be glad, . . . take what's at hand because tomorrow never comes, it's always today. *(She begins to cry)* Awwww, I didn't mean it that way . . . I forgot your name. *(He brushes her tears away)* You act like I belong to you. You're jealous of a picture?

TOMMY That's how women are, always studyin' each other and wonderin' how they look up 'gainst the next person.

BILL *(A bit smug)* That's human nature. Whatcha call healthy competition.

TOMMY You think she's pretty?

BILL She was, perhaps still is. Long, silky hair. She could sit on her hair.

TOMMY *(With bitter arrogance)* Doesn't *everybody?*

BILL You got a head like a rock and gonna have the last word if it kills you. Baby, I bet you could knock out Muhammad Ali in the first round, then rare back and scream like Tarzan . . . "Now, I am the greatest!" *(He is very close to her and is amazed to feel a great sense of physical attraction)* What we arguin' bout? *(Looks her over as he looks away. He suddenly wants to put the conversation on a more intimate level. His eye is on the bed)* Maybe tomorrow would be a better time for paintin'. Wanna freshen up, take a bath, baby? Water's nice n' hot.

TOMMY *(Knows the sound and turns to check on the look. Notices him watching the bed. Starts weeping)* No, I don't! Nigger!

BILL Was that nice? What the hell, let's paint the picture. Or are you gonna hold that back too?

TOMMY I'm posin'. Shall I take off the wig?

BILL No, it's a part of your image, ain't it? You must have a reason for wearin' it.

(TOMMY *snatches up her orange drink and sits in the model's chair*)

TOMMY (*With defiance*) Yes, I wear it cause you and those like you go for long, silky hair, and this is the only way I can have some without burnin' my mother-grabbin' brains out. Got it? (*She accidentally knocks over container of orange drink into her lap*) Hell, I can't wear this. I'm soaked through. I'm not gonna catch no double pneumonia sittin' up here wringin' wet while you paint and holler at me.

BILL Bitch!

TOMMY You must be talkin' 'bout your mama!

BILL Shut up! Aw, shut-up! (*Phone rings. He finds an African throw-cloth and hands it to her*) Put this on. Relax, don't go way mad, and all the rest-a that jazz. Change, will you? I apologize. I'm sorry. (*He picks up phone*) Hello, survivor of a riot speaking. Who's calling? (TOMMY *retires behind the screen with the throw. During the conversation she undresses and wraps the throw around her. We see* TOMMY *and* BILL, *but they can't see each other*) Sure, told you not to worry. I'll be ready for the exhibit. If you don't dig it, don't show it. Not time for you to see it yet. Yeah, yeah, next week. You just make sure your exhibition room is big enough to hold the crowds that's gonna congregate to see this fine chick I got here. (*This perks* TOMMY'S *ears up*) You ought see her. The finest black woman in the world . . . No, . . . the finest *any* woman in the world . . . This gorgeous satin chick is . . . is . . . black velvet moonlight . . . an ebony queen of the universe . . . (TOMMY *can hardly believe her ears*) One look at her and you go back to Spice Islands . . . She's Mother Africa. . . . You flip, double flip. She has come through everything that has been put on her . . . (*He unveils the gorgeous woman he has painted* . . . "Wine In The Wilderness." TOMMY *believes he is talking about her)* Regal . . . grand . . . magnificent, fantastic. . . . You would vote her the woman you'd most like to meet on a desert island, or around the corner from anywhere. She's here with me now . . . and I don't know if I want to show her to you or anybody else . . . I'm beginnin' to have this deep attachment . . . She sparkles, man, Harriet Tubman, Queen of the Nile . . . sweetheart, wife, mother, sister, friend. . . . The night . . . a black diamond . . . A dark, beautiful dream . . . A cloud with a silvery lining . . . Her wrath is a storm over the Bahamas. "Wine In The Wilderness" . . . The memory of Africa . . . The *now* of things . . . but best of all and most important . . . She's tomorrow . . . she's my tomorrow . . . *(TOMMY is dressed in the African wrap. She is suddenly awakened to the feeling of being loved and admired. She removes the wig and fluffs her hair. Her hair under the wig must not be an accurate, well-cut Afro . . . but should be rather attractive natural hair. She studies herself in a mirror. We see her taller, more relaxed and sure of herself. Perhaps braided hair will go well with Afro robe)* Aw, man, later. You don't believe in nothin'! *(He covers "Wine In The Wilderness." Is now in a glowing mood)* Baby, whenever you ready. *(She emerges from behind the screen. Dressed in the wrap, sans wig. He is astounded)* Baby, what. . . ? Where . . . where's the wig?

TOMMY   I don't think I want to wear it, Bill.

BILL   That is very becoming . . . the drape thing.

TOMMY   Thank you.

BILL   I don't know what to say.

TOMMY   It's time to paint. *(Steps up on the model stand and sits in the chair. She is now a queen, relaxed and smiling her appreciation for his past speech to the art dealer. Her feet are bare)*

BILL   *(Mystified by the change in her. Tries to do a charcoal sketch)* It is quite late.

TOMMY   Makes me no difference if it's all right with you.

BILL   *(Wants to create the other image)*   Could you put the wig back on?

TOMMY You don't really like wigs, do you?

BILL Well, no.

TOMMY Then let's have things the way you like.

BILL *(Has no answer for this. He makes a haphazard line or two as he tries to remember the other image)* Tell me something about yourself, . . . anything.

TOMMY *(Now on sure ground)* I was born in Baltimore, Maryland and raised here in Harlem. My favorite flower is "Four O'clocks," that's a bush flower. My wearin' flower, corsage flower, is pink roses. My mama raised me, mostly by herself, God rest the dead. Mama belonged to "The Eastern Star." Her father was a "Mason." If a man in the family is a "Mason" any woman related to him can be an "Eastern Star." My grandfather was a member of "The Prince Hall Lodge." I had a uncle who was an "Elk," . . . a member of "The Improved Benevolent Protective Order of Elks of the World": "The Henry Lincoln Johnson Lodge." You know, the white "Elks" are called "The Benevolent Protective Order of Elks" but the black "Elks" are called "The *Improved* Benevolent Protective Order of Elks of *the World.*" That's because the black "Elks" got the copyright first but the white "Elks" took us to court about it to keep us from usin' the name. Over fifteen hundred black folk went to jail for wearin' the "Elk" emblem on their coat lapel. Years ago, . . . that's what you call history.

BILL I didn't know about that.

TOMMY Oh, it's understandable. Only way I heard 'bout John Brown was because the black "Elks" bought his farmhouse where he trained his men to attack the government.

BILL The black "Elks" bought the John Brown Farm? What did they do with it?

TOMMY They built a outdoor theatre and put a perpetual light in his memory, . . . and they buildin' cottages there, one named for each state in the union and . . .

BILL How do you know about it?

TOMMY Well, our "Elks" helped my cousin go through school with a scholarship. She won a speaking contest and wrote a composition titled "Onward and Upward, O, My Race." That's how she won the scholarship. Coreen knows all that Elk history.

BILL *(Seeing her with new eyes)* Tell me some more about you, Tomorrow Marie. I bet you go to church.

TOMMY Not much as I used to. Early in life I pledged myself in the A.M.E. Zion Church.

BILL *(Studying her face, seeing her for the first time)* A.M.E.

TOMMY A.M.E. That's African Methodist Episcopal. We split off from the white Methodist Episcopal and started our own in the year Seventeen hundred and ninety six. We built our first buildin' in the year 1800. How 'bout that?

BILL That right?

TOMMY Oh, I'm just showin' off. I taught Sunday School for two years and you had to know the history of A.M.E. Zion ... or else you couldn't teach. My great, great grandparents was slaves.

BILL Guess everybody's was.

TOMMY Mine was slaves in a place called Sweetwater Springs, Virginia. We tried to look it up one time but somebody at Church told us that Sweetwater Springs had become a part of Norfolk ... so we didn't carry it any further ... As it would be a expense to have a lawyer trace your people.

BILL *(Throws charcoal pencil across room)* No good! It won't work! I can't work anymore.

TOMMY Take a rest. Tell me about you.

BILL *(Sits on bed)* Everybody in my family worked for the Post Office. They bought a home in Jamaica, Long Island. Everybody on that block bought an aluminum screen door with a duck on it, ... or was it a swan? I guess that makes my favorite flower crab grass and hedges. I have a lot of bad dreams. *(TOMMY massages his temples and the back of his neck)* A dream like suffocating, dying of suffocation. The worst kinda dream. People are standing in a weird looking art gallery, they're looking and laughing at everything I've ever done. My work begins to fade off the canvas, right before my eyes. Everything I've ever done is laughed away.

TOMMY Don't be so hard on yourself. If I was smart as you I'd wake up singin' every mornin'. *(There is the sound of thunder. He kisses her)* When it thunders that's the angels in heaven playin' with their hoops, rollin' their hoops and bicycle wheels in the rain. My Mama told me that.

BILL I'm glad you're here. Black *is* beautiful, you're beautiful, A.M.E. Zion, Elks, pink roses, bush flower, . . . blooming out of the slavery of Sweetwater Springs, Virginia.

TOMMY I'm gonna take a bath and let the riot and the hell of living go down the drain with the bath water.

BILL Tommy, Tommy, Tomorrow Marie, let's save each other, let's be kind and good to each other while it rains and the angels roll those hoops and bicycle wheels. *(They embrace. The sound of rain)*

(Music in as lights come down. As lights fade down to darkness, music comes in louder. There is a flash of lightning. We see TOMMY *and* BILL *in each other's arms. It is very dark. Music up louder, then softer and down to very soft. Music is mixed with the sound of rain beating against the window. Music slowly fades as gray light of dawn shows at window. Lights go up gradually. The bed is rumpled and empty.* BILL *is in the bathroom.* TOMMY *is at the stove turning off the coffee pot. She sets table with cups and saucers, spoons.* TOMMY's *hair is natural, she wears another throw [African design] draped around her. She sings and hums a snatch of a joyous spiritual)*

TOMMY "Great day, Great day, the world's on fire, Great day . . ." *(Calling out to* BILL *who is in bath)* Honey, I found the coffee, and it's ready. Nothin' here to go with it but a cucumber and a Uneeda biscuit.

BILL *(Offstage. Joyous yell from offstage)* Tomorrow and tomorrow and tomorrow! Good mornin', Tomorrow!

TOMMY *(More to herself than to* BILL*)* "Tomorrow and tomorrow." That's Shakespeare. *(Calls to* BILL*)* You say that was Shakespeare?

BILL *(Offstage)* Right, baby, right!

TOMMY I bet Shakespeare was black! You know how we love poetry. That's what give him away. I bet he was pass-in'. *(Laughs)*

BILL *(Offstage)* Just you wait, one hundred years from now all the honkys gonna claim our poets just like they stole our blues. They gonna try to steal Paul Laurence Dunbar and LeRoi and Margaret Walker.

TOMMY *(To herself)* God moves in a mysterious way, even in the middle of a riot. *(A knock on the door)* Great day, great day the world's on fire . . . *(Opens the door. OLD-TIMER enters. He is soaking wet. He does not recognize her right away)*

OLDTIMER 'Scuse me, I must be in the wrong place.

TOMMY *(Patting her hair)* This is me. Come on in, Edmond Lorenzo Matthews. I took off my hair-piece. This is me.

OLDTIMER *(Very distracted and worried)* Well, howdy-do and good mornin'. *(He has had a hard night of drinking and sleeplessness)* Where Billy-boy? It pourin' down some rain out there. *(Makes his way to the window)*

TOMMY What's the matter?

OLDTIMER *(Raises the window and starts pulling in the cord, the cord is weightless and he realizes there is nothing on the end of it)* No, no, it can't be. Where is it? It's gone! *(Looks out the window)*

TOMMY You gonna catch your death. You wringin' wet.

OLDTIMER Yall take my things in? It was a bag-a loot. A suit and some odds and ends. It was my loot. Yall took it in?

TOMMY No. *(Realizes his desperation. She calls to BILL through the closed bathroom door)* Did you take in any loot that was outside the window?

BILL *(Offstage)* No.

TOMMY He said "no."

OLDTIMER *(Yells out window)* Thieves, . . . dirty thieves . . . lotta good it'll do you . . .

TOMMY *(Leads him to a chair, dries his head with a towel)* Get outta the wet things. You smell just like a whiskey still. Why don't you take care of yourself. *(Dries off his hands)*

OLDTIMER Drinkin' with the boys. Likker was everywhere all night long.

TOMMY You got to be better than this.

OLDTIMER Everything I ever put my hand and mind to do, it turn out wrong, . . . Nothin' but mistakes . . . When you don' know, you don' know. I don' know nothin'. I'm ignorant.

TOMMY Hush that talk . . . You know lotsa things, everybody does. *(Helps him remove wet coat)*

OLDTIMER Thanks. How's the trip-tick?

TOMMY The what?

OLDTIMER *Trick-tick.* That's a paintin'.

TOMMY See there, you know more about art than I do. What's a trip-tick? Have some coffee and explain me a trip-tick.

OLDTIMER *(Proud of his knowledge)* Well, I tell you, . . . a trip-tick is a paintin' that's in three parts . . . but they all belong together to be looked at all at once. Now . . . this is the first one . . . a little innocent girl . . . *(Unveils picture)*

TOMMY She's sweet.

OLDTIMER And this is "Wine In The Wilderness" . . . The Queen of ᴛhe Universe . . . the finest chick in the world.

TOMMY *(Tommy is thoughtful as he unveils the second picture)* That's not me.

OLDTIMER No, you gonna be this here last one. The worst gal in town. A messed-up chick that—that—*(He unveils the third canvas and is face to face with the almost blank canvas, then realizes what he has said. He turns to see the stricken look on* TOMMY's *face)*

TOMMY The messed-up chick, *that's* why they brought me here, ain't it? That's why he wanted to paint me! Say it!

OLDTIMER No, I'm lyin', I didn't mean it. It's the society that messed her up. Awwwwww, Tommy, don't look that-a-way. It's art, . . . it's only art . . . He couldn't mean you . . . it's art . . . *(The door opens.* CYNTHIA *and* SONNY-MAN *enter)*

SONNY-MAN Any body want a ride down . . . down . . . down

... downtown? What's wrong? Excuse me ... *(Starts back out)*

TOMMY *(Blocking the exit to* CYNTHIA *and* SONNY-MAN*)* No, come on in. Stay with it ... "Brother" ... "Sister." Tell 'em what a trip-tick is, Oldtimer.

CYNTHIA *(Very ashamed)* Oh, no.

TOMMY You don't have to tell 'em. They already know. The messed-up chick! How come you didn't pose for that, my sister? The messed-up chick lost her home last night, ... burnt out with no place to go. You and Sonny-man gave me comfort, you cheered me up and took me in, ... *took me in!*

CYNTHIA Tommy, we didn't know you, we didn't mean ...

TOMMY It's all right! I was lost but now I'm found! Yeah, the blind can see! *(She dashes behind the screen and puts on her clothing, sweater, skirt etc.)*

OLDTIMER *(Goes to bathroom door)* Billy, come out!

SONNY-MAN Billy, step out here, please! *(*BILL *enters shirtless, wearing dungarees)* Oldtimer let it out 'bout the triptych.

BILL The rest of you move on.

TOMMY *(Looking out from behind screen)* No, don't go a step. You brought me here, see me out!

BILL Tommy, let me explain it to you.

TOMMY *(Coming out from behind screen)* I gotta check out my apartment, and my clothes and money. Cynthia, ... I can't wait for anybody to open the door or look out for me and all that kinda crap you talk. A bunch-a liars!

BILL Oldtimer, why you ...

TOMMY Leave him the hell alone. He ain't said nothin' that ain' so!

SONNY-MAN Explain to the sister that some mistakes have been made.

BILL Mistakes have been made, baby. The mistakes were yesterday, this is today ...

TOMMY Yeah, and I'm Tomorrow, remember? Trouble is I was Tommin' to you, to all of you, ... "Oh, maybe they gon' like me." . . . I was your fool, thinkin' writers and painters know moren' me, that maybe a little bit of you would rub off on me.

CYNTHIA We are wrong. I knew it yesterday. Tommy, I told you not to expect anything out of this . . . this arrangement.

BILL This is a relationship, not an arrangement.

SONNY-MAN Cynthia, I tell you all the time, keep outta other people's business. What the hell you got to do with who's gonna get what outta what? You and Oldtimer, yak-kin' and yakkin'. *(To* OLDTIMER*)* Man, you mouth gonna kill you.

BILL It's me and Tommy. Clear the room.

TOMMY Better not. I'll kill him! The "black people" this and the "Afro-American" . . . that . . . You ain' got no use for none-a us. Oldtimer, you their fool too. 'Til I got here they didn't even know your damn name. There's something inside-a me that says I ain' suppose to let *nobody* play me cheap. Don't care how much they know! *(She sweeps some of the* books *to the floor)*

BILL Don't you have any forgiveness in you? Would I be beggin' you if I didn't care? Can't you be generous enough . . .

TOMMY Nigger, I been too damn generous with you, al-ready. All-a these people know I wasn't down here all night posin' for no pitcher, nigger!

BILL Cut that out, Tommy, and you not going anywhere!

TOMMY You wanna bet? Nigger!

BILL Okay, you called it, baby, I did act like a low, degraded person . . .

TOMMY *(Combing out her wig with her fingers while holding it)* Didn't call you no low, degraded person. Nigger! *(To* CYNTHIA *who is handing her a comb)* "Do you have to wear a wig?" Yes! To soften the blow when yall go up side-a my head with a baseball bat. *(Going back to taunting* BILL *and ignoring* CYNTHIA's *comb)* Nigger!

BILL That's enough-a that. You right and you're wrong too.

TOMMY Ain't a-one-a us you like that's alive and walkin' by you on the street . . . you don't like flesh and blood niggers.

BILL   Call me that, baby, but don't call yourself. That what you think of yourself?

TOMMY   If a black somebody is in a history book, or printed on a pitcher, or drawed on a paintin', . . . or if they're a statue, . . . dead, and outta the way, and can't talk back, then you dig 'em and full-a so much-a damn admiration and talk 'bout *"our"* history. But when you run into us livin' and breathin' ones, with the life's blood still pumpin' through us, . . . then you comin' on 'bout how we ain' never together. You hate us, that's what ! *You hate black me!*

BILL   *(Stung to the heart, confused and saddened by the half truth which applies to himself)*   I never hated you, I never will, no matter what you or any of the rest of you do to *make* me hate you. I won't! Hell, woman, why do you say that! Why would I hate you?

TOMMY   Maybe I look too much like the mother that give birth to you. Like the Ma and Pa that worked in the post office to buy you a house and a screen door with a damn duck on it. And you so ungrateful you didn't even like it.

BILL   No, I didn't, baby. I don't like screen doors with ducks on 'em.

TOMMY   You didn't like who was livin' behind them screen doors. Phoney Nigger!

BILL   That's all! Damnit! don't go there no more!

TOMMY   Hit me, so I can tear this place down and scream bloody murder.

BILL   *(Somewhere between laughter and tears)*   Looka here, baby, I'm willin' to say I'm wrong, even in fronta the room fulla people . . .

TOMMY   *(Through clenched teeth)*   Nigger.

SONNY-MAN   The sister is upset.

TOMMY   And you stop callin' me "the" sister, . . . if you feelin' so brotherly why don't you say *"my"* sister? Ain't no we-ness in your talk. "The" Afro-American, "the" black man, there's no we-ness in you. Who you think *you* are?

SONNY-MAN   I was talkin' in general er . . . *my* sister, 'bout the masses.

TOMMY   There he go again. "The" masses. Tryin' to make

out like we pitiful and you got it made. You the masses your damn self and don't even know it. *(Another angry look at* BILL*)* Nigger.

BILL *(Pulls dictionary from shelf)* Let's get this ignorant "nigger" talk squared away. You can stand some education.

TOMMY You *treat* me like a nigger, that's what. I'd rather be called one than treated that way.

BILL *(Questions* TOMMY*)* What is a nigger? *(Talks as he is trying to find word)* A nigger is a low, degraded person, *any* low degraded person. I learned that from my teacher in the fifth grade.

TOMMY Fifth grade is a liar! Don't pull that dictionary crap on me.

BILL *(Pointing to the book)* Webster's New World Dictionary of The American Language, College Edition.

TOMMY I don't need to find out what no college white folks say nigger is.

BILL I'm tellin' you it's a low, degraded person. Listen. *(Reads from the book)* Nigger, N-i-g-g-e-r, . . . A Negro . . . A member of any dark-skinned people . . . Damn. *(Amazed by dictionary description)*

SONNY-MAN Brother Malcolm *said* that's what they meant, . . . nigger is a Negro, Negro is a nigger.

BILL *(Slowly finishing his reading)* A vulgar, offensive term of hostility and contempt. Well, so much for the fifth grade teacher.

SONNY-MAN No, they do not call low, degraded white folks niggers. Come to think of it, did you ever hear whitey call Hitler a nigger? Now if some whitey digs us, . . . the others might call him a nigger-*lover*, but they don't call him no nigger.

OLDTIMER No, they don't.

TOMMY *(Near tears)* When they say "nigger," just dry-long-so, they mean educated you and uneducated me. They hate you and call you "nigger," I called you "nigger" but I love you. *(There is dead silence in the room for a split second)*

SONNY-MAN *(Trying to establish peace)* There you go. There you go.

CYNTHIA *(Cautioning* SONNY-MAN*)* Now is not the time to talk, darlin'.

BILL You love me? Tommy, that's the greatest compliment you could . . .

TOMMY *(Sorry she said it)* You must be runnin' a fever, nigger, I ain' said nothin' 'bout lovin' you.

BILL *(In a great mood)* You did, yes, you did.

TOMMY Well, you didn't say it to me.

BILL Oh, Tommy, . . .

TOMMY *(Cuts him off abruptly)* And don't you dare say it now. I'm tellin' you, . . . it ain't to be said now. *(Checks through her paper bag to see if she has everything. Starts to put on the wig, changes her mind, holds it to end of scene. Turns to the others in the room)* Oldtimer, . . . my brothers and my sister.

OLDTIMER I wish I was a thousand miles away, I'm so sorry. *(He sits at the foot of the model stand)*

TOMMY I don't stay mad, it's here today and gone tomorrow. I'm sorry your feelin's got hurt, . . . but when I'm hurt I turn and hurt back. Somewhere, in the middle of last night, I thought the old me was gone, . . . lost forever, and gladly. But today was flippin' time, so back I flipped. Now it's "turn the other cheek" time. If I can go through life other-cheekin' the white folk, . . . guess yall can be other-cheeked too. But I'm goin' back to the nitty-gritty crowd, where the talk is we-ness and us-ness. I hate to do it but I have to thank you 'cause I'm walkin' out with much more than I brought in. *(Goes over and looks at the queen in the "Wine In The Wilderness" painting)* Tomorrow-Marie had such a lovely yesterday. *(BILL takes her hand, she gently removes it from his grasp)* Bill, I don't have to wait for anybody's by-your-leave to be a "Wine In The Wilderness" woman. I can be it if I wanta, . . . and I *am*. I am. I am. I'm not the one you made up and painted, the very pretty lady who can't talk back, . . . but I'm "Wine In The Wilderness" . . . alive and kickin', me . . . Tomorrow-Marie, cussin' and fightin' and lookin' out for my damn self 'cause ain' nobody else 'round to do it, dontcha know. And, Cynthia, if my hair is straight, or if it's natural, or if I wear a wig, or take it off, . . . that's all right; because wigs . . . shoes . . . hats . . . bags . . . and even this . . . *(She picks up the African throw she wore a few moments before . . . fingers it)* They're just what you call . . . access . . . *(Fishing for the word)* . . . like what you wear with your Easter outfit . . .

CYNTHIA Accessories.

TOMMY Thank you, my sister. Accessories. Somethin' you add on or take off. The real thing is takin' place on the inside . . . that's where the action is. That's "Wine In The Wilderness," . . . a woman that's a real one and a good one. And yall just better believe I'm it. *(She proceeds to the door)*

BILL Tommy. *(She turns. He takes the beautiful queen, "Wine In The Wilderness" from the easel)* She's not it at all, Tommy. This chick on the canvas, . . . nothin' but accessories, a dream I drummed up outta the junk room of my mind. *(Places the "queen" to one side)* You are and . . . *(Points to* OLDTIMER*)* . . . Edmund Lorenzo Matthews . . . the real beautiful people, . . . Cynthia . . .

CYNTHIA *(Bewildered and unbelieving)* Who? Me?

BILL Yeah, honey, you and Sonny-man, don't know how beautiful you are. *(Indicates the other side of model stand)* Sit there.

SONNY-MAY *(Places cushions on the floor at the foot of the model stand)* Just sit here and be my beautiful self. *(To* CYNTHIA*)* Turn on, baby, we gonna get our picture took.
    *(*CYNTHIA *smiles)*

BILL Now there's Oldtimer, the guy who was here before there were scholarships and grants and stuff like that, the guy they kept outta the schools, the man the factories wouldn't hire, the union wouldn't let him join . . .

SONNY-MAN Yeah, yeah, rap to me. Where you goin' with it, man? Rap on.

BILL I'm makin' a triptych.

SONNY-MAN Make it, man.

BILL *(Indicating* CYNTHIA *and* SONNY-MAN*)* On the other side, Young Man and Woman, workin' together to do our thing.

TOMMY *(Quietly)* I'm goin' now.

BILL But you belong up there in the center, "Wine In The Wilderness" . . . that's who you are. *(Moves the canvas of "the little girl" and places a sketch pad on the easel)* The nightmare, about all that I've done disappearing before my eyes. It was a good nightmare. I was painting in the dark, all head and no heart. I couldn't see until you came, baby. *(To* CYNTHIA, SONNY-MAN *and* OLDTIMER*)* Look at Tomorrow. She came through the biggest riot of all, . . . somethin' called "Slavery," and she's even comin' through the "now" scene, . . . folks laughin' at her, even her own folks laughin' at her. And look *how* . . . with her head high up like she's poppin' her fingers at the world. *(Takes up charcoal pencil and tears old page off sketch pad so he can make a fresh drawing)* Aw, let me put it down, Tommy. "Wine In The Wilderness," you gotta let me put it down so all the little boys and girls can look up and see you on the wall. And you know what they're gonna say? "Hey, don't she look like somebody we know?" *(*TOMMY *slowly returns and takes her seat on the stand.* TOMMY *is holding the wig in her lap. Her hands are very graceful looking against the texture of the wig)* And they'll be right, you're somebody they know . . . *(He is sketching hastily. There is a sound of thunder and the patter of rain)* Yeah, roll them hoops and bicycle wheels.

> *(Music in low. Music up higher as Bill continues to sketch)*

CURTAIN

About the Authors

ALICE GERSTENBERG was born c. 1893 in Chicago and attended college at Bryn Mawr. Her first novel, *Unquenchable Fire*, was published when she was twenty years old. At about the same time, her play *Overtones* was produced by the Washington Square Players, the group that was later to be the basis of the Theatre Guild. Alice Gerstenberg was probably the first expressionistic playwright in America, using the technique of inner and outer characterization a decade before Eugene O'Neill. She founded the Playwrights Theatre in Chicago where she was also the director. She wrote a number of plays, of which an adaptation of *Alice in Wonderland* (1915) was one of the most successful.

LILLIAN HELLMAN was born in 1907 in New Orleans, and attended New York University and Columbia University. Her first play, *The Children's Hour*, ran for 691 performances on Broadway in 1934 and was successfully revived in 1952. It has twice been made into a film, first in 1936 under the title *These Three*, for which Ms. Hellman wrote the screenplay, and again in 1962. Her other plays include *The Little Foxes; Another Part of the Forest; Watch on the Rhine*, which won the New York Critics Circle Award as the best play of 1941; and *Toys in the Attic*, which won the same award in 1960. She has written a number of screenplays in addition to *These Three*; among them *Dead End* (1937) and *The Searching Wind* (1946)i. In 1969 she published a memoir, *An Unfinished Woman*. She has been awarded the Gold Medal of the American Academy of Arts and Letters for distinguished achievement in the theatre.

CLAIRE BOOTHE (LUCE) was born in 1903 in New York City. One of her first plays, *The Women* (1936), was her most successful; it has been filmed twice, the last tme in 1956 under the title *The Opposite Sex*. Her other plays include *Abide with Me; Kiss the Boys Goodbye*; and *Margin for Error*. Outside the theatre world she has had several successful careers. She was an editorial writer for *Vogue* magazine in 1929, and managing editor of *Vanity Fair* in 1933. She married Henry R. Luce of *Time-Life* in 1935, and during World War II was a war correspondent for her husband's publications. From 1943 to 1947 she was a member of Congress. President Eisenhower appointed her ambassador to Italy in 1953, where she served until 1956. In 1970 she wrote a one-act play on women's liberation, *A Doll's House 1970*, whose title was subsequently changed to *Slam the Door Softly*.

DORIS LESSING was born in 1919 in Persia. When she was five, her family moved to Southern Rhodesia, where she lived until 1949 when she settled in England. A year later she published her first novel, *The Grass Is Singing*. She is best known for *The Golden Notebook*, which has been recognized by many women as an important book about self-realization. She has written two plays: *Each His Own Wilderness* (1958), which was performed at London's Royal Court Theatre, and *Play with a Tiger* (1962), which was produced at the Comedy Theatre, London.

NATALIA GINZBURG was born in 1916 in Palermo, Italy. The daughter of a famed biologist, she spent her childhood in Turin. She has been married twice and has three children. She has written three plays: *I Married You for Fun* (1965); *The Secretary* (1968); and *The Advertisement*, which was given its world premiere by the National Theatre in Brighton, England, in 1968. Almost simultaneously the play was produced on BBC radio. Both productions starred Joan Plowright. She has written six novels, five of which have been translated into English. She admits to being influenced by Harold Pinter. "What interests me most," she has said, "is the absurdity of real people."

MEGAN TERRY was born in 1932 in Seattle, Washington. She studied theatre in the West and Canada before coming east to be a member of the Open Theatre and director of its playwrights' workshops, which placed a heavy emphasis upon the improvisation of actors as a device to help the playwright form his piece. Some of Megan Terry's plays are *Eat at Joe's; Keep Tightly Closed in a Cool Dry Place; Magic Realists; Ex-copper Queen on a Set of Pills;* and *Viet Rock*. In February 1972 she joined with five other female playwrights to form the Women's Theatre Council, a group founded to direct, produce and encourage the plays of women. As she said then: "Jane Austen wrote under her embroidery. My grandmother wrote, and no one knew it until she died. The fact that we exist will give other women a chance to come out."

MAUREEN DUFFY was born in 1933. She attended the University of London, and has written five novels and a collection of poetry, as well as several plays. *Rites* was produced in London in the spring of 1969.

ALICE CHILDRESS, born in Charleston, South Carolina, grew up in Harlem and became interested in the theatre while she was in grade school. For twelve years she was a member of The American Negro Theatre, which produced such successes as *Striver's Row* and *Anna Lucasta*. Her own career as a writer began in 1949 with a one-act play, *Florence,* for which she received twenty dollars. In 1952 *Gold Through the Trees* became the first play written by a black woman to be performed professionally on the American stage; *Trouble in Mind* won an "Obie" in 1955 for the best off-Broadway play. Her other plays include *Wedding Band; Mojo; Martin Luther King at Montgomery, Alabama;* and *Just a Little Simple*, an adaptation of Langston Hughes's *Simple Speaks His Mind.* In 1971 she edited *Black Scenes,* the first collection of scenes chosen for the training of black actors. At present she lives and writes in Harlem.

About the Editors

VICTORIA SULLIVAN was educated at Radcliffe, Barnard and Columbia Graduate School. The mother of two, she is an assistant professor in the English Department of City College, where she has taught courses in poetry, modern fiction, the hero, and literature and Women's Liberation. She has published poetry in little magazines, movie criticism in the *New York Times*, and had a play produced.

JAMES HATCH received his Ph.D. in theatre from the University of Iowa, and has taught theatre arts at the University of California at Los Angeles and the Cinema Institute of Cairo. Winner of the "Obie" award for the best off-Broadway musical of the 1961–62 season, *Fly Blackbird*, he is also the author of *Liar, Liar*, a children's musical; *Black Image on the American Stage*, a bibliography of 2,000 plays; and many articles on theatre for *The Nation* and the *Village Voice*. He is the editor of the anthology *Black Theatre USA, 1847–1972* and is associate professor of English at the City College of New York.